Marx for Our Times

Marx for Our Times

Adventures and Misadventures
of a Critique

◆

DANIEL BENSAÏD

Translated by Gregory Elliott

VERSO
London • New York

This book is supported by the French Ministry for Foreign
Affairs as part of the Burgess Programme, headed for the French
Embassy in London by the Institut Français du Royaume Uni

Liberté • Égalité • Fraternité
RÉPUBLIQUE FRANÇAISE

This edition first published by Verso 2002
© Verso 2002
Translation © Gregory Elliott 2002
First published as *Marx l'intempestif*
© Librairie Arthème Fayard 1995

1 3 5 7 9 10 8 6 4 2

Verso
UK: 6 Meard Street, London W1F 0EG
USA: 180 Varick Street, New York, NY 10014–4606
www.versobooks.com

Verso is the imprint of New Left Books

ISBN 1–85984–712–9

British Library Cataloguing in Publication Data
A catalogue record for this book is available from the British Library

Library of Congress Cataloging-in-Publication Data

A catalog record for this book is available from the Library of Congress

Typeset in 10/12pt Baskerville by
SetSystems Ltd, Saffron Walden, Essex
Printed by Biddles Ltd, Guildford & King's Lynn
www.biddles.co.uk

For Hippolyte

Contents

Preface to the English Edition
The Archipelago of
a Thousand Marxisms

This book is the result of work undertaken during the 1980s. The French version appeared in October 1995, the same year as its companion text, *La Discordance des temps*. Back in those times of counter-reformation and neo-liberal reaction, Marx had become a 'dead dog'. Such Marxism as survived was under attack on all sides. In itself, a critical rereading of Marx represented a gesture of resistance, a refusal to submit to adverse currents, a decision to think against the grain, in the conviction that a founding critique like that contained in *Capital* could not be obsolete. For its actuality is that of its object, its intimate and implacable enemy: capital itself – an insatiable vampire and fetish-automaton now more invasive than ever.

In his *Recollections* of the June Days of 1848, de Tocqueville recalls the fear of a fellow deputy who, as the gunfire was ringing out, came upon two young servants musing about putting an end to the power of their masters. He was, recounts the author of *The Ancien Régime and the Revolution*, 'very careful not to show that he had heard the monkeys', who 'made him very frightened'. And so this good bourgeois prudently waited until the day after the insurrection had been defeated, before dismissing the insolent brats and sending them back to their hovels. In the same passage, Tocqueville evokes his meeting on the rue Saint-Honoré with 'a crowd of workers anxiously listening to the gunfire':

> They wore blouses, which, as we all know, are their fighting as well as their working clothes; they were not actually carrying arms, but one could see from the look of them that they were pretty near to taking them up. With hardly restrained delight they noted that the sound of the firing seemed to be getting closer, which meant that the rebels were gaining ground. I had guessed before this that the whole of the working class backed the revolt, either actively or in

its heart; this proved it to me. In fact the spirit of insurrection circulated from end to end of that vast class and all its parts, like blood in the body; it filled places where there was no fighting as much as those that formed the battlefield; and it had penetrated into our houses, around us, above us, below us. Even the places where we thought we were the masters were creeping with domestic enemies; it was as if an atmosphere of civil war enveloped the whole of Paris, and, no matter where one withdrew, one had to live in it.[1]

Reading this evocation of bourgeois *grande peur* before the 'spirit of insurrection', one imagines the slight smile on the lips of the spectre haunting Europe in the spring of 1848: the spectre of communism. A century and a half after the opening declaration of the *Communist Manifesto*, the spectre seemed to have vanished beneath the rubble of really non-existing socialism. The hour of Counter-Reformations and Restorations had struck. Francis Fukuyama decreed the end of history. In *The Passing of an Illusion*, François Furet claimed to close the file on communism: the issue was settled. Immobilized in its market eternity, capitalism had become the untranscendable horizon of all time. Death of Marx and the avant-gardes? End of history, end of communism?

Ends never finish ending. History strikes back. After Seattle, Genoa and Porto Alegre, it has got its colour back. Ghosts are stirring. Revenants are arriving to disturb the peace of the established order. Close on twenty-five years ago, *Newsweek* solemnly proclaimed the death of Marx on its front cover. By 1993, the labour of mourning was over. There would, Jacques Derrida wrote in his *Specters of Marx*, be 'no future without the memory and the inheritance of Marx: in any case of a certain Marx . . . [and] at least one of his spirits'. For, he added, '*there is more than one of them, there must be more than one.*'[2] The same year, Gilles Deleuze told a journalist from *Le Nouvel Observateur* that he did not understand what it meant when people claimed that Marx was wrong, and still less when they claimed that Marx was dead: the urgent task of analyzing the world market and its transformations could not dispense with Marx. 'My next book – and it will be my last', confided Deleuze, 'will be called *Grandeur de Marx*.' Unfortunately, he did not live to complete the project.

Today, Marx is the subject of colloquia and seminars; he is even included in the prestigious 'La Pléiade' collection published by Gallimard. He has been immortalized in academia and publishing; his future seems assured. Communism is a different matter. The word seems forever associated with the bureaucratic crimes committed in its name, as if Christianity was exclusively identified with the Inquisition, dragonnades and forcible conversions.

After the Congress of Vienna in 1815, in an age of Restoration when the names of Robespierre and Saint-Just had become unpronounceable, and the workshops of Silesian and Lyonnais weavers simmered with anger, communism was initially a conspiratorial term, whispered like some good news, the 'secret name' (in Heine's words) counterposing proletarian rule to the bourgeois regime. It made its first appearance as part of a resumption of the subterranean advance towards equality. In 1840, the first communist banquet in Belleville added a new word – communism – to the republican motto of liberty, equality and solidarity. More than a doctrine, communism is, in the first instance, this real movement, this accumulation of constantly renewed experience, this upsurge of hope that puts suppression of the existing order on the agenda. How could a 'secret name', which rallies resistance, dissidence and rebelliousness from one person to the next, from strikes to riots, be over and done with?

In retrospect, it is easy to pick out the threads of the event and to discover what was being woven silently and obscurely. Since the early 1990s, released from his 'isms' by the fall of the Berlin Wall and the break-up of the Soviet Union, Marx has been out of quarantine. We no longer have the excuse of his capture by the bureaucracy and confiscation by the state to duck the responsibility of rereading and interpreting him. The debate might have remained academic had it not begun to resonate with a revival of struggle. In France, we had the red anger of December 1995, a great surge of winter resistance, the frail rebirth of a 'left of the left'.

But what can resistance achieve when the horizon of expectations has collapsed? After the disasters that had piled up in the twentieth century, amid the troubling silence of better futures that had ceased to resonate, it was very tempting to revert back from 'scientific socialism' to 'utopian socialism'; to escape the dogmatic illusions of the former only to succumb to the senile, exhausted chimeras of the second, without even the excuse of the innocence or enthusiasm of their original *élan*.

According to Derrida once again, the essential question – a question that is always fresh – is not communism, but capital and the formation of surplus-value in its new forms: capital obviously does not operate in the way it did in the nineteenth century (only an idiot would ignore the fact); and yet it operates.[3] To see what it is up to, to escape its phantasmagorias, to respond to its enigmas – this remains the business of Marx, and of communism. As long, says Daniel Singer, as capital works.

Inheriting is never an automatic process: it poses questions of legitimacy and imposes responsibilities. A theoretico-political legacy is never straightforward: it is not some possession that is received and banked. Simultaneously instrument and obstacle, weapon and burden, it is always to be transformed. For everything depends upon what is done with this inheritance lacking owners or directions for use.

As Eustache Kouvélakis has stressed, Marxism is, in its very constitution, 'crisis theory' [*pensée de la crise*].[4] Its first wave of diffusion, at the end of the nineteenth century, coincided with what Georges Sorel was already calling its 'decomposition'. This crisis betokened a 'pluralization' of the legacy from the very start and the onset of tendency struggles which, echoing the challenges of the epoch, have run through the field of theory ever since. Thus, the crisis of the 1980s had some features in common with previous crises. Once again, the research programme derived from Marx's founding *oeuvre* confronted the questions posed by a period of expansion and transformation of the capitalist system itself. The practices and forms of the social movement have been tested by changes in social relations, the division of labour, and the organization of production. To these recurrent features, the end of the historical sequence dubbed the 'short twentieth century' added the collapse of the societies and orthodoxies that had been presented as the earthly embodiment of the spectre of communism for more than half a century.

Under the impact of the neo-liberal counter-reformation, the 1980s were years of lead for militant Marxism. In France, Mitterrandism opened up careers to the appetite for social promotion. Those disappointed in Maoism largely realigned themselves with a human rights anticommunism, delighted at the chance to be on the side of the angels after having played the fool for too long. Others indulged in 'weak thought' and postmodern resignation. In his *Confession d'un enfant du siècle*, Musset evoked a sense of something vague and floating in connection with the Restoration, marking the transition between a finished past and an uncertain future. A disenchanted generation lived through the age wrapped in the mantle of egotism. In the absence of more noble enterprises and ambitions, in this 'hideous sea of action without a goal', the time was ripe for the cynicism of the victors, for trifling entertainments and minor virtues. Faced with a new reaction and restoration, are we in our turn going to be reduced to minimalism and miniaturism? Are we going to be shipwrecked on the dark sea of action without a goal?

In France, the strikes of winter 1995 in defence of public services and social security marked an anti-neo-liberal turn, subsequently confirmed on an international scale by the demonstrations against capitalist globalization: 'The world is not for sale! The world is not a commodity!'. On the rubble of the twentieth century, the 'thousand Marxisms' referred to by the philosopher André Tosel have begun to blossom.[5] The sky has not turned crimson, but the climate is improving. In 1993 appeared Derrida's

Specters of Marx and *The Weight of the World* directed by Pierre Bourdieu. In autumn 1995, at the very moment the strike movement was getting underway, the first 'International Marx Conference' was held on the initiative of the journal *Actuel Marx*. *Marx l'intempestif* appeared in October. The press could only marvel at this intellectual resurrection paralleling the 'return of the social question'.

Since then, the Fondation Saint-Simon (think-tank of a temperate liberalism) has been wound up, whereas various spaces for militant reflection have opened up on the left of the left, like the Fondation Copernic, whose appearance echoed the renewal of union and social movements (feminist, unemployed, anti-racist movements, Attac, etc.). This renaissance, as yet modest, also finds expression in France in the flourishing of a new social cinema, the hatching of critical journals, and the increased publication of literature inspired by Marxism.

In this context, the ramification of a 'thousand Marxisms' appears as a moment of liberation in which thought breaks its doctrinal shackles. It indicates the possibility of starting over anew, overcoming the traumatic experiences of a tragic century without making a clean sweep of the past. Plural and actual in equal measure, these Marxisms evince a commendable curiosity and promising richness. Yet their proliferation poses the question of what, underneath the differences and disciplinary fragmentation, constitutes the common core of a research programme with one and the same name. Can we still speak of Marxism, or must we make do (as the formula of the Catalan philosopher Fernandez Buey has it) with a Marx 'without isms' and a deconstructed Marxism? What, asks André Tosel, is the minimal consensus as to what may legitimately be called a Marxist interpretation? According to him, these thousand Marxisms, present and future, pose the question of minimum theoretical agreement over the field of legitimate disagreements. Their generous multiplicity can in fact lead to the dissipation of the theoretical core and its dissolution into a postmodernist cultural broth.

The long theoretical fast of the Stalinist period has whetted the appetite for rediscovery. The millstone of state Marxism and the experience of inquisitorial excommunications have likewise fuelled a profound and legitimate aspiration to freedom of thought, of which the great heretics of a previous age (Ernst Bloch, the late Lukács, Louis Althusser, but also Henri Lefebvre or Ernest Mandel) were the precursors. Eustache Kouvélakis underscores the new, converse risk that the thousand Marxisms will peacefully coexist on a becalmed stage from which the exigency of controversy seems strangely absent. This danger goes hand in hand with the institutional rehabilitation of a Marx subjected to the proprieties of an academic Marxology bereft of subversive designs. In *Specters of Marx*, Derrida had already cautioned against the temptation to play off Marx against Marxism, neutralizing political imperatives in tranquil exegesis.

The basis of this threat lies in the discordance between the rhythms of intellectual recovery and those of social mobilization, in the ongoing split between theory and practice which, according to Perry Anderson, has long characterized Western Marxism. As Alex Callinicos has stressed,[6] in its proud adherence to the unity of theory and practice, Marxism is subject to a double criterion of judgement. If it has not been seriously refuted at a theoretical level, it has unquestionably been affected by the grave political defeats of the past century.

Some recently prestigious and seemingly promising 'schools' of Marxism have not withstood the ordeal of the neo-liberal reaction and social defeats of the 1980s. Contributions to the recent *Dictionnaire Marx contemporain* foreground the parallel crisis of three of them.

The coherence of the so-called Regulation School was always open to doubt. As early as his stocktaking of 1987, Robert Boyer acknowledged its difficulties and impasses.[7] Clearly abandoning reference to Marxism, it was not long before it stopped existing as a genuine school, torn as it was between the increasingly managerialist trajectory of Michel Aglietta, Boyer's adherence to conventions theory, and the non-existent ecological 'new paradigm' promised by Alain Lipietz. As early as 1995, the inspirational core of the current had switched from a post-Fordist perspective to a historical compromise with patrimonial capitalism, with some like Aglietta going so far as to praise employee shareholding, and others transforming themselves into advisers to human resources directors.[8]

Nor has the current of Analytical Marxism survived the watershed of the 1990s as such. Rational Choice Marxism and some of its distinguished sponsors have failed the test of social remobilization and struggle against imperial globalization. From the outset, the group was marked by a certain eclecticism, pulled between the Marxist problematic of Robert Brenner, Erik Olin Wright or G. A. Cohen, and a Philippe van Parijs who never claimed to have much in common with any form of Marxism. Jon Elster himself ended up conceding the impossibility of seriously combining Marxism with game theory and methodological individualism. If his works, or those of John Roemer, can be stimulating, their farewell to Marx supplies candid clarification.[9]

Finally, the current known as Italian *operaismo*, exemplified in the 1960s and 70s by the research of Raniero Panzieri, Mario Tronti and Toni Negri, has not withstood the changes of the last two decades, industrial decentralization and the social defeats of the industrial working class. It would seem that the disappointed 'workerism' of yesteryear has today found expression in disaffection with Marx's legacy. Mario Tronti expresses a species of 'theoretical despair', while the latest works of Toni Negri remain ambiguous. Reading *Empire*, it is not clear whether what is involved is the new form – in sum, the 'highest stage' – of imperialism, or a qualitatively different reality – a-centric, a-cephalous and rhizomatic – in which the relations of domination and inequality between North and South are dissolved in the 'frictionless space' of the world market. Likewise, it is no longer clear if the (sociologically vacant) concept of 'multitude' is simply a new (postmodern?) name – a kind of pseudonym – for the globalized proletariat, or a dissolution of classes into the diverse subjectivities oppressed by capital and their reticulate counter-power.

Even so, the research programme inspired by Marx remains robust. But it only has a genuine future if, rather than seeking refuge in the academic fold, it succeeds in establishing an organic relationship with the revived practice of social movements – in particular, with the resistance to imperialist globalization.

For that is where Marx's actuality finds striking expression: in the privatization of the world, in the capital-fetish, and its lethal course in the frenzied acceleration of the chase for profits and the insatiable conquest of space subject to the impersonal law of the market. The theoretical and militant *oeuvre* of Marx was produced in the age of Victorian globalization. The rapid development of railways, of the telegraph and steam navigation was the contemporary equivalent of internet and satellite telecommunications; credit and speculation underwent impetuous development; the barbarous union of the market and technology was celebrated; 'industrialized killing' made its appearance. It was then too that the workers' movement of the First International emerged. The 'critique of political economy' conducted in *Capital* unquestionably remains the foundational reading of the hieroglyphs of modernity and the starting point for a research programme that has yet to be exhausted.

The crisis of liberal globalization and its apologetic discourses, which has now become open, represents the basis for the renaissance of Marxism. This is attested by such Marxological works as those of Enrique Dussel or Jacques Bidet, as well as, in the field of economics, those of Robert Brenner in the United States, Francisco Louça on long waves, and Gérard Duménil and Jacques Lévy; or by politically oriented research on the logics of globalization, like that by François Chesnais or Issac Joshua in France. Under the impetus provided by David Harvey, the exploration of a 'historical-geographical materialism' is extending the tracks opened up by Henri Lefebvre on the production of space. Feminist studies are renewing reflection on the relations between social classes and gender or community identities. Cultural studies, especially as represented by the works of Fredric Jameson or Terry Eagleton, are developing new perspectives for the critique of aesthetic representations, ideologies and forms. The critique of political philosophy is finding new inspiration with the essays of Domenico Losurdo or Ellen Meiksins Wood on liberalism; with a critical rereading of major figures like Georg Lukács or Walter Benjamin; with the examination of a critical historiography on the French Revolution; with new readings of the Marxist corpus by young philosophers; with the inquiries of jurists and academics into the metamorphoses and uncertainties of law; with debates about the role of science and technology, and democratic control over them, as in the contributions to a critique of political ecology by authors like John Bellamy Foster, Ted Benton, Michel Husson, Jean-Marie Harribey, Jean-Paul Deléage, and José Manuel Naredo; with an original interpretation of Lacanian psychoanalysis in Slavoj Žižek; with the confrontation between the Marxist legacy and bodies of work such as those of Hannah Arendt or Pierre Bourdieu. *Oeuvres* like that of Alex Callinicos, engaged in the great controversies of the present, illustrate the possibility and vitality of a militant Marxism.

This flowering meets the requirements of rigorous research while avoiding the trap of academic exegesis. It demonstrates the extent to which the spectres of Marx still haunt our present, and how mistaken it would be to oppose an imaginary golden age of 1960s Marxism (when E. P. Thompson legitimately set about the 'poverty of theory') to the sterility of contemporary Marxisms. The 1980s were relatively barren, but the new century promises more than a few oases.

No doubt the molecular labour of theory is less visible than it was previously. It has no master-thinkers comparable in renown to the old ones. It is also wanting in dialogue with a political project capable of assembling and combining energies. But it is probably deeper, more collective, freer, and more secular. And hence rich in future promise.

Daniel Bensaïd, February 2002

Notes

1. Alexis de Tocqueville, *Recollections*, trans. George Lawrence, Macdonald, London 1970, pp. 142–3.
2. Jacques Derrida, *Specters of Marx: The State of the Debt, the Work of Mourning, and the New International*, trans. Peggy Kamuf, Routledge, London and New York 1994, p. 13.
3. Ibid.

4. Eustache Kouvélakis, 'Crises du marxisme, transformation du capitalisme', in Jacques Bidet and Kouvélakis, eds, *Dictionnaire Marx contemporain*, Presses Universitaires de France, Paris 2001, pp. 41–56.
5. André Tosel, 'Devenir du marxisme: de la fin du marxisme-léninisme aux mille marxismes, France-Italie 1975–1995', in ibid., pp. 57–78.
6. Alex Callinicos, 'Où va le marxisme anglo-saxon?', in ibid., pp. 79–95.
7. See Robert Boyer, *La Théorie de la régulation: une analyse critique*, La Découverte, Paris 1987.
8. See Michel Husson's merciless article, 'L'école de la régulation de Marx à Saint-Simon: un aller sans retour?', in *Dictionnaire Marx contemporain*, pp. 171–82.
9. For a balance-sheet, see Callinicos, 'Où va le marxisme anglo-saxon?'.

The Inaudible Thunder

> When *Das Kapital* interrupted the course and rent the fabric of this whole historical movement, it was like an inaudible thunderclap, a silence, a margin.
>
> (Gérard Granel, Preface to Husserl, *La Crise des sciences européennes*)

> *Capital* is an essentially subversive work. It is such less because it leads, by way of scientific objectivity, to the necessary consequence of revolution, than because it includes, without formulating it too explicitly, a mode of theoretical thinking that overturns the very idea of science.
>
> (Maurice Blanchot, 'Marx's Three Voices')

As Isabelle Stengers has suggested, 'remaining faithful to a line of thinking first of all involves learning to resist it.' Committed to such resistance *vis-à-vis* Marx and what he took from his epoch, I have set out to discover what remains actively current in his many voices.

Marx's actuality attaches, in the first instance, to the universalization and morbid energy of capital itself. Having become global, capital is more than ever the spirit of an age bereft of spirit, marked by the impersonal power of the reign of commodities. It is our leaden horizon, our sad lot. As long as capital continues to dominate social relations, Marx's theory will retain its currency, its endless renewals constituting the reverse side and negation of universal commodity fetishism.

'Written in black and white', *Capital* 'painted it red' and sent 'European humanity' into crisis.[1] Far from muffling its 'inaudible thunder', accelerating global upheaval finally makes it possible to hear it.

Marx's Three Critiques

This does not mean pitting some original, authentic Marx against counter-feit versions, or restoring a truth seized from us long ago, but disturbing the heavy slumber of orthodoxies. So multifaceted an *œuvre* is sustained by its diverse and contrasting interpretations. The contradictory multi-plicity of established 'Marxisms' derives from the comparative undecida-bility of texts in which a critical decipherment of social hieroglyphics is intimately bound up with the practical subversion of the existing order. Registering a directly critical voice, a political voice that is 'always excessive . . . since excess is its only measure', and the indirect voice of scientific discourse, Maurice Blanchot notes that these discourses are held together by 'disparity'. They are not juxtaposed, but intertwined and intermingled. Diversity of registers should not be confused with vulgar eclecticism, and 'Marx does not live comfortably with this plurality of languages, which always collide and disarticulate themselves in him.'[2]

Torn between his fascination with the physical model of positive science and his loyalty to 'German science', between the siren calls of progress and rejection of its artificial paradises, Marx quarrels with his own shadow, and wrestles with his own spectres. His thought, riddled with unresolved contradictions, is far from homogeneous. But neither is it incoherent or inconsistent. The core of his research programme still makes it possible to question the universe we inhabit, with a view to changing the world. It cannot be employed for eclectic collages and media rush jobs. What we are dealing with is not a doctrine, but the theory of a practice open to several readings. Not any readings whatsoever: not everything is permiss-ible in the name of free interpretation; not everything is valid. Text and context specify constraints, define a field of variations compatible with its own aporias, and consequently invalidate the results of misinterpretation.

Thus, Marx's theory is sometimes defined as a philosophy of history, its meaning and culmination; sometimes as a sociology of classes and method of classification; and sometimes as an enterprise in scientific economics. None of these definitions survives a rigorous reading. While it is by no means easy to state what Marx's theory is, at least it is possible to clarify what it is not.

It is not a speculative philosophy of history. Professedly a deconstruc-tion of universal History, it opens the way to a history that promises no salvation, offers no guarantee to redress injustice – not even the faintest possibility. A profane history emerges whose trajectory is unsettled, in that it is determined conjointly by struggle and necessity. Hence there is no question of founding a new philosophy of some unidirectional history. What we have, instead, is a new way of writing history, whose alphabet is suggested by the *Grundrisse*. *Capital* thus indissociably deploys a new representation of history, and a conceptual organization of time as a social relation: cycles and turnovers, rhythms and crises, strategic moments and contretemps. The old philosophy of history thus fades into a critique of commodity fetishism on the one hand, and political subversion of the existing order on the other.

Marx's theory is not an empirical sociology of classes, either. Contrary to positive reason, which arranges and classifies, inventories and itemizes, soothes and assuages, it brings out the dynamics of social conflict and renders the phantasmagoria of commodities intelligible. Not that the various social antagonisms (of sex, status or nation) are reducible to class relations. The diagonal of the class front links and conditions them, but without conflating them. From this kind of perspective, the other (alien on account of his or her religion, traditions, origins, chapel or parish) can always become one of us through a process of real universalization. That is why social classes are never objects or categories of sociological classification, but the very expression of historical development

Finally, Marx's theory is not a positive science of the economy conforming to the then dominant model of classical physics. A contemporary of the sciences of evolution and the advance of thermodynamics, it is recalcitrant to the compartmentalized, one-sided rationality of the scientific division of labour – all the more so since the strange choreography of commodities and currencies inclines it towards the then unknown logics of systems and information. Just as it would be anachronistic to make Marx's theory the conscious pioneer of the latest epistemology, so it is clear that the erratic behaviour of capital inflects it towards unexplored paths. Paradoxically, here Marx rediscovers the synthesizing ambitions of the old metaphysics, which he explicitly adopts in the shape of 'German science' [*deutschen Wissenschaft*]. Revival of this tradition enables him to tackle the non-linear logics, laws of tendency, and conditional necessities of what Gramsci shrewdly identified as a 'new immanence'.

These three critiques – of historical reason, economic reason, and scientific positivity – match and complement one another. They are directly relevant to current questions about the end of history and the representation of time; about the relationship between class struggle and other types of conflict; about the destiny of the hard sciences tormented by the uncertainties of the narrative sciences. If it is not a philosophy of history, a sociology of class, or a science of the economy, what is Marx's theory? By way of a provisional response, we might say: not a doctrinal system, but a critical theory of social struggle and the transformation of the world.

Vectors of Possibility

In his sketch of a new way of writing history, Marx stresses the role of the asynchrony or non-contemporaneity of economic, juridical and aesthetic spheres. The dynamic of social conflict operates in the rifts and fractures of this discordance of temporalities. Marx's thought is itself situated at the meeting point where the metaphysical legacy of Greek atomism, Aristotelian physics and Hegelian logic is put to the test of the Newtonian epistemological model, the flourishing of historical disciplines, and rapid developments in the knowledge of the living being. Profoundly anchored in its present, it oversteps and exceeds that present in the direction of the past and the future. That is why the echo of its discourse was *practically inaudible* to contemporaries insensitive to the art of contretemps. It was easier for inheritors and epigones to translate it into the humdrum music of the dominant positivism and reassuring odes to progress.

Positioned at the intersection of typically non-contemporaneous tracks, Marx emerges today as an audacious vector of possibilities. As the crust of orthodoxies flakes off, it is an auspicious moment to revive long disdained or ignored potentialities. In search of this untimely Marx, torn between present, past and future, I have traversed the variegated landscape of a century of readings and commentaries. The approaches of Karl Kautsky or Rosa Luxemburg, Nicolai Bukharin or Karl Korsch, Louis Althusser or Roman Rosdolsky, do not lead to the same Marx. We must therefore choose our path and our company. For my part, I have prioritized two other great intermediaries: Walter Benjamin and Antonio Gramsci. Their tragic destinies as outsiders enabled them to hear what remained inaudible to the majority of Marx's professed disciples, anxious to translate his unusual words into a familiar language, which was inevitably that of the dominant ideology. Against the somnolent cult of progress and its often illusory promises, they approached Marx via remarkably convergent, difficult and unfrequented roads. From his *Moscow Diary* (1927) to the *Theses on the Philosophy of History* (1939), Benjamin deepened his Messianic critique of temporal abstraction. At the same moment, in the experience of defeat, Gramsci drew the consequences of the inherently uncertain character of the conflict in his *Prison Notebooks* (1930–36): the only thing that could be forecast was class struggle – not its precise occasions. The result was a conception of politics as strategy and error as the risk inherent in any decision.

The vitality of a theory is tested by the refutations to which it is subject and the mutations it can experience without disintegrating. Engaging in this game of contradiction, I have often prioritized confrontation with Karl Popper and the current of 'Analytical Marxism'.

• With Popper, because his critique of Marxist historicism – which to my mind is largely unfounded – pervaded the ideological counter-offensive of the 1970s in France, preparing the way for the social, political and moral counter-reformation whose damage we are assessing today. Popper's epistemology, although questionable, is definitely more valuable than his vague philosophy, which in its turn is better than vulgar Popperianism reduced to an ideological commonplace.

• With Analytical Marxism (G.A. Cohen, Jon Elster, John Roemer, Erik Olin Wright), because throughout the 1980s the merit of these authors was to pose fundamental questions about history, progress and class in the light of the tragic experiences of the twentieth century. They sought to save Marx from his archaism by formulating a general theory of history (Cohen) or exploitation (Roemer), informed by recent developments in game theory and theories of justice. The result – recognized as such – was the methodical destruction of the central theoretical core of Marx's thought (value theory, abstract labour, the relation between value and prices), which illustrates the incompatibility between any radical methodological individualism and a critical theory of social conflict.

More generally, the bankruptcy of the state policies implemented in Marx's name since the late 1920s supposedly demonstrates the impossibility of combining two distinct research programmes: the critique of political economy and the theory of history; an analysis of social conflict and an understanding of historical evolution. Their hastily proclaimed identity served scientifically to justify the necessity of a socialist alternative, 'historical Marxism' drawing its mythical power and eliciting credulity from a link that could not be demonstrated. The fusion of history, science and ethics, however, is characteristic of positivist catechisms and the freemasonry of *raison d'état*, rather than the subversive thought of Marx himself. In truth, what is dying is the historical cult of modernity, of which the established Marxisms were ultimately only variants.

Uncertain, history neither promises nor guarantees anything. Undecided, the struggle is not destined to redress injustice. Science without ethics does not prescribe the good in the name of the true.

The three parts of this book take up Marx's three great critiques (of historical reason, economic reason and scientific positivism). But in order to remain within the requisite limits, it has been necessary to be selective, at the risk of being criticized for neglecting some aspect or other.[3] I have also opted to let the texts speak for themselves. Their polysemy often says more than any commentary could – and says it better. Hence this decision is not academic: assembling and juxtaposing extracts make it possible to outline the constellation of an epoch, to awaken echoes under the impact of the present.

I am indebted to all those who have contributed to this book, whether by their advice and criticism, their articles and works, their bibliographical information, or simply their conversation. In particular, I thank Antoine Artous, Michel Husson, Samuel Joshua, Vincent Jullien, Georges Labica, Nicole Lapierre, Francisco Louça, Michaël Löwy, Henri Maler, Sophie Oudin, Edwy Plenel, Miguel Romero, Pierre Rousset, Catherine Samary, Isabelle Stengers, Stavros Tombazos, Charles-André Udry, and Robert Went. I am equally grateful to Olivier Bétourné for his pertinent suggestions.

Finally, this book owes a great deal to François Maspero, whose editorial efforts saved so many essential texts from oblivion or indifference. In this way, he helped to transmit a theoretical heritage to us, and open up the horizon of a many-sided controversy.

Notes

1. Gérard Granel, Preface to Edmund Husserl, *La Crise des sciences européennes*, Gallimard, Paris 1976, p. vii.
2. Maurice Blanchot, 'The Three Voices of Marx', in Blanchot, *Friendship*, trans. Elizabeth Rottenberg, Stanford University Press, Stanford, CA 1997, pp. 98–100.
3. Readers thirsting for more are referred to my *La Discordance des temps. Essais sur les crises, les classes, l'histoire* (Éditions de la Passion, Paris 1995), containing chapters on crises and 'long waves' that illustrate the 'new appreciation of time' introduced here, as well as chapters on castes and bureaucracy, the social relations of sex, or the link between globalization and the retreat into identity. In a sense, *La Discordance des temps* represents the counterpoint and complement to *Marx for Our Times*.

From the Sacred to the Profane
Marx's Critique of Historical Reason

> *History* does *nothing . . .*
> (Engels, *The Holy Family*)

A New Way of Writing History

Marx is sometimes condemned for economic determinism, and sometimes for historical teleology. In practical terms, these cardinal sins allegedly translate into either a fanatical voluntarism, hastening the course of history towards some guaranteed 'happy ending', or a bureaucratic passivity confident in the mechanics of progress.

Vices sometimes have their virtue. Calvinist predestination originally contained a strong practical impulse, and a certain kind of determinism could develop into 'a spirit of initiative and into an extreme tension of collective will'. Confidence in an emancipated future was likewise 'a tremendous force of moral resistance', in which '[r]eal will takes on the garments of an act of faith'.[1] Gramsci interpreted such ambivalence as the expression of a profound popular religiosity, whose stubborn faith is resistant to the intellectual power of discursive argument.

Some 'Marxists' have indeed happily spun out the metaphor of the 'Tribunal of History', with its 'tracks' and 'detours', as if a one-way street led to the foot of the oak tree where, in the manner of Saint Louis, justice will finally be done. According to this religious interpretation, that which is untimely is deviant and erroneous, a plot. The collapse of the bureaucratic regimes today affords us the opportunity to reread Marx, dismantling the wall of a 'Marxism' that petrified into ideology, an orthodoxy formed largely in ignorance of his thought. Does Marx subscribe to the prospect of an end of history? The prospect of a classless society, of the extinction of the state, and of the unlimited satisfaction of needs might make it legitimate to think so:

> It may be supposed that a socialist society in this sense would be a state of complete satisfaction, an *ultimate society* with no incentive or need for further development. While Marx does not express his vision in these terms, he does not rule out such an interpretation either, and it is encouraged by his view of socialism as the removal of all sources of human conflict and a state in which the essence of humanity is empirically realized. Communism, he says, 'is the

solution to the riddle of history and is aware of that fact'; the question then arises whether it is not also the termination of history.[2]

The 'ultimate society'? The 'termination of history'? These are not Marx's formulas; they are the preserve of his commentators. Characterization of communism as the 'solution to the riddle of history' belongs to a period when Marx specifies that by communism he means nothing other than the '*real* movement'.[3] The key to the mystery thus supposedly consists in the 'real movement' whereby history is, inextricably, history in the making and the critical theory of its own development.

As early as 1845, Engels categorically rejected any personification of history promoted to the rank of a power in its own right:

> *History* does *nothing*, it 'possesses *no* immense wealth', it 'wages *no* battles'. It is *man*, real, living man who does all that, who possesses and fights; 'history' is not, as it were, a person apart, using man as a means to achieve *its own* aims; history is *nothing but* the activity of man pursuing his aims.[4]

For the 'first premise of all human history is, of course, the existence of living human individuals'.[5] It would be difficult to find a more categorical rejection of any fetishized representation of history. The history that 'does' something is invariably a sacred history, supposed to act instead of human individuals and behind their backs; a philosophical, speculative history: the history of the ideologues. Profane history has no ends of its own.

These fiery words are from Engels's pen. But *The Holy Family* was a joint text, mainly written by Marx. A year later, *The German Ideology* hammered the point home: future history should not be regarded as the aim of past history. Such self-professed incredulity was fraught with consequences. To overturn the dictatorship of ends is to de-moralize history (to renounce definitively the notion that it has a moral). To de-moralize it is to politicize it, and open it up to strategic conceptualization. Conceiving the abolition of capital not as the 'end of history', but as the end of 'prehistory', is no mere literary coquetry or wordplay.

Without drawing all the consequences, Ruge had anticipated this alteration whereby time becomes political; and Kierkegaard, while bitterly regretting the fact, likewise observed in 1847 that everything was becoming political. Marx, for his part, would never give an inch. The rest is another story.

The Poverty of Popperianism

In the indictment of historical teleology, Karl Popper's role is that of relentless public prosecutor.[6] Hegel and Marx are in the dock. The Hegelian farce of a history destined to accomplish a final cause has, he maintains, lasted long enough. An 'open society' and a closed history (one whose last word has already been written) are incompatible. The last consistent avatar of Hegelian historicism, and an 'intellectual fifth column' in the camp of humanism, 'Marxism' must be destroyed as a matter of urgency. Marx is indeed the false prophet of the purest, most widely diffused, and most formidable form of historicism the world has known. In particular, he is responsible for the confusion between social forecasting and historical prediction, and the reduction of historical causality to the model of natural causality. Inverting the original efficient cause into final cause, and subjecting the present to the despotic power of history, he allegedly exploited the authority of scientific determinism in the service of historical finalism. Without this confusion, the reasonable idea that social evolution is governed by certain causes would not have led to historicism and its practical ravages.

According to Popper, historicism is a religion of earthly salvation wherein God's judgements are disclosed in and through the course of history. Yet in the usual sense of the word, history does not exist. There is no such thing as history as a unified, meaningful structure; and hence no meaning or direction to history.[7] Were history to be our judge, it would endlessly celebrate the *fait accompli*. From the outset, its sinister tribunal would be the preserve of the victors, whose arrogant domination it would perpetuate – until victory changed sides, carrying justice and judges off in its train.

Reducing social science to history defined as the study of the 'laws of social evolution', historicism, according to Popper, is divided into anti- and pro-naturalistic currents. The first current – active – seeks to bend the course of history to its will. The second – passive – submits to evolutionary laws. Incapable of knowing whether these laws obtain beyond observation periods, we can never be certain of possessing a fixed, universal law. Thus the omnipotence of history induces a relativism that is ruinous for knowledge.[8]

Marx does not fit into this latter structure. Suspected of activism, he should be assigned to the anti-naturalistic camp. On the other hand, his interest in the laws of physics and chemistry pushes him into the pro-naturalistic camp.[9] Popper handles this difficulty by indicting the

paradoxical alliance between historicism and utopianism, between submission to the laws of history and the unrelenting desire to force its
course. On the pretext of epistemological rigour, it is then a question of
contrasting two types of politics: the historicist voluntarism of any revolutionary project and the 'piecemeal social engineering' of a reasonable
reformism. The main route to practical results in the social and natural
sciences alike, humble repair work is thus dignified with the patience of
scientific precision.

Since the 1970s and the success of *The Poverty of Historicism*, this line of
argument has become the stock in trade of contemporary anti-Marxism in
France. In truth, the fad for scientistic readings of Marx prompted an
epistemological critique of him in response. Popper seemed best placed
to refute official Marxism's exorbitant claim to be engaged in science,
and to annex the truth to history.

In his debate with Carnap and the Vienna Circle in the 1930s, Popper
criticized logical positivism for losing sight of the privileged moment of
scientific discovery and daring conjecture. The logical purification of
science by the elimination of meaningless statements involved an illusion.
In order to meet the requirements of non-relativism, a critical, dynamic
conception of scientific knowledge had to expose itself to the test of
refutation. According to this epistemology of hazardous conjectures,
irrefutability constituted the typical vice of pseudo-scientific 'knowledge'.
An 'unfalsifiable' discourse (Marxism, say, or psychoanalysis) which does
not subject its predictions to the test of refutation, and constantly hits
upon new justifications for itself, is precisely what characterizes non-
science.

Although it is undeniably fertile, Popperian epistemology, from *The
Logic of Scientific Discovery* and *Conjectures and Refutations* to *Objective Knowledge*, lapses into ideology when it reduces all scientificity to its own criteria.
The mediocre philosophy of *The Poverty of Historicism* (published, it should
be recalled, in 1944–45, at a time when Marxism was widely identified
with Stalinist orthodoxy), and of *The Open Society and its Enemies*, exemplifies this error. But when he maintains that a world in which objective
knowledge exists as social progress without a sovereign subject is not
wholly determined or predictable, Popper is closer to Marx than he
imagines.

If human knowledge is cumulative, Popper argues, it is not possible to
anticipate today what will be known only in the future. Growth in
knowledge alters the path as it goes along. Accordingly, for strictly logical
reasons, predicting the future course of history is precluded. In and
through a reflexive knowledge of it, historical development yields some-

thing inherently novel, whose role and significance are never immediately fixed, but only provisional, open to subsequent correction and interpretation. It is true that Marx states that he is seeking to discover economic laws as rigorous as those of the so-called exact sciences, yet he invariably founders on the recalcitrant, non-linear logic of 'laws of tendency'. Now, according to Popper, the confusion between 'laws' and 'trends' is responsible for the 'central doctrines of evolutionism and historicism'.[10] By way of proof, he cites John Stuart Mill's *Logic*, with its aim 'by a study and analysis of the general facts of history to discover . . . the law of progress; which law, once ascertained, must . . . enable us to predict future events, *just as after a few terms of an infinite series in algebra we are able to detect the principle of regularity in their formation, and to predict the rest of the series to any number of terms we please*'.[11] The 'historical laws of succession' stated by Comte or Mill resemble nothing so much as 'a collection of misapplied metaphors'.[12]

What are we to conclude from this? That knowledge of social, psychic, or historical phenomena belongs irrevocably to the obscure domain of ideology or myth? Making falsifiability the exclusive criterion of science prompts such a conclusion. Following in the tradition of Rickert and Dilthey, Popper distinguishes between explanatory and interpretative sciences in scientific knowledge. The former deal with the general and the quantifiable; the latter with the singular and the qualitative: 'I wish to defend the view, so often attacked as old-fashioned by historicists, that *history is characterized by its interest in actual, singular, or specific events, rather than in laws or generalizations*.'[13]

Dreaming of a predictive capacity comparable to that of the natural sciences is supposedly the cardinal sin common to all varieties of historicism. Popper concedes that social and historical development is not purely random: 'trends exist, or more precisely, the assumption of trends is often a useful statistical device'.[14] The important thing is not to confuse them with physical laws; not to assign tendencies the force of laws.

This profession of faith is aimed more at 'Marxism' than at Comte or Mill, but Marx did not pursue this model of historical predictability. *Capital* is not the science of the laws of history, but a 'critique of political economy'. It does not seek to establish the coherence of a universal History, but to disentangle tendencies and temporalities that counteract, without abolishing, one another. The texts devoted to particular historical conjunctures (the 1848 revolutions, the American Civil War, the Paris Commune) respond point by point to Popper's charges. They are not only literary masterpieces (as is commonly agreed), but also examples of a knowledge of history in the making. This historical present is not a link in some mechanical sequence of effects and causes, but a contemporaneity full of possibilities, where politics takes precedence over history in deciphering tendencies that do not possess the force of law.

What is foreshadowed is another kind of knowledge, resistant to the canons of Newtonian physics. It produces a positive knowledge quite differently, along with a capacity to act on reality. Popper accepts that any causal explanation of a singular event can be called 'historical'. To explain why and how it came about is, in sum, to 'tell its history'. Faithful to the evidential form of inquiry that originally characterized history, the 'narrative sciences' thus elude the simplistic verdict of refutation. They permit several narratives of the same history, and involve the postulate that narrative pluralism does not cancel the substance of what is narrated. From the critique of political economy, via the disciplines of evolution, to psychoanalysis, various so-called human sciences practise this type of knowledge. Polemicizing against their 'historicist' pretensions to predict the future then emerges as a trivial quarrel. If '[a] prediction is a social happening which may interact with other social happenings, and among them with the one which it predicts', it can also contribute to creating, hastening or averting the predicted event.[15]

More surprising is to find as attentive a reader of Marx as Jon Elster, eminent representative of the Anglo-Saxon school of analytical Marxism, repeating the same grievances. He applies himself to documenting the articles that appeal to 'the functionalist notion of free-floating intentions, purposes that can be imputed to no specific actor, only to "history"'.[16] Like Smith's invisible hand or Mandeville's hive, history allegedly plays the role of grand organizer of collective destinies in Marx, condemning individuals to execute its grand design unconsciously. Elster sees this as the result of a close bond between a strong inclination to functional explanation and the philosophy of history: 'It was certainly because Marx believed history to be directed towards a goal – the advent of communist society – that he felt justified in explaining, not only patterns of behaviour, but even individual events, in terms of their contribution to that end.'[17] Thus, the early works exhibit 'a fairly consistent teleological attitude towards history'.[18]

Yet Elster is forced to concede that *The Holy Family* and *The German Ideology* explicitly contradict this problematic. As a faithful reader of the relevant texts, he cannot be unaware of the 'settlement of accounts' with 'our erstwhile philosophical consciousness' in 1845–46:

History is nothing but the succession of the separate generations, each of which uses the materials, the capital funds, the productive forces handed down to it by all preceding generations, and thus, on the one hand, continues the traditional activity in completely changed circumstances and, on the other, modifies the old circumstances with a completely changed activity. *This can be speculatively distorted so that later history is made the goal of earlier history,* e.g., the goal ascribed to the discovery of America is to further the eruption of the French Revolution.[19]

Or again: 'In this way [i.e. Stirner's procedure] it is infinitely easy to give history "unique" turns, as one has only to describe its very latest result as the "task" which "in truth it originally set itself".' Thus, the 'task' the institution of landed property originally set itself was the eviction of men in favour of sheep, as is evident from Scotland; or – to take another example – the advent of the Capet dynasty 'set itself the task' of sending Louis XVI to the guillotine. The ritual formula 'Now, at last, *one* can state it' is the password for this apologetic vision of history.[20]

A more radical secularization of history, a firmer repudiation of 'speculative artifices' and retrospective illusions, can scarcely be imagined! Present and future history is not the goal of past history. A banal 'succession of generations', it has no more meaning than the dreary genealogy of whales. In these transitional years, when he was shedding his old skin, Marx had no mania for posteriority. He did not march to the beat of ultimate promises and last judgements. His critique is bound up with the poverty of the present: 'If we have no business with the construction of the future or with organizing it for all time there can still be no doubt about the task confronting us at present: the *ruthless criticism of the existing order.*'[21] Elster cites these texts, which contradict his own thesis, but only to dispatch them forthwith by presenting them as adventitious and inconsistent. His only concession is that he has 'no explanation for the stark contrast between *The German Ideology* and the other works'[22] – as if what was involved was some sort of enormous theoretical lapsus, immediately forgotten in favour of the developmental schema that works 'from the future to the present and not the other way round'. This account is all the more incoherent in that *The German Ideology* resumes and systematizes the themes of *The Holy Family.*

These themes are those of the 'settlement of accounts'. Yet to settle accounts with the erstwhile philosophical consciousness from the standpoint of the class struggle and the critique of political economy is also to settle them with the *speculative philosophy of history.* It is to overturn 'sacred history', with its lost paradises and promised lands, in the name of 'profane history'.[23] It is to think in the present, not the future anterior.

Faced with the positive refutation represented by the texts, Elster does not yield. Marx supposedly never envisaged 'the possibility that communism might occur prematurely, and like the Asiatic mode of production become a dead end of history'.[24] His whole approach to history 'can . . . be subsumed, perhaps, under the more general heading of *teleology*. The invisible hand upholding capital is one of the two main forms of teleology in Marx, the other being the necessity of the process that will ultimately destroy it.'[25] A prudent and modest 'perhaps', for the evidence adduced is not on a par with the conjecture.

This evidence boils down to a few letters and occasional articles. Making Russia or the English bourgeoisie characters, or erecting history into 'modern *fatum*' – these were current journalistic practices. We may detect in them the index of an anthropomorphic representation of history, but it is (to say the least) abusive to identify them as irrefutable proof of a fully fledged teleological conception. The notion of 'historical necessity' can refer to a problematic that is determinist or finalist; or it can express a 'trend' or 'law of tendency', the concept of which is examined in *Capital*. What, in fact, is a *historical* necessity that is open to 'factual' singularities? In 1849, in the *Neue Rheinische Zeitung*, Marx exhorted the workers and petty bourgeois 'to suffer in modern bourgeois society, which by its industry creates the material means for the foundation of a new society that will liberate you all', rather than to 'revert to a bygone form of society which . . . thrusts the entire nation back into medieval barbarism'. Projecting on to Marx the shadow of his posterity and the interpretation of the epigones, Elster's retrospective reading perceives this as the rough draft of Stalinist sermons on the course of history: 'Substitute the peasantry for the petty bourgeoisie, and primitive socialist accumulation for modern bourgeois society, and you have the classic justification for Stalinism.'[26]

'Marx's faith, I believe,' writes Popper, 'was fundamentally a faith in the open society.'[27] Elster goes further: 'We should retain the respect for the individual that is at the core of Marx's theory of communism, but not the philosophy of history that allows one to regard pre-communist individuals as so many sheep for the slaughter.'[28] Despite the misunderstandings or caricatures, this concern betrays a genuine difficulty. Popper and Elster refuse to take Marx *en bloc*. They cannot, in fact, establish any consistency between *the philosophy of history they attribute to him and the open theory of conflict they acknowledge in him*. They are thus reduced to making him into an eclectic, incoherent thinker. How can 'faith in the open society' and the cult of a closed history, the communist primacy of the individual and historical indifference to the lot of the masses, be reconciled?

Marx employs an 'immanent teleology' misunderstood by most of his critics, who are ignorant of Spinoza. As for utopia, it persists at the price of various subtle changes – not as some arbitrary invention of the future, but as a project that forces itself on to the horizon of the future. Henceforth, what we are confronted with is not some future City or better world, but a logic of emancipation rooted in conflict.[29]

The Alphabet of the New Historiography

While Marx is reviled as a philosopher of history, his interventions on the subject belong to the period when he was breaking with the Hegelian legacy. After the 'settlement of accounts', we no longer find any trace of a philosophy of history in his work. It is no longer his problem: he has changed terrain.

The Holy Family and *The German Ideology* thus conclusively renounce any notion of historical transcendence. Historical religiosity is systematically liquidated:

> The Hegelian philosophy of history is the last consequence, reduced to its 'clearest expression', of all this *German historiography for which it is not a question of real, nor even of political, interests, but of pure thoughts,* which must therefore appear to Saint Bruno [Bauer] as a series of 'thoughts' that devour one another and are finally swallowed up in 'self-consciousness'; and even more consistently the *course of history* must appear to Saint Max Stirner, who knows not a thing about real history, as a mere 'tale of knights, robbers and ghosts', from whose visions he can, of course, only save himself by 'unholiness'. *This conception is truly religious . . .*[30]

In 1844, Stirner denounced humanist revolts against God as 'theological', and atheists converted to the cult of abstract Man as 'pious folk'. We are never done with religiosity! Secularization can never go far enough! Marx, in his turn, challenges 'the Ego' on the terrain of secularization. Philosophers for whom history is the realization of an Idea, and the past the path traced towards the crowning achievement of the present, are given a pitilessly hard time:

> If for once these theorists treat really historical subjects, as for instance the eighteenth century, they merely give a history of ideas, separated from the facts and the practical development underlying them; and even that merely *in order to represent that period as an imperfect preliminary stage, the as yet limited predecessor of*

the truly historical age, i.e., the period of the German philosophic struggle from 1840 to 1844. As might be expected when the history of an earlier period is written with the aim of accentuating the brilliance of an unhistoric person and his fantasies, all the really historic events, even *the really historic interventions of politics in history*, receive no mention. Instead we get a narrative based not on research but on *arbitrary constructions* and literary gossip . . .[31]

How can Elster reduce this anti-religious and anti-teleological problematic to a species of inexplicable accident in Marx's thought? Quite the reverse: it involves a crucial moment of clarification and focusing, in which Marx renounces a 'truly religious conception' of the 'course of history' once and for all. He turns his back on grand 'narratives' and other historical 'constructions' so arranged as to lead up to the present, construed as the outcome of these imperfect stages. With all due respect to Fukuyamas past, present and future, who make Marx 'the great author of universal history in the nineteenth century', universal History, for him, is nothing but a (bad) novel!

Henceforth, what is at issue is taking history seriously – no longer as a religious abstraction, of which living individuals are merely the humble creatures, but as the real development of conflictual relations.

First of all – *contra* Stirner, caught out on his chosen ground of desacralization – Marx denounces a literally idealist history:

> In the foregoing presentation [he] conceives history merely as the product of abstract thoughts – or rather, of his notions of abstract thoughts – as governed by these notions, which, in the final analysis, are all resolved into the 'holy'. This domination of the 'holy', of thought, of the Hegelian absolute idea over the empirical world he further portrays as a historical relation existing at the present time, as the domination of the holy ones, the ideologists, over the vulgar world – as a *hierarchy*. In this hierarchy, what previously appeared *consecutively* exists *side by side*, so that one of the two co-existing forms of development rules over the other. Thus, the youth rules over the child, the Mongol over the Negro, the modern over the ancient, the selfless egoist (*citoyen*) over the egoist in the usual sense of the word (bourgeois), etc. . . . The 'destruction' of the 'world of things' by the 'world of the spirit' appears here as the 'domination' of the 'world of thoughts' over the 'world of things'. The outcome, of course, is bound to be that the domination which the 'world of thoughts' exercises from the outset in history is at the end of the latter also presented as the real, actually existing domination of the thinkers – and, as we shall see, in the final analysis, as the domination of the speculative philosophers – over the world of things, so that Saint Max has only to fight against thoughts and ideas of the ideologists and to overcome them, in order to make himself 'possessor of the world of things and the world of thoughts'.[32]

An apologia for domination, this sacred representation is consecrated, at the 'end of history', with the tyranny of thinkers exercising domination in the name of the Idea.

Next, *contra* Proudhon, Marx denounces the hypostasis of categories:

> We shall concede that economic relations, viewed as *immutable laws, eternal principles, ideal categories*, existed before active and energetic men did; we shall concede further that these laws, principles and categories had, since the beginning of time, slumbered 'in the impersonal reason of humanity'. We have already seen that, with all these changeless and motionless eternities, there is no history left; there is at most history in the idea, that is, history reflected in the dialectic movement of pure reason. M. Proudhon, by saying that, in the dialectic movement, ideas are no longer '*differentiated*', has done away with both the *shadow of movement* and the *movement of shadows*, by means of which one could still have created at least a semblance of history.[33]

This history of the idea is precisely the negation of history as an interplay of conflictual, determinate and random relations. The hypostasis of impersonal reason and impersonal history proceed in tandem. But history is nothing outside 'active and energetic men'.

From 1847, the page of the universal History dear to speculative philosophy is definitively turned. For Hegel, 'all that has happened and is still happening is only just what is happening in his own mind'. The philosophy of history is nothing but the history of his philosophy. 'There is no longer a "history according to the order in time", there is only "the sequence of ideas in the understanding".'[34] The charge is too unambiguous for it to be legitimate to turn Marx's own critique of speculative philosophy back against him. Aware of what he has rejected, he is equally conscious of the consequent task: nothing less than the *invention of another way of writing history*.

History becomes universal not because it aims at the fulfilment of its Idea, or because it aspires to a goal from which it retrospectively derives its meaningful unity, but quite simply as a function of a process of real universalization. If 'the actual empirical existence of men' already unfolds 'on a world-historical level', if '*world-historical*, empirically universal individuals' replace 'local ones', it is because of the actual globalization of the economy and communications. History then escapes the detached abstraction of individuals, becoming the '*world-historical existence of individuals*, i.e., existence of individuals which is directly linked up with world history'.[35] It is no more the fulfilment of a generic destiny than the present is the predetermined goal of the past.

Ten years later, Marx returned to these ideas in the introductory drafts of the *Grundrisse*. There he records eight telegraphic points under the rubric '*Notabene* in regard to points to be mentioned here and not to be forgotten':

(1) *War* developed earlier than peace; the way in which certain economic relations such as wage labour, machinery etc. develop earlier, owing to war and in the armies etc., than in the interior of bourgeois society. The relation of productive force and relations of exchange also especially vivid in the army.

(2) *Relation of previous ideal historiography to the real. Namely of the so-called cultural histories,* which are only histories of religions and of states. (On that occasion something can also be said about the various kinds of previous historiography. The so-called objective. Subjective (moral among others). The philosophical.)

(3) *Secondary and tertiary* matters; in general, *derivative, inherited,* not original relations of production. Influence here of international relations.

(4) *Accusations about the materialism of this conception. Relation to naturalistic materialism.*

(5) *Dialectic of the concepts of productive force (means of production) and relations of production,* a dialectic whose boundaries are to be determined, and which does not suspend the real difference.

(6) *The uneven development of material production relative to e.g. artistic development.* In general, the concept of progress not to be conceived in the usual abstractness. Modern art etc. This disproportion not as important or so difficult to grasp as within practical-social relations themselves. E.g. the relation of education. Relation of the *United States* to Europe. But the really difficult point to discuss here is how relations of production develop unevenly as legal relations. Thus e.g. the relation of Roman private law (this less the case with criminal and public law) to modern production.

(7) *This conception appears as necessary development.* But legitimation of chance. How. (Of freedom also, among other things.) (Influence of means of communication. World history has not always existed; history as world history a result.)

(8) *The point of departure obviously from the natural characteristic;* subjectively and objectively. Tribes, races etc.[36]

These brief remarks contribute to deconstructing the notion of 'ideal history' in favour of a *new way of writing history.* In line with the upheaval represented by the discovery of real history, this new historiography will be, quite simply, the 'critique of political economy'. Deepening the rupture with the speculative notion of universal History, this programmatic text introduces the notion of *uneven development* or *uneven relationship* between the different spheres of social activity, a critical approach to the abstract notion of progress, and a problematic relationship between historical chance and historical necessity. What is done away with is a representation of history as linear in its course and homogeneous in its moments, a history wherein the flow of time and meaning coincide. The relation between real history and written history cannot be reduced to the narrative that is supposed to impose order on the chaos of the facts.

Essays in objective, subjective or philosophical historiography to date have resulted in an *ideal history incapable of generating an understanding of real history*. A new way of writing history involves a theoretical revolution. It is no longer a question of taking possession of a transparent, meaningful totality. Thus, war has its own political and technological logic, which is not directly reducible to that of society. It develops social relations that do not correspond to those of society as a whole, or anticipate their subsequent forms. More generally, every social formation comprises relations of production that are derivative, transposed, unoriginal; whose comprehension involves 'international relations'. There is disjunction, discrepancy, discordance, 'uneven relation', and 'uneven development' between material production and artistic production, between legal relations and relations of production. A concrete social formation is irreducible to the homogeneity of the dominant production relation. The different forms of production (material, legal, artistic) do not proceed at the same rhythm. Each has its own rhythm and its own temporality.

The new way of writing history invoked by Marx thus introduces the decisive notions of contretemps or non-contemporaneity. The preface to the first edition of *Capital* echoes the notes of the *Grundrisse* on this score: 'Alongside the modern evils, we are oppressed by a whole series of inherited evils, arising from the passive survival of archaic and outdated modes of production, with their accompanying train of anachronistic social and political relations. We suffer not only from the living, but from the dead.'[37] This anachronism will astonish those who make do with the rigid 'correspondence' between infrastructure and superstructure in the 1859 Preface to *A Contribution to the Critique of Political Economy*. Marx, by contrast, insists on the discordance of temporalities.[38]

Do the texts contradict one another? Perhaps. Yet we must reiterate the continuity between the *Grundrisse* and *Capital* on this score. 'Correspondence' does not imply 'adequacy'. It merely delimits a bundle of possibilities. Contretemps, on the other hand, is the real world of politics, aesthetics, theory. Thus: '[t]he tradition of the dead generations weighs like a nightmare on the minds of the living. And, just when they appear to be engaged . . . in the creation of something which does not yet exist

. . . they timidly conjure up the spirits of the past to help them; they borrow their names, slogans and costumes . . .'[39] The present is always played out in the garb and cast-offs of another age, under assumed names, with words derived from the mother tongue, until the new language is finally mastered to the point where the old one can be forgotten. Far from being effaced in its wake, the past continues to haunt the present. Politics is precisely the point where these discordant times intersect. In Freudian archaeology, we re-encounter these active survivals and interwoven times, in which nothing that has once been formed disappears, and where anything that has been preserved can reappear.[40]

In articulating these temporalities, which are heterogeneous *vis-à-vis* one another, Marx inaugurates a non-linear representation of historical development, and opens the way to comparative research. The concepts of 'combined and uneven development' introduced by Parvus and Trotsky from 1905 onwards, and of 'non-contemporaneity' developed by Ernst Bloch, are directly in line with Marxian intuitions that remained untapped for a long time.[41]

On the eve of the 1848 revolutions, the atmosphere was thick with ghosts. That of communism, certainly. But Stirner also saw man metamorphosing into an obscure, deceptive spook: 'Yes, the whole world is haunted! . . . Ghosts in every corner!'[42] – ghosts and fetishes of truth, law, order, the good, honour, fatherland. Dehumanized humanity completely disappears into its own ideal. It is wandering like an accursed spirit that vanishes at cockcrow.

This spectral history was pregnant with events. Spectres and revenants creeping into the interstices of dis-adjusted times, the contretemps of a time out of joint, heralded their imminence.

The notes in the *Grundrisse* underline the principal consequences of this revolution in historicity. The heterogeneity of historical development is incompatible with the image of a unidirectional progress, which posits (as Nietzsche might put it) the absolute homogeneity of everything that occurs. Progress could scarcely emerge unscathed from the rejection of universal History. Marx soberly notes the fact. Generally speaking, the concept of progress should no longer be conceived 'in the usual abstractness', which makes of it a sort of destiny or providence (with technological progress mechanically entailing social and cultural progress). This abstractness assumes a notion of time as homogeneous and empty; merely by virtue of its flow, the passage of time ('the hand of time', in Darwin's phrase) vouchsafes progress. Here, on a route that has already been laid down, there are no slowdowns, no diversions, no stops. The uneven development of social, legal or cultural spheres, in contrast, obliges us to conceive a progress that is neither automatic nor uniform. History is not a long, tranquil stream. The reverse side of technological progress is social (or ecological) regression. Here we register progress; there regression. 'Progress', writes Robert Bonnaud, 'is divided; it is its own enemy.'[43] It changes front and direction.

Zeitwidrig! Non-contemporaneity, non-linearity. Discordance of spheres and times. Time punctuated by alternation and intermittence. The broken time of politics and strategy.

Open to the rhythmical contradictions of cycles and genealogies, this 'historical materialism' cannot be confused with 'naturalistic materialism'. Every individual is involved in a multiplicity of times in which economic cycles, organic cycles, ecological cycles, and the deep trends of geology, climate and demography intervene. Swaying this way and that, time is replete with the opportunities and auspicious moments once foreshadowed by the *kairos* of the Sophists. Duration no longer acts in the manner of a cause, but of a chance. The dialectic between forces and relations of production, 'whose boundaries are to be determined', 'does not suspend the real difference'. Chance is no longer an accident or parasitic on causality, but the direct correlate of 'necessary development', the other of necessity, the chance of *this* necessity, just as freedom is not caprice, but freedom from a constraint. Determinate, historical development remains full of junctions and bifurcations, forks and points.

This conceptual revolution abolishes the universal History that introduces order into historical chaos. It makes it possible to re-examine the forms of historiography itemized by Hegel: original history, reflective history and philosophical history. History is not inherently and invariably universal. It becomes so in and through a process of actual universalization. Then, and only then, can we begin to conceive it as constantly evolving universality. Against any normative Eurocentrism, this simple remark opens the way to comparative anthropology and history.

As early as the 1843 Introduction to the *Contribution to the Critique of Hegel's Philosophy of Right*, Marx grasped the paradoxical specificity of German history, condemned to share restorations with modern peoples, but not their revolutions. Political in France, the revolution was philosophical in Germany – not in the vulgar sense of a purely fantastical parody of the missing revolution, but in that it expressed uneven development between economic, political and philosophical instances on a European scale. In the combination of these unevennesses, something that was advanced was simultaneously backward, and vice versa. Germany's political and economic 'backwardness' determined its philosophical 'advance', whereas England's economic 'advance' concealed a political and philosophical 'backwardness'. The advanced and the backward are combined without compensating for one another. They form asymmetrical pairs. Marx invites us to consider the contretemps of these temporal orders: 'we Germans have lived our future history in thought, in *philosophy*. We are the *philosophical* contemporaries of the present without being its *historical* contemporaries.'[44] Non-contemporary contemporaries; 'malcontemporaries' . . .

History knows no one-way streets – whether longitudinally, following the sequence of centuries; or in cross-section, when one society lives the life of another in thought, while the latter acts out the thought of the former, without philosophy and history, economics and politics, ever achieving reconciliation in the tranquil harmony of some simple 'correspondence'. Construed as 'backwardness' in relation to an imaginary temporal norm, anachronism ends up imposing itself not as a residual anomaly, but as an essential attribute of the present. Non-contemporaneity is not reducible to the immaterial unevenness of its moments. It is also their combined development in a novel historical space–time.[45]

Here we are far removed from the crude Meccano of base and superstructure, yet the critique of historical reason does not result in some impotent or aestheticizing contemplation of sound and fury. The dialectic of the forces and relations of production sheds light on historical development. But concepts do not exhaust reality. Marx firmly recalls the 'boundaries' of this dialectic, 'which does not suspend the real difference'. For explanatory necessity does not abolish chance, and the 'how' of history 'necessarily' refers to the aleatory instance of the struggle.

Universal History is not the fulfilment of a destiny or a script. As the result of a process of actual universalization of consciousness (especially through the development of communications), it is itself a historical product requiring explanation, not the explanatory principle.

History possesses no philosophical meaning. Yet it can be understood politically and thought strategically.

Announced by the *Grundrisse*, the new way of writing history is set to work in *Capital*. As both the index and the text attest, however, there is no longer any question of History as such.

Apes, Acorns and Humans

Some of the polemics against Marx's determinism derive from sheer ignorance or a deliberate amalgam between his theory and a certain doctrinal 'Marxism'. Thus, Kolakowski ponders Marxism 'as a means of predicting the future':

> No student can fail to recognize that in Marx's view history as he knew and analysed it derived its meaning not from itself alone but from the future that lay before mankind. We can understand the past only in the light of the new world of human unity to which our society is tending – this is the Young Hegelian point of view, which Marx never abandoned. Marxism, then, cannot be accepted without the vision of the communist future; deprived of that, it is no longer Marxism.[46]

Quite the opposite: Marx categorically rejected the 'Young Hegelian' viewpoint attributed to him here.

Bogged down in received ideas, Kolakowski confuses logical *démarche* and philosophy of history. When Marx sees in humanity a key to the anatomy of the ape, he specifies that '[b]ourgeois society is the most developed and the most complex historic organization of production'. That is why:

> The categories which express its relations, the comprehension of its structure, thereby also allow insights into the structure and relations of production of all the vanished social formations out of whose ruins and elements it built itself up, whose partly still unconquered remnants are carried along within it, whose mere nuances have developed explicit significance within it, etc.[47]

To detect in this line of thought evidence of a determinist or teleological conception of history is a gross misinterpretation. At issue is a problem of knowledge. The most developed form discloses the secrets of less developed forms. This categorically does not mean that the destiny of the ape is humanity, its only possible development, its sole genuinely possible future. We are in no way obliged to *regard humanity as the goal of the ape.*[48] Between them lie many bifurcations.

From his prison cell, Gramsci ridiculed the 'vulgar, fatalistic and positivist evolutionism' attributed to Marx:

> The problem might be formulated as follows: each 'acorn' can think that it will become an oak. Were acorns to have an ideology, it would precisely consist in feeling 'pregnant' with oaks. But in reality, 999 acorns out of a thousand serve as pig food and at most go to making sausages and mortadella.[49]

So there is no terminus of history; no *colline inspirée* of the sort imagined by Maurice Barrès, from which to complete the ascent; no summit from which the plain crossed blind is offered to a triumphant gaze; no retrospective revelation of the meaning of it all – only mortadella and sausages.

The temporal category of knowledge is not that of a future which will have the final word, but that of the present furnishing the keys to an understanding of the past. The fact that a developed form makes it possible to shed light on embryonic forms, a complex category on a simple category, does not mean that *this* development is the only possible future of *that* embryo. The categories of the bourgeois economy doubtless make it possible to take a new look at all forms of society, but *cum grano salis*, for they do not exempt us from elaborating the categories specific to those social formations. Denouncing the retrospective illusion whereby a society invariably tends to conceive the past as its necessary genesis, Marx rejects a species of inverted determinism: earlier societies, he says,

> can contain [the categories of bourgeois economy] in a developed, or stunted, or caricatured form etc., but always with an essential difference. The so-called historical presentation of development is founded, as a rule, on the fact that the latest form regards the previous ones as steps leading up to itself, and, since it is only rarely and only under quite specific conditions able to criticize itself . . . it always conceives them one-sidedly.[50]

The unilateral relationship of the latest form to past forms eliminates an abundance of possibilities, and mutilates necessity by severing it from the relevant chance.

The upshot of seeking to explain history by history is to go round in circles. This circle must be broken, the question turned around, and the totality broached. History must no longer be posited as the explanatory principle, but as that which is to be explained.

The new historiography thus demands elucidation of the actual internal structure of the mode of production. Logical order takes precedence over genetic order, which conceptual amateurs persist in confusing with empirical history. This knowledge is not articulated in the form of historical forecasts disguised as scientific predictions. On the contrary, Marx denounces inventors of a normative state ('what must be created'), or of an ideal to which society should conform. His anti-utopian aim is to disentangle a bundle of possibilities – not to predict the necessary course of history, but to think the bifurcations emerging out of the present instant.[51]

Marx's theory thus plunges into the innermost depths of the contemporary world, to unravel the knots of a time full of lumps, wrinkles and folds. 'In order to develop the laws of bourgeois economy,' he writes,

> it is not necessary to write the *real history of the relations of production*. But the correct observation and deduction of these laws, as having themselves become in history, always leads to primary equations . . . which point towards a past

lying behind this system. These indications, together with a correct grasp of the present, then also offer the key to the understanding of the past – a work in its own right which, it is to be hoped, we shall be able to undertake as well. This correct view likewise leads at the same time to the points at which the suspension of the present form of production relations gives signs of its becoming – foreshadowings of the future. Just as, on one side the pre-bourgeois phases appear as *merely historical,* i.e. suspended presuppositions, so do the contemporary conditions of production likewise appear as engaged in *suspending themselves* and hence in positing the *historic presuppositions* for a new state of society.[52]

No more, but no less either.

A new temporality of knowledge is asserted here. Past societies are not in themselves, in their immediacy, historical. They become such under the impact of the present. Knowledge of the past cannot consist in donning its cast-offs, slipping into its shoes, or taking in the completed picture of universal History in some panoramic view. It does not pertain to the horizontal order of inspection, or to magisterial overview.

It is vertical in character, digging and delving into the depths of the present, where the keys to the coffers of the past as well as the gates to the future lie buried. Its aim is not to lay claim to control of them, but to permit a fleeting glimpse, through a half-opened door and in flickering torchlight, of the still unsettled landscape of what is desirable. A *prefiguration of the future* lacks the certainty of a predictable end. It is simply the 'birth of a movement'. The current moment, which is constantly tipping over into the past, becomes conscious of its own cancellation and supersession – in a word, its own nascent historicity. It in turn thus becomes the 'historical presupposition for a new state of society'. Of this new state, which is already being cancelled, the present can know nothing definite and say nothing positive. It can merely catch the moment of the negative in passing, as it sends up blinding, evanescent flares of possibility.

Marx, who was not given to wild imaginings, refused to draft blueprints for posterity, or to stoke up the fire under the cooking-pots of the future. He did not construct plans for a perfect society that charlatans would gladly flog on the black market. He was content to wedge open the door through which a faint glimmer of the future filtered.[53]

Were Marx to have adopted the Hegelian theodicy of spirit, the mechanical sequence of modes of production leading to communism would simply mark out the stages of an inexorable march towards paradise regained. His famous letters on Russia to Vera Zasulich categorically contradict this linear vision.[54] In them, he defends the possibility of Russian society being spared the travails of capitalist accumulation. This possibility derived from the articulation of the Russian rural commune and the industrial development of the most advanced countries. The combination of collective working of the land with the most advanced techniques (chemical fertilizers, farming machinery) made it possible to achieve a productivity superior to that of the capitalist agrarian enterprise straight away:

> because in Russia, thanks to a combination of unique circumstances, the rural commune, which is still established on a national scale, can gradually be freed of its primitive characteristics and develop directly as an element of collective production on a national scale: it is precisely owing to the *contemporaneity* of capitalist production that it can appropriate all its positive properties, without experiencing the dreadful episodes.

This letter from 1882 takes up the notion of 'contemporaneity' introduced in the notes of 1857: *the (international) contemporaneity of non-contemporaneous (national) situations makes it possible to disrupt the stages of an alleged historical normality*! The theoretical ground covered by Marx between 1845 and 1882 was considerable, but the enemy remained the same: historical fetishism.

A letter of 1877 to the editorial board of the *Otechestvenniye Zapiski* clearly echoes the passages from *The Holy Family* and *The German Ideology*. Marx's critic:

> insists on *transforming my historical sketch of the genesis of capitalism in Western Europe into an historico-philosophic theory of the general path of development prescribed by fate to all nations, whatever the historical circumstances in which they find themselves,* in order that they may ultimately arrive at the economic system which ensures, together with the greatest expansion of the productive powers of social labour, the most complete development of man. But I beg his pardon ... Events strikingly analogous but taking place in different historical surroundings led to totally different results. *By studying each of these forms of evolution separately and then comparing them one can easily find the clue to this phenomenon, but one will never arrive there by using as one's master key a general historico-philosophical theory, the supreme virtue of which consists in being supra-historical.*[55]

Marx definitively rejects any supra-historical general schema clamped on to the determinate unpredictability of actual historical development. This did not prevent the epigones (whether social democrats or Stalinists) imagining a mechanical succession of modes of production, even if it meant suppressing those, like the Asiatic mode of production, which might have upset this neat arrangement.[56]

How is this combination of laws and randomness, tendencies and events, economic determinations and political bifurcations, to be conceived? And what of 'the transition' leading beyond the capitalist mode of production? The four-centuries-long transition involved in the genesis of capital, which was sporadic and uneven, supplies some valuable pointers. It was not accomplished solely on the basis of economic forces or relations, but by way of wars, conquests, state intervention, religious conflicts, and legal reforms.[57]

Marx seems to be torn between two incompatible ideas. On the one hand, he cannot stop himself conceiving the transition to socialism as a protracted process, modelled on the transition to capitalism. According to this hypothesis, capitalism itself develops the conditions of its own negation, and the transformation will supervene at the appointed time, given that '[m]ankind . . . inevitably sets itself only such tasks as it is able to solve'.[58] The Kautskyist orthodoxy of the Second International unilaterally developed this interpretation. Here revolutions partake of an organic, quasi-natural maturation of the social process. In a sense, they *make themselves*, without needing to be made. Reduced to the role of educator, the Party's task is to awaken the consciousness of the masses, transmitting the lessons of experience and overseeing the swelling pile of electoral votes and trade-union enrolments.

On the other hand, Marx clearly appreciates the asymmetry of conditions between bourgeois and proletarian revolutions. The bourgeoisie possesses the means of production before controlling political power. Master of the age, it produces and fashions its organic intellectuals. The proletariat, in contrast, is subject to absolute domination. Losing autonomy in their labour, succumbing to the need to sell themselves as a commodity, proletarians enter the iron circle of alienation. Condemned as they are, under the lash of the commodity, to mark time in the circus of the dominant ideology, the best party pedagogy (propaganda) is insufficient to end their servitude. Rebellion and insurrection are required for that. Revolutionary politics consists in seizing those exceptional moments when the spell of fetishism can be broken.

How do we reconcile the maturity of the process and the aleatory instance of action? How do we combine the slowness of the former with the rapidity of the latter? How can we master the switch in rhythm whereby revolutionary days are suddenly equivalent to centuries? How can we ensure that the revolution cuts through the knot of contradictions at the right moment – neither too soon, nor too late? If too soon, the impossible transition will fall into the rut of the 'vulgar communism' denounced as early as the 1844 *Manuscripts*. If too late, humanity will have let itself in for who knows what, with no guarantee that it will one day be able to make good what has been botched or bungled. Revolutions never occur on the stroke of time. They persistently miss their deadline. They seem condemned to the infernal dialectic of the 'already no longer' and the 'still not', to falling vertiginously between 'the already-there of the not-yet' and 'the already-no-longer of the still'.[59]

The agonizing riddle of socialist revolutions brings this unsettling situation to a head. How, from having been nothing, do we become everything? How do we accomplish this giant leap without bones getting broken!

As early as the 1848 revolutions, Marx was conscious of the peculiarity of socialist revolutions:

> Bourgeois revolutions, such as those of the eighteenth century, storm quickly from success to success. But . . . they soon reach their apogee, and society has to undergo a long period of regret until it has learned to assimilate soberly the achievements of its periods of storm and stress. Proletarian revolutions, however, . . . constantly engage in self-criticism, and in repeated interruptions of their own course. They return to what has apparently been accomplished in order to begin the task again; with merciless thoroughness they mock the inadequate, weak and wretched aspects of their first attempts; they seem to throw their opponent to the ground only to see him draw strength from the earth and rise again before them, more colossal than ever; they shrink back again and again before the immensity of their own goals, until the situation is created in which any retreat is impossible, and the conditions themselves cry out: *Hic Rhodus, hic salta!* Here is the rose, dance here![60]

Bourgeois and proletarian revolutions also differ in their temporality. For the bourgeoisie, the conquest of political power is the culmination of an already established hegemony. For the proletariat, it is the key to social and cultural emancipation. Bourgeois revolution sanctions changes that have already occurred. Proletarian revolution initiates a period of uncertainty and chaos. Whereas the relation of exploitation and the contract of commodity exchange automatically reproduce the encounter between bourgeois and proletarians, no social mechanism guarantees the withering away of commodity categories and the reproduction of a non-capitalist social order. Time is fractured, folds back in on itself, and then swells abruptly.

The pages of *The Eighteenth Brumaire* are of particular importance today. Conscious that there is no spontaneous harmony between economic and political temporalities, Marx leaves the last word to the 'circumstances' charged with restoring harmony. For no one controls social conflict, or the date of its explosion. Riots and revolutions do not obey the injunctions of theory. Untimely and non-quotidian, they are never where you would expect them to be in the routine flow of work and days. Hence the specificity of the political and the event. Their temporality scarcely chimes with the 'march of history' commonly attributed to Marx and Engels. Often accused of severe determinism, the latter perfectly understood politics as a rent in the horizon of what had been determined:

> In my opinion the colonies proper, i.e., the countries occupied by a European population – Canada, the Cape, Australia – will all become independent; on the other hand, the countries inhabited by a native population, which are simply subjugated – India, Algeria, the Dutch, Portuguese and Spanish possessions – must be taken over for the time being by the proletariat and led as rapidly as possible towards independence. How this process will develop is difficult to say . . . *It seems to me that we can only make rather futile hypotheses about the social and political phases that these countries will then have to pass through before they can likewise arrive at socialism.*[61]

Deconstructing Universal History

The texts of Marx's that might justify the charge of a teleological vision of history were influenced by a rapidly developing science of living beings.[62] Numerous metaphors thus designate capital as an organism whose growth constitutes a vital process; its circulation is frequently compared with the circulation of blood; and competition is held to reproduce its 'internal living organization'.

The accusation of mechanical determinism, which appears at first sight to be of more substance, draws arguments from the ambiguities of progress. You do not have to posit an implacable causality or last judgement to reckon that what follows represents progress over what precedes it. The criterion can remain soberly comparative. If, from 1858 on, Marx refuses the 'abstract notion of progress', easily confused with habit and routine, how does he conceive it? His whole logic is opposed to a one-sidedly quantitative vision of progress. The reduction of human relations to a cold cash nexus and the mere piling up of commodities cannot constitute evidence of civilization. The development of the productive forces, albeit necessary, does not in and of itself amount to a sufficient condition. The most frequently invoked criteria are social rather than technological: the relations between men and women (in the 1844 *Manuscripts*); the conquest of creative free time, as against the enslaved and alienated time of compulsory labour (in the *Grundrisse*); the enrichment of the species and the individual personality through the development and diversification of needs.

Chronological order is in no sense a guarantee. If we need to be convinced of this, it is enough to read Engels's magnificent pages in *The Peasants' War in Germany*. In real history, the vanquished are not necessarily wrong; nor are the victors necessarily right. The critical gaze of the oppressed on the 'changeovers' of progress even seems to deny the civilizing mission elsewhere attributed to capitalism. But, says Marx,

> The question is, can mankind fulfil its destiny without a fundamental revolution in the social state of Asia? If not, whatever may have been the crimes of England she was the *unconscious tool of history* in bringing about that revolution. Then, whatever bitterness the spectacle of the crumbling of an ancient world may have for our personal feelings, we have the right, in point of history, to exclaim with Goethe:
>
> > 'Should this torture then torment us
> > Since it brings us greater pleasure?'[63]

The conclusion is not in any doubt. Marx's attitude to the annexation of California and Texas by the United States confirms it. Just as 'non-historic peoples' are sacrificed to the dynamism of historic nations, so colonization involves a civilizing mission, notwithstanding its horrors. Explicit support-ers of colonization within the Second International, like David or Van Kol, were able to draw on these texts to justify their largely uncritical support for the imperialist expeditions of the early twentieth century.[64]

Yet Marx expresses some unease over an unresolved contradiction. The colonial role of England will be 'progressive' if, and only if, humanity does not succeed in revolutionizing social relations in Asia. Then, and only then, will it be possible to consider that it performed this role, while not forgetting that it did so through 'crimes'. This idea of a *relative progress* is not reducible to the meagre comparative relationship between a before and an after. It takes account of missed opportunities and defeated possibilities. 'Progress' with respect to a despotic feudal state is not necessarily such with respect to lost possibilities; and it is not enough coldly to consider the role of British colonialism in Asia as progressive by default to absolve its misdeeds. The quotation from Goethe illustrates this painful contradiction. Under the reign of private property, 'there comes a stage when productive forces . . . are no longer productive but destruc-tive forces'.[65]

This is indeed the problem. Marx deconstructs the notion of universal History. Each present affords a multiplicity of possible lines of develop-ment. But they do not all possess the same index of normality. The majority orthodoxy of the Second and Third Internationals alike happily treated the disruptions of capitalism in clinical terms. Anti-Stalinist oppositions themselves often applied the vocabulary of 'degeneration' and 'deformation' to the bureaucratic societies. Contrasting monstrosities with healthy development, 'Marxism' without Marx thus equipped itself with a veritable teratological discourse. Gramsci, perceptive as ever, accused Bukharin's *Historical Materialism* of judging the past as 'irrational' and proposing 'a historical treatise on teratology'.[66]

Darwin, however, was already conscious of the problematic relationship between the normal and the pathological: 'monstrosities cannot be separated by any clear line of distinction from mere variations ... By a monstrosity I presume is meant some considerable deviation of structure in one part, either injurious to or not useful to the species.'[67] These theoretical difficulties increase when we quit biology for history. As Canguilhem clearly saw, the distinction between the normal and the pathological then assumes a value judgement immanent in the process:

> There is no fact which is normal or pathological in itself. An anomaly or a mutation is not in itself pathological. These two express other possible norms of life. If these norms are inferior to specific earlier norms in terms of stability, fecundity, variability of life, they will be called pathological. If these norms in the same environment should turn out to be equivalent, or in another environment, superior, they will be called normal. Their normality will come to them from their normativity. The pathological is not the absence of a biological norm: it is another norm but one which is, comparatively speaking, pushed aside by life.[68]

Analogously, we could say that there is no abnormality in history, but at most anomalies. Treating Nazism or Stalinism as pathological forms, rather than seeing them as entirely original historical phenomena, results in simultaneously valorizing the normal societies from which they deviate, and minimizing the specific import of their temporary 'deviancy'. Stalinism and Nazism are neither monsters nor exceptions: they reveal 'other possible norms of life'. They must be fought not in the name of some nonexistent historical norm, but in the name of a project that assumes responsibility for its own evaluative criteria.

Like life, history is a variation of forms and an invention of modes of behaviour. It is not surprising to find in Hegel a logic of history and in Marx a logic of capital conceived as logics of a living organism. Life posits its own values in seeking to prevail over death and counteracting increasing entropy. It is also possible to imagine society resisting its own death throes. Rejected forms are such not by virtue of a clear line of demarcation between the normal and the pathological, but in the name of constantly renewed resistance to its own morbidity. Gramsci probably had this in mind when he grasped 'in every instant of unfolding history' a struggle 'between the rational and the irrational':

> Let us take 'irrational' to mean that which will not prevail ultimately, will never become part of actual history, but which in reality is itself rational because it is necessarily bound up with what is rational, is a moment of the rational that must be taken into consideration. For while, in history, the general always prevails, *the particular also struggles to assert itself in so far as it determines a certain development of the general – and not some other development. . . . Only the struggle, with its outcome – and not even its immediate outcome, but rather the one expressed in a permanent victory – will decide what is rational or irrational,* i.e. what is 'worthy' of triumphing, because it continues in its own way and transcends the past.[69]

Normality and rationality are always partial and provisional, permanently subject to confirmation. There is nothing to say that the supposedly 'normal' or 'rational' is guaranteed a future. Even incomplete, normality remains normality, and poses the problem of its criterion. If God is indeed dead, and science does not dictate moral standards, only two solutions remain. Either the judgement of History returns surreptitiously to pronounce the closing words of the fable; or a class standpoint determines 'its' norm in self-referential fashion. In this instance, we are dealing not with a transcendental normality but with an immanent rationality giving expression, in the mode of strategic choice, to a desirable state of affairs that is simultaneously an optative necessity and an effective possibility.

The last hypothesis seems to accord better with Marx's problematic.[70] It is no accident that his critique started out by desacralizing the Family and History conjointly. Henceforth the course of history no longer follows the one-way street that would endow it with meaning. It breaks up into branches, large and small, that always begin afresh. Each critical point of bifurcation poses its own questions and demands its own answers.

The critique of the speculative philosophy of history leads Marx radically to recast the conceptual field, and change theoretical priorities. On the one hand, explains Jean-Marie Vincent,

> the class struggle must be conceived as a struggle against prehistory, against the primacy of a closed past, which also means a struggle for the reactivation of the unexplored, untapped potential of an eclipsed and buried past. In this sense, there can be no linearity to social progress and no unsuccessful supersession without a recovery of what has previously gone unvalidated. The front of progress therewith transcends the usual limits of temporality; as Bloch observes, it is established in an elastic temporality that traverses epochs. Nothing has been definitively settled because for the moment nothing has truly been played out.[71]

On the other hand, shattering the fetish of history liberates the categories that allow us to conceive it differently. What emerges from the ruins of universal History is a 'rhythmology' of capital, a conceptualization of crises, and a historicity in which politics 'attains primacy over history'.[72] In *The German Ideology*, Marx invokes the 'really historic interventions of politics in history'. They herald the intelligibility of real history, which presupposes the destruction of its own myth.

The disproportion between the endless commentaries on the putative 'Marxist philosophy of history' and the scant attention paid to this conceptual revolution is a cause for surprise. For from the *Grundrisse* onwards, history in the then current sense recedes from Marx's theoretical discourse. And 'when *Capital* interrupted the course and rent the fabric of this whole historical movement, it was like an inaudible thunderclap, a silence, a margin'.[73]

We are still in the process of learning to attend to that silence.

Notes

1. Antonio Gramsci, *Selections from the Prison Notebooks*, ed. and trans. Quintin Hoare and Geoffrey Nowell Smith, Lawrence & Wishart, London 1971, pp. 370, 336.
2. Leszek Kolakowski, *Main Currents of Marxism*, vol. I, trans. P.S. Falla, Oxford University Press, Oxford 1978, p. 141; emphasis added.
3. Karl Marx and Frederick Engels, 'The German Ideology', in Marx and Engels, *Collected Works*, vol. 5, Lawrence & Wishart, London 1976, p. 49.
4. Karl Marx and Frederick Engels, 'The Holy Family', in Marx and Engels, *Collected Works*, vol. 4, Lawrence & Wishart, London 1975, p. 93.
5. Marx and Engels, 'The German Ideology', p. 31.
6. See Karl Popper, *The Open Society and its Enemies*, 2 vols, Routledge, London 1994.
7. 'We must find our justification in our work, in what we are doing ourselves, and not in a fictitious "meaning of history" ... Although history has no ends, we can impose these ends of ours upon it; and *although history has no meaning, we can give it a meaning* ... It is we who introduce purpose and meaning into nature and into history': Popper, *The Open Society and its Enemies*, vol. 2, p. 278.
8. In order to expose the 'poverty of historicism', Popper assembles a harlequinade of ready-made quotations from Comte or John Stuart Mill, rather than Marx or Hegel: see *The Poverty of Historicism*, Routledge & Kegan Paul, London 1957.
9. In general, Popper evinces a highly superficial and unsure grasp of Marx's thought:

    If we now proceed to a criticism as well as to an appreciation of Marx's 'historical materialism', or of so much of it as has been presented so far, then we may distinguish two different aspects. The first is historicism ... This ..., I think, must be dismissed. The second is economism ..., i.e. the claim that the economic organization of society ... is fundamental for all social institutions and especially for their historical development. This claim, I believe, is perfectly sound, so long as we take the term 'fundamental' in an ordinary vague sense, not laying too much stress upon it ... Marx himself undoubtedly did so. Owing to his Hegelian upbringing, he was influenced by the ancient distinction between 'reality' and 'appearance', and by the corresponding distinction between what is 'essential' and what is 'accidental'. (*The Open Society and its Enemies*, vol. 2, pp. 106–7).

Or again: 'although *Capital* is, in fact, largely a treatise on social ethics, these ethical ideas are never represented as such' (ibid., p. 199). In a brief essay entitled *Pour l'incertain* (Syllepse, Paris 1990), Jean-Loup Englander endeavours to rectify Marx's scientistic inclinations by means of Popperian epistemology. It would be more judicious to revisit Marx in the light of contemporary scientific developments than to 'Popperianize' him without querying Popper's own epistemology.

10. Popper, *The Poverty of Historicism*, p. 116.
11. John Stuart Mill, quoted in ibid., pp. 117–18.
12. Ibid., p. 119.
13. Ibid., p. 143.
14. Ibid., p. 115.
15. Ibid., p. 15.
16. Jon Elster, *Making Sense of Marx*, Cambridge University Press/Éditions de la Maison des Sciences de l'Homme, Cambridge and Paris 1985, pp. 17–18.
17. Ibid., p. 29.
18. Ibid., p. 109.
19. Marx and Engels, 'The German Ideology', p. 50; emphasis added.
20. Ibid., p. 146.
21. Karl Marx, letter to Arnold Ruge of September 1843, in Marx, *Early Writings*, trans. Rodney Livingstone and Gregor Benton, Penguin/NLR, Harmondsworth 1975, p. 207.
22. Elster, *Making Sense of Marx*, p. 109.
23. Marx precisely accused Proudhon of remaining on the terrain of 'sacred history' and a formal genealogy of ideas: 'In short, it is not history but trite Hegelian trash, it is not profane history – history of man – but sacred history – history of ideas': letter to Annenkov of 28 December 1846, in Marx and Engels, *Selected Correspondence*, Progress Publishers, Moscow 1975, p. 31.
24. Elster, *Making Sense of Marx*, p. 309.
25. Ibid., p. 514.
26. Ibid., p. 117.
27. Popper, *The Open Society and its Enemies*, vol. 2, p. 200.
28. Elster, *Making Sense of Marx*, p. 118. Louis Dumont and Michel Henry identify a radical theory of individuality in Marx: see Louis Dumont, *Homo aequalis*, vol. 1, Gallimard, Paris 1977; Michel Henry, *Marx, une philosophie de la réalité*, 2 vols, Gallimard, Paris 1976.
29. See Marx and Engels, 'The German Ideology'; Yirmiyahu Yovel, *Spinoza and Other Heretics*, vol. 2, Princeton University Press, Princeton, NJ 1989. On the adventures of utopia in Marx's *œuvre*, see Henri Maler's subtle study *Convoiter l'impossible*, Albin Michel, Paris 1995.
30. Marx and Engels, 'The German Ideology', p. 55; emphasis added.
31. Ibid., p. 57; emphasis added.
32. Ibid., pp. 172–3. Max Stirner's *The Ego and its Own* was published in 1844.
33. Karl Marx, 'The Poverty of Philosophy', in Marx and Engels, *Collected Works*, vol. 6, Lawrence & Wishart, London 1976, p. 170. The same critique is to be found in the famous letter to Annenkov of 28 December 1846:

> Mr. Proudhon sees in history a series of social developments; he finds progress realised in history; finally he finds that men, as individuals, did not know what they were doing and were mistaken about their own movement, that is to say, their social development seems at first glance to be distinct, separate and independent of their individual development. He cannot explain these facts, and the hypothesis of universal reason manifesting itself is pure invention. Nothing is easier than to invent mystical causes, that is to say, phrases which have no sense at all. (Marx and Engels, *Selected Correspondence*, p. 30)

34. Marx, 'The Poverty of Philosophy', p. 165.
35. Marx and Engels, 'The German Ideology', p. 49; emphasis added.
36. Karl Marx, *Grundrisse*, trans. Martin Nicolaus, Penguin/NLR, Harmondsworth 1973, pp. 109–10.
37. Karl Marx, *Capital*, vol. 1, trans. Ben Fowkes, Penguin/NLR, Harmondsworth 1976, p. 91.
38. We re-encounter this notion of 'contretemps' or 'anachrony' in Jacques Derrida: 'We no longer realize the wear, we no longer take account of it as of a single age in the progress of history. Neither maturation, nor crisis, nor even agony . . . Contretemps. *The Time is out of joint* . . . the age is off its hinges. Everything, beginning with time, seems out of kilter, unjust, dis-adjusted' (*Specters of Marx*, trans. Peggy Kamuf, Routledge, New York and London 1994, p. 77).
39. Karl Marx, 'The Eighteenth Brumaire of Louis Bonaparte', in Marx, *Surveys from Exile*, Penguin/NLR, Harmondsworth 1973, p. 146.
40. Sigmund Freud, 'Civilization and its Discontents', in Freud, *Civilization, Society and Religion*, Penguin, Harmondsworth 1985, pp. 255 ff.
41. At the beginning of the twentieth century, historians interested themselves in these curious effects of contretemps. In his *La Théorie de l'histoire*, Xenopol stressed that social facts 'do not always follow an even, parallel line of march'. Some 'lag behind as if to rest, gather their strength, and later catch up with those that have preceded them', whereas others seem to regress 'before rushing forward' again. In *Les Alternances du progrès*, Robert Bonnaud in particular cites the works of Paul Lacombe, *De l'histoire considérée comme science* (1894), and of Xenopol, whose *Théorie* was published in French in 1904. He perceives in them an invitation to 'rhythmology'. His periodization, articulated around the 'turning points of acts', 'phase' and 'episode', replete with chains and overlaps, beckons towards a heroic exploration in the interlace of these complex temporalities. For Robert Bonnaud's work, see *Le Système de l'histoire* (Fayard, Paris 1989), *Y-a-t-il des tournants historiques mondiaux?* (Kimé, Paris 1992), and *Les Alternances du progrès* (Kimé, Paris 1992). The last of these places particular emphasis on the necessity of a 'rhythmology': 'May the economists, drawn to the study of qualitative cycles by quantitative cycles, roused from their beatitude by the end of the *trente glorieuses* and what some characterize as the descending part of the Kondratieff wave, by the same token closely study Hirschman's wave, complete it, correct it, take inspiration from it, multiply the outlines. Qualitative rhythms exist. The science of those rhythms deserves to exist' (p. 87).
42. Max Stirner, *The Ego and its Own*, trans. Steven Tracy Byington, Cambridge University Press, New York 1995, pp. 36, 42.
43. Bonnaud, *Les Alternances du progrès*, p. 11.
44. Karl Marx, 'A Contribution to the Critique of Hegel's Philosophy of Right. Introduction', in Marx, *Early Writings*, p. 249. 'What things are contemporary?', asks Michel Serres, when 'we are always simultaneously making gestures that are archaic, modern, and futuristic': Serres with Bruno Latour, *Conversations on Science, Culture, and Time*, trans. Roxanne Lapidus, University of Michigan Press, Ann Arbor 1995, pp. 45, 60.
45. Lenin with his theory of the 'weakest link', and Trotsky with his theses on 'uneven and combined development' and 'permanent revolution', drew the strategic conclusions from this new way of writing history.
46. Kolakowski, *Main Currents of Marxism*, vol. 1, p. 371.
47. Marx, *Grundrisse*, p. 105.
48. In *La Violence capitalisée* (Cerf, Paris 1986), Bernard Guibert offers the following stimulating comments on the 'anatomical' understanding of history: 'An understanding of history occurs *a posteriori*. The logical is the historical condensed. Anachronism is thus itself directed by an irreversibility; the cone of light (of space and time) that accompanies capital in its trajectory precludes understanding any history other than its own and retrospectively. Capital recaps its history. In this sense only, the anatomy of humanity is a key to the anatomy of the ape' (p. 29).
49. Antonio Gramsci, *Quaderni del carcere*, vol. II, ed. Valentino Gerratana, Einaudi, Turin

1975, p. 1192. In the same notebook, Gramsci inveighed against 'fetishistic history' and the illusion of origins whereby the germs of a concrete fact are sought in prior history, in the same way as 'the hen is sought in the fertilized egg'.

50. Marx, *Grundrisse*, p. 106.
51. 'As so often when he is examining concrete historical problems, Marx substitutes the concept of "alternatives" for that of "necessity" ': Agnes Heller, *The Theory of Need in Marx*, Allison & Busby, London 1976, p. 75.
52. Marx, *Grundrisse*, pp. 460–1.
53. Having reached this point, we might ask whether theoretical blindness or bad faith is prevalent when an author as meticulous as Elster persists in denouncing 'Marx's constant tendency to fuse, or confuse, philosophy of history and historical analysis' (*Making Sense of Marx*, p. 437).
54. See Maurice Godelier, *Les Sociétés précapitalistes et le mode de production asiatique*, CERM/Éditions Sociales, Paris 1967, pp. 318–42.
55. Marx and Engels, *Selected Correspondence*, pp. 293–4; emphasis added.
56. As Kolakowski notes, the Asiatic mode of production 'may appear no more than a detail in his philosophy of history, but if it is accepted it calls for the revision of a number of stereotypes, especially those connected with historical determinism and the idea of progress' (*Main Currents of Marxism*, vol. 1, p. 351). This is the least that can be said. For Stalinist orthodoxy, elimination of the Asiatic mode of production had obvious implications. If the majority of humanity lived under modes of production alien to the chronological succession between feudalism and capitalism, no schema of unified development, or theory of revolution by stages, survived; and then – who knows? – there might no longer be a way of presenting really existing socialism as 'post-capitalism' or a 'transition' necessary to socialism. In fact, this 'post-' is meaningless. The bureaucratic societies were never post-capitalist. Neither temporally: they remained contemporaneous with the dominant world capitalist system; nor from the viewpoint of labour productivity, which never caught up with that of the imperialist metropoles. A better understanding of them would have required conceiving history according to the articulation of the world system of domination and dependency and according to the non-contemporaneity of its space–time.
57. See Maurice Godelier's article 'Les contextes illusoires de la transition au socialisme', *Actuel Marx*, special issue on 'Fin du communisme', Presses Universitaires de France, Paris 1991.
58. Marx, Preface to *A Contribution to the Critique of Political Economy*, in *Early Writings*, p. 426.
59. Jacques Derrida, *Glas*, Denoël, Paris 1981, p. 305.
60. Marx, 'The Eighteenth Brumaire of Louis Bonaparte', p. 150.
61. Engels, letter to Kautsky of 12 September 1882, in Marx and Engels, *Selected Correspondence*, p. 331; emphasis added.
62. Nineteenth-century biology is shot through with methodological inquiries that intersect with those of the critique of political economy. Unlike physics, biology works not with mechanical causalities, but with significant structures. Hence its readily teleological perspective. Defending the fertility of such an approach, Georges Canguilhem distinguishes between a transcendental teleology and what he calls an organismic teleology: prioritizing the whole organism in no way requires conferring some providential design on it.
63. Marx, 'The British Rule in India' (1853), in *Surveys from Exile*, p. 307.
64. See Roman Rosdolsky, *Engels and the 'Nonhistoric' Peoples: The National Question in the Revolution of 1848*, trans. John-Paul Himka, Critique Books, Glasgow 1987. It is important to remember that Marx and Engels's texts predated the appearance of what Lenin, Luxemburg, Bukharin and Hilferding were to characterize as modern imperialism. On the congresses of the Second International and the colonial question, see Stuart Schram and Hélène Carrère d'Encausse, *Marxism and Asia*, Allen Lane, London 1969.
65. Marx and Engels, 'The German Ideology', p. 52.

66. Gramsci, *Selections from the Prison Notebooks*, p. 449.
67. Charles Darwin, *The Origin of Species*, Penguin edn, London 1985, pp. 72, 101.
68. Georges Canguilhem, *The Normal and the Pathological*, trans. Carolyn R. Fawcett, Zone Books, New York 1991, p. 144.
69. Gramsci, *Quaderni del carcere*, vol. II, pp. 689–90; emphasis added.
70. Strategic thinking remained in its early stages in Marx. Practically absent from the ranks of the Second International, it would fully emerge only with Lenin. On this topic, the reader is referred to the research of Henri Maler. For him, strategy and utopia are two mutually exclusive poles, and the critique of utopia is 'by definition strategic'. Yet in Marx, the strategic pole remains in its infancy: strategy is merely 'the translation of history as expressed in the language of theory'. This false start for strategy permitted the surreptitious return of an unguided utopia.
71. Jean-Marie Vincent, *Critique du travail*, Presses Universitaires de France, Paris 1987, p. 45. See also Stéphane Moses, *L'Ange de l'Histoire*, Seuil, Paris 1991; Daniel Bensaïd, *Walter Benjamin, sentinelle messianique*, Plon, Paris 1991.
72. Walter Benjamin, *The Arcades Project*, trans. Howard Eiland and Kevin McLaughlin, Belknap/Harvard University Press, Cambridge, MA and London 1999, pp. 388–9.
73. Gérard Granel, Preface to Husserl, *La Crise des sciences européennes*, Gallimard, Paris 1976, p. vii.

2

Time Out of Joint
(On Analytical Marxism)

The age of restoration is upon us. A restoration of order? If so, only on a scale with the attendant disorders. Of progress? There is reason to doubt it. The partial eclipse of the class struggle is conducive to the seductions of the market, and the escalation of local and parochial conflicts.

For a long time, Germany, Latin Europe and central Europe exerted influence as living sources of theoretical Marxism. In the 1980s, renovation seemed to be sweeping in from the north. The current of 'analytical' or 'rational choice' Marxism has generated some meticulous textual studies. *Analytical Marxism* is the manifesto-title of a collection edited in 1986 by John Roemer, with contributions from Jon Elster, G.A. Cohen, Erik Olin Wright, Robert Brenner, Adam Przeworski, and Allen Wood. Most of these authors concur in contrasting 'methodological individualism' with 'methodological collectivism'. Wright characterizes the current as 'one intellectual tendency within this newly influential academic Marxism'. Without minimizing the disagreements between these researchers on nearly all the crucial practical questions, he stresses their shared methodological commitment: respect for 'conventional scientific norms'; emphasis on 'systematic conceptualization' ('careful attention to definitions of concepts and to the logical coherence of repertoires of interconnected concepts'); commitment to 'fine-grained specification of the steps in the theoretical arguments linking concepts', with 'the use of explicit, systematic models'; and the significance accorded to 'the intentional action of individuals within both explanatory and normative theories'. More circumspect than most of his colleagues about 'methodological individualism', Wright candidly poses the question of 'what remains Marxist' about analytical Marxism.[1]

These authors share the conviction that Marxism must aspire to the status of authentic social science. Inspired by pragmatics and game theory, their approach assumes a consensus on what science does, and on its criteria. Empirical research plays a decisive role. Much time is to be spent 'defending specific definitions' and examining the logical interdependence of concepts: 'a necessary condition for the development of powerful theories is the elaboration of logically coherent concepts'. Wright thus justifies recourse to abstract models, 'sometimes highly formalized', borrowed from game theory. Finally, although the question is the most controversial one within the group, stress is laid on 'micro-foundations' and the behaviour of rational agents.[2] General equilibrium theory, 'rational choice' models, and neoclassical economics supply instruments that make it possible to theorize preference-formation, and anticipate the foundations of a materialist psychology.

Ellen Meiksins Wood presents this 'rational choice Marxism' as 'Cohen on history plus Roemer on class and exploitation'.[3] A priori, there is nothing obvious about this pairing. Once classes are dissolved into the interaction of individual interests, history seems bound to become immobilized in an endlessly resumed game. The games succeed one another without continuity or progress. Meaning evaporates in an indifferent combinatory of endowments and motivations. Yet history does not draw to a close in the uniform repetition of its figures. It advances through the elimination of forms of property and exploitation that have become socially obsolete. In so far as fewer and fewer production goods can function under the regime of private property, the arrow of historical time simultaneously marks out a constraining technological determinism and an irreversible process of socialization of property.

Marx as Theoretician of the Historical Norm?

Even among resolute opponents of the Stalinist counter-revolution, we often encounter a nostalgia for historical norms. The revolution is alleged to have 'degenerated' or 'deviated'. Having come off its tracks, history should end up being put back on them, after a more or less protracted 'detour' or skid.

Elster and Cohen thus claim to be responding to the challenge represented by the appearance of a novel social formation in the twentieth century: bureaucratic totalitarianism. What place can Stalinism have in a rational representation of history? Does it ruin any idea of progress? Does it return history to a Shakespearian aesthetic of sound and fury? What are its implications today? These are legitimate questions, but the answers are hazardous. From the preface to *Capital*, Elster retains the idea that 'the conditions of a viable communism must emerge endogenously if they are to emerge at all'. For they are not bound to emerge. An irrational faith to the contrary would betray a stubborn teleological premiss:

> Communism will occur, hence any necessary conditions for its emergence will also occur. In this sense Marx's developmental scheme works from the future to the present, not the other way round. He did not consider the possibility that communism might occur *prematurely*, and like the Asiatic mode of production become a dead end of history.[4]

'Prematurely': that is the fatal word. Debates on the correct rhythm of history generally invoke the well-known passage from the 1859 Preface to *A Contribution to the Critique of Political Economy*:

> In the social production of their existence, men inevitably enter into definite relations, which are independent of their will, namely relations of production *appropriate* to a given stage in the development of their material forces of production ... At a certain stage of development, the material productive forces of society come into conflict with the existing relations of production or – this merely expresses the same thing in legal terms – with the property relations within the framework of which they have operated hitherto. From forms of development of the productive forces these relations turn into their fetters. Then begins an era of social revolution ... No social order is ever destroyed before all the productive forces for which it is sufficient have been developed, and new superior relations of production never replace older ones before the material conditions for their existence have matured within the framework of the old society. Mankind thus inevitably sets itself only such tasks as it is able to solve, since closer examination will always show that the problem itself arises only when the material conditions for its solution are already present or at least in the course of formation.[5]

Despite (or because of) its didactic intentions, this text poses more problems than it resolves. G.A. Cohen's commentary on it begins by dissociating the productive forces from the economic structure; they constitute not a relation, but a property or an object, which has primacy, being the driving force. Next, he insists upon the notion of *correspondence*. The 'relations of production [correspond] to a given stage in the development of [the] material forces of production'. Hence the famous formula: 'No social order is ever destroyed before all the productive forces for which it is sufficient have been developed.' Cohen concludes from this that 'we may attribute to Marx ... not only a *philosophy* of history, but also what deserves to be called a *theory* of history, which is not a reflective construal, from a distance, of what happens, but a contribution to understanding its inner dynamic'.[6]

Faithful to the title of his major work, Cohen presents a resolute 'defence' of this theory. From *The German Ideology* to *Theories of Surplus-Value*, he itemizes the evidence for a rigorous determination of the relations of production by the level of development of the productive forces, since, according to Marx, no revolution can succeed before capitalism has raised labour productivity to the requisite level. Otherwise, once the dominant class has been expropriated, the labouring class will not be capable of founding a socialist community. For without the indispensable practical premiss of a high level of productivity, forced socialization would result merely in the generalization of penury. Far from leading to the genuine emancipation of wage-labourers, state appropriation of the means of production can betoken the generalization of wage-labour in the form of 'vulgar communism' (what we might today translate as 'bureaucratic collectivism'). 'Premature' attempts to transform social relations would thus be condemned to capitalist restoration in the worst imaginable conditions.

Several questions are conflated here. In opposition to utopian communists, Marx insisted on the preconditions of socialism. According to his emphatic expression of this point, with the socialization of penury 'all the old filthy business would necessarily be restored'.[7] This reminder is always useful. Thus, the critique of productivism often gives rise to naivety. If it involves exposing the false neutrality of the productive forces, and emphasizing their ambivalence (as a factor of potential progress *and* destruction), this century's disasters are enough to establish its pertinence – without any need to trot out Robinsonnades of zero growth and an economy of hunter-gatherers. There is no single, exclusive, and socially neutral potential development of the productive forces. Various paths, with different social and economic consequences, can always be envisaged. But the satisfaction of new, diverse human needs on the basis of a reduction in labour time, and hence the emancipation of humanity from compulsory labour, cannot be achieved without an expansion of the productive forces.

If the proletariat is reckoned to play a key role in this transformation, it is particularly because the technical and social division of labour creates the conditions for a conscious (political) organization of the economy in the service of human needs. An effective socialization of production thus requires a determinate level of development. In an increasingly globalized economy, this minimum threshold is not fixed from country to country. Relative and mobile, it varies as a function of the bonds of dependency and solidarity within the world economy. The less developed a country is, the more reliant it is on the international balance of forces.

Admitting these constraints does not require the 'defence', Cohen-style, of a 'theory of history' inspired by the determinist orthodoxy of the

Second International: 'It is an old-fashioned historical materialism which I defend, a traditional conception, in which history is, fundamentally, the growth of human productive power, and forms of society rise and fall according as they enable or impede that growth.'[8] Capitalism, Cohen argues, was necessary in so far as it extended humanity's control over nature. Against the current of the soft new utopias, Cohen insists on the primacy of the productive forces, maintaining that when Marx claimed that the relations of production 'corresponded' to the productive forces, he meant that the former were 'adequate' for the latter. Substituting 'adequacy' for 'correspondence' does not advance things an inch. Do the relations and forces correspond, or are they adequate? This correspondence determines a field of possibilities. It does not dictate unambiguous relations of adequacy. The forces are determinant in the last instance. But 'determination in the last instance' is always the index of a difficulty, as well as a solution. Thus, the productive forces include enhancement of the power of human labour. The relations of production determine the productive forces through productivity and labour capacity. Growth of the productive forces and class struggle are not extraneous to one another. They simply pertain to two distinct levels of determination, from the most abstract to the most concrete, in understanding historical development.[9]

Wright summarizes the theory of history *à la* Cohen in the form of a series of propositions:

1. capitalism becomes an obstacle to itself;
2. its contradictions create the preconditions for socialism;
3. they also produce the (proletarian) class capable of resolving them;
4. the sole historical alternative to capitalism is socialism.

This logical formalization obeys the principle of the excluded middle. Bureaucratic regimes thus necessarily pertain to the alternative categories of capitalism (albeit state capitalism), or socialism (albeit 'really existing'). Conscious of the excessive rigidity of this binary schema, Wright amends it by introducing two variants:

3a. the transformative capacity of the proletariat may prove to be blocked indefinitely;
4b. it is legitimate to imagine post-capitalist alternatives other than socialism.[10]

These corrections scarcely relax an ossified understanding of 'historical materialism' wrongly attributed to Marx. An axiom of 'historical materialism' has supposedly always been that 'historical development occur[s] along a single developmental trajectory' – that there is only one route, and that historical junctions simply represent detours on this compulsory route.[11]

How can history as the development of the productive forces and as the history of class struggle be reconciled? Elster detects 'a major difficulty in Marxism' here: 'There is no hint of any mechanism by which the class struggle promotes the growth of the productive forces.'[12] Rather than developing this hypothesis, he, too, plays the trump card of Marx's 'teleological view of history'. In Marx there is a 'very intimate . . . relation between his philosophy of history and his predilection for functional explanation. It was certainly because Marx believed history to be directed towards a goal . . . that he felt justified in explaining, not only patterns of behaviour, but even individual events, in terms of their contribution to that end'.[13] Summing up Marx's theory as 'an amalgam of methodological collectivism, functional explanation and dialectical deduction', Elster does not bother with nuances or scruples: 'These can all be subsumed, perhaps, under the more general heading of *teleology*. The invisible hand upholding capital is one of the two main forms of teleology in Marx, the other being the necessity of the process that will ultimately destroy it.'[14] Beneath the mystifications and marvels of commodity fetishism, Marx unveils the profane reality of the objectified relations between human beings. The functionalism tracked by Elster appears as the shadow cast by the classical intentionality that has taken refuge in his own 'methodological individualism'. Incapable of grasping Marx's novel 'laws of tendency', and the necessity shot through with chance that is characteristic of them, Elster dismantles and reassembles the tedious Meccano of forces and relations, infrastructures and superstructures.

So where are the 'particular events' explained by the end of history in Marx, who analyses the Eighteenth Brumaire, the Civil War, or the Paris Commune in their factual, determinate and contingent singularity, and leaves the question of capitalist development historically open? Elster never succeeds in reuniting what his claim has artificially separated: the productive forces and the class struggle – as if the modalities of class struggle were extraneous and irrelevant to the development of the forces, and as if class struggle were not already among the determinants of the productive forces! By resisting the exploitation of their labour-power, wage-labourers tend to liberate new productive forces, and hit upon new seams of productivity. This 'inner' or 'immanent' law of development does not in any way imply a transcendental, teleological view. The expansion of the productive forces does not preclude the decline or disappearance of vanquished civilizations. Rome can always be sacked, and empires collapsing into barbarism is not an invention of film-makers or science-fiction writers.

Blinded by the one-sided primacy of the productive forces, Cohen and Elster are on the wrong track. Where Marx searches out the secret of economic cycles and rhythms to renew historiography, they strive to construct an unavailable theory, and therefore miss the real contradiction of a 'transition' inscribed in a rigorously immanent representation of historical development. Maurice Godelier has revealed the hesitations of a Marx tempted to conceive the passage from capitalism to socialism in the manner of the transition between feudalism and capitalism. By virtue of a quasi-natural genetic law, communism should be engendered out of the very entrails of capital, prior to being able to dominate it. The germs of the future society supposedly develop in the pores of the existing society in a long gestation process. In one sense (but one sense only), this is indeed the case. The accumulation of capital brings about the concentration of the labour force, the expansion of productive capacity, expanded co-operation of labour, a tendency towards the socialization of production, an unprecedented flowering of science and technology, and increasing integration of intellectual labour into the productive forces. The class struggle leads to the blossoming of new possibilities and new rights.

Far removed from triumphalist representations of it, history is not reducible to a zero-sum game. Its cumulative development is marked by the growth of science and technology. The emergence of a new mode of production is not the sole possible result of the preceding mode of production; it is not the only conceivable way in which it can be historically surpassed. It is merely inscribed in a determinate field of real possibilities. Assessment of historical progress in terms of advances and regressions on a chronological axis conceives disaster as a return to a bygone past or its residues, instead of sounding the alarm bells against novel, original and wholly contemporaneous forms of a barbarism that is always the barbarism of a particular present – a barbarism for our time.

Understood in a non-mechanical, non-unilateral way, the productive forces come back into their own here. The forces and relations of production are the two aspects of the process by which human beings produce and reproduce their conditions of existence. Unless ruination supervenes – and this is a permanent possibility – the development of the productive forces is cumulative and irreversible. The upshot is not automatic social and cultural progress, but simply the possibility of progress. Otherwise, any emancipatory project would be a product of sheer ethical voluntarism, or utopian arbitrariness. To say that the growth of the productive forces is signposted, that its film cannot be rewound, means that humanity does not revert from capitalism to feudalism and from feudalism to Antiquity. History does not backtrack. It can nevertheless cloak the worst novelties in the misleading guise of old cast-offs.

Socialism or Barbarism? Not 'socialism or the status quo', 'socialism or the lesser evil', 'socialism or regression'! Not progress or regression, but a genuine bifurcation. The dialectic of possibilities is likewise cumulative. The destruction of emancipatory potentialities creates unknown – and no less terrifying – threats.

Correspondence and Optimality

For Elster, as for Cohen, the primacy of the productive forces 'may involve the *level* of development of the productive forces, their *rate of change*, or both'. We must therefore specify what is meant by 'correspondence' (or non-correspondence), on which the possibility and actuality of a systemic transformation depend. A rupture in correspondence emerges not as an absolute blockage, but as a loss of optimality: 'the theory says that the level of the productive forces determines which relations are optimal for their further development. It says, moreover, that optimal relations tend to be realized. This is probably the version that best captures Marx's more general, theoretical statement.'[15] The passage from the 1859 Preface asserting that no social formation disappears 'before all the productive forces for which it is sufficient have been developed' (and referring to 'new superior relations of production'), as well as the admiring pages in which Marx describes the progressive role of capital in revolutionizing the productive forces, may indeed be construed in terms of optimality. The relations of production would then become outmoded as a consequence of exhausted correspondence.

Revolutionary change would be on the agenda when the relations of production become 'sub-optimal' for the productive forces. This thesis supposedly explains the factual reality of the Russian Revolution, as well as the bureaucratic collapse of socialist construction:

It is quite conceivable that the time at which communism would be superior to capitalism in this respect [the free and full development of the individual] is earlier than the time at which it becomes technically superior ... The idea would be that the superiority of communism would explain the communist revolution in all countries but the first in which it occurred ... The first appearance of communism on the historical world scene could be more or less accidental, but its subsequent diffusion would be rationally grounded. An obvious condition is that the revolution should not occur too early in the first country. Having dismissed the proposal that communism will occur in the pioneer country *because* it is more efficient, it remains essential that it should be introduced at a moment *when* communism – immediately or ultimately – can develop the productive forces more rapidly than capitalism, since otherwise there will be no success to inspire the latecomers.[16]

Since the actual and the possible are incommensurable, the key problem is that of the starting point. The alleged superiority of communism as a project is not verifiable. Its practical superiority would subsequently ensure its progressive, rational diffusion. This is why the initial victory would necessarily be 'accidental'. In 1917, all in all, the dice fell badly. A bad draw and a bad start: rather than initiating the triumph of more successful relations of production, we are back to square one.

Faced with this historical unreason, Elster quotes Trotsky in his support: 'But societies are not so rational in building that the dates for proletarian dictatorship arrive exactly at that moment when the economic and cultural conditions are ripe for socialism.'[17] For Trotsky, as for Marx, history is not so simple. A political crisis and ripe economic conditions do not necessarily coincide. 'In fact', adds Elster, 'I shall argue that they are so irrational in building that these two factors tend systematically not to coincide.'[18] The clocks are not synchronized; temporalities are not uniform. Structured like a language, politics, like the unconscious, has its displacements and condensations. Not content with not being rational, might history be a tiny bit perverse?

More subtle than a mechanistic schema of the collapse of capitalism under the impetus of the productive forces, Elster's thesis displaces the problem without resolving it. We would need to be able to determine the *optimal correspondence* between forces and relations of production – something he carefully avoids. A first difficulty concerns the very determination of the productive forces:

> The notion of *development* of the productive forces is multiply ambiguous. It is unclear whether the exploitation of economies of scale counts as such development. Also, it is unclear whether the productive forces develop when they allow for a greater surplus under constant environmental and demographic conditions, or when they allow for a greater surplus under the actual, possibly changed conditions.[19]

The concept of productive forces in fact raises a problem that is common to most of Marx's basic concepts: their descriptive enumeration varies with the level of determination of the concept.[20]

The notion of correspondence thus involves a relation of relative reciprocity. As approximations referring to social reproduction as a whole, optimality and sub-optimality cannot be quantitatively defined exclusively at the economic level of production or distribution. Moreover, this is why Marx sometimes seems to accept exploitation and injustice . . . in the name of correspondence. Ricardo 'wants *production for the sake of production* and this with *good reason*'. Good reason? Are primitive accumulation and factory despotism novel ruses of historical reason? 'Production for its own sake means nothing but the development of human productive forces, in other words the *development of the richness of human nature*', even if it 'takes place at the cost of the majority of human individuals and even classes'. From Ricardo's standpoint – which is that of political economy, not its critique – there is nothing 'base' about equating proletarians with beasts of burden or machinery, for that is indeed how things stand *within the framework of capitalist relations of production*. 'This is stoic, objective, scientific', Marx ironizes.[21]

No yardstick allows us to decide that a mode of production has reached its limits, except for the (productive) power of labour itself, expressing an alternative positive historical possibility in and through its rebellions and insurrections. No mechanical law presides over the triumphant ineluctability of revolutions. 'Correspondence' is not a simple adequation of two terms (infrastructure and superstructure); it merely indicates a relationship of formal non-contradiction or compatibility.[22] Reciprocally, the discordance of times determines the general character of an epoch. 'An epoch of social revolution', according to Marx. A bundle of possibilities: nothing more.

Was socialism 'premature' in Russia at the beginning of the twentieth century? The question assumes a historical norm of reference: 'We noted . . . that a theory of history is not answerable to *abnormal* occurrences, but we did not specify *criteria of normality*.'[23] And for a very good reason. How can we define normality amid the singular shapes of history? To declare what functions 'normally' healthy is tautological. *A fortiori*, Cohen is well aware of this when it comes to social relations:

> To be sure, we could not make it a defining property of a normal society that it tends to increase its productive power . . . Nor, for the same reason, could it be a defining feature of a normal society that its production relations are adjusted

to its productive forces ... Finally, we should expect any concept of a *normal society* to be less clear and less easy to apply than that of a *healthy organism.* We must remember that the matter of history resists very refined conceptualization.[24]

Cohen cautiously imparts to the primacy of the productive forces a sense that is more explanatory than causal. He distinguishes between three grades of potentiality:

1. in certain conditions, x will become y;
2. in certain normal conditions, x will become y;
3. in all normal conditions, x will become y.

These grades, stated in the form of laws, once again refer to the presumed normality of history. What do these 'normal conditions' mean in the case of singular situations? Historical necessity and possibility permit of only conditional predictions, in the manner of Lenin announcing 'the impending catastrophe and how to combat it'! Unlike predictions in physics, historical anticipation is expressed in a strategic project.

This constitutes a change of register and rationality. A radial schema replaces the straight line. For historical development is not reducible to a monotonous alternation between correspondence and non-correspondence. It involves what is actual and what is possible. In the perpetual struggle between the rational and the irrational, irrationality is in reality the reverse side of rationality and 'a moment that must be taken into consideration'.[25] Something which will never become real history is irrational.

The theoreticians of analytical Marxism might also ponder whether capitalism has not lasted too long, and at what cost. Remedying prematurity by senility, they could seek the ideal average, and trace the correct dividing line where change would have occurred at just the right point in the century. Marx does not engage in this kind of chronological speculation. For him, it is enough to have a handle on the contradictions and conflicts of the epoch, where what is at stake is what is actually possible.

According to Lenin, his was the 'era of war and revolutions'. The rest was a matter for politics, not prediction. Everything is created 'according to struggle and necessity' – both together, not one without the other. And the time of the world is displayed in history 'as a unity of the rule and the vicissitudes of the future'.[26]

Intermittence and Contretemps

Notwithstanding the numerous explicit texts on this point, Elster persists in detecting 'a theory of history, of the successive modes of production' in Marx. He attributes to him 'a fairly consistent teleological attitude towards history', even though it means he cannot explain the contrast between *The German Ideology* and the subsequent major texts, 'except possibly [by] the influence of Engels'.[27] This explanation is as convenient as it is inconsistent. The texts of 1846 are in no sense careless juvenilia that deviate from a generally consistent position. There is a strict continuity between them and *The Holy Family*. The *Grundrisse* and the 1859 *Contribution* echo them faithfully:

> The so-called historical presentation of development is founded, as a rule, on the fact that the latest form regards the previous ones as steps leading up to itself, and, since it is only rarely and only under quite specific conditions able to criticize itself . . . it always conceives them one-sidedly.[28]

It is impossible to imagine a more emphatic dismissal of retrospective illusions about the course of history as a process whose unfolding conspires to bring about the consecration of a present that is ineluctable, and hence legitimate.

Correspondence of the forces and relations of production, historical necessity and possibility: they bring us back to the question of the transformation of societies, 'premature' revolutions, and abortive transitions. Not content with attributing to Marx the 'supra-historical schema' he manifestly condemned, Elster accuses him of having imagined a communism that arrives at the appointed hour, instead of considering the disastrous consequences of its premature advent. This 'prematurity' scarcely has any meaning. An event that is inserted like a dutiful link into the orderly sequence of days and tasks is no longer an event, but mere routine. History is composed of eventful singularities. An event can be adjudged premature by reference to an imaginary deadline, but not in the tremulous horizon of real possibilities. Those who accuse Marx of being a determinist are often the very same people who reproach him for being insufficiently determinist! For the 'legal' Marxist Struve, as for the Mensheviks, a socialist revolution in Russia in 1917 seemed monstrously premature. The question re-emerges today, at the hour of reckoning. Would it not have been wiser and preferable to respect the rhythms of history, to allow objective conditions and Russian capitalism to mature, to allow Russian society time to modernize?

Who composes the score, and who beats time? According to Elster,

[t]wo spectres haunt the communist revolution. One is the danger of premature revolution, in a combination of advanced revolutionary ideas and miserable conditions in a country not yet ripe for communism. The other is the risk
of preempted revolutions, of reforms introduced from above to defuse a
dangerous situation.[29]

If such things as premature revolutions exist, then there must also be
overripe revolutions. Resolved not to succumb to lullabies about the
radiant future, Cohen prefers to note that 'what a weak capitalism makes
possible is *potentially reversible* subversion of the capitalist system, *not*
construction of socialism'. He still does not always succeed in eluding the
formalistic traps of the 1859 Preface: 'the anti-capitalist revolution can be
premature and can therefore fail in its socialist object'.[30] An explanation
of Stalinism that boils down to the immaturity of historical conditions
thus invalidates a priori all strategic debate on the seizure of power in
1917, the chances of a German revolution in 1923, the significance of the
NEP and the various conceivable economic policies, in favour of a
mechanistic fatalism.

Does the weakening of capitalism make 'subversion' possible? Maybe.
Is it the case that it does not, *ipso facto*, render the 'construction of
socialism' possible? That is another claim – and a claim too far. It is to
play fast and loose with the crucial notion of possibility. If 'possible' means
potential in the sense of current possibility, subversion and construction
are conditionally compossible, though not inevitably connected. Otherwise, subversion would be consumed in a gallant last stand, and fade into
resignation. Marx (and Lenin) were more concrete. For them, there was
no question of instituting communism in Russia 'immediately', only of
initiating a socialist transition. They did not envisage classifying countries
on a 'scale of maturity', as a function of the growth of the productive
forces. On the contrary, Marx's response to Vera Zasulich on the actuality
of socialism in Russia insists upon two elements: the existence of a still
collective form of agrarian property; and the combination of Russian
capitalist development with the global development of the productive
forces.[31] The 'maturity' of the revolution is not determined in a single
country according to a unified, homogeneous time. It is worked out in
the discordance of times. Uneven and combined development makes its
possibility actual. The chain can be snapped at its weakest link. On the
other hand, socialist transition can be conceived only in a perspective that
is international from the outset. The theory of permanent revolution,
which systematizes these intuitions, has always been contested in the name
of a rigorously determinist vision of history; and Stalinist orthodoxy

precisely reduced Marx's theory to the skeleton of a 'supra-historical schema' that could no longer accommodate the Asiatic mode of production.

The fate of the Russian Revolution after 1917 – the bureaucratic Thermidor, the Stalinist terror, the tragedy of the camps – did not result mechanically from its putative prematurity. Economic, social and cultural circumstances played a determinate role. But they did not constitute an ineluctable fate, independent of concrete history, the state of the world, political victories and defeats. The German revolution of 1918–23, the second Chinese revolution, the victory of fascism in Italy and Nazism in Germany, the crushing of the Viennese Schutzbund, the Spanish Civil War, the collapse of the Popular Fronts – these represented so many bifurcations for the Russian Revolution itself.

How is this tendential development to be reconciled with its negation, which results from general commodity fetishism and the reification of social relations? Marx reiterates that the infernal waltz of wage-labour and capital reproduces the physical and mental mutilation of the worker, the subjugation of people to things, and universal subjection to the dominant ideology and its phantasmagorias. The 'prematurity' of the revolution then takes on a meaning of which Cohen and Elster have no inkling. In some sense, it is *structural and essential*. It is not restricted to a particular country or moment. In so far as the conquest of political power precedes social transformation and cultural emancipation, making a start is always a perilous leap – and possibly a fatal one. Its suspended time is conducive to bureaucratic usurpation and totalitarian confiscation.

For Elster, according to the 'Marxist philosophy of history', capitalism is an unavoidable step on the road to communism. Inasmuch as communism becomes a real possibility only at a certain threshold of development, capitalism contributes to creating the conditions for it. This banal truism does not in any way authorize the reciprocal proposition: that capitalism is always and everywhere a requisite (unavoidable) step towards the predetermined end of communism. To say: (a) that communism presupposes a determinate degree of development of the productive forces (labour productivity, skilled labour force, flourishing science and technology), to which capitalist growth contributes; and (b) that capitalism constitutes a stage and an unavoidable preparatory phase on the plotted path of the march to communism – these are not equivalent. The second formula lapses into the speculative illusion so often scoffed at by Marx, whereby 'later history is . . . the goal of earlier history', and 'the latest form regards the previous ones as steps leading up to itself'.[32]

Historical Necessity and Real Possibilities

A revolution 'just on time', without risks or surprises, would be an uneventful event, a sort of revolution without the revolution. Realizing a possibility, revolution is in essence untimely and, to some extent, always 'premature': a creative imprudence.

If humanity poses only the problems that it can resolve, should not everything occur at the appointed hour? If a social formation never disappears before the development of all the productive forces for which it is sufficient, why force fate, and at what cost? Was it premature or pathological to proclaim the primacy of the right to existence over the right to property as early as 1793? To demand social equality by the same token as political equality? Marx explicitly asserts the reverse: the birth of a new right expresses the actuality of the conflict. Revolutions are the sign of what humanity *can historically* resolve. In the nonconforming conformity of the epoch, they are a potentiality and possibility of the present, at once opportune and inopportune, too soon and too late, poised between the no longer and the not yet: a possibility whose last word has not been spoken.

Does siding with the oppressed when the objective conditions for their liberation are not ripe betray a teleological vision? If so, the 'anachronic' struggles of Spartacus, Münzer, Winstanley and Babeuf, in their optimism, made a date with a preordained end in mind. The opposite interpretation seems to chime better with Marx's thought: no pre-set course of history, no predestination, justifies resignation to oppression. Non-current, untimely, 'mal-contemporaneous', revolutions cannot be assimilated to the pre-established schemas of 'supra-history' or 'pallid, supra-temporal models'. Their occurrence does not observe the dispositions of a universal History. They are engendered at ground level, out of suffering and humiliation. It is always right to rebel.

If 'correspondence' has the force of normality, should we embrace the cause of the victors in opposition to impatience construed as a provocation? Without hesitation or reservation, Marx was on the side of the beggars in the German peasants' war, the Levellers in the English Revolution, the Equals in the French Revolution, the communards set to be crushed by Versailles.

It is conceivable for the era of revolutions to drag on in worsening times that are out of joint; for the productive forces to continue to grow with their train of damage and destruction; for the dark side of progress to prevail over its bright side. Henri Lefebvre evokes this 'growth without development', in which the divorce between the forces and relations of production translates into greater irrationality.

The present is the central temporal category of an open-ended history. Freed from the myths of origins and ends, it is the time of politics that 'attains primacy over history', as strategic conceptualization of struggle and decisions: 'A historical materialist cannot do without the notion of a present which is not a transition, but in which time stands still and has come to a stop.'[33]

Saint Augustine implored God to teach him how he reveals future things – or, more precisely, 'the present of future things' – to the prophets. For 'it is not strictly correct to say that there are three times', linked by an order of chronological succession. Rather, there are three modes of one and the same time, which is triply present: 'a present of past things, a present of present things, and the present of future things'.[34] The present redistributes meaning, scans the field of what is potential from the vantage point of its 'maybes', and invents new opportunities.

In these intertwined, intersecting, interwoven times, there is no longer room for oracular prediction of an implacable fate, only for conditional anticipation, for an indication of what will happen 'if', and only if, the community of unbelievers forgets its traditions. A traitor to inevitability, the prophet defies fate. It is no longer a question, once launched, of hurtling down the slope to a dead stop; or of proceeding straight along the chain of causes and effects. Unlike oracles, prophecy is conditional. In contrast to vulgar messianism, with its resigned anticipation, the active messianism of prophecy touches the sorrows of the present:

> There is no set time for the arrival of the Messiah that they can count on and decide that it is close or distant. The incumbency of the commandments does not depend on the appearance of the Messiah. . . . If we do what we have to do, we or our children or our grandchildren may be privileged by God to witness the coming of the Messiah, and life will be more pleasant . . . Inasmuch as Daniel has proclaimed the matter a deep secret, our sages have interdicted the calculation of the time of the future redemption, or the reckoning of the period of the advent of the Messiah, because the masses might be mystified or bewildered should the Messiah fail to appear as forecast . . . That is why they have uttered the imprecation, 'May the calculators of the final redemption come to grief.'[35]

In fact, the prophet does not indulge in the 'fervour of anticipation'. He strives to thwart the decrees of fate by announcing the evil that lies in store if . . . Conditional, messianic prophecy is not the anticipation of an event foretold, be it confident or resigned, but an awakening to the possibility of its advent. A reflexive knowledge, in which what is known incessantly modifies what is possible, its temporal mode is the present, not the future.

Prophecy, then, is the emblematic figure of all political and strategic discourse. In 'The Impending Catastrophe and How to Combat It', Lenin deciphers various tendencies in the belief that stating them conditionally makes what seems inevitable avoidable. Catastrophe is certain *if* . . . Hence it is not fated.

Marx opposes the 'historically necessary' abolition of classes to their 'logically impossible' equalization. This historical necessity does not in any sense involve a mechanical fatality. The specificity of political economy requires that we revise the concepts of chance and law, and distinguish between necessity in the 'speculative-abstract' sense and necessity in the 'historical-concrete' sense. According to Gramsci, 'necessity exists when there exists an efficient and active *premiss*, consciousness of which in people's minds has become operative, proposing concrete goals to the collective consciousness and constituting a complex of convictions and beliefs which acts powerfully in the form of "popular beliefs" '.[36]

Immanent, 'historical necessity' states what must and can be, not what will be: 'Real possibility and necessity are . . . only *seemingly* different . . . this necessity is at the same time *relative*.' Real possibility becomes necessity. It begins with the unity, '*still external to itself*', of the possible and the actual. It is not yet determined as contingency. For necessity, adds Hegel, real in itself, is equally contingency: 'This is manifest at first in this manner: though the really necessary is a necessary *as regards form*, as regards content it is limited, and through this has its contingency . . . Here, therefore, the unity of necessity and contingency is present *in itself* or *in principle*; this unity is to be called absolute actuality.'[37]

As early as his thesis on the philosophy of nature in Democritus and Epicurus, Marx handled this dialectic perfectly:

> Chance, for Epicurus, is a reality which has only the value of possibility. *Abstract possibility*, however, is the direct *antipode of real possibility*. The latter is restricted within sharp boundaries, as is the intellect; the former is unbounded, as is the imagination. Real possibility seeks to explain the necessity and reality of its object; abstract possibility is not interested in the object which is explained, but in the subject which does the explaining. The object need only be possible, conceivable. That which is abstractly possible, which can be conceived, constitutes no obstacle to the thinking subject, no limit, no stumbling-block. Whether this possibility is also real is irrelevant, since here the interest does not extend

to the object as object . . . Necessity appears in finite nature as *relative necessity*, as *determinism*. Relative necessity can only be deduced from *real possibility*. . . . Real possibility is the explication of relative necessity.[38]

Possibility is inscribed in this interplay of the necessary and the contingent, in the movement from formal necessity, via relative necessity, to absolute necessity. It is distinct from merely formal possibility (or non-contradiction), as from abstract or general possibility. As a determinate possibility, it carries within it an 'imperfection', with the consequence that 'possibility is at the same time a contradiction or an impossibility'.

Marx, 'thinker of possibility', thus plays with several modes: contingent possibility, whose link with reality (according to Hegel) determines contingency; 'being *in potentia*' as a determinate capacity (according to Aristotle) to receive a given form (the transition from potentiality to actuality is then the unitary moment *par excellence* of chance and necessity); finally, historical possibility (real or effective – *wirklich*), which is the unity of contingent possibility and being *in potentia*. *Capital* says nothing else: there is no absolute necessity, no Laplacean demon. Chance and necessity are not mutually exclusive. The determinate contingency of the event is not arbitrary and capricious; it simply derives from a non-formal causality: 'The reverse rather is true, namely, that such a petty and contingent circumstance is the occasion of the event *only* because the latter has determined it to be such.'[39]

Necessity delineates the horizon of struggle. Its contingency averts the decrees of fate.

The penultimate chapter of Volume One of *Capital*, 'The Historical Tendency of Capitalist Accumulation', has inspired many mechanistic professions of faith in the certain collapse of capitalism under the weight of its own contradictions, and many polemics. Marx writes: 'capitalist production begets, with the inexorability of a natural process, its own negation. This is the negation of the negation.'[40] This is indeed a curious text. On the one hand, it lucidly anticipates the tendencies towards the concentration of capital, the industrial application of science and technology, the contradictory socialization of the major means of production, and the globalization of commodity relations: forecasts that have largely been confirmed. On the other hand, it appears to deduce a law of absolute pauperization and increasing social polarization from capitalist development. Yet Marx's polemics against Lassalle and his 'iron law of wages' preclude any mechanistic interpretation of pauperization. By contrast, the idea that capital concentration and the 'very mechanism of

capitalist production' have the effect of swelling the ranks of the proletariat and automatically enhancing its resistance, organization and unity
breaks – at least in part – with the general logic of *Capital*.

The stress laid on the 'immanent laws of capitalist production' results
here in an objectification and naturalization of historical 'fate'. The
aleatory instance of struggle vanishes without trace into the formalism of
the negation of the negation – as if time, solely by flowing, could
guarantee that the expected hour will strike punctually on the clock of
history. Yet 'history does nothing': men and women make it, and in
circumstances not of their own choosing.

This controversial chapter from Volume One is too prominent for us
to be able to regard it as a mere blunder. Instead, it underscores an
unresolved contradiction between the influence of a naturalistic model of
science ('the inexorabililty of a natural process') and the dialectical logic
of an open-ended history. In *Anti-Dühring*, Engels strove to counter trivial
interpretations that turn the 'negation of the negation' into an abstract
machine and a formal pretext for false predictions:

> But what role does the negation of the negation play in Marx? ... by
> characterizing the process as the negation of the negation Marx *does not intend
> to prove that the process was historically necessary*. On the contrary: only after he has
> proved from history that in fact the process has partially already occurred, and
> partially must occur in the future, he in addition characterizes it as a process
> which develops in accordance with a definite dialectical law. It is therefore once
> again a pure distortion of the facts by Herr Dühring when he declares that the
> negation of the negation has to *serve here as the midwife to deliver the future from
> the womb of the past*, or that Marx wants anyone to be convinced of the necessity
> of the common ownership of land and capital ... *on the basis of credence in the
> negation of the negation*. Herr Dühring's total lack of understanding of the nature
> of dialectics is shown by the very fact that he regards it as a mere proof-
> producing instrument, as a limited mind might look upon formal logic or
> elementary mathematics.[41]

Duly noted: (1) the negation of the negation is not a new *deus ex machina*,
or a midwife of history; (2) one cannot extend it credit and draw drafts
on the future, trusting exclusively in its law. 'Historical necessity' does not
license reading the cards and issuing predictions. It operates in a field of
possibilities, where the *general* law applies in and through a *particular*
development. Dialectical logic and formal logic definitely do not sit
comfortably together. Having reached this critical point, the 'extremely
general' law is silent. It must defer to politics or history. To dot the i's
and cross the t's, Engels returns to the attack:

And so, what is the negation of the negation? An *extremely general* – and for this reason extremely far-reaching and important – law of development of nature, history, and thought; a law which, as we have seen, holds good in the animal and plant kingdoms, in geology, in mathematics, in history and in philosophy . . . *It is obvious that I do not say anything concerning the particular process of development* of, for example, a grain of barley from germination to the death of the fruit-bearing plant, if I say that it is a negation of the negation . . . The bare knowledge that the barley plant . . . [is] governed by negation of the negation does not enable me . . . to grow barley successfully . . . just as little as the bare knowledge of the laws of determination of sound by the dimensions of the strings enables me to play the violin.[42]

If the negation of the negation 'consists in the childish pastime of alternately writing and cancelling *a,* or in alternately declaring that a rose is a rose and that it is not a rose, nothing eventuates but the silliness of the person who adopts such a tedious procedure'.[43]

To demand more from a dialectical law than its generality would yield an empty formalism. Historical development is no more deducible from the negation of the negation than an individual grain of barley. No formula can replace the concrete analysis of the concrete situation, of which *The Peasants' War in Germany, The Eighteenth Brumaire,* and *Class Struggles in France* furnish so many examples. The thorny question is then no longer that of the determinism unjustly attributed to Marx, but the notion that there exists, among the various possibilities, a 'normal' course of development and deviant monstrosities.[44]

Ten years after the publication of *Capital* Volume One, Engels's comments on 'The Historical Tendency of Capitalist Accumulation' cleared up ambiguities that were perfectly understandable in the intellectual context of the period. It is striking that he felt the need to intervene on this point, and that he did it in this fashion – all the more so since *Anti-Dühring* was written in close collaboration with Marx. Henceforth, the controversial chapter of *Capital* was inseparable from the commentary that clarified and emended it.

Determinate necessity is not the opposite of chance, but the corollary of determinate possibility. The negation of the negation states what must disappear. It does not dictate what must occur.

Progress in the Balance

Like the history of organisms, social history comprises 'a staggeringly improbable series of events, sensible enough in retrospect . . ., but utterly unpredictable'.[45] In 1909, Charles Walcott discovered the fossils known as the Burgess Shale in the Canadian Rockies. His overriding concern was to fit these organisms into an evolutionary schema progressing from the most simple to the most complex. In the 1970s, the reopening of the file by a group of researchers led, through a series of monographic studies accepting their anatomical oddity as another possible norm, to a 'quiet revolution'. Today, the Burgess creatures (*Opabinia, Hallucigenia, Anomali-caris*) are no longer regarded as elementary forms of known species. They are simply taken as evidence of the Cambrian explosion of life – organic constructs and possibilities that came to nothing.

Such a discovery dashes the dominant idea of evolution, symbolized by the ladder of continuous progress or the 'inverted cone' of growing diversity and complexity. History increases the diversity of species, but it prunes the branches and restricts the initial disparity between different forms of anatomical organization. Following the Copernican and Darwinian revolutions, interpretation of the Burgess Shale delivers a further blow to anthropocentrism. Humanity is merely a cosmic accident, or 'one bauble on the Christmas tree of evolution'. We may no longer 'grasp all that came before us as a grand preparation, a foreshadowing of our eventual origin'.[46] This presumptuous view made the human avatar the original goal of five million years of bodges and experiments! Following its own paths, geology thus deepened the young Marx's critique of 'speculative distortions' whereby 'later history is made the goal of earlier history', and *Homo sapiens* the goal of *Opabinia*: 'the diversity of possible itineraries does demonstrate that eventual results cannot be predicted at the outset'.[47]

Yet another effort, human beings, if you want to become utter non-believers! – renounce the retrospective illusion whereby nothing other than what is could have been, and the gradualist illusion of continuous modifications.[48] Just as military or political victories do not prove what is true or right in history, survival has no value as proof in palaeontology. It is precisely what must be explained. Unlike vulgar Darwinists, Darwin was conscious that adaptive responses to environmental changes by individual variation and natural selection did not necessarily constitute progress (by what criteria?) but, rather, evolution without plan or direction. In his theory of evolution, 'historical science *par excellence*', the winners transmit more copies of their own genes to future generations – 'nothing else'.[49] Operating according to strictly Baconian principles, selection exercises its driving force through random genetic variation and adaptation. Darwin himself refused to represent it in terms of progress and categorically rejected the terms 'lower' and 'higher', convinced as he was that there was no immanent tendency to progress in development. Evolution is a tree- or bush-like formation, rather than a gradual ladder. In it, previous forms are not the rough drafts of more developed forms; and non-contemporaneity permits the survival of 'archaic' ancestors when their descendants are already differentiated.

Reinterpreted, the Burgess Shale rehabilitates the contingency of evolution without a goal and history as an explanatory, rather than a normative, principle. Its oddities and imperfections are often more eloquent than its regularities. Henceforth we are obliged to regard 'the "pageant" of evolution as a staggeringly improbable series of events, sensible enough in retrospect and subject to rigorous explanation, but utterly unpredictable and quite unrepeatable'.[50]

Despite his discoveries, Darwin had difficulty escaping the progressivist ideology of his age. To some extent his dilemma was identical to that of Marx, who recognized in *The Origin of Species* the 'historical foundation of [his own] conception'. Darwin's Darwinism is, in fact, neither an environmental determinism nor a mere animal parable of market competition. Anticipating some recent interpretations of Darwin, Marx drew inspiration from 'accumulation through heredity' as a motor principle. In insisting on the dialectic of cumulation (necessary) and invention (contingent), Darwin avoided the mechanistic trap: 'the various organisms themselves are formed as a result of "accumulation" and are only "inventions", gradually accumulated inventions of living beings'.[51] Darwin's time proceeds 'by errors'.[52]

Étienne Balibar rounds off Marx's disquieting suggestion that 'history advances by the bad side', by adding: and yet it advances! Indeed, cases where the 'failures' and 'mistakes' of 'victorious defeats' have played an unexpected role are not rare.[53] Balibar stresses the important role of the 'bad side' – the defeat that wrecks the vision of a world unified by the irresistible march of the proletariat. After 1848, and again after 1871, the impact of events prompted a critique of the idea of progress. It necessitated conceptualizing 'singular historicities'. This conclusion is hardly compatible with the hypothesis of an absolute historical yardstick of progress. Marx's endeavour aims to hold both ends of the chain: to extricate himself from the abstraction of universal History (the 'floating universal') without lapsing into the insane chaos of absolute singularities ('what only happens once'); and without resorting to the trump card of progress. In so far as universalization is a process, progress is not conjugated in the present indicative, only in the future anterior: conditionally. But if quotidian progress consists in winning more than one loses, assessment of it is condemned to the vulgar calculation of profit and loss. This boils down to discounting the temporality of the measurement itself: the fact that today's gains become tomorrow's losses, and vice versa.

The standard notion of progress, in effect, supposes a fixed scale of comparison and final statement of account. For liberal optimism both past and present, 'any change at all can qualify as progress . . . From the perspective of the total cosmic process, . . . [retrogression] is not possible.' In other words, belief in historical progress 'rules out . . . contingency'.[54] The extent to which interwar social-democratic and Stalinist politicians shared this quietism cannot be stressed enough; nor can what it cost them to perceive, in repeated catastrophes, merely 'backwardness' and 'retardation'.

In the third of his 'Theses on the Philosophy of History', Benjamin conveys this retrospective, definitive determination of progress by means of the image of an unpronounceable Last Judgement:

> A chronicler who recites events without distinguishing between major and minor ones acts in accordance with the following truth: nothing that has ever happened should be regarded as lost for history. To be sure, only a redeemed mankind receives the fullness of its past – which is to say, only for a redeemed mankind has its past become citable in all its moments. Each moment it has lived becomes a *citation à l'ordre du jour* – and that day is Judgment Day.[55]

An exhaustive recapitulation of moments, their summons to appear, is conceivable only at the last hour, at the limit point of the Judgement that conceals itself on the horizon of an open-ended history. The meaning of progress thus hangs on the dream of a redeemed humanity. Meanwhile, every classification and division remains provisional. Thwarting the ordered, victorious discourse of the historian, the patient inventory of the chronicler records events none of which can be neglected, for their significance will be disclosed only much later, under the resurrectionary impact of the future.

The abstraction of progress and universal History are linked. Completion of the latter is the only thing that would make it possible to validate the course pursued by the former. In the absence of this ending, from whose vantage point humanity would contemplate its finished work with satisfaction, this improbable day when the final word will be spoken, profane history expires in a haemorrhage of meaning.

Historically and socially determinate, and coupled with the regression that accompanies it like its shadow, progress is never absolute and definitive. Thus, the progress accomplished by capital consists in altering the form of slavery, with the metamorphosis of feudal exploitation into capitalist exploitation. The abstractly 'progressive' expropriation of the peasantry 'is written in the annals of mankind in letters of blood and fire'.[56] Faced with the ravages of agrarian transformation in Russia (deforestation, agricultural crisis), Engels refused to regard its human and ecological disasters as the inevitable incidental costs of modernization: 'And we are supposed to console ourselves with the thought that all this must ultimately serve the cause of human progress!'.[57] Always deferred, progress also comprises the pitiless violence employed against the vanquished, its perfection and technical refinement, which scarcely square with the edifying picture of a triumphal march of history.

The generalization of commodity production leads to a globalization of exchange and communication; yet the world market is articulated in a hierarchy of domination and dependency. The international extension of the class struggle bursts through the narrow horizons of hearth and home, universalizes a logic of solidarity, tends towards self-negation in the abolition of every relation of oppression; yet the dynamic of the conflict crystallizes new divisions, new lines of fracture, new national and religious particularisms. Far from civilizing standards of behaviour, the trade of all with all extends the theatre of war in space and time. The rapid development of production, science and technology discloses hitherto unknown human needs and capacities, summons into being a magnificent range of tastes, creations, differences. But reification and alienation turn humanity into a mass besotted by the spectacle of its own fetishes. Increased labour productivity frees time for individual and collective creativity, permitting new forms of social interaction and consciousness. But the 'miserable' measurement of all wealth and exchange by abstract labour-time transforms an extraordinary potential liberation into unemployment, exclusion, and physical and spiritual poverty.

The great disillusionment with progress can induce dazed contemplation of the kaleidoscopic shapes of a history without rhyme or reason, allowing space only for moral indignation or aesthetic pleasure, for cries of protest without any echo or enigmatic silence. If all that remains is the sound and fury of the struggle, how can the chaos of battle be avoided? How can a principle of intelligibility and critical judgement be salvaged? Doubtless by beginning with a reconsideration of the criteria of a progress ensnared in its own contradictions. Those proposed by Marx are not so bad: real historical universalization; enrichment of individuals and species by the diversification of needs and capabilities; suppression of compulsory labour in favour of time for free creation; transformation of social and affective relations between men and women. These criteria are incomparably richer than industrial production statistics or approval ratings in opinion polls.

Why these rather than others? Simply because these 'values' are the immanent product of the social relation of humanity with nature and itself, the historical and cultural result of its own humanization, to the exclusion of any divine transcendence. Facts and values, ethics and politics, responsibility and conviction no longer work separately, in mutual indifference. In radically rejecting historical fetishism, the abstraction of progress, and the closure of meaning, Marx uncovers more promising potentialities than the meagre dialectic of the forces and relations of production.

According to G.A. Cohen, '[t]he growth of human power is the central process of history': 'The need for that growth explains why there *is* history. . . . For Hegel men have history because consciousness needs time and action to come to know itself, for Marx because men need time and action to prevail against nature.'[58] The separation of history and politics (understood as strategy of conflict) issues in a lapse back into speculative representations of history, without elucidating the 'need for that growth'. It simply seems to echo the law of evolution and progress: 'in one particular sense the more recent forms must . . . be higher than the more ancient; for each new species is formed by having had some advantage in the struggle for life over other and preceding forms'.[59] This statement confuses chronological succession with causal link.

Acknowledging that 'Marx did not see history as simply a form of linear progress', Elster is content to register 'an interesting contrast . . . between Marx's theory of perpetual progress of the productive forces and the more gloomy view of the perpetual destruction of nature'.[60] Incapable of conceptualizing progress and regression in their contradictory unity, he simply detects a theoretical inconsistency. The link between a progress reduced to rapid technological development of the productive forces and shattered social integration is broken. All that remains is a laboured collage of the positive odyssey of technology and a new theodicy of spirit.

Inseparable from assertions of the rationality of history, the idea of progressive evolution is the latest avatar of a philosophy of universal History from which Marx supposedly never succeeded in extricating himself. On this point, Balibar follows the findings of analytical Marxism. He observes, however, that the idea of progress has virtually disappeared from *Capital*:

[W]hat interests Marx is not *progress*, but the *process*, which he makes the dialectical concept *par excellence*. Progress is not something given or pre-programmed; it can only result from the development of the antagonisms which comprise the process and, as a consequence, it is always relative to those antagonisms. Now, process is neither a moral (spiritualist) concept, nor an economic (naturalist) one. It is a logical and political concept . . .[61]

Having attributed an evolutionist and progressivist conception of universal History to Marx, Balibar interprets his last texts on Russia as 'an astonishing turnabout, induced by a question from outside': 'Marx's *economism* gave birth to its opposite: a set of *anti-evolutionist* hypotheses.'[62]

This hypothesis of a late reversal, as absolute as it was spectacular, is scarcely plausible. We may concede that the rejection, as early as 1845, of a fetishistic or 'supra-historical' history, in favour of profane history, could coexist with incompatible evolutionistic generalizations (to whose influence the 1859 Preface attests). It remains the case that the spectre of a homogeneous, linear, universal History is exorcized by the concept of a branching history, whose significance is identified by Balibar:

> Marx resorted less and less to pre-existing *models* of explanation and increasingly *constructed a rationality* which had no real precedent. That rationality is neither the rationality of mechanics, physiology, or biological evolution, nor that of a formal theory of conflict or strategy, though it has recourse to all of these from time to time. In the incessant transformation of its conditions and forms, the class struggle is its own model.[63]

A rationality that 'had no real precedent' – and is to be found at the point where the critique of historical reason, the critique of political economy, and the critique of scientific positivism converge.

Notes

1. Erik Olin Wright, 'What is Analytical Marxism?', in Wright, *Interrogating Inequality*, Verso, London and New York 1994, pp. 181–2. This question had already been posed by John Roemer: 'But why should this kind of work be called Marxist? I am not sure that it should' (Roemer, ed., *Analytical Marxism*, Cambridge University Press/Éditions de la Maison des Sciences de l'Homme, Cambridge and Paris 1986, p. 2).
2. Wright, *Interrogating Inequality*, pp. 186–91. Wright challenges the straightforward identification of analytical Marxism with methodological individualism: 'a number of Analytical Marxists have been explicitly critical of methodological individualism and have argued against the exclusive reliance on models of abstract rationality as a way of understanding human action' (p. 190).
3. Ellen Meiksins Wood, 'Rational Choice Marxism: Is the Game Worth the Candle?', *New Left Review*, no. 177, September/October 1989, p. 43.

4. Jon Elster, *Making Sense of Marx*, Cambridge University Press/Éditions de la Maison des Sciences de l'Homme, Cambridge and Paris 1985, p. 309; emphasis added.
5. Karl Marx, Preface to *A Contribution to the Critique of Political Economy*, in Marx, *Early Writings*, Penguin/NLR, Harmondsworth 1975, pp. 425–6.
6. G.A. Cohen, *Karl Marx's Theory of History: A Defence*, Clarendon Press, Oxford 1978, p. 27.
7. Karl Marx and Frederick Engels, 'The German Ideology', in Marx and Engels, *Collected Works*, vol. 5, Lawrence & Wishart, London 1976, p. 49.
8. Cohen, *Karl Marx's Theory of History*, p. x.
9. See Isaac Joshua, *La Face cachée du Moyen Age*, La Brèche, Paris 1988.
10. Erik Olin Wright, 'Capitalism's Futures', in *Interrogating Inequality*, pp. 114–16.
11. Ibid.
12. Elster, *Making Sense of Marx*, p. 318.
13. Ibid., p. 29.
14. Ibid., p. 514.
15. Ibid., p. 300.
16. Ibid., pp. 290, 292–3.
17. Trotsky, *History of the Russian Revolution*, quoted in ibid., p. 293.
18. Elster, *Making Sense of Marx*, p. 293.
19. Ibid., p. 300.
20. In addition, the notion of 'material productive forces' can induce error if it is forgotten that material is contrasted with formal, and does not imply a restrictive conception. Thus, the material productive forces are never reducible to some trivial materiality. The occurrences of the concept indicate that they include natural resources (raw materials, energy) and technological resources (machines, processes), as well as the organization of labour, scientific knowledge and the way in which it is produced. Far from playing the role of a simple motor under the bonnet of the relations of production, they are themselves determined by the latter, from the angle both of the organization of labour and of the practical utilization of knowledge. Criticizing the schema of 'historical motor' according to Cohen, Michel Vadée notes:

> Forces and means are two different categories as commonly understood. In reality, things are not so simple. In labour that is no longer simple labour, particularly in developed capitalist production (industrial machinofacture), the productive forces are means and the means of production are forces: a dialectical identity obtains between them. Forces and means pass into one another. It is pointless trying to maintain an absolute distinction between them, as can be seen from the synoptic tables displaying the diverse species of forces and relations of production, where the ambiguities and oddities or surprising lacunae are apparent. (*Marx penseur du possible*, Klincksieck, Paris 1993, p. 398)

21. Karl Marx, *Theories of Surplus-Value*, Part II, trans. Renate Simpson, Lawrence & Wishart, London 1969, pp. 117–19.
22.

> In German, to correspond (*sich entsprechen*) and to contradict (*sich widersprechen*) are diametrically opposed. This is not the case in French – hence our use of the term *discordance* to bring out what is immediately visible in German. Correspondence can also be expressed by *Überstimmung*, which has the same root as *Bestimmung* (determination), *stimmen* meaning to agree in the various senses of the word. These correspondences are untranslatable. (Vadée, *Marx penseur du possible*, p. 154)

23. Cohen, *Karl Marx's Theory of History*, p. 156; emphasis added.
24. Ibid., pp. 156–7; emphasis added.
25. Antonio Gramsci, *Quaderni del carcere*, vol. II, ed. Valentino Gerratana, Einaudi, Turin 1975, pp. 689–90.
26. Jean-Toussaint Desanti, *Réflexions sur le temps*, Grasset, Paris 1993, p. 25.

27. Elster, *Making Sense of Marx*, pp. 107, 109.
28. Karl Marx, *Grundrisse*, trans. Martin Nicolaus, Penguin/NLR, Harmondsworth 1973, p. 106.
29. Elster, *Making Sense of Marx*, p. 531.
30. Cohen, *Karl Marx's Theory of History*, p. 203.
31. On this point, see Marx's letters to Vera Zasulich, in Maurice Godelier, ed., *Sur les sociétés précapitalistes*, CERM/Éditions Sociales, Paris 1967. See also Leon Trotsky, *The Permanent Revolution*, Pathfinder Press, New York 1978; Lenin, 'The Development of Capitalism in Russia', in *Collected Works*, vol. 3, Progress Publishers, Moscow 1964 ('The Tasks of the Proletariat in the Present Revolution'), in *Collected Works*, vol. 24, Progress Publishers, Moscow 1964; Alain Brossat, *La Théorie de la révolution permanente chez le jeune Trotsky*, Maspero, Paris 1972; and the historical works of E.H. Carr and Theodor Shanin.
32. Marx and Engels, 'The German Ideology', p. 50; Marx, *Grundrisse*, p. 106. Suppressing the thorny question of the Asiatic mode of production, Stalin wanted to reduce concrete history to a 'supra-historical' schema of successive modes of production. This ideological operation served immediately political interests (the 'construction of socialism in one country', international alliances, the bloc of four classes).
33. Walter Benjamin, 'Theses on the Philosophy of History', XVI, in Benjamin, *Illuminations*, trans. Harry Zohn, Fontana, London 1973, p. 264.
34. Saint Augustine, *Confessions*, XI, 20, trans. R.S. Pine-Coffin, Penguin, London 1961, p. 269. In Heidegger, by contrast, 'being-towards-death' makes the present conditional on the future. Whereas the primacy of the past determines the historical, in historicality the future takes precedence as an expression of the finitude of temporality: 'Inauthentic history goes in search of modernity in order to free itself from the weight of the past, whereas authentic history involves the return of the possible' (Françoise Dastur, *Heidegger et la question du temps*, Presses Universitaires de France, Paris 1990). See also Françoise Proust, *L'histoire à contretemps*, Cerf, Paris 1994.
35. Maimonides, *Epistles of Maimonides*, trans. Abraham Halkin, Jewish Publication Society, Philadelphia 1993, pp. 32–3, 116. Jews were forbidden to foretell the future.
36. Antonio Gramsci, *Selections from the Prison Notebooks*, ed. and trans. Quintin Hoare and Geoffrey Nowell Smith, Lawrence & Wishart, London 1971, pp. 412–13.
37. G.W.F. Hegel, *Science of Logic*, trans. A.V. Miller, Allen & Unwin, London 1969, pp. 549–50.
38. Karl Marx, 'Difference between the Democritean and Epicurean Philosophy of Nature' (1841), in Karl Marx and Frederick Engels, *Collected Works*, vol. 1, Lawrence & Wishart, London 1975, pp. 43–5. On the category of the possible in Marx, see Vadée, *Marx penseur du possible*; Henri Maler, *L'utopie selon Karl Marx*, L'Harmattan, Paris 1994.
39. Hegel, *Science of Logic*, p. 562.
40. Karl Marx, *Capital*, vol. 1, trans. Ben Fowkes, Penguin/NLR, Harmondsworth 1976, p. 929.
41. Frederick Engels, *Anti-Dühring*, trans. Emile Burns, Progress Publishers, Moscow 1947, pp. 162–5; emphasis added.
42. Ibid., pp. 172–3; emphasis added.
43. Ibid., p. 173.
44. Ernest Mandel frequently refers to historical 'detours' and 'deviations'. Nevertheless, he indicates that the problem is normality, rather than historical determinism:

> It should be stressed, however, that the question of whether capitalism can survive indefinitely or is doomed to collapse is not to be confused with the notion of its inevitable replacement by a *higher* form of social organization, i.e. with the inevitability of socialism. It is quite possible to postulate the inevitable collapse of capitalism without postulating the inevitable victory of socialism. . . . The system cannot survive, but may give way either to socialism or to barbarism. (Introduction to Karl Marx, *Capital*, vol. 3, Penguin/NLR, Harmondsworth 1981, p. 79)

68   FROM THE SACRED TO THE PROFANE

45. Stephen Jay Gould, *Wonderful Life*, Hutchinson Radius, London 1990, p. 14.
46. Ibid., pp. 44–5.
47. Ibid., p. 51.
48. Gould, in contrast, insists on 'hopeful monsters' and 'punctuated equilibria', arguing that punctual changes are at least as important as imperceptible accumulation, and that the history of the earth is punctuated by a series of pulsations that force reluctant systems to pass from one steady state to the next. See Gould, *The Panda's Thumb*, Penguin, Harmondsworth 1983, pp. 149–61.
49. Stephen Jay Gould, *An Urchin in the Storm*, Penguin, London 1990, p. 30.
50. Gould, *Wonderful Life*, p. 14.
51. Karl Marx, *Theories of Surplus-Value*, Part III, trans. Jack Cohen, Lawrence & Wishart, London 1972, pp. 294–5.
52. See Michel Serres (with Bruno Latour), *Conversations on Science, Culture, and Time*, trans. Roxanne Lapidus, University of Michigan Press, Ann Arbor 1995, p. 188.
53. See Étienne Balibar, *The Philosophy of Marx*, trans. Chris Turner, Verso, London and New York 1995, pp. 97–100.
54. Georg Simmel, *The Problems of the Philosophy of History*, trans. Guy Oakes, Free Press, New York 1977, pp. 180, 182.
55. Benjamin, 'Theses on the Philosophy of History', p. 256.
56. Marx, *Capital*, vol. 1, p. 875.
57. Engels, letter to Danielson, 15 March 1892. For his part, Labriola roundly condemned the 'Madonna Evoluzione' that confuses natural evolution and social development.
58. Cohen, *Karl Marx's Theory of History*, p. 23.
59. Charles Darwin, *The Origin of Species*, Penguin, London 1985, p. 336.
60. Elster, *Making Sense of Marx*, pp. 304, 58.
61. Balibar, *The Philosophy of Marx*, p. 100.
62. Ibid., p. 108.
63. Ibid, p. 96. On this non-positivist rationality, see also George E. McCarthy, *Marx's Critique of Science and Positivism*, Kluwer, Dordrecht and London 1983.

3

A New Appreciation of Time

Louise Michel has recounted the circumstances in which the communard Cipriani suddenly felt like stopping time on the clock of the Hôtel de Ville. Unwittingly repeating the gesture of rebels of 1830, he shot at the clock-face, which shattered. It was five past four on a lousy January day. At that very moment, his friend Sapia was killed by a bullet straight in the chest.

What is time? How is it to be told? A new way of writing history is a new way both of listening to time and of composing it. Punctuated by events, history no longer possesses the meaningful unity of a universal History governed by an alliance between order and progress. From its fractures issues a vortex of cycles and spirals, revolutions and restorations, 'historical monsoons' and 'oscillations', 'which advance none the less'.[1]

Dreams and Nightmares of History

In universal History, according to Bossuet, Providence pursues a design that prepares from the very origin of the world what is to be completed at the end of time.[2] As secularized in Kant, this grand design becomes a 'plan of nature', by which human beings, 'while pursuing their own ends, each in his own way and often in opposition to others, . . . are unwittingly guided'. In his 'Idea for a Universal History with a Cosmopolitan Purpose', the first proposition subscribes to the existence of a teleological order: '*All the natural capacities of a creature are destined sooner or later to be developed completely and in conformity with their end.*' Far from enjoining resignation to the decrees of fate, acknowledgement of such a goal, where necessity is conjugated in the conditional, remains a civic principle of freedom: 'And the point of time at which this degree of development is reached must be the goal of man's aspirations (at least as an idea in his mind)'.[3]

More generally, classical German philosophy is resistant to the historicist schemas commonly attributed to it. Led astray by legends about the end of history, careful readers will be surprised to discover in the philosopher of Jena a critique of historical reason in the making: a contrast between (abstract) empty time and full time ('full of struggle'); repudiation of an abstract (one-sidedly quantitative) conception of progress; rejection of a purely formal generalization of the course of history. Kojève, on the other hand, in proclaiming that history was over, and that nothing remained to be done, forced the interpretation of Hegel in the direction of historical closure. But the German language is badly adapted to the ambiguities of 'end', as both intended goal and final stage. The relevant Hegelian categories are 'result' [*Resultät*] or 'goal' [*Zweck*], rather than 'ending' [*Ende*] or 'closure' [*Schluss*].

Moments of the concrete unity of nature with motion, space and time are interconvertible in Hegel in a way that is familiar to strategists, who have always known how to 'give ground in order to win time'. As commonly represented, there exists a space and there *also* exists a time. But philosophy, says Hegel, contests this 'also', for time is the 'truth of space'.[4] He thus rejects the abstract representation of a linear time: the forms of past, present and future coincide in the singularity of the now.

The dissociation of history and the logic that problematizes it in Hegelian philosophy yields some caricatural interpretations. Contrary to such clichés, Hegel precisely refuses to see in the development of human societies the abstract, irrational necessity of blind destiny. If universal history is a tribunal, it is not simply the verdict of might, but the development of self-consciousness and the freedom of the spirit. The march of the universal spirit transcends passions great and small, subjective 'viewpoints', moments in which specific forms disappear. But concrete history 'is a progress not in empty time but in time infinitely filled and full of struggle'.[5] For in philosophy, it is always the present that is at issue. In philosophy? And what about politics? When it comes to the present and the unfolding of its possibilities, politics assumes primacy over history. In the Europe of the Treaty of Vienna, this primacy had, alas, been abruptly terminated: while speculative philosophy seized upon a non-practical concept of freedom, universal history lapsed back into an evolutionary formalism in which great men drop to the ground like spent cartridges, after playing a role that invariably transcends them.

This theodicy of the spirit attaining self-knowledge reduces history to 'the necessary development ... of the *moments* of reason'. Hence its formidable juridical dispensation. World history becomes 'a court of judgement'. This formal rationalization does not, however, completely stifle rebellion against the appalling emptiness of physical time: 'history is the process whereby the spirit assumes the shape of events'.[6] To acknowledge the role of events in historical genesis is to open up a space for possibility between what is (but need not have been) and what is not (but has not exhausted its potential to be).

Obsession with the desired end of history is much more apparent in Comte or Cournot than in Hegel. The former sees history concluding in the consecration of the positive spirit; the latter sees it extinguished in the meaningless eternity of the marketplace of opinions.

Obsessed with the urgency of 'overseeing the organic termination of revolution', Comte dreams of history as non-revolutionary progress. Henceforth, only the positive spirit can 'adequately represent all the major historical phases as so many determinate stages of the same basic evolution, in which each results from its predecessor and prepares for the next according to invariant laws that determine its particular part in the common progress'. Governed by *invariant laws*, this evolution dispels a major anxiety and betrays a desire to accumulate without any risk. The triumph of positivism 'will restore order in society', and finally guarantee 'a genuinely normal state of affairs'.[7]

For Cournot, universal history culminates in journalism. The event is abolished in the *fait divers* or the sporting exploit: newspapers supplant history. The ruination of the grand narrative of history could not be better expressed.

After Hegel, how is historical time to be conceptualized? According to Paul Ricoeur, leaving Hegelianism behind signifies renouncing the attempt to 'decipher the supreme plot', the 'plot of all plots' that can simultaneously ground the meaningful unity of history and the ethical unity of humanity.[8] This exodus is indissociable from the name of Marx and the way in which he multiplied time, according to the plural rhythms and cycles of a broken political temporality. Time is no longer the motor of history, its secret energetic principle, but the conflictual social relation of production and exchange.

The present is no longer a mere link in the chain of time, but a moment for selecting among possibilities. The acceleration of history is not that of a time intoxicated by speed, but the effect of the furious turnover of capital. Revolutionary action is not the imperative of a proven capacity to make history, but engagement in a conflict whose outcome is uncertain. Hypothetical and conditional, bristling with discontinuities, the impossible totalization of historical development opens out into a multiplicity of pasts and futures.[9] For every epoch, the historical present represents the result of a history that has been made and the inaugural force of an adventure that is beginning anew. At issue is a specifically political present, strategically identified with the notion of the 'given and inherited *circumstances*' in which 'men make their own history'. Politics is the modality of this making of history. In politics, a practical sense of what is possible averts any utopianism swept up in the pursuit of an indeterminate future.

If the space for experimentation contracts with the fading of a horizon of expectation capacious enough to encompass hope and fear, desire and volition, prudent calculation and hazardous wager, this practical sense is threatened with collapse. Without a determinate aim for the future, expectation is thrown into turmoil. Recollection of a past that repeats itself without any variation becomes delirious. '[W]hen expectation takes refuge in utopia and when tradition becomes only a dead deposit', the present in its entirety is abandoned to the morbidity of its own crisis.[10] Without any guarantee of success, political struggle then strives to prevent the tension culminating in the immaterial rupture of disjointed times. Only determinate expectation and recollection can sustain the pursuit of a goal that is not an end.

'The universal history of Hegel is the dream of history.'[11] Marx does not pursue this dream. Delivering a wake-up call, he interrupts the nightmare instead.

Time as a Social Relation

In the space–time couplet of the old metaphysics, space features as a placid element of unchanging objectivity and mathematical eternity. Always in motion, time does not stay in one place. The past is already no longer; and the future is not yet. The present vanishes into a series of new instants, which are neither exactly identical nor utterly different. Time exists only through the metamorphoses of this punctual present, whose changeable persistence defies the logic of the same and the other.

In secularizing time, modern science believed it could avoid these existential torments. From the Renaissance onwards, social time supplanted solar time. The reassuring signs of the calendar and the uneven hours of the seasons were erased in indifferently divisible equal hours. Clocks and dials multiplied. The year Spinoza wrote his 'geometry of the passions', storage of energy by the spring made it possible for Huyghens to invent newly accurate, portable clocks. The age of divine watchmakers and men-machines had dawned.

General commodity exchange strips human relations of their sacred aura. Henceforth the abstractions of chronometry and money go hand in hand. Time is money; money is time. Capital times become the time of capital, 'a time endowed with some rather strange qualities: variable, linear, segmented, measurable, and above all "manipulable" by the thread of a fantastic accounting'.[12] The desolate space and time of physics now constitute the formal conditions of any knowledge, whether of nature or the economy. Crowning the victorious coalition of the absolute and the true against the apparent and the commonplace, Newton contrasts the 'absolute, true and mathematical' time, space and motion of physics with 'relative, apparent and commonplace' time, space and motion.

Hollowed out and calculated, won and lost without being lived, this time is no longer that of gods and signs, labours and days, calendars and confessions. Like some spiteful evil genius, it henceforth seems to be pulling the strings of the social bond. It is the market measure of everything, starting with human activity reduced to a mere 'temporal shell'. Yet economic time remains distinct from mechanical time with its clocks, psychological time with its duration, and political time with its revolutions and restorations. Perhaps history is simply a bridge spanning these unconnected, incommensurable temporalities.

A game of invisible hands: those of the market, those of time. For Adam Smith, the 'hand of the market' fashions the social bond. For Darwin, the 'hand of time' contains the small differences that make for major bifurcations. Convinced that it suffices to tolerate delays, to await the end of the tunnel or the crisis (which cannot last for ever, since nothing does, as is attested by the gnawing progress of the clock), rhetoricians and journalists put their confidence in the passage of time.

Yet time has nothing to do with it; and it has no hands. It does not work for us, or dispense justice, or attend to our wounds. It unties no knots simply by virtue of passing. That requires the fingers of the event, which belongs to another order and a different register. Insatiable Chronos is finished. In Marx, as in Proust, lost time is the time without quality of a chronometrical God. Bereft of memory or music, mere yardstick of an unbearable history, this desperately empty time of chronometric and monetary abstraction strings its dismal periods together, in keeping with the utterly immaterial alterations of mere progression that distressed Hegel so much. Holding market fashion and death in check, time regained will be that of work salvaged and creative activity.

Fascinated by the temporal regularities of Newtonian physics, Marx nevertheless continued to conceptualize time starting from Democritus and Epicurus, Aristotle and Hegel. Epicurus's time is the active form of the world, 'the fire of essence, eternally consuming appearance', 'change as change'. It 'emerges when the accidentals of bodies, perceived by the senses, are thought of as accidentals': 'sensuous perception reflected in itself is time itself, and there is no going beyond it'.[13]

The new way of writing history heralded by Marx breaks with the sacred time of salvation, as well as with the abstract time of physics. It involves rediscovering the sense of rhythms and beginnings, combining regularity and novelty, and constructing the concept of a time whose categories (crises, cycles, turnovers) are yet to be invented. Capital is a specific, contradictory conceptual organization of social time. This radical desa-cralization of time consolidates the representation of a rigorously imma-nent history. Marx could hardly go any further. His programmatic anticipations scanned the available horizon. But the critique of political economy could not venture beyond

> the points at which the suspension of the present form of production relations gives signs of its becoming – foreshadowings of the future . . . The contemporary conditions of production likewise appear as engaged in *suspending themselves* and hence in positing the *historic presuppositions* for a new state of society.[14]

Nothing more.

An economy of time: 'to this all economy ultimately reduces itself'. But what of the time inscribed in the motion of capital, which punctuates its cycles, resonates with its drives, vibrates with its desires, and can be heard ticking? Cycles, turnovers and crises: fractured time set in motion. Articu-lating these temporalities, Marx's work was that of a pioneer: 'First of all, he had to fashion all the conceptual categories relative to the time factor: cycle, turnover, turnover time, turnover cycle. He quite legitimately criti-cized classical theory for having neglected the time factor.'[15]

Capital Volume One – the book of stolen time – reveals the incredible secret of the surplus-value extorted in the subterranean sites of produc-tion, safe from prying eyes. Volume Two – the book of the metamorphoses and circulation of capital – explores the syllogisms of time. And Volume Three – the book of the process of reproduction as a whole – rediscovers the living time of conflicts and crises via competition and the transforma-tion of surplus-value into profit.

In Volume One, *linear production time* unveils the mystery of surplus-value. Behind the mystificatory phenomena of exchange, in the basements where the alchemy of production is carried on, the endless struggle over the division between necessary labour and surplus labour determines the shifting line of the rate of exploitation. The line dividing this time in two is displaced according to the class struggle. Despite its apparent mechani-cal banality, production time, in which commodities are reduced to the abstraction of value and labour is reduced to the abstraction of a non-qualitative time, is a social time from the outset.

Tyrannical, this time of troubles subjugates and mortifies bodies. Human beings find themselves in the same condition as instruments of labour:

> Every day brings a man twenty-four hours nearer to his grave, although no one can tell accurately, merely by looking at a man, how many days he has still to travel on that road. This difficulty, however, does not prevent life insurance companies from using the theory of averages to draw very accurate, and what is more, very profitable conclusions about the length of a man's life. So it is with the instruments of labour. It is known by experience how long on the average a machine of a particular kind will last.[16]

Descent into the inferno of capital thus reveals an infernal alchemy, in which moments of time are the elements of profit and the worker is reduced to 'personified labour-time'.

Marx examines this temporal despotism, whose ritual is disclosed in factory reports and investigations, with horrified care and attention:

> 'The time [of work] shall be regulated by a public clock', for example the nearest railway clock, by which the factory clock is to be set. The manufacturer has to hang up a 'legible' printed notice stating the hours for the beginning and ending of work and pauses allowed for meals.[17]

Under the cyclopean surveillance of the clock, the hunt is henceforth on for scraps of time. It aims to convert duration into intensity, to gain from the latter what has been lost in the former, to close up 'the pores of the working day' in order to 'compress' labour itself.

The antinomies of capital (use-value/exchange-value, concrete labour/abstract labour) issue from the open fracture of the commodity in Volume One. The unity of use-value and exchange-value expresses a clash of temporalities. The time of general/abstract labour exists only in and through concrete/particular labour. As the establishment of a relation between these two times, value emerges as an abstraction of social time. Reciprocally, time is established as a measure that must itself be measured. The determination of socially necessary labour-time refers to the motion of capital as a whole.[18]

The mysteries of measurement encountered in Volume One reappear with *circulation* in Volume Two. Nestling in the commodity, surplus-value can evaporate if it is not generated anew at each cycle of its metamorphoses. It increases and multiplies by completing the cycle of the turnover of capital. Set against the labour-time that posits value, circulation time initially appears as an obstacle or negation, an inroad on surplus labour-time and an indirect increase in necessary labour-time, and hence as the threat of a possible devalorization – as opposed to a positive creation – of value. If turnover does not create surplus-value, its acceleration multiplies it in line with its own velocity:

> Thus a moment enters *into value-determination* which indeed does not come out of the direct relation of labour to capital. The frequency with which the same capital can repeat the production process (creation of new value) in a given period of time is evidently a condition not posited directly by the production process itself. . . . Thus, in addition to the labour time realized in production, the *circulation time* appears as the *time of devaluation* . . . *Circulation time* is therefore not a positive value-creating element . . . It is therefore in fact a deduction from *surplus labour time*, i.e. an increase of *necessary labour time*.[19]

The 'negative time' of circulation contributes to an increase in value through the furious acceleration of its turnovers. Volume Two thus elaborates new factors of capital efficiency, its expansion and contraction, which are independent of its value.

Circulation time is broken down into segments corresponding to the various metamorphoses of capital. The sequence of the purchase of production goods corresponds to the period in which capital takes the shape of money-capital; that of sale to the period when it is found in the form of commodity-capital. In its frantic course, capital switches guises with the briskness of a triathlethe. Considered as a whole, it is 'simultaneously present, and spatially coexistent, in its various phases'. Each part passes successively from one phase and form to another, functioning in each of them in turn:

> The forms are therefore fluid forms, and their simultaneity is initiated by their succession. Each form both follows and precedes the others, so that the return of one part of capital to one form is determined by the return of another part to another form. Each part continuously describes its own course, but it is always another part of capital that finds itself in this form, and these particular circuits simply constitute simultaneous and successive moments of the overall process. It is only in the unity of the three circuits that the continuity of the overall process is realized . . . The total social capital always possesses this continuity, and its process always contains the unity of the three circuits.[20]

In the accumulation of capital, this double mechanism of sites and sequences thus goes beyond the inert juxtaposition of space and time to attain the Hegelian 'also' of a historical space–time.

Reproduction time is the organic time of capital. In it, labour-time and circulation time are conjoined in the unity of the overall process. If value is an abstraction of time, and time is the measure of all wealth, the determination of 'socially necessary' labour-time can occur only retrospectively, through the self-development of time in the expanded reproduction and accumulation of capital. To ensure its own expanded reproduction, capital consumes living labour, and does so without respite – at the risk (if the crucial step is missed, if use-value fails to coincide with exchange-value, if the cogwheel breaks) of the arrhythmias of crisis.[21]

The mechanical time of production, the chemical time of circulation, and the organic time of reproduction are thus coiled and slotted inside one another, like circles within circles, determining the enigmatic patterns of historical time, which is the time of politics.

Time Measured and Time as Measure

Any economy is an 'economy of time'. The category of time is at the heart of the critique of political economy. Many superficial readers stick with this observation, forgetting that economy signifies not only thrift, but also a rational organization of time. Time is the measure of social relations. But what is the measure of the measure? What is the measure of time?

Just as history is its own knowledge, so time is held to be its own measure. A time is said to be long or short, hence measurable. But the present possesses no duration. We think we are measuring time; but we are simply measuring intervals. So how are we to measure this perpetual fading in which eternity unravels? The present is incapable of measuring either the past or the future. Saint Augustine was haunted by this puzzle: 'when a body moves, it is by time that I measure how long its motion lasts'; yet there exists no regular, homogeneous motion making possible a precise measurement of time.[22]

Now, we measure stretches of time, homogeneous and yet different, according to whether they bring pleasure or suffering, expectation or oblivion. Between abstract time, a kind of transcendental referent, and concrete time, which is existential and immanent in motion, Augustine defined time, irreducible to an essence, as a *relation* of duration between movements, the measurement of a movement that lasts relative to another. And yet, if '[b]y means of time I measure the movement of bodies . . . what means do I use to measure time?'.[23] For such a measure to be conceivable, whatever is subject to constant transformation and differentiation must be suspended, the diversity of forms of movement standardized, and duration spatialized. For the 'absolute' time of classical physics to be able to flow in homogeneous, uniform fashion, the measure had to be abstracted from the movement, the time-measure from real time. In the same way, capital reduces the particular time of practical know-how, beautiful works and human effort, which are always unique, to an abstract social time.

A new technology of time then makes it possible to reduce concrete labour to abstract labour: 'the two material bases on which the preparations for which machine-operated industry proceeded within manufacture . . . were the *clock* and the *mill . . .* The clock was the first automatic device applied to practical purposes; the whole theory of the *production of regular motion* was developed through it.' The clock suggested the idea of automatic devices, and 'Vaucanson's experiments on these lines had a tremendous influence on the imagination of the English inventors.'[24] The logic of capitalist production prompts Marx to an extraordinary anticipation of the practical modes of abstraction of labour subsequently developed by Taylorism and the relationship between horology, abstract labour and automatization. The robot is the culmination and ultimate truth of 'unskilled labour' – mere support of the relation of exploitation, animate abstract labour, or 'personified labour-time'. This reduction of being to time is the very essence of alienation as self-estrangement.

It is now commonplace to reduce Marx's thought to a dated Newtonianism. Yet for him, separating time from development represented a speculative artifice *par excellence.* The antinomics of content and form, measure and substance, derive from it.[25] How much time is a particular movement equivalent to? What is this time-standard that manifests itself only as space (a segment of duration, a surface swept by the hand of the dial, the fluid volume of the hourglass)? And why should time measure motion, rather than motion measuring time?

Time measured and time as measure? Intertwined in the grip of their co-determination, time and motion measure one another in a whirlwind relationship of paradoxical reciprocity: 'Not only do we measure change by time, but we also measure time by change, because they are determined by each other.'[26] In *Capital*, the reflexivity of time illuminates the mysteries of value and its metamorphoses. How can we find an 'invariable measure of value' that would itself be of 'invariable value' – in other words, 'since value itself is a precipitate of the commodity, a commodity of invariable value'? For the exchange-value of commodities to be expressible in money, a unity must be assumed, a '*homogeneity* which makes them the same – makes them *values*'. 'The problem of an "invariable measure of values" was simply a spurious name for the quest for the concept, the nature, of *value* itself, the definition of which could not be another value.' The self-determination of value is resolved into the development of '*labour-time*, social labour as it presents itself specifically in commodity production'. For commodities to be measurable by the quantity of labour embodied in them, different kinds of labour must in fact be 'reduced to uniform, simple labour, average labour, ordinary unskilled labour'; 'an hour of more intensive labour . . . counts as much . . . [as an hour of] more extensive labour'. 'Only then can the amount of labour embodied in [commodities] be measured according to a common measure, according to time.'[27]

Thus, value is 'measured by time' or, more precisely, the labour-time 'required to produce labour capacity'. The value added to value by abstract labour 'is exactly equal to its duration'.[28] If value and duration are deemed equal, it is because their common measure is time. But the time that measures value is not time in general. As a measure, it exists only ideally. In practice, it is always *socially determined* as necessary labour-time, for it cannot act directly as its own measure. The measure must itself be measured:

> The difference between price and value, between the commodity measured by the labour time whose product it is, and the product of the labour time against which it is exchanged, this difference calls for a third commodity to act as a measure in which the real exchange value of commodities is expressed. *Because price is not equal to value, therefore the value-determining element – labour time – cannot be the element in which prices are expressed, because labour time would then have to express itself simultaneously as the determining and the non-determining element, as the equivalent and non-equivalent of itself.* Because labour time as the measure of value exists only as an ideal, it cannot serve as the matter of price-comparisons.[29]

In following the development of capital, which determines labour-time socially, the critique of political economy tackles the enigmas of a measure that is itself subject to measurement.

The value of a commodity would remain constant if the time required for its production likewise remained so. In the event, however, it constantly varies with the productivity of labour. The determination of social labour-time thus contradicts the formal definition of time. At issue now is the time that the society recognizes in and through the general exchange of commodities. When social labour-time is no longer validated by society, because the cycle between selling and buying is interrupted, the social expels the social, according to Marx. The value of labour-power involves variations in value bound up with the conditions of its own (re)production. Thus, the value of a machine is determined not by the time that *was* required for its production in practice, but by the time *currently necessary* for its reproduction. Hence the need for capital to be productively consumed as rapidly as possible.

The time and motion of capital are therefore determined reciprocally. Social time measures the accumulation of capital, whose turnovers determine the social substance of time. So time appears simultaneously as a measure of value and as its substance. This substance is continually modified according to the changing conditions of social production. Incredibly mystical, it is every bit as strange as the measure whose measurements vary with what is measured. Value is determined by the labour-time socially necessary for the production of the commodity, which is itself fluctuating and flexible like a measuring instrument that varies with the object to be measured.

Value that has 'become autonomous in money', vampiric automaton, capital runs through the cycle in which the commodity features now as money, now as means of production, and now once again as commodity. These temporal metamorphoses are expressed in money:

> If money appears as the general commodity in all places, so also does it in all times. It maintains itself as wealth at all times. Its specific durability. It is the treasure which neither rust nor moths eat up. All commodities are only transitory money; money is the permanent commodity. Money is the omnipresent commodity; the commodity is only local money. But accumulation is a process which takes place in time.[30]

So the close relationship between time and money is clarified.

The idea of an accumulation that unfolds 'in time' appears to revert to an abstract temporal referent, preceding social relations. The process of capital is, however, 'at the same time its becoming, its growth, its vital process'. 'If', says Marx, 'anything needed to be compared with the circulation of the blood, it was not the formal circulation of money, but the content-filled circulation of capital.' The interruption of circulation induces apoplexy. Capital is therefore a matter of metabolism, of blood flows and cardiac arrests:

> All moments of capital which appear involved in it when it is considered from the point of view of its general concept obtain an independent reality, and further, only show themselves when it appears as real, as many capitals. The inner, living organization, which takes place in this way within and through competition, thus develops all the more extensively.[31]

Guided by the specific object of his research, Marx explores a pluralization of duration. Against any historical transcendence, he conceives an original temporality in which time is no longer either the uniform referent of physics, or the sacred time of theology. Subject to historical and economic rhythms, organized into cycles and waves, periods and crises, the profane time of *Capital* links the contrary temporalities of production and circulation, the antagonistic requirements of labour and capital, the contrasting forms of money and commodity. Combining measure and substance, it represents a *social relation* in motion.

Ontological Critique and Messianic Critique

The bourgeoisie hauled itself into power under the sign of History. Bereft of heroic genealogies, it possessed the sulphurous connivance of time and money by way of legitimate title. Its affairs served the cause of progress. Progress was its business. Hence its pious conviction that the best is always certain, and that the worst is simply its shadow. Once historical reason had allied with *raison d'État*, this optimism, which was initially a vehicle for audacity and rebelliousness, turned apologetic.

As early as 1871, Nietzsche saw through the dangers of an 'excess of history': the arrogance of an era convinced that it embodied the acme of justice; the invariably harmful belief in 'the old age of mankind'; the 'awareness of being a latecomer and an epigone'; the unchecked reign of contempt and cynicism. In this 'fever of history' that was consuming the century, 'admiration for the "power of history" ... transforms every moment into a naked admiration for success and leads to an idolatry of the factual'. He 'who has once learned to bend his back and bow his head before the "power of history" at last nods "Yes" like a Chinese mechanical doll to every power ... and moves his limbs to the precise rhythm at which any "power" whatever pulls the strings'.[32]

Marx – why refuse to admit it? – was a pioneer of this critique of historical reason – an enormous undertaking in which mystical critique and profane critique, romantic critique and revolutionary critique, sometimes coincided and mingled, while continuing their contest. Between the two stood various intermediaries, whose ambiguities have been endlessly debated by posterity: the Blanqui of *L'Éternité par les astres* (1871); the Nietzsche of *Untimely Meditations* (1871); the Péguy of *Clio* (1913); the Sorel of *Illusions du progrès* (1908). Ushered in with the disaster of August of 1914, the 'era of wars and revolutions' was to allow less and less space for those who straddled two worlds. The critique of historical reason was to become the stake of a fight to the death.

Lukács and Heidegger? No: Benjamin against Heidegger.[33]

It is not enough to contrast the qualities of the seasons and days with the dismal indifference of clocks and currencies. The critique of homogeneous, empty time is divided between a psychological and an aesthetic critique, attentive to the lived experience of duration, and a social critique implying a revolution in the conception of time. Recalcitrant to prescribed routes and goals, Marx, for his part, repudiated the 'historico-philosophic theory of the general path of development prescribed by fate to all nations' that is so often attributed to him: the 'master key [of] a general historico-philosophical theory' will only ever labour the obvious.[34] Just as Marx rejected every 'supra-historical' schema, Heidegger denounced the teaching of history dressed up as a supra-temporal model. For him, '[t]he theme of historiology is neither that which has happened just once for all nor something universal that floats above it', but the possibility of an existence for death.[35] Far from universal pictures, edifying tales, golden legends, history is written in the tension between abstract universality and the uniqueness of the event, on the shifting sand of possibility where shapes appear that might not have existed, and are destined to be effaced. Neither the struggle nor Being exists in time. They are determined by what attaches to time, by the set of temporal properties of being and of social relations.

Temporality does not, as such, exist. It 'temporalizes itself'. For Marx, it does so in the present, starting from the process of production and reproduction, where the unsettled political patterns of the struggle arise. For Heidegger, it is temporalized in the future, whose primacy reveals anticipation of the extreme possibility, and authenticates 'Being-towards-death'. Thus, in a way, what has been springs from the future which, in turn, holds it open.

Heidegger intends to extract the temporality of Being from the ontic banality of ordinary time. He rejects the ordinary conception that derives from a levelling of original time, and merely represents an official, datable time, caught up in the ritual of temporal institutions. Understood as one 'now' after another in an ongoing sequence, the vulgar, calculated time of chronometers pits a deadly technology against meditation on what is peculiar to time. To the transformation of qualitative duration into quantity and space is counterposed the irreducible originality of that which, in the course of time, passes and, passing constantly, remains *qua* time.[36]

In deciphering its profane rhythms, Marx radicalizes the secularization of quotidian time. Convinced that there is no other time than ours, the time of labour and effort, agony and love, he thinks the conceptual organization of this meagre 'ontic' time, and plunges headlong into the cycles, turnovers, and non-linear trajectories in which time and motion are mutually determined. If *Capital* can be read as an 'ontology of social being', it is solely as a rigorously negative ontology.

Heidegger ontologizes and resacralizes; Marx secularizes and deontologizes. Both refuse the models – 'supra-historical' for the latter, 'supra-temporal' for the former – of the historians' Reason. For Heidegger, the relentless knowledge of historical studies oscillates between an overly abstract universality and an unduly concrete singularity. He therefore echoes the different way of writing history announced as a project by Marx. But the difference between a history governed by the future, whose possibilities are rooted in desire, and a history whose strategic potential is formed and confounded in the present of the struggle, remains an insuperable one.

Heidegger cites at length Count Yorck's correspondence with Dilthey. With history, 'what makes a spectacle and catches the eye is not the main thing'. What is required is to penetrate 'the basic character of history as "virtuality"' and, in order to do this, to elaborate on the generic difference between 'the ontic and the Historical', immediately replaced by the difference between the ontic and the ontological.[37] This surreptitious deposition of the historical by the ontological is not self-evident. While the relation of Being to being restores the separation between transcendental subject and empirical object that Being-in-the-world claimed to suppress, a generic difference separates the ontic and the historical. The sleight of hand is not without consequence. Ontic, progress is ontologically contemptible for Heidegger. Historical, it is open to political criticism for Lukács, yet not condemned to the aristocratic contempt of Being.

A goodly measure of thoughtlessness or blindness is required for a one-sided insistence on the similarity between Heidegger's 'cosmic-historic vision and Marx's historico-practical conception', on their 'common denominator' and shared 'radical critique of the world' – going so far as to argue, without batting an eyelid, that 'Heidegger's essential contribution is to help us understand what Marx said'.[38] Forced comparisons are unavailing: the historicality of Being and the class struggle cannot be superimposed upon one another. Historicality intervenes as a determination prior to what is called history, as a sort of *ante-* or pre-history. Unlike this historicality, whose 'secret reason' reposes in Being-for-death, history in Heidegger sometimes designates being (understood as a past that no longer has any effect on the present); sometimes the past (in the sense of source without any particular primacy); sometimes the whole of the being that changes over time; and sometimes, finally, what is traditional. These four senses totalize the adventure of history. For Heidegger, the historians' thematization of history is the necessary condition for the construction of a historical world in the sciences of the spirit.

In Nietzsche's view, 'monumental history', the preserve of men of action and power, expresses retrospective faith in humanity in a relay race that conserves past grandeur regardless of the losers, who are consigned to oblivion. From the past it derives its momentum to forge ahead, while trampling the eternal victims underfoot. The passion of ordinary men endlessly rehearsing their regret for what is no longer, 'antiquarian' history expresses a taste for the conservation and veneration of past splendours, but gives way to desiccated reverence for a tradition that has deteriorated into habit. Finally, 'critical history' resolves to dissolve part of its past by hauling it before justice. These three ways of broaching history combine in the historicality to which only an elite has aesthetic access.

Hegel actualizes the past; the Young Hegelians actualize the future. The past is determinate; the future is indeterminate, albeit determinable. The present decides between them. It is the interval – very small, but finite – in which events are neither past nor future. For Nietzsche, this dispute of rhythms and sequences expresses the will to act against time, hence on time, and in favour of future times. 'Like to like!', he proclaims: 'Otherwise you will draw the past down to you.' 'Do not', he says, 'believe historiography that does not spring from the heads of the rarest minds.' He affirms in the same breath the critical pre-eminence of the present over the past, as long as it expresses '*the fullest exertion of the vigour of the present*', on the basis of which the past may legitimately be interpreted: '[O]nly when you put forth your noblest qualities in all their strength will you divine what is worth knowing and preserving in the past.'[39] The capacity to reconfigure time derives exclusively from the 'vigour of the present' and its equal standing with the past, in opposition to idolatry of the factual.

Heidegger, on the other hand, means to banish from temporality the pervasive sense of the relations between past, present and future, derived from the 'ordinary conception of time'. *Now–then–previously* designate the structure of ordinary datability. The 'temporalization' of time on the basis of the future inscribes every temporality in the horizon of Being-for-death. The result is anxiety without fear, authentic experience of which implies a rigorous depoliticization of time. The temporalization of time [*die Zeitigung der Zeit*] demands, indeed, a revision of the banal schema of horizontal *ekstases* in which we imagine our daily lives, while not daring to think them. The future is what advances towards us; the present [*Gegenwart*] an anticipation-towards or an anticipation-against; the past, a Being-towards the authentic. What is yet to be confers on the past its meaning or vacuity; it all depends. The anticipation of the future reopens the past in the direction of the future, to the point of rescinding the dominion of the past over the present.

In the depths of time and language, the temporality of speech is one in which the past is weeded, and branches out towards the future. Grammatical logic thus posits experience of the future as a junction of possibilities. Before tipping over into a linear past, the future is trimmed into its present evolution. On the other hand, it is supposedly difficult to grasp a future linearity derived from the tangle of the past.[40] Difficult to comprehend? According to the 'logic of time', no doubt. But in 'the politics of time', what becomes of such 'pruned' possibilities? Are they forever swallowed up in the capacious dustbin of history? Or does some meticulous rag-and-bone man have the power to salvage them? Bygone days are irreducible to a string of faded days. Through the recollection of past conjunctures, '[t]o approach . . .' "what has been" means to treat it not historiographically, as heretofore, but politically, in political categories'.[41] Treating history politically means conceiving it from the standpoint of its strategic moments and points of intervention. 'Presence of mind' is the quality – political *par excellence* – of this 'art of the present'.

Summoning the past to appear contradicts the postulate of an irreversible, unmodifiable time. Critical history cannot cancel what was; but it can redistribute its meaning. Bringing the past back into play can, however, take one of two routes: either ontological, with Heidegger and the temporality that is temporalized on the basis of the future; or political, with Benjamin and the messianic possibility that is conjugated in the present.

According to Heidegger, '[e]ven in expecting, one leaps away from the possible and gets a foothold in the actual. It is for its actuality that what is expected is expected. By the very nature of expecting, the possible is drawn into the actual, arising out of the actual and returning to it.'[42] But this expectation is anticipation of death and the thought of its imminence. In Benjamin, political (strategic) anticipation appears as the precise negation of this ontological anticipation. Whereas Heidegger keeps open the 'having-been' to celebrate the reunion of Being, Benjamin cuts back the undergrowth of madness and myth in order to uncover the traces of a past that awaits salvation. Messianic anticipation is never the passive certainty of an advent foretold, but akin to the concentration of a hunter on the lookout for the sudden emergence of what is possible.

According to Jacques Rancière, the 'Marxist manner' of elaborating 'a way of thinking that is not concerned with events' leads to a 'predominance of a future, alone fit to explain the past'. Thus, immaturity and tardiness of 'the forces of the future' were held responsible for stagnation, regression, the 'repetition of the past in place of the execution of the tasks of the present'.[43] We shall leave to Rancière the responsibility for this structural 'manner', his allusive indictment of which avoids any serious examination of the question. The roads of the return to Marx are, if not impenetrable, at least many and varied. Remote from the dominant 'manner' and its 'supra-historical' schemas, the paths of Benjamin and Gramsci are not the least legitimate available.

For them, the granular time of history is neither the fulfilment of an origin, nor the pursuit of an end. For Ernst Bloch, the primacy of the future delineates the utopian horizon of hope. For Heidegger, it haunts the anticipated meditation of Being-for-death. For Whitehead, it saves the present from the collapse that lies in wait for it. The Benjaminian categories of time are triply organized in the present: present of the past; present of the future; present of the present. Every past is reborn in the present-becoming-past. Every present fades in the future-becoming-present. In the constellation of eras and events, the present indefinitely appeals to another present, in a discontinuous interplay of echoes and resonances.

In the 'dialectical concept of historical time', the present of the past responds to the present of the future, memory to expectation: 'we are expected'. To anticipate this present laden with messianic debts is the political task *par excellence.*

The Primacy of Politics over History

The mystery of time is responsible for numerous misunderstandings. Labour–time is first of all the site of an opposition between the abstraction of dead labour and the concreteness of living labour, between homogeneous duration and variable intensity. Stavros Tombazos makes his way through the extraordinary landscape of these contradictions. He observes: 'Capital is precisely a conceptual organization of time. It is neither a thing, nor a simple social relation, but a living rationality, an active concept, abstraction *in actu*, as Marx writes on several occasions. *Capital* is the logic of its history.'[44]

Overcoming the antinomies of linear and cyclical time, measure and substance, ontological and physical time, a new temporality emerges:

The relationship between the abstract, logical laws immanent in operative economic rationality, and historical time, is not one of separation, but of mutual communication and fertilization. The former is realized in concrete historical forms, economico-institutional and political, which periodically enter into crisis and develop by leaps. Through fluctuations in the rate of profit and crises, capital punctuates history and orients its direction without determining it mechanically. It reduces the role of chance, without abolishing it. History is in no sense predetermined fate. Major crises are the moments when the homogeneous time of history is interrupted, the hour of probabilities and possibilities. Capital produces its concrete contents and enters into conflict with them. Surmounting these conflicts, which is always possible and more or less probable depending on the case, is the peace that capital concludes with itself, ensuring it a new period of growth.[45]

A conflict of temporalities, the relation between use-value and exchange-value pertains to a logic in which the classical laws of causality and equilibrium prove powerless. The disequilibrium inherent in the arrhythmias of capital 'dictates a lot more than a complement to equilibrium analysis: it demands different concepts, which are non-mathematizable and superior to the logic of identity'.[46]

It would be absurd to claim that Marx possessed the keys to this logic of disequilibrium. But the fact is that the critique of political economy impels him beyond the categories of classical determinism and the representations of time bound up with it.

Time stretched and torn apart; concentrated, staccato, broken time: the worst of times, the best of times.

The repetition of 'nows' confers on each instant its messianic opportunity. Thus: '[a] historical materialist cannot do without the notion of a present which is not a transition, but in which time stands still and has come to a stop. For this notion defines the present in which he himself is writing history.'[47] This is a suspended present, which is not a transition but a fork and bifurcation; a strategic present for those who stand still on the threshold of time. An art of time and contretemps, strategy has as its temporal mode the present and as its cardinal virtue 'presence of mind'.

Although he is often credited with discovery of the 'continent of history' or paternity of a 'science of history', Marx did not construct any universal History. Combining critique and politics, he fashioned the concepts of a conflictual rationality. Politicized, history becomes intelligible to anyone who wishes to engage in action to change the world. 'Politics attains primacy over history.'[48]

Politics? Conceptualization of the event that breaks through the barrier of time. Its primacy derives from the reciprocal determination of history and memory, anticipation and commemoration, strategic project and recomposed past. The speculative philosophies of universal History presupposed an 'empty, homogeneous' time, embodying causality itself. This abstract time of classical physics and the labour-commodity is dashed by the experiences that interrupt its course. The Benjaminian critique of historical reason thus leads 'from a time of necessity to a time of possibilities':[49] a secret history, whose messianic potentialities subvert the fatality of appearances, and where each present instant and every commemorated expectation is laden with a particular meaning. Whereas the recapitulative meaning of universal History is lost in the silence of the Last Judgement, the dialectical concept of historical time involves overturning the habitual categories of catastrophe, critical instant and progress.

Catastrophe now gives way to the concept of 'missed opportunity'; the critical instant to the concept of the disastrous continuation of the 'status quo'; and genuine progress to the strictly factual concept of the 'first measure of the Revolution' – not as willed acceleration, but as a caesura in temporal uniformity.

Lacerated and torn, messianic time destroys the myth of a homogeneous history of being, its beginnings and decline. With all due respect to those readers who would like to see his 'historical materialism' as a strange coquetry or a regrettable misunderstanding, Benjamin acknowledges in Marx a critique of historical reason and a new representation of time as a social relation. This critical temporality makes it possible to conceptualize anachronisms and contretemps, as well as the disquieting contemporaneity of possibilities none of which pertains to the past of the other. It also makes it possible to understand why the 'old demons' are always ageless and wholly current.

A common misinterpretation waxes ironic about the impotent 'ardour' of messianic anticipation. On the contrary, the 'messianic concept' expresses the tension and anxiety of what is merely possible. Like commemoration, which has the curious ability to 'modify what science has observed', its anticipation is active. In 'this dialectical revolution of commemoration', there is no fatality of the past, no dictatorship of the *fait accompli*. In exchange, Benjamin proposes 'a historical materialism that has abolished the idea of progress' to make way for interruptions and transitions.[50]

Far removed from the 'duty to remember' and other commemorative pedagogies, commemoration, according to Benjamin, is a struggle for the oppressed past in the name of defeated generations. It does not lend itself to commemorative reconciliations and consensual memories. It involves no closed cases, only the 'redemptive shocks' and 'regenerating cata-clysms' that were dear to Blanqui. The inspired 'remembrance' of the Hebraic tradition is thus inscribed in the stake of the event: for Benjamin, memory is always at war. Such is indeed the consequence of political primacy and the acute sense of imminent danger. Without the least nostalgia for a hidden God, or the slightest temptation to piety, Benjamin opposes to the fetishism of history its profane politicization.

At a disturbing, critical moment, when so many rational minds allowed themselves to be exploited, he demonstrated a lucidity and firmness against the prevailing current that will be sought in vain among professional politicians. In February 1927, he left Moscow in tears, suitcase on his lap. His grief was not purely romantic, but also derived from having seen the party of the victors in action, with their appetite for power, their 'gold-digging' frenzy, their ongoing counter-revolution. In 1937, he did not share the great illusion of the Popular Fronts, and condemned the minor concessions that paved the way for major capitulations and disasters. After the victory of Nazism, he identified the overwhelming responsibility of social-democratic and Stalinist politicians with great precision: their shared, chloroforming confidence in 'progress', their 'mass base', and the strength of their apparatuses. This threefold confidence constituted the essence of what must in fact be dubbed a bureaucratic culture of resignation.[51]

Every instant witnesses a confrontation between the rational and the irrational, between possibilities that attain effective history and those that are provisionally or definitively eliminated. The struggle alone decides between them. That is why the 'scientific' pretension to predict the future of society is derisory: 'In reality one can "scientifically" foresee only the struggle, but not the concrete moments of the struggle.'[52] In practice, the only foresight is strategic.

So, we have a time out of joint, full of gaps, which is messianic in a sense unsuspected by commonplace critique. Tuned into its 'revolutionary frequency', Marx explored a 'punctuated anachrony'. Discovering in its palpitations the play of potentiality from which the event issues, he deconstructed physical temporality in order to reconstruct a social tem-porality. This syncopated history is set against the 'history without events' – a succession of trivial incidents in which nothing happens – evoked in *The Eighteenth Brumaire*.

Full of new arrivals and old ghosts, revolution is the event *par excellence*. Not current, untimely, all in all it 'never occurs in the present'. It is always too soon *and* too late. Revolution haunts the margins of politics. Beyond it stretch indistinct lands and unnamed regions, which exceed the limits of what can be conceived. The ancients, so it is said, reckoned for a long time that war, inaccessible to thought, pertained to ritual and myth. Our era has encompassed wars and revolutions in the horizon of knowledge. It has connected rebellion and thought.

Very early on, Marx grasped that '[e]very revolution dissolves the *old order of society*; to that extent it is *social*'. He also understood that '[e]very revolution brings down the *old ruling power*; to that extent it is *political*'. 'But', he wrote, 'whether the idea of a *social revolution* with a *political soul* is paraphrase or nonsense there is no doubt about the rationality of a *political revolution* with a *social soul*.' Revolution as such – 'the *overthrow* of the existing ruling power and the *dissolution* of the old order' – is thus, in the first instance, 'a *political act*'. Without revolution, socialism cannot become a reality: 'It stands in need of this political act just as it stands in need of *destruction* and *dissolution*. But as soon as its *organizing functions* begin and its *goal*, its *soul* emerges, socialism throws its *political* mask aside.'[53]

As 'overthrow', revolution is a political act; as 'dissolution', socialism is a social process. It is simultaneously a protracted intellectual and ethical revolution, slowly undermining the foundations of empires, and a revolution astonished at its own sudden eruption. Uniting ruptures and continuities, tradition and genuine novelty, a combination of mingled times, it traces the boundary where what is conceivable fades into the uncertainties of choice. Exceeding the critique of political economy, it is poised on the threshold of strategic reason, replete with its concepts studded with junctions and bifurcations.

This world is one of 'explosions, cataclysms and crises', whose contradictions are resolved in the violence of decisiveness.

Notes

1. The work of Robert Bonnaud, particularly *Les Alternances du progrès* (Kimé, Paris 1992), contains a scholarly anthology of this rhythmical terminology.
2. See Jacques-Bénigne Bossuet, *Discourse on Universal History*, trans. Elborg Forster, University of Chicago Press, Chicago and London 1976.
3. Immanuel Kant, 'Idea for a Universal History with a Cosmopolitan Purpose', in Kant, *Political Writings*, trans. H.B. Nisbet, Cambridge University Press, Cambridge 1991, pp. 41–3.
4. Astrophysicians have undertaken to calculate the exchange rate of space in time: in the cosmic bank, a second of time is said to be worth 300,000 kilometres of space (Trinh Xuan Thuan, *La Mélodie secrète*, Fayard, Paris 1989).
5. G.W.F. Hegel, 'Berlin Introduction' (1820) in Hegel, *Introduction to the Lectures on the History of Philosophy*, trans. T.M. Knox and A.V. Miller, Clarendon Press, Oxford 1985, p. 44.

6. G.W.F. Hegel, *Elements of the Philosophy of Right*, trans. H.B. Nisbet, Cambridge University Press, Cambridge 1991, pp. 372–4. See also Eugène Fleischmann, *Hegel et la politique*, Gallimard, Paris 1993.

7. Auguste Comte, 'Le Fondateur de la société positiviste à quiconque désire s'y incorporer', 8 March 1848. A heavy dose of bad faith is required to confuse the thought of Marx with that of Comte, even if this confusion has been propagated by the 'orthodox Marxism' of the Third International. Thus, Bukharin's *Historical Materialism* brought down upon it the wrath of Gramsci, who detected in it 'an adaptation of formal logic to the methods of physical and natural science'. The law of causality and a quest for historical normality had, he explained, been substituted for the historical dialectic. Gramsci denounced the premature desire to 'write an elementary handbook' and censured its 'vulgar evolutionism', the result of which was a theory of history and politics conceived as sociology. 'Sociology', he wrote, 'has been an attempt to create a method of historical and political science in a form dependent on a pre-elaborated philosophical system, that of evolutionist positivism.' Its alleged laws were invariably 'tautologies and paralogisms', 'a duplicate of the observed fact itself', and had 'no causal value' (see Antonio Gramsci, *Selections from the Prison Notebooks*, trans. Quintin Hoare and Geoffrey Nowell Smith, Lawrence & Wishart, London 1971, pp. 425–37).

   In *Capital*, Marx devoted no more than an unobtrusive footnote to Comte: 'Hence Auguste Comte and his school might just as well have shown that feudal lords are an eternal necessity, in the same way as they have done in the case of the lords of capital' (*Capital*, vol. 1, trans. Ben Fowkes, Penguin/NLR, Harmondsworth 1976, p. 451 n. 18). In a letter of 7 July 1866 to Engels, he made his opinion clear: 'I am studying Comte on the side because the British and French make so much fuss over that fellow. What captivates them is the encyclopaedic form, the synthesis. But compared with Hegel it is wretched (in spite of the fact that Comte being a mathematician and physicist is, by profession, superior to him, i.e., superior in details; but even here Hegel is infinitely greater when one considers the whole). And this trashy positivism appeared in 1832!' (Marx and Engels, *Selected Correspondence*, Progress Publishers, Moscow 1975, p. 169). In Marx's view, positivism deserves neither the scientific respect owed political economy, nor the political respect due to the utopians.

   Comte and Marx are incompatible. Everything opposes them: the one conceptualizes the completion of revolution and the consolidation of order; the other conceptualizes subversion and the permanence of revolution. Detractors of a positivist Marx close their eyes to this stubbornly obvious fact, as if the radical opposition between Comtean sociology and the critique of political economy were accompanied by some covert complicity.

8. Paul Ricoeur, *Time and Narrative*, vol. 3, trans. Kathleen Blamey and David Pellauer, University of Chicago Press, Chicago 1988, pp. 206, 259.

9. '[D]oing means that reality is not totalizable': ibid., p. 231.

10. Ibid., p. 235.

11. Maurice Merleau-Ponty, *In Praise of Philosophy*, trans. John Wild and James M. Edie, Northwestern University Press, Evanston, (IL) 1963, p. 49. Against the grain of current interpretations of Marx, Merleau-Ponty clearly grasped the theoretical upheaval involved in the demand that we awaken from the slumber of universal History:

   Marx himself discovers a historical rationality immanent in the life of men. For him, history is not merely the order of fact or of reality on which philosophy, with its rationality, will confer the right to exist. History is rather the situation in which all meanings are developed . . . It is not directed at the beginning by an idea of universal or total history. We must remember that Marx insisted on the impossibility of thinking the future. It is rather the analysis of the past and present which enables us to perceive in outline a logic in the course of things which does not guide from the outside . . . Hence there is no universal history. Perhaps we shall never advance beyond pre-history. Historical meaning is immanent in the inter-human event, and is as fragile as the event . . . Every appeal to universal history cuts off the meaning of the specific event, and renders effective history insignificant. (ibid., pp. 50–53)

12. Eric Alliez, *Capital Times*, trans. Georges Van Den Abbeele, University of Minnesota Press, Minneapolis and London 1996, pp. 22–3.
13. Karl Marx, 'Difference between the Democritean and Epicurean Philosophy of Nature', in Marx and Frederick Engels, *Collected Works*, vol. 1, Lawrence & Wishart, London 1975, pp. 63–5. Marx was equally familiar with Lucretius, for whom time had no existence in itself: it was things, and the passing of things, that rendered past, present and future perceptible.
14. Karl Marx, *Grundrisse*, trans. Martin Nicolaus, Penguin/NLR, Harmondsworth 1973, p. 461.
15. Henryk Grossmann, *Marx, l'économie politique classique et le problème de la dynamique*, Champ Libre, Paris 1975, p. 139.
16. Marx, *Capital*, vol. 1, pp. 312–13.
17. Ibid., p. 394.
18. 'Being a possibility that lasts, value is thus not limited to immediate utilization; it refers to the continuity of human needs and their satisfaction. Duration, time, thus becomes a constitutive element of value' (Fleischmann, *Hegel et la politique*, pp. 309–11).
19. Marx, *Grundrisse*, pp. 538–9.
20. Karl Marx, *Capital*, vol. 2, trans. David Fernbach, Penguin/NLR, Harmondsworth 1978, p. 184.
21. Production time, circulation time and overall reproduction time correspond, as has been indicated, to the three volumes of *Capital*. Here I have been inspired by Stavros Tombazos's remarkable work *Les Catégories du temps dans l'analyse économique*, Cahiers des saisons, Paris 1994.
22. Saint Augustine, *Confessions*, trans. R.S. Pine-Coffin, Penguin, London 1961, p. 272.
23. Ibid., p. 274.
24. Letter from Marx to Engels of 28 January 1863, in Marx and Engels, *Selected Correspondence*, Progress Publishers, Moscow 1975, p. 129.
25. Here we once again discover the inspiration of Feuerbach, for whom '[t]he only means by which *opposite* or *contradictory determinations* are *united* in one and the same being in a way corresponding to reality is in *time*': 'Principles of the Philosophy of the Future', trans. Zawar Hanfi, in Ludwig Feuerbach, Karl Marx and Friedrich Engels, *German Socialist Philosophy*, Continuum, New York 1997, p. 70.
26. Aristotle, *Physics*, trans. Robin Waterfield, Oxford University Press, Oxford 1996, Book IV, chapter xiv, p. 109.
27. Karl Marx, *Theories of Surplus-Value*, Part III, trans. Jack Cohen, Lawrence & Wishart, London 1972, pp. 133–5, 308, 135.
28. Karl Marx, 1861–63 Manuscripts, in Marx and Engels, *Collected Works*, vol. 30, Lawrence & Wishart, London 1988, pp. 42, 82.
29. Marx, *Grundrisse*, pp. 139–40.
30. Ibid., p. 231.
31. Ibid., pp. 715, 520.
32. Friedrich Nietzsche, 'On the Uses and Disadvantages of History for Life', in Nietzsche, *Untimely Meditations*, trans. R.J. Hollingdale, Cambridge University Press, Cambridge 1997, pp. 101–2, 105.
33. In his courses of 1968–70, Lucien Goldmann drew the parallel between Lukács and Heidegger. Much more so than Lukács, Walter Benjamin, whose unmatched sense of danger immediately divined the significance of *Being and Time*, is the 'anti-Heidegger' of the interwar period.
34. Letter from Marx of November 1877 to the editorial board of the *Otechestvenniye Zapiski*, in *Selected Correspondence*, pp. 293, 294.
35. Martin Heidegger, *Being and Time*, trans. John Macquarrie and Edward Robinson, Blackwell, Oxford and Cambridge, MA 1992, p. 447.

36. On this, see Françoise Dastur's valuable little book *Heidegger et la question du temps*, Presses Universitaires de France, Paris 1990.
37. Heidegger, *Being and Time*, pp. 451–3.
38. This anthology is collected in Pierre Bourdieu, *The Political Ontology of Martin Heidegger*, trans. Peter Collier, Polity, Cambridge 1991, p. 95. The last formula derives from Jean Beaufret; the others are from Henri Lefebvre, François Chatelet, and Kostas Axelos.
39. Nietzsche, 'On the Uses and Disadvantages of History for Life', p. 94.
40. 'On the other hand, it is difficult to grasp what a linearity for the future accompanied by a ramification towards the past would correspond to' (Jean-Louis Gardiès, *La Logique du temps*, Presses Universitaires de France, Paris 1975, p. 97). Our experience of the future can 'perfectly coincide with a fork diagram in which each fork represents one of the multiple possibilities. In general, it is only at the moment when future time becomes present that all its branches are pruned, with the exception of a single one that then becomes the unique line whose origin is marked by the present, and which we call the past.'
41. Walter Benjamin, *The Arcades Project*, trans. Howard Eiland and Kevin McLaughlin, Belknap/Harvard University Press, Cambridge, MA and London 1999, p. 392.
42. Heidegger, *Being and Time*, p. 306.
43. Jacques Rancière, *The Names of History*, trans. Hassan Melehy, University of Minnesota Press, Minneapolis and London 1994, p. 31.
44. Tombazos, *Les Catégories du temps dans l'analyse économique*, p. 11.
45. Ibid.
46. Ibid.
47. Walter Benjamin, 'Theses on the Philosophy of History', XVI, in Benjamin, *Illuminations*, trans. Harry Zohn, Fontana, London 1982, p. 264. The formula is similar to that of Nietzsche in 'On the Uses and Disadvantages of History for Life': 'He who cannot sink down on the threshold of the moment and forget all the past, who cannot stand balanced like a goddess of victory without growing dizzy and afraid, will never know what happiness is' (p. 62).
48. Benjamin, *The Arcades Project*, pp. 388–9.
49. Stéphane Moses, *L'Ange de l'Histoire*, Seuil, Paris 1992, p. 23.
50. Ibid., p. 163: 'The most precise formula for the philosophy of history underlying Jewish messianism is perhaps the following: there are too many constraints or too much meaning at the origin of history for it to be absolutely unpredictable; but there are not enough for it to be wholly determined' (ibid., p. 195).
51. Benjamin, 'Theses on the Philosophy of History', X, p. 260.
52. Gramsci, *Selections from the Prison Notebooks*, p. 438. For Gramsci, Croce's error consists in 'exclud[ing] the moment of struggle' (p. 118). The open-ended dialectic of struggle restores the possibility of error in politics, rather than seeing in all decisions and conduct simply the manifestation of an essence. When this is done, there is no room for errors, only betrayals and misconduct. To make a mistake is then already to be guilty (first principle of totalitarian logic). For Gramsci, by contrast, it is not decreed that the tendencies of the structure 'must necessarily be realized'. Whereas '[m]echanical historical materialism does not allow for the possibility of error, but assumes that every political act is determined, immediately, by the structure', Gramsci knows that a political act can perfectly well have been 'an error of calculation': 'If, for every ideological struggle within the Church one wanted to find an immediate primary explanation in the structure one would really be caught napping: all sorts of politico-economic romances have been written for this reason', he remarks (p. 408).
53. Karl Marx, 'Critical Notes on the Article "The King of Prussia and Social Reform by a Prussian"', in Marx, *Early Writings*, trans. Rodney Livingstone and Gregor Benton, Penguin/NLR, Harmondsworth 1975, pp. 419–20.

PART II

Struggle and Necessity
Marx's Critique of Sociological Reason

> . . . all things come to pass through conflict.
>
> (Heraclitus)

> Le Nouvel Observateur: In your view, which left-wing value should be promoted as a matter of urgency?
>
> Marguerite Duras: Class struggle.
>
> N.O.: Pardon?
>
> M.D.: Apart from reinstating class struggle, I don't see . . .
>
> (*Le Nouvel Observateur*, 2 April 1992)

4

Classes, or The Lost Subject

'The history of all hitherto existing society is the history of class struggles.' Whether it is dealing with the relations of production or historical development, 'class struggle' is at the centre of Marx's thought. Yet 'Marxist' common sense seems oblivious of how easy it is to cite canonical texts containing the notion of class, yet how difficult it is to find a precise definition of class. At most we glean some pedagogical approximations: 'In so far as millions of families live under economic conditions of existence that separate their mode of life, their interests and their cultural formation from those of the other classes and bring them into conflict with those classes, they form a class.' Or we get a terse characterization of the proletarian (not the proletariat) as 'he who lives without capital and ground rent from labour alone, and from one-sided, abstract labour at that'.[1] On the occasion of a new edition of the *Communist Manifesto* in 1888, Engels specified in a footnote: 'By proletariat [is meant] the class of modern wage labourers who, having no means of production of their own, are reduced to selling their labour power in order to live'[2] – this is sketchy. These occasional formulas do not constitute a reference point for defining class.

Troubled by this lacuna, numerous authors (for example Schumpeter, Aron, or Dahrendorf) readily attribute it to Marx's alleged conflation of science and philosophy, economy and sociology. It is true that Marx proceeds not by definitions (enumeration of criteria) but by the 'determination' of concepts (productive/unproductive, surplus-value/profit, production/circulation), which tend towards the concrete as they are articulated within the totality. The (unfinished) last chapter of *Capital*, devoted to classes, contrives to keep us in suspense. Ralf Dahrendorf has attempted to reconstruct its probable content on the basis of scraps and fragments taken from the preceding 51 chapters of Volume Three, just as the skeleton of a great saurian is reconstructed on the basis of bone fragments. The exercise carries little conviction.[3]

The interrupted pages of *Capital* leave unanswered many questions, pregnant with consequences, about how to understand the evolution of classes in developed capitalist societies (their transformation and internal differentiation); and in non-capitalist (or bureaucratic) societies, often reduced to formal characterizations derived sometimes from the primacy of the economy (plan versus market), sometimes from the primacy of the political ('dictatorship of the proletariat'), and sometimes from a vague sociology of power ('workers' state').[4]

Marx's Unobtainable Sociology

'Curiously enough, Marx has never, as far as we know, worked out systematically what it is plain was one of the pivots of his thought.' Schumpeter entertains the notion that this task might have been deferred. Equally plausible is that 'some points about it remained unsettled in his own mind, and that his way toward a full-fledged theory of classes was barred by certain difficulties he had created for himself by insisting on a purely economic and over-simplified conception of the phenomenon.'[5] What is even more 'curious' is that this judgement of Schumpeter's on the subject of classes could also be applied to the absence of a discourse on method, a theory of crises, an explicit theory of time, which unquestionably are likewise so many 'pivots of his thought'. We might even be led to believe that Marx, ensnared in his own traps, spent his time creating diversions by resolving secondary questions.

Anyway, what exactly did he spend his time doing? Treating his dreadful boils, sharing family problems, putting off his creditors, doing jobbing journalism to pay his debts, treating his Uncle Philip harshly, keeping up a voluminous correspondence, conspiring, and organizing the working-class movement. Above all, writing and rewriting *Capital*.

This is where we must seek the key to a theory of classes *in actu* – unsatisfactory, perhaps, but certainly not 'over-simplified'. The oversimplification is Schumpeter's. Marx, he claims, froze classes at the moment of their abstraction, as a structural potentiality of the mode of production, before the development of the social formation produced the complex differentiation of the division of labour, its organization and juridical relation to the state. This is to set little store by the logic of *Capital*, where the end is always-already contained in the origin. Thus, the results of circulation and reproduction are already present in value and surplus-value, which 'presuppose' the class struggle and the determination of *socially necessary* labour-time. Proceeding from the abstract to the concrete, in this optic the theory of classes cannot be reduced to a static operation of definition and classification. It refers to a system of relations structured by struggle, whose complexity is displayed to the full in the political writings (*Class Struggles in France*, *The Eighteenth Brumaire*, *The Civil War in France*), where Marx offers his last word on the subject.

Schumpeter is well aware that the notion of class has several possible senses. Prisoner of an intellectual division of labour compartmentalized into so many watertight 'subject matters', he detects a deliberate confusion between different disciplines, like economics and sociology. This mixture of genres, which animates Marx's theory, fascinates him: 'There cannot be any doubt about the access of vitality which comes to analysis thereby. The ghostly concepts of economic theory begin to breathe. The bloodless theorem descends into *agmen, pulverem et clamorem.*'[6] Rejecting this seductive profusion, which seems to him to be a threat to science, Schumpeter prefers to ignore the movement from the abstract to the concrete. For him, the 'stratifying principle consists in the ownership, or the exclusion from ownership, of means of production. . . . We have thus, fundamentally, two and only two classes.'[7] An oversimplified 'definition' if ever there was one. . . .

The simple opposition between wage-labour and capital is not located at the level of the social formation in Marx, but at the first level of determinate abstraction – the sphere of production. In its deep structure, each society boils down to a fundamental, conflictual class opposition.

The determination of class relations in the sphere of production precisely represents merely the first word of Marx's analysis, and he does not leave it there. Disregarding Engels's clarification that the only human history reducible to class struggles is written history, subsequent to the dissolution of primitive communist society, Schumpeter condemns the abusive extension of the notion of class to all societies, including 'non-historical epochs', with the exception of primitive communism and the classless society of the future. This effaces the specific articulations of these societies and systematically reduces classes to 'purely economic phenomena, and even phenomena that were economic in a very narrow sense'. Marx thereby denied himself the possibility of 'a deeper view of them'. This impasse is a political one. In fact, the reductive definition of classes allowed 'a bold stroke of analytic strategy', in the shape of an 'ingenious tautology': private property having been placed at the heart of the definition of classes, its abolition would automatically open to a classless society.[8]

According to Schumpeter, a class is 'something more than an aggregation of class members. It is something else . . . A class is aware of its identity as a whole, sublimates itself as such.'[9] This observation poses a

logical problem whose elucidation would obviate a number of miscon-
ceived debates on borderline cases or individual statuses. The notion of
class in Marx is reducible neither to an attribute of which the individual
units comprising it are the bearers, nor to the sum of these units. It is
something else: a relational totality, not a mere sum. This old problem
has continued to rack logicians:

> We must not forget that in social science the term 'class' has a different sense
> from its meaning in the mathematical sciences, which use it to denote a
> property. The bourgeoisie and the proletariat are social classes; and it would be
> a misconstrual to regard bourgeoisie or proletariat as properties of some
> particular individual. Here, in the social sciences, the mereological usage of
> 'class' is appropriate. The proletariat is a group of people, a composite object,
> in which the various proletarians are constitutive pieces of the solar system, in
> the same way that the various bees are the constitutive elements of a swarm of
> bees. The people who make up a given social class are obviously interdependent
> in ways other than the constitutive pieces of an inanimate object or a herd of
> animals. In this instance, dependencies of a social, specifically human character
> come into play – for example, those attendant on the use of language to
> communicate, or conscious co-operation, etc. Nevertheless, this in no way alters
> the fact that the relation between a social class and the members of this class is
> a relation established between a composite object and its own constitutive
> elements. Class is here construed in 'mereological' fashion.[10]

But the dialectic finds it difficult to accommodate logical formalism.

Does not making class a higher reality than the individuals who
comprise it succumb to the fetishistic illusions that transform society,
history or class into so many mythical subjects? Marx specifically accuses
Proudhon of treating society as if it were a 'person'. Denouncing this
'fiction' of the society-person, he scoffs at those who 'make a thing out of
a word'. His approach precludes treating class as a person or as a unified,
conscious subject, on the model of the rational subject of classical
psychology. Class exists only in a conflictual relationship with other classes.
In his marginal annotations to the manuscript of *The German Ideology*,
Marx criticizes German philosophers for their formal understanding of
the concept of class and for reducing individuals to mere specimens of an
abstraction that dominates them. In particular, he criticizes Stirner for his
frequent assertion that everyone is what they are by virtue of the state, in
the same way that the bourgeois is a specimen of the bourgeoisie – as if
the bourgeoisie existed prior to the individuals who comprise it. The
crystallization of personal relations into class relations does not thereby
dissolve them into a hypostatized mechanism of imaginary 'persons'. The
dynamic reality of classes never falls into the inert domain of pure

objectivity. Their cohesion is irreducible to the formal unity of a simple collection of individuals.[11] These early works should obviously not be conflated with the concept of class developed in *Capital*. Nevertheless, they conclusively rule out both representing class as a super-subject and reducing it to a simple pattern of inter-individuality.

To demand of Marx a 'sociology' that conforms to the academic criteria of the discipline is a nonsense. No one is less sociological (in this conventional sense) than Marx. His 'critical sociology' is a negative sociology, or 'anti-sociology'.[12] Sociological inquiry can generate useful information; but information does not constitute thought and factual information does not constitute knowledge. In his repeated attacks on Bukharin's *Historical Materialism*, Gramsci stresses the irreducible antagonism between the two approaches. Seeking to adapt formal logic to the methods of the physical and natural sciences, Bukharin's manual yields a vulgar evolutionism. Despite its pedagogical intentions, the very idea of such a manual is incongruous, in the case of a theory 'that is still at the stage of discussion, polemic and elaboration': 'the vulgar contention is that science must absolutely mean "system", and consequently systems of all sort are built up. . . . The *Manual* contains no treatment of any kind of dialectic.' This defect could have two origins: 'on the one hand, a theory of history and politics conceived as sociology . . . and on the other hand a philosophy proper, this being philosophical alias metaphysical or mechanical (vulgar) materialism'. The attempt to reduce 'the philosophy of praxis to a form of sociology' in fact reveals a desire – at once both illusory and disturbing – to hold 'the whole of history in the palm of its hand'. The real issue is to know what sociology amounts to as a separate discipline, and its role in the historical development of culture. Based on a 'vulgar evolutionism', in Gramsci's eyes it is an attempt to apprehend the social 'in a form dependent on . . . evolutionist positivism'. In a critical perspective on the existing order, by contrast, what would be required would be to find the most appropriate literary form to avoid a *sociological* exposition.[13] Hence *Capital* as a *non-sociological* exposition.

The genesis of *Capital* constitutes a 'theoretical event' in its own right, comprising ruptures and continuities. This mutation could not fail to have consequences for the conceptualization of classes. In the grip of the economic crisis of 1857–58, Marx worked feverishly on the composition of the *Grundrisse*: 'so that I at least get the outlines clear before the *déluge*'.[14] So it was an urgent piece of work. At the same time – 'by mere accident' – he rediscovered Hegel and his *Logic*. Chance sometimes has its necessity.

Knowledge is not a simple collection of facts. The difficulty resides in the transition from facts to knowledge, in the relation of logical categories to their content. 'Through its formal and abstract thinking, [which is] lacking all basic import, this enlightenment has emptied all content out of religion', leaving only 'the lifeless water of the understanding, with its generalities and its abstract rationalism'. Even so, it is not enough to oppose to these abstractions the immediate and chaotic concreteness of 'life' or romantic 'nature'. Partial determinations are one-sided, and need to be transcended by the authentic concrete that approximates to the whole. 'A philosophizing *without system* cannot be scientific at all': 'A content has its justification only as a moment of the whole, outside of which it is only an unfounded presupposition or a subjective certainty. Many philosophical writings restrict themselves like this – to the mere utterance of *dispositions* and opinions.'[15]

Thus Hegelian logic develops a radical critique of empiricism. Rather than searching for the true in thinking, the latter refers to experience, postulating that what is true must exist in reality and exist for perception. It thus recognizes a principle of freedom (human beings must see for themselves), but universality, Hegel objects, is something other than large numbers. Kant's critical philosophy, he states, shares with empiricism the error of taking experience as the sole foundation of knowledge, not as truths, but as knowledge of phenomena, inevitably resulting in epistemological relativism.[16]

The genesis of *Capital* presupposes this critique of empiricism and Kantian philosophy. Most of Marx's detractors (the 'sociology of class' is the most blatant example) unimaginatively follow the opposite route, criticizing the unfinished determinations of the dialectical totality in the name of the metaphysical categories of empirical perception. In the 1857 Introduction, Marx explains the transition from the abstract to the concrete as a 'synthesis of many determinations' and 'unity of the diverse'.[17] The concrete is not the empirical immediate datum of statistical investigation but a conceptual construction, or thought-concrete.

The possibility of scientific knowledge is inscribed in the distance between the empirically given and this constructed concrete. Starting from the domination of the whole over the parts, the plan of the *Grundrisse* no longer follows the descriptive categories of classical economics. Neither historical exploration nor analysis of the 'factors of production', it announces the dialectical synthesis of a system and its history. An interpretative abstraction from actual societies, 'capital' becomes the key to the totality in the capitalist mode of production. That is why, as 'the all-dominating economic power of bourgeois society', capital 'must form the starting-point as well as the finishing-point, and must be dealt with before landed property'.[18]

The initial plan of *Capital* in six volumes envisaged a volume on the state and another on foreign trade (or the world market). Yet the subject matter of these unwritten volumes is not exhausted by the final four-volume plan. Marx explained this by suggesting that the other volumes would have led him beyond his specific task (the critique of political economy), since they would have introduced new conceptual determinations and new degrees of concreteness. The study of the state would have required elucidation of the relation between production and the institutionalization of law, the division of labour, and ideological apparatuses. An account of the world market would have demanded a study of the relations between classes, nations and states. Even so, the state and the world market have not disappeared. Moments and mediations of reproduction, they are constantly presupposed and, in some sense, 'already given'.[19]

Production and the Relation of Exploitation

Classes reveal themselves in and through the movement of *Capital*. If this disclosure is logically completed in Volume Three, with the 'process of production as a whole', the question is dealt with on several occasions in the process of production.

1. Class polarization features in Volume One, Chapter 10 on 'The Working Day': 'Hence, in the history of capitalist production, the establishment of a norm for the working day presents itself as a struggle over the limits of that day, a struggle between collective capital, i.e. the class of capitalists, and collective labour, i.e. the working class.'[20] This transition from abstract social relations, corresponding to the *level of production* (capital/labour), to classes proper (at the *level of struggle*), already *presupposes* a permanent conflict over the division of time between necessary labour and surplus labour (at the level of overall reproduction).

2. Marx proceeds to explain (Chapter 14 on 'The Division of Labour and Manufacture') that the tendency of manufacture to convert

a partial task into the life-long destiny of a man corresponds to the tendency shown by earlier societies towards making trades hereditary. The trades either became petrified into castes, or, in cases where definite historical conditions produced a variability in the individual which was incompatible with a caste system, they hardened into guilds. Castes and guilds arise from the action of the same natural law that regulates the differentiation of plants and animals into species and varieties, except that, when a certain degree of development has been reached, the heredity of castes and the exclusiveness of guilds are ordained as a law of society.[21]

3. The subject of classes reappears in Part 7 in the chapter on 'The General Law of Capitalist Accumulation':

within the capitalist system all methods for raising the social productivity of labour are put into effect at the cost of the individual worker . . . all means for the development of production undergo a dialectical inversion so that they become means of domination and exploitation of the producers; they distort the worker into a fragment of a man, they degrade him to the level of an appendage of a machine, they destroy the actual content of his labour by turning it into a torment; they alienate . . . from him the intellectual potentialities of the labour process in the same proportion as science is incorporated in it as an independent power; they deform the conditions under which he works, subject him during the labour process to a despotism the more hateful for its meanness; they transform his life-time into working-time . . .[22]

In so far as it presupposes an account of the antagonistic relationship of exploitation, the presentation of the labour theory of value and surplus-value sets about a theoretical approach to classes from Volume One onwards. But many mediations between this truncated and fragmented producer and the fully determined class remain.

4. Far from conferring on the proletariat the image of a mythical subject, from Volume One onwards Marx poses with the utmost clarity the contradiction of its condition and the enigma of its emancipation, on which (in his view) the future of humanity depends:

The advance of capitalist production develops a working class which by education, tradition and habit looks upon the requirements of that mode of production as self-evident natural laws. The organization of the capitalist process of production, once it is fully developed, breaks down all resistance. The constant generation of a relative surplus population keeps the law of the supply and demand of labour, and therefore wages, within narrow limits which correspond to capital's valorization requirements. The silent compulsion of economic relations sets the seal on the domination of the capitalist over the worker. Direct extra-economic force is still of course used, but only in exceptional cases. *In the ordinary run of things*, the worker can be left to the 'natural laws of production', i.e. it is possible to rely on his dependence on capital, which springs from the conditions of production themselves, and is guaranteed in perpetuity by them.[23]

Things were different during the 'historical genesis' of capitalist production, when the bourgeoisie could not dispense with 'constant state intervention'. Alienation and fetishism are rooted in the production relation. The conditions of exploitation render the direct producer a physically and intellectually stunted being, to the extent that, 'in the ordinary run of things', submission reproduces submission, allowing the state seemingly to hold itself in reserve from the sphere of production.

How, being nothing, to become everything? Such is the unresolved mystery of emancipation starting out from a condition of subjection and alienation. The answer is found in political confrontation and class struggle: only struggle can break this vicious circle.

Volume One does not develop a systematic, complete conception of classes. The relation of exploitation between wage-labour and capital is only the first and most abstract of their determinations. At this level, the question of classes enters from two angles:

- to introduce the specificity of modern classes, grounded in the formal freedom of labour-power compared with caste and guild societies;
- to introduce the presupposition of the relation of exploitation: the class struggle, which determines the socially necessary labour-time for the reproduction of labour-power.

Circulation and Productive Labour

Volume Two deals with class relations in the unity of production and circulation. Before our very eyes, circulating capital accomplishes the endlessly renewed marvel of its metamorphoses. It steps out of one guise and slips into another. From money (M) it becomes means of production (P), then commodity (C), and then money again (M'), and so on. When the worker is separated from the means of production (the very precondition of the capitalist process of production), when the means of production confront the owner of labour-power as someone else's property, '[t]he class relation between capitalist and wage-labourer already exists':

- This is a *sale and purchase*, a money relation, but a sale and purchase in which it is presupposed that the buyer is a capitalist and the seller a wage-labourer; and this relation does in fact exist, because the conditions for the realization of labour-power, i.e. means of subsistence and means of production, are separated, as the property of another, from the possessor of labour-power.
- It goes without saying, therefore, that the formula for the circuit of money capital . . . is the self-evident form of the circuit of capital only on the basis of already developed capitalist production, because it presupposes the availability of the class of wage-labourers in sufficient numbers throughout society.
- Industrial capital is the only mode of existence of capital in which not only the appropriation of surplus-value or surplus product, but also its creation, is a function of capital. It thus requires production to be capitalist in character; its existence includes that of the antagonism between capitalists and wage-labourers.
- The wage-labourer lives only from the sale of his labour-power [for money] . . . His payment must . . . be constantly repeated at short intervals, to enable him to repeat the purchases . . . that are needed for . . . self-maintenance. Hence the capitalist must constantly confront him as money capitalist, and his capital as money capital.[24]

In Volume One, the class relation took the form of an antagonistic relation of exploitation between the worker as producer and the capitalist as industrial capitalist, as a division between necessary labour and surplus labour. Volume Two develops the metamorphoses of the circuit of capital. This process is a succession of acts of buying and selling. The relation of exploitation emerges here as that between the worker as wage-labourer selling his labour-power and the capitalist as possessor of money-capital. What is at stake in this relation is grasped from the angle not of the division of labour-time, but of conflictual negotiations over labour-power as a commodity.

Often construed as a purely economic description of the process of circulation, Volume Two provides the material for a political theory of classes for Biagio De Giovanni, who writes that the

> form of circulation of capital becomes decisive for the very morphology of classes. The antagonism corresponds to the space of circulation, not in as much as the acuteness of the contradiction in production is weakly reflected there, but in so far as the contradiction is extended over the whole form of the process and patiently reconstructed in its various forms.[25]

The circulation process destroys the simplicity of the patterns of production in Volume One, and complicates their phenomenology. It constructs the 'social patterns' and the relations between them.

Indeed, it is as legitimate to seek the morphology of classes at the level of Volume Two as Volume One, to which most popularizers confine themselves. Specific to the sphere of circulation, the relation of buying and selling labour-power is no less constitutive of the class relation than the relation of exploitation disclosed in Volume One. For exploitation to become possible, the labourer and the means of production must be separated; and 'this separation is abolished only through the sale of labour-power to the owner of the means of production, a sale which signifies that the buyer is now in control of the continuous flow of labour-power to the owner of the means of production, a flow which by no means has to stop when the amount of labour necessary to reproduce the price of labour-power has been performed.' Marx then specifies:

> The capital relation arises only in the production process because it exists implicitly in the act of circulation, in the basically different economic conditions in which buyer and seller confront one another, in their class relation . . . It goes without saying, therefore, that the formula for the circuit of money capital: M-C . . . P . . . C'-M', is the self-evident form of the circuit of capital only on the basis of already developed capitalist production, because it presupposes the availability of the class of wage-labourers in sufficient numbers throughout society.[26]

And, consequently, the class struggle.

Thus each volume of *Capital* contributes its specific determination.[27] In Volume One, the class relation receives an initial basic determination: that of the relation of exploitation. In Volume Two, it receives a new and essential – but not definitive – determination: that of productive or indirectly productive labour, which has generated so many controversies and misunderstandings. But why seek the last word for a theory of classes in the sphere of circulation? Marx broaches the subject systematically only in Volume Three, in the framework of his study of reproduction as a whole.

Reproduction as a Whole and the Enigma of the Unfinished Chapter

Here, once again, we change register. When it comes to production and reproduction as a whole, classes are no longer exclusively determined by the extraction of surplus-value, or by the categories of productive and unproductive labour. They are determined by the combination of the relation of exploitation in production, the wage relation and the productivity/non-productivity of labour in circulation, and the distribution of revenue in reproduction as a whole.

Can we now include among the proletariat public-sector wage-labourers who participate in reproduction? With the result that what – from the viewpoint of circulation in Volume Two – was unproductive labour becomes indirectly productive in Volume Three, when it is considered from the standpoint of the capitalist dynamic as a whole? It can indeed be deduced from the logic of *Capital* that workers in the sphere of circulation (transport, trade, credit, advertising), who yield surplus-value to their employer and are subject to conditions of exploitation comparable to those endured by workers in production, fall under the same class determination. If Volume Three deals with the process of reproduction as a whole, it does not tackle the conditions of reproduction (education, health, housing), which would require the introduction as such of the state's mediation. In *Theories of Surplus-Value*, Marx simply evokes the 'immaterial' forms of labour that are 'transitional' to capitalist production (mentioning the 'educational factories' whose teachers are productive not *vis-à-vis* their pupils, but *vis-à-vis* the educational establishment), insisting on the notion of the collective worker.[28]

There is no eluding the logical architecture of *Capital.*

In Volume Three, classes form the subject of a specific chapter once the theoretical conditions for a systematic approach have finally been met. The partial determinations of classes, at the level of the extraction of surplus-value in the production process and the sale of labour-power in the circulation process, are now integrated into the overall dynamic of competition, equalization of the profit rate, the functional specialization of capitals, and the distribution of revenue.

Only now can classes appear as something other than a sum of individuals performing a similar social function:

> From what has been said so far [about the equalization of the profit rate through competition], we can see that each individual capitalist, just like the totality of all capitalists in each particular sphere of production, participates in the *exploitation of the entire working class by capital as a whole*, and in the level of this exploitation; not just in terms of general class sympathy, but in a direct economic sense, since, taking all other circumstances as given, including the value of the total constant capital advanced, the *average rate of profit depends on the level of exploitation of labour as a whole by capital as a whole* . . . We thus have a mathematically exact demonstration of why the capitalists, no matter how little love is lost among them in their mutual competition, are nevertheless united by a real freemasonary *vis-à-vis* the working class as a whole.[29]

Thus class relations cannot be reduced to a direct confrontation between boss and worker in the workplace. Exploitation, a social phenomenon, always presupposes the metabolism of competition, the formation of an average profit rate, and the determination of socially necessary labour-time.

The famous Chapter 52 of Volume Three, left unfinished, opens with a claim:

> The owners of mere labour-power, the owners of capital and landowners, whose respective sources of income are wages, profit and ground-rent – in other words wage-labourers, capitalists and landowners – form the three great classes of modern society based on the capitalist mode of production.[30]

The three 'great classes' (not the only ones) thus seem to be definitively determined by the source of their income.

As a classic capitalist country, England perfectly illustrates the tendency to increasing class polarization announced in the *Communist Manifesto*. The capitalist mode of production tends 'to divorce the means of production ever more from labour and to concentrate the fragmented means of production more and more into large groups, i.e. to transform labour into wage-labour and the means of production into capital'. Yet 'even here', in this paradigmatic country, 'this class articulation does not emerge in pure form': 'Here, too, middle and transitional levels always conceal the boundaries (although incomparably less so in the countryside than in the towns).'[31] In other words, the actual social formation is never reducible to the bare skeleton of the mode of production. Polarization operates, but without reducing the spectrum of positions, statuses and intermediate classes that complicate the class front. Far from dispelling this blurring by some kind of urban purity of capitalist relations, Marx observes, the town reinforces it relative to the countryside. We are miles away from a simplistic conception of classes. To clarify the problem, we must turn back from the immediate data of sociology to theory.

Marx writes: 'The question to be answered next is: "What makes a class"?, and this arises automatically from answering another question: "What makes wage-labourers, capitalists and landowners the formative elements of the three great social classes?"'[32] In other words, revenue determines class, and – vice versa – the owners of capital, land and labour-power constitute the three great classes. . . . The trap closes in a patent tautology.

But what is *a* class? '*At first sight*, the identity of revenues and revenue sources.'[33] Wages, profit or ground rent are the common denominator of a vast social group forming a class. But 'at first sight' only.

Marx does not make do with this first glance. The claim is immediately corrected by an objection: 'from this point of view, however' – the criterion of revenue – one would slip into the fragmentation of a descriptive sociology, since 'doctors and government officials would also form two classes, as they belong to two distinct social groups, the revenue of each group's members flowing from its own source'.[34]

There would never be an end to it. Classes would be dissolved into status groups and socioprofessional categories: 'The same would hold true for the *infinite fragmentation of interests and positions* into which the division of social labour splits not only workers but also capitalists and landowners – the latter, for instance, into vineyard-owners, field-owners, forest-owners, mine-owners, fishery-owners, etc.' 'At this point,' Engels notes laconically, 'the manuscript breaks off', leaving a major theoretical question begging.

From Karl Renner to Ralf Dahrendorf, attempts to pick up the thread of the interrupted manuscript and reconstruct the unfinished chapter are too numerous to count. For Dahrendorf, the theory of classes in Marx is not a theory of social stratification, but an instrument for explaining overall social change.[35] The issue is not to know what a society looks like at a given moment, but how to change the social structure. Dahrendorf's interpretation is, however, mortgaged to the idea that class theory represents the problematic link in Marx's work between sociological analysis and philosophical speculation. When he proposes to arrange a set of quotations from Marx in systematic order, and articulate them in a coherent text, Dahrendorf, far from following the logic of the unfinished chapter, leaves the terrain of *Capital* to venture into a theory of interests and ideology, struggle and class consciousness, which refers to a different level of analysis. He extracts fragments from *The German Ideology* or *The Poverty of Philosophy* (for example: '[t]his mass is thus already a class as against capital, but not yet for itself . . . the struggle of class against class is a political struggle').[36] Absorbed in this labour of montage, he forgets that the approach to class in these texts is bound up with the anthropological conception of alienation in the young Marx; and that it is necessarily modified by the theory of surplus-value, profit and capital accumulation.

Faced with the blank page of the unfinished chapter, it would be more coherent to imagine Marx poised to change problematics once again. The route from the concrete to the concrete is never the shortest one; it often ends in a cul-de-sac. Determination of classes exclusively by revenue leads to their infinite erosion and disappearance as operational concepts. In accordance with the counsel of the 1857 Introduction, it is time to reconvene, in its unity, the set of determinations encountered on the long journey of *Capital*: the relation of exploitation that accounts for surplus-value; the wage relation that makes the worker by turns a buyer and seller of commodities; directly and indirectly productive labour; the social division of labour; and the nature and amount of income. This hypothesis seems to be more in line with Marx's conception of class, which does not draw up socioprofessional tables, string together statistics, or labour over borderline cases in the class structure.

Where positivist sociology claims to 'treat social facts as things', Marx always treats them as relations. He does not define his object once and for all by criteria or attributes; he pursues the logic of its multiple determinations. He does not 'define' *a* class; he apprehends relations of conflict between classes. He does not photograph a social fact labelled 'class'; he has his sights set on the class relation in its conflictual dynamic. *An* isolated class is not a theoretical object, but a nonsense.

The unfinished chapter can thus be read as an additional step in the determination of the concrete. Determined at the level of the production process as a whole, classes can still receive new determinations involving analysis of the family, education, the state and, further still, the political struggle proper. The unfinished path of *Capital* should be intersected starting from the opposite direction, leading from class struggle as a political struggle to the mode of production. The abandoned volume on the state would then represent the vanishing point of an unobtainable theory of classes, to which death, definitively halting Marx's pen, was not the only obstacle.

Social Classes and Political Representation

The whole set of determinations – not only economic, but also political – converges behind the 'superficial appearance [that] veils the *class struggle*'. Confrontation between political parties discloses its reality even as it dissimulates it. It discloses it in mystified form. On the basis of different property forms and social conditions of existence, there arises, in fact, a 'whole superstructure of different and specifically formed feelings, illusions, modes of thought and views . . . The whole class creates and forms these out of its material foundations and the corresponding social relations.' Accordingly: '[i]n historical struggles one must make a still sharper distinction between the phrase and fantasies of the parties and their real organization and real interests, between their conception of themselves and what they really are'.[37]

Revolutionary theory has something in common with psychoanalysis. Political representation is not the simple manifestation of a social nature. Political class struggle is not the superficial mirroring of an essence. Articulated like a language, it operates by displacements and condensations of social contradictions. It has its dreams, its nightmares and its lapses. In the specific field of the political, class relations acquire a degree of complexity irreducible to the bipolar antagonism that nevertheless determines them.

1. In the sphere of the political, the relations of production are articulated with the state: 'the *material interest* of the French bourgeoisie is most intimately imbricated precisely with the maintenance of that extensive and highly ramified state machine'. It is precisely through this 'imbrication' that class fractions are differentiated, political representations developed, and alliances forged. It is also the site where class relations and the bureaucratic corps of the state interact, perpetuating the hierarchical structure of pre-capitalist societies. Thus: '[b]ureaucracy is only the low and brutal form of a centralization still burdened with its opposite, feudalism'. And it is not disagreeable to the second Bonaparte to find himself 'forced to create, alongside the real classes of society, an artificial caste for which the maintenance of his regime is a question of self-preservation'.[38]

2. Starting from the basic classes, determined by antagonistic relations of production, these intersecting articulations multiply the differentiations. From *Class Struggles in France* to *The Civil War in France*, Marx meticulously follows the dialectic between social relations and political representation:

> because the democrat represents the petty bourgeoisie, a *transitional class* in which the interests of the two classes meet and become blurred, he imagines he is elevated above class antagonisms generally. The democrats admit that they are confronted with a privileged class, but assert that they, along with all the rest of the nation, form the *people*.[39]

If the middle classes experience the polarization of the basic classes, they none the less play a role of their own. In the Paris Commune:

> For the first time in history the petty and middling middle class has openly rallied round the workmen's revolution, and proclaimed it as the only means

of their own salvation and that of France! . . . The principal measures taken by the Commune are taken for the salvation of the middle class . . .[40]

The Society of 10 December is construed as the product of the lumpen-proletariat, 'the refuse of all classes':

Under the pretext of founding a charitable organization, the Paris lumpenpro-letariat had been organized into secret sections . . . Alongside decayed roués of doubtful origin and uncertain means of subsistence, alongside ruined and adventurous scions of the bourgeoisie, there were vagabonds, discharged soldiers, discharged criminals, escaped galley slaves, swindlers, confidence tricksters, *lazzaroni*, pickpockets, sleight-of-hand experts, gamblers, *maquereaux*, brothel-keepers, porters, pen-pushers, organ-grinders, rag-and-bone merchants, knife-grinders, tinkers, and beggars: in short, the whole indeterminate frag-mented mass, tossed backwards and forwards, which the French call *la bohème* . . .[41]

3. If the proletariat is the potentially emancipatory class, this potential is not realized automatically. *Capital* underscores the obstacles to the development of class consciousness inherent in the reification of social relations. To these obstacles peculiar to the production relation are added the specific effects of practical victories and defeats: 'the workers . . . renounced the honour of being a conquering power, gave themselves up to their fate and proved that the defeat of June 1848 had rendered them incapable of fighting for years'. The non-linearity of the class struggle ultimately expresses its structural specificity under the rule of capital:

Bourgeois revolutions, such as those of the eighteenth century, storm quickly from success to success. They outdo each other in dramatic effects; men and things seem set in sparkling diamonds and each day's spirit is ecstatic. But they are short-lived; they soon reach their apogee, and society has to undergo a long period of regret until it has learned to assimilate soberly the achievements of its period of storm and stress. Proletarian revolutions, however, such as those of the nineteenth century, constantly engage in self-criticism, and in repeated interruptions of their own course. They return to what has apparently already been accomplished in order to begin the task again; with merciless thorough-ness they mock the inadequate, weak and wretched aspects of their first attempts; they seem to throw their opponent to the ground only to see him draw new strength from the earth and rise again before them, more colossal than ever; they shrink back again and again before the indeterminate immensity of their own goals, until the situation is created in which any retreat is impossible . . .[42]

4. Finally, the relationship between social structure and political struggle is mediated by the relations of dependence and domination

between nations at the international level. Thus: '[t]he English have all that is needed *materially* for social revolution. What they lack is *the sense of generalization and revolutionary passion.*' The reasons for this have nothing to do with temperature or climate:

> England can not be considered simply as one country among many others. It must be treated as the metropolis of capital. . . . In dragging down the working class in England still further by the forced immigration of poor Irish people, the English bourgeoisie has not merely exploited Irish poverty. It has also divided the proletariat into two hostile camps.[43]

It is in this sense that 'a people that oppresses another people forges its own chains': 'The English proletariat is actually becoming more and more bourgeois, so that the ultimate aim of this most bourgeois of all nations would appear to be the possession, *alongside* the bourgeoisie, of a bourgeois aristocracy and a bourgeois proletariat.'[44]

So the social structure of class does not mechanically determine political representation and conflict. If a state or a party has a class character, their relative political autonomy opens up a wide range of variations in the expression of this 'nature'. The irreducible specificity of the political makes the social characterization of the state, parties – and, *a fortiori*, theories – a highly perilous exercise.

On the basis of fragments from *The Poverty of Philosophy* and *The Eighteenth Brumaire*, this non-correspondence between social structure and political representation has often been treated in terms of the discrepancy between class-for-itself and class-in-itself:

> *In so far as* millions of [peasant] families live under economic conditions of existence that separate their mode of life, their interests and their cultural formation from those of the other classes and bring them into conflict with those classes, they form a class. *In so far as* these small peasant proprietors are merely connected on a local basis, and the identity of their interests fails to produce a feeling of community, national links, or a political organization, *they do not form a class.* They are therefore incapable of asserting their class interest in their own name . . .[45]

On the one hand, the peasants constitute a class 'in so far as . . .'; on the other, they do not 'in so far as . . .'. They thus seem to constitute a class *objectively* (sociologically), but not *subjectively* (politically).

Object and subject, being and essence are bound up with one another in the development of classes. In the *dynamic* of class relations, the subjectivity of consciousness cannot arbitrarily emancipate itself from the structure, any more than the objectivity of being can be passively detached from consciousness. This problematic is opposed to any mechanical conception of a necessary transition from the in-itself to the for-itself, from the unconscious to the conscious, from the pre-conscious social to the conscious political, with time acting as a neutral go-between. Class consciousness and unconsciousness are intertwined in a perverse embrace, and both are consistently mistaken.

The notions of class-in-itself and class-for-itself, by no means frequent in Marx, belong to the philosophical representation of the proletariat characteristic of the early works, illustrated by the famous letter to Ruge of September 1843 in which Marx evokes the 'consciousness of itself' that the proletariat 'will be obliged to acquire, whether or not it wants to'. Analogous formulations recur in *The Poverty of Philosophy*: they are inscribed in the problematic of the self-development of historical subjectivity, and betray the strong influence of Hegelian phenomenology as a science of consciousness and self-consciousness, and nostalgia for what Lukács embraced in his later work as an 'ontology of social being'.[46] In certain early works, the proletariat appears to be still ontologically 'compelled as proletariat to abolish itself'. Its fate is in some sense determined by its being: 'It is a question of *what the proletariat is*, and what, in accordance with this *being*, it will historically be compelled to do.'[47]

This destiny still figures prominently in the letter to Weydemeyer of 5 March 1852, in which Marx sums up his own contribution:

> What I did that was new was to demonstrate: 1) that the *existence of classes* is merely linked to *particular historical phases in the development of production*, 2) that class struggle necessarily leads to the *dictatorship of the proletariat*, 3) that this dictatorship itself only constitutes the transition to the *abolition of all classes* and to a *classless society*.[48]

Hegelian interpretations of Marx have drunk their fill at these sources. The proletariat, writes Labriola in his text on the *Communist Manifesto*, 'is a necessary result of modern history, has for its mission to succeed the bourgeoisie, and to succeed it as the producing force of a new social order in which class antagonisms shall disappear'.[49] In *History and Class Consciousness*, Lukács develops this dialectic of the in-itself and the for-itself more subtly, mediated by the totality: 'The self-knowledge, both subjective and objective, of the proletariat at a given point in its evolution is at the same time knowledge of the stage of development achieved by the whole society.' The result is a kind of theoretical ultra-Bolshevism on the question of party organization. Elevated into the fulfilment of the 'for-itself', the latter becomes the 'form taken by the class consciousness of the proletariat', invested with 'the sublime role of *bearer of the class*

consciousness of the proletariat and the consciousness of its historical vocation'.
More 'Leninist' than Lenin, paradoxically, Lukács thus lapses back into
the conflation of party and class that the author of *What is to be Done?*
precisely set out to avoid. In the dominant discourse of the Second
International, this confusion tended to identify the party with the multiform historical movement of the class. In Lukács, the tendency is to
absorb the class into the party: 'it is the proletariat that embodies this
process of consciousness. Since its consciousness appears as the immanent
product of the historical dialectic, it likewise appears to be dialectical.
That is to say, this consciousness is nothing but the expression of historical
necessity.'[50]

In contrast, the *Grundrisse* and *Capital* present themselves as a labour of
mourning for ontology, a radical deontologization, after which no space
remains for any 'world beyond' [*arrière-monde*] whatsoever, any dual content, any dualism of the authentic and the inauthentic, science and
ontology. There is no longer any founding contrast between Being and
existence, nothing behind which there lies concealed some other thing
that does not come to light. The appearance of the commodity, of social
labour-time, of classes, is inextricably the appearance and the travesty of
their being: Being is resolved into existence, class essence into class
relations. Reduced to a pathetic philosophical incantation, the obscure
disclosure of the in-itself in the for-itself evaporates in its own conceptual
impotence.

The conclusion to Volume One of *Capital* takes up the idea of the
proletariat's 'historical mission' and its practical conditions of possibility,
which consist in the very expansion and concentration of capitalist
production. Yet *Capital* also states the converse theory of the infernal cycle
of reification.

1. According to Marx, 'economy in the use of means of production . . .
appears as a power inherent in capital and a method specific to and
characteristic of the capitalist mode of production'. This is:

> all the less surprising in that it corresponds to the semblance [*der Schein*] of the
> matter and that the capital relation actually does conceal the inner connection
> [*innern Zusammenhang*] in the state of complete indifference, externality and
> alienation [*Ausserlichkeit* and *Entfremdung*] in which it places the worker *vis-à-vis*
> the conditions of realization of his own labour.

Since the 'means of production' are for him 'a means for exploiting
labour', the worker tends to regard them with indifference, even hostility.

He behaves towards the social character of labour (the labour of others) as if it were 'a power that is alien to him'.[51]

2. 'Yet there is more to this than the alienation and indifference that the worker, as the bearer of living labour, has towards the economical, i.e. rational and frugal use of his conditions of labour.' The 'squandering of the life and health of the worker, and the depression of his conditions of existence'; physical and psychological mutilation – these become a means of raising the rate of profit.[52] Consequently:

> Capital shows itself more and more to be a social power, with the capitalist as its functionary – a power that no longer stands in any possible kind of relationship to what the work of one particular individual can create, but an alienated social power [*als entfremdete gesellschaftliche Macht*] which has gained an autonomous [*verselbständigte*] position and confronts society as a thing [*eine Sache*], and as the power that the capitalist has through this thing. The contradiction between the general social power into which capital has developed and the private power of the individual capitalists over these social conditions of production develops ever more blatantly . . .[53]

3. With the externalization [*Veräusserlichung*] of capital in the form of interest-bearing capital, 'the capital relationship attains its most superficial and fetishized form' [*erreicht seine äusserlischste und fetischertigste Form*], the 'alienated form of the capital relation'. In it, 'capital obtains its pure fetish form' [*seine reine Fetischform*]: 'capital's determinations are dissolved and its real elements are invisible'. Living capital now presents itself as a pure object; money becomes pregnant, and 'interest accrues to it no matter whether it is asleep or awake'![54] Interest-bearing capital:

> displays the conception of the capital fetish [*Kapitalfetisch*] in its consummate form, the idea that ascribes to the accumulated product of labour, in the fixed form of money at that, the power of producing surplus-value in geometric progression by way of an inherent secret quality, as a pure automaton . . . The product of past labour, and past labour itself, is seen as pregnant in and of itself with a portion of present or future living surplus labour.[55]

4. Capital is 'the products and conditions of activity of labour-power, which are rendered autonomous *vis-à-vis* this living labour-power and are personified in capital through this antithesis'. The result is 'a definite social form, and at first sight a very mysterious form': the means of labour as an alienated form that has become autonomous *vis-à-vis* labour-power (which is decidedly not the same thing as the loss of an anthropological essence). 'Just as the products become an independent power *vis-à-vis* the producers in capital and in the capitalist . . . so land is personified in the

landowner.' The result is also a 'mystification' that transforms social relations 'into properties of these things themselves (commodity)' and 'the relation of production itself into a thing (money)'. Hence the appearance of a 'bewitched and distorted world'.[56]

Value, an autonomous social relation, is imposed on individuals as a natural law. Its very elements become ossified in autonomous forms. 'The division of profit into profit of enterprise and interest . . . completes the autonomization of the form of surplus-value, the ossification of its form as against its substance, its essence.' Indeed, a portion of profit becomes completely detached from production: 'If capital originally appeared on the surface of circulation as the capital fetish . . . so it now presents itself once again in the figure of interest-bearing capital as its most estranged and peculiar form.'[57]

The discovery of abstract labour-time leads ineluctably to that of commodity fetishism. Hence 'the bewitched, distorted and upside down world', 'this autonomization and ossification of the different social elements of wealth', 'this personification of things and reification of the relations of production' [*Verdinglichung* and *Versachlichung*] – in short, a veritable 'religion of everyday life'.[58]

In these conditions, by what miracle could the proletariat free itself from the spells of an enchanted world? Without underestimating his aporias, it is still Marx that we must start from if we are to have any hope of overcoming the contradiction. The mystifications of the commodity universe present social relations as things. Marx conceives them as conflictual relations. Rather than photographing them at rest, he penetrates their innermost dynamic. Rather than seeking a criterion for classifying individuals, he unearths the lines of polarization between vast groups, whose contours and borders are fluctuating. Rather than setting off in search of a principle of classification, he travels an infinite path of determinations, aiming for the totality without attaining it. Rather than separating subject and object, he starts from their amorous embraces and reversals. Classes do not exist as separable entities, but only in the dialectic of their struggle. They do not disappear when the more vital or conscious forms of struggle die down. Heterogeneous and uneven, consciousness is inherent in the conflict that commences with the sale of labour-power and resistance to exploitation – and is unceasing.

Notes

1. Karl Marx, 'The Eighteenth Brumaire of Louis Bonaparte', in Marx, *Surveys from Exile*, Penguin/NLR, Harmondsworth 1973, p. 239; 'Economic and Philosophical Manuscripts', in Marx, *Early Writings*, trans. Rodney Livingstone and Gregor Benton, Penguin/NLR, Harmondsworth 1975, p. 288.
2. Karl Marx and Frederick Engels, 'Manifesto of the Communist Party', in Marx, *The Revolutions of 1848*, Penguin/NLR, Harmondsworth 1973, p. 67 n. 12.
3. See Ralf Dahrendorf, *Class and Class Conflict in Industrial Society*, Stanford University Press, Stanford, CA 1957.
4. For 'determinate abstraction', readers are referred to Chapter 8 below ('A New Immanence'). Pursuing this logic, it would have been illuminating to compare the class relation with other types of conflictual relation (hierarchical, sexual, national). The interested reader can consult my *La Discordance du temps*, Éditions de la Passion, Paris 1995.
5. Joseph A. Schumpeter, *Capitalism, Socialism and Democracy*, Routledge, London 1992, pp. 14–15.
6. Ibid., pp. 45–6.
7. Ibid., p. 15.
8. Ibid., p. 19. An analogous but more developed line of criticism features in Anthony Giddens, *A Contemporary Critique of Historical Materialism* (Macmillan, London and Basingstoke 1981). According to Giddens, the class relation can be regarded as the structural principle of society only under capitalism. Capitalist society nevertheless remains shot through with multiple forms of exploitation and domination that are not reducible to class relations. He therefore criticizes Marx for a dual reductionism: making class conflict an explanatory principle for all social formations; and allotting it excessive explanatory power in the case of capitalist society. This critique is based on a re-examination of the articulation of domination and exploitation in social relations. On Giddens's theses, see Erik Olin Wright, 'Giddens's Critique of Marxism', *New Left Review*, no. 138, March/April 1983.
9. Joseph Schumpeter, *Imperialism and Social Classes*, Basil Blackwell, Oxford 1951, p. 140.
10. Jozef Kotarbinski, *Leçons sur l'histoire de la logique*, Presses Universitaires de France, Paris 1964, p. 278. 'Mereology' refers to the theses of the Polish logician Stanislaw Lesniewscki.
11. For Michel Henry, 'the productive forces and social classes are not primary realities or explanatory principles, but the very things that are to be explained'. It was 'Marxism' that turned them into basic concepts against 'the thought of Marx' (Henry, *Marx, une philosophie de la réalité*, Gallimard, Paris 1976, pp. 226, 239).
12. The term 'sociology' appeared in 1838 in Comte's 47th *Cours de philosophie politique*. Whereas political philosophy, natural law or classical economics pertained to the period when revolution was in gestation, sociology emerged as an ideological product of the post-revolutionary period. With a great flourishing of societies, journals and congresses at the end of the nineteenth century and the beginning of the twentieth, it was codified as an enterprise of depoliticization (naturalization) of the social, and as an antidote to the class struggle. For Comte, what was at issue was 'ending' the revolution. In the name of social laws, Durkheim would strive to demonstrate that 'revolutions are as impossible as miracles' (Émile Durkheim, 'La philosophie dans les universités allemandes', *Revue internationale de l'enseignement*, vol. XIII, 1887). On this critique and the 'sociology of sociology', see Göran Therborn, *Science, Class and Society*, New Left Books, London 1976. From the outset, sociology drew inspiration from biology (Bichat, Cabanis) and mechanics, in order to reduce politics to a sociological determinism: 'Sociology emerged as a discourse on politics after the bourgeois revolution and came to maturity as a discourse on economics before the threat of a proletarian revolution' (*Science, Class and Society*, p. 417).

13. Antonio Gramsci, *Selections from the Prison Notebooks*, ed. and trans. Quintin Hoare and Geoffrey Nowell Smith, Lawrence & Wishart, London 1971, pp. 425–34.
14. Letter from Marx to Engels of 8 December 1857, in Marx and Engels, *Collected Works*, vol. 40, Lawrence & Wishart, London 1983, p. 217.
15. G.W.F. Hegel, *The Encyclopedia Logic*, trans. T.F. Geraets, W.A. Suchting and H.S. Harris, Hackett Publishing Company, Indianapolis and Cambridge 1991, pp. 21, 39: 'Each of the parts of philosophy is a philosophical whole, a circle that closes on itself; but in each of them the philosophical Idea is in a particular determinacy or element. Every single circle also breaks through the restriction of its element as well, precisely because it is inwardly [the] totality, and it grounds a further sphere. The whole presents itself therefore as a *circle of circles*' (p. 39; emphasis added).
16. Ibid.
17. See Karl Marx, *Grundrisse*, trans. Martin Nicolaus, Penguin/NLR, Harmondsworth 1973, p. 101 (trans. modified).
18. Ibid., p. 107.
19. On the plan and general logic of *Capital*, see my essay 'Introduction aux lectures du *Capital*', in *La Discordance des temps*.
20. Karl Marx, *Capital*, vol. 1, trans. Ben Fowkes, Penguin/NLR, Harmondsworth 1976, p. 344.
21. Ibid., p. 459.
22. Ibid., p. 799.
23. Ibid., p. 899; emphasis added.
24. Karl Marx, *Capital*, vol. 2, trans. David Fernbach, Penguin/NLR, Harmondsworth 1978, pp. 115, 117–18, 135–6, 119.
25. Biagio De Giovanni, *La teoria politica delle classi nel capitale*, De Donato, Bari 1976, p. 16.
26. Marx, *Capital*, vol. 2, pp. 115, 117–18.
27. For De Giovanni (*La teoria politica delle classi nel capitale*), Volume Two of *Capital* contains the essentials of the political theory of classes. This polemical approach has the merit of running counter to received ideas according to which class relations can be reduced to the relation of exploitation in production, and of drawing attention to the often underestimated importance of Volume Two. Nevertheless, it has the defect of fixing the theory of classes at the level of circulation, rather than logically pursuing the dynamic of their determination in reproduction as a whole.
28. '[A]ll together, as a workshop, they are the living production machine of these *products* – just as, taking the production process as a whole, they exchange their labour for capital and reproduce the capitalists' money as capital, that is to say, as value producing surplus-value, as self-expanding value' (Karl Marx, *Theories of Surplus-Value*, Part I, trans. Emile Burns, Lawrence & Wishart, London n.d., pp. 398–9); 'If we consider the aggregate *worker*, i.e. if we take all the members comprising the workshop together, then we see that their *combined activity* results materially in an *aggregate* product which is at the same time a *quantity of goods*' ('Results of the Immediate Process of Production', in *Capital*, vol. 1, p. 1040).
29. Karl Marx, *Capital*, vol. 3, trans. David Fernbach, Penguin/NLR, Harmondsworth 1981, pp. 298–300; emphasis added.
30. Ibid., p. 1025.
31. Ibid.
32. Ibid., pp. 1025–6.
33. Ibid., p. 1026; emphasis added.
34. Ibid.
35. Dahrendorf, *Class and Class Conflict in Industrial Society*.
36. Karl Marx, 'The Poverty of Philosophy', in Marx and Engels, *Collected Works*, vol. 6, Lawrence & Wishart, London 1976, p. 211.
37. Marx, 'The Eighteenth Brumaire of Louis Bonaparte', pp. 173–4.
38. Ibid., pp. 186, 245 n. 53, 243.

39. Ibid., pp. 179–80.
40. Karl Marx, 'First Draft of "The Civil War in France"', in Marx, *The First International and After*, Penguin/NLR, Harmondsworth 1974, p. 258.
41. Marx, 'The Eighteenth Brumaire', p. 197.
42. Ibid., pp. 194, 150.
43. Karl Marx, 'The General Council to the Federal Council of French Switzerland' (1870), in Marx, *The First International and After*, p. 116.
44. Letter from Engels to Marx of 7 October 1858, in Marx and Engels, *Collected Works*, vol. 40, Lawrence & Wishart, London 1983, p. 344.
45. Marx, 'The Eighteenth Brumaire of Louis Bonaparte', p. 239; emphasis added.
46. André Tosel maintains that this ontology 'inherits the philosophy of history without sharing its certainties, without guaranteeing its claims, [and that] it moves in the element of an objective teleology that is finite and dramatically open' (*Idéologie, symbolique, ontologie*, Éditions du CNRS, Paris 1987, p. 100). He is right to stress that such an ontology resumes the philosophy of history abandoned as early as *The Holy Family*, albeit a philosophy attenuated in its 'claims' and certainties. In the same collection, Costanzo Preve explicitly adopts it: 'As an ontology of social being, the philosophy of historical materialism comprises an ethics, an aesthetics, a philosophy of nature, and a philosophy of history' (p. 111).
47. Karl Marx and Frederick Engels, 'The Holy Family', in Marx and Engels, *Collected Works*, vol. 4, Lawrence & Wishart, London 1975, pp. 36–7.
48. Letter from Marx to Joseph Weydemeyer of 5 March 1852, in Marx and Engels, *Selected Correspondence*, Progress Publishers, Moscow 1975, p. 64.
49. Antonio Labriola, *Essays on the Materialist Conception of History*, trans. Charles H. Kerr, Monthly Review Press, New York and London 1966, p. 27.
50. Georg Lukács, *History and Class Consciousness*, trans. Rodney Livingstone, Merlin, London 1971, p. 23, 41, 177.
51. Marx, *Capital*, vol. 3, p. 178. This is the price to be paid for the general, undifferentiated abstract character of labour itself: 'the basis of *value* is the fact that human beings relate to each other's labour as equal, and general ... This is an abstraction' (Karl Marx, 1861–63 Manuscripts, in Marx and Engels, *Collected Works*, vol. 30, Lawrence & Wishart, London 1988, p. 232).
52. Ibid., p. 179. Inquests on workers and the numerous testimonies of those who have gone into factories to work provide ample proof. Simone Weil's *Journal d'usine* describes in a quasi-clinical manner this daily temptation to 'stop thinking', this 'situation that makes thought shrivel up' and 'rebellion become impossible except in sudden flashes': 'A manifestly inexorable and unchanging oppression does not generate rebellion in response, but submission. At Alsthom, I scarcely rebelled except on Sundays ... Outside of exceptional moments that cannot, I believe, be induced, or avoided, or even foreseen, the pressure of necessity is always for the most part sufficiently strong to maintain order': Weil, *La Condition ouvrière*, Gallimard, Paris 1979, pp. 21, 28, 145.
53. Marx, *Capital*, vol. 3, p. 373.
54. Ibid., pp. 516–17. Marx writes: 'In interest-bearing capital, therefore, this automatic fetish [*dieser automatische Fetisch*] is elaborated into its pure form, self-valorizing value, money breeding money, and in this form it no longer bears any marks of its origin. The social relation is consummated in the relationship of a thing, money, to itself' (ibid., p. 516).
55. Ibid., pp. 523–4.
56. Ibid., pp. 954–5, 963–6.
57. Ibid., p. 968.
58. Ibid., p. 969.

5

Class Struggle is No Game (Marx *contra* Game Theory and Theories of Justice)

The neoliberal offensive, the failure of the bureaucratic regimes, and the partial eclipse of the class struggle have encouraged some curious amalgams between class struggle, market categories, and contract theory. Despite some important differences, most of the representatives of 'analytical Marxism' are influenced by methodological individualism.[1] For Elster, 'all social phenomena ... are in principle explicable in ways *that only involve individuals* – their properties, their goals, their beliefs and their actions'.[2] Social conflict is engendered by exploitation as a form of interaction. By contrast, Marx's 'methodological collectivism' supposedly entails the dissolution of individuals, their desires, interests and preferences, into the undifferentiated abstraction of class or history.

Yet as early as *The German Ideology*, Marx categorically condemned the hypostases of history, society or class. Moreover, Elster recognizes the coexistence in the *Grundrisse* of a collectivist approach (dissolution of individual behaviour into the social macro-subject) and an individualist approach attentive to 'micro-motives' and 'micro-behaviour'. According to him, Marx cleverly included private interests in the social conditions of reproduction from the beginning. Its form and content are then determined by impersonal constraints. Indeed. But is this a clever trick, as Elster claims?

Socially determined, individuals in Marx do not thereby disappear into the class of which they are, as it were, the cloned representatives. The relation of exploitation (the establishment of an average rate of profit) determines the collective interest of capital *vis-à-vis* labour. Real-life capitalists are none the less pitted against one another by the harsh law of competition. Similarly, while workers have an interest in collectively resisting the extortion of surplus-value, they are subject to incessant competition and devastating rivalry on the labour market. Marx firmly holds on to both ends of the chain. He equally dismisses the tyrannical abstraction of the collective and that of egotistical individuality.

The string of quotations to which Elster proceeds destroys the inner dynamic of the thinking in *Capital*, and obscures what is decisively at stake in its organization. Marx:

> believed it possible to deduce the economic categories from one another in a way reminiscent of what Hegel had done for ontology. Yet, unlike the Hegelian categories, the economic ones also succeed each other chronologically, in the order of their historical appearance. Hence Marx had to confront the question of how the logical sequence is related to the historical one, without being able, however, to provide a consistent answer. If we attempt a synthesis of the *Grundrisse* and the opening chapters of *Capital I*, the logical or dialectical sequence embodies the following stages: product – commodity – exchange value – money – capital – labour . . . roughly the same sequence is retained. . . .[3]

Roughly! The crucial issue is the opening and the plan of *Capital*, on which Marx worked himself into the ground for a decade, proceeding from one reorganization after another, before opting for the commodity (rather than products in general). Elster looks to 'the motives of individual economic agents' for an explanation of saving and investment, which cannot be deduced from 'a conceptual analysis of money'.[4] This is to miss the essential point. Capitalism is general commodity production. In the first instance, it crystallizes in the sphere of circulation, at the point of contact between two societies. Strictly speaking, the capitalist mode of production becomes dominant when capital seizes hold of production, and productive capital subordinates commercial capital and finance capital to itself. The commodity then encapsulates the social relation as a whole. The rest follows. Self-valorizing value, capital is no less concrete than *individual economic agents* and their *motivations*. Neither autonomous nor sovereign, these subjects of rational calculation presuppose an idea of reason, a use of language, and a definition of interests that are by no means self-evident. Properly understood, what is individual interest, its rational pursuit, and the sovereign will pursuing it? The notions of interest, reason and will are heavily laden with philosophical assumptions.

Whereas the 'motives' of agents are a matter for a classical economic psychology, Marx regards capital as a social relation. From this standpoint, saving and investment are a product of unintentional fluctuations in the rate of exploitation, the renewal of fixed capital, and the rhythms of capital turnover. If the deceptive game of mirrors between methodological collectivism and methodological individualism is rejected, 'analytical

Marxism' appears in its very formulation as a combination of chalk and cheese. I have attempted to demonstrate this in connection with the theory of history. I shall now do the same *vis-à-vis* the theory of justice and exploitation.

A Non-Juridical Conception of Justice

Methodological individualism confidently espouses a theory of justice, defining a principle of fair allocation to govern reciprocal exchange between individuals in society. Social classes are supposedly either purely imaginary products of 'methodological collectivism', submerging the reality of irreducible interests in abstraction; or a useful device for classification on the basis of the unstable aggregate of individual motives. Everything is then played out in the calculated relation of the individual to the group, and game theory is more operational than class theory. Analytical Marxism is thus led to a wholesale revision of the conception of social class elaborated by Marx.

Starting from the works of Roemer and Elster, this question has given rise to a productive debate.[5] Norman Geras poses the issue of whether the condemnation of capitalism in Marx is rooted in a principle of justice. He begins by itemizing arguments contrary to this hypothesis:

- In good contractual logic (including the purchase and sale of labour-power), 'sold' labour-power belongs to the capitalist, who is henceforth legally entitled to use it without any restrictions other than those prescribed by law. The capacity to generate surplus-value possessed by this remarkable commodity is simply a 'windfall' for the buyer, not an injustice to the 'seller'.
- The wage relation cannot be deemed 'just' or 'unjust'. Conceptions of justice are, in fact, historical – that is to say, relative to a particular mode of production. Just as slavery is not 'unjust' from the standpoint of a slave society, exploitation is not 'unjust' by the contractual rules specific to general commodity production.
- The notion of distributive justice, which is theoretically questionable, fosters the practical illusion that exploitation can be corrected or eliminated by reforming income distribution. But it would be as absurd to demand fair remuneration on the basis of the wage system as to claim freedom on the basis of slavery.
- Invoking principles of justice inevitably entails a formalism that is inconceivable in the absence of the state and institutions that are, in

fact, condemned to wither away. Communist society is firmly located 'beyond justice'. 'Equal right' thus remains a bourgeois right by virtue of the fact that it is inscribed in the horizon of justice. By contrast, the needs principle, which is opposed to the abstract equivalence of the commodity order, is no longer a principle of distributive justice.

Geras offers a symmetrical refutation of this set of arguments, likewise grounded in a reading of Marx:

- Marx regarded exchange as an exchange of equivalents only from the formal viewpoint of circulation. From the standpoint of production, the wage relation cannot be regarded as an exchange of equivalents: hence the notion of 'surplus-labour' supplied 'gratis'.
- This is why Marx so frequently refers to 'robbery' in the context of exploitation. While the extortion of surplus-value is legal and legitimate for the capitalist, it remains robbery from the viewpoint of those who are exploited, who in this instance represent universal justice. 'From what Marx says about capitalist robbery', Geras concludes, 'we can infer a commitment to independent and transcendent standards of justice.'[6]
- The idea that right cannot transcend the economic structure may then be understood not in a relativist sense, but in a realist sense, illustrated by Marx's passionate interest in the distribution of free time and, more generally, social wealth.
- It is therefore appropriate to distinguish justice as an institution (according to positive law) and justice in the broad sense: 'Marx had . . . a non-juridical conception of justice.'[7] For him, need and effort constitute distributive criteria that are more pertinent than individual property, and more realistic than evasive recourse to the trump card of an 'abundance' that is as uncertain as it is indefinable.
- Capital is thus open to condemnation not only because it incites the resistance of the oppressed, but also because it is unjust.

Having expounded thesis and antithesis, Geras proposes his own synthesis under the heading 'Marx against Marx':

(a) Does the wage relation represent an exchange of equivalents? Yes and no. *Yes*, as an exchange of commodities; *no*, as a relation of production. What we have is two legitimate perspectives on one and the same phenomenon. In this instance, which is the 'appropriate' viewpoint? To the enormous confusion of his interpreters, Marx never stopped simultaneously asserting equivalence in exchange and unequal exchange. The fact that exploitation is intolerable to the oppressed does not signify that it is unjust in their eyes, for such a judgement assumes the presence in this outlook of a conception of justice. Yet Marx repeats that exploitation is robbery! How could robbery be other than unjust? It must in fact be conceded that exploitation can be both unjust and just at one and the same time. It is not unjust from the standpoint of the bourgeois right that legitimates it. It is unjust from the standpoint of the right of the oppressed, who assert themselves by resisting it. Between these two rights – an established right and a nascent right – force decides. There is nothing to guarantee that its verdict will be just. So does the choice between the two principles of justice boil down to a cold calculation of interest, there being no criterion ultimately capable of deciding between them?

(b) Geras offers a solution: 'Marx did think capitalism was unjust but he did not think he thought so.'[8] A curious escape clause: Marx's blindness about himself derived from too narrow a conception of justice, confusing justice and juridical norms on the one hand, justice and the distribution of consumer goods on the other. Even so, almost despite himself, Marx could not avoid a wider conception of justice, consonant with a universality that was not immediate but 'tendential', breaking through. Private property titles could then be deemed unjust in the name of a moral universality. Geras is conscious of the fact that such an interpretation might have something paradoxical about it: 'Some will doubtless find it mildly shocking that I attribute to Marx what is in effect a notion of natural right.'[9] Yet even in *Capital*, we find formulas characterizing land as an 'inalienable condition of existence'. Taken together with the multiple denunciations of private property as usurpation and exploitation as robbery, such formulas offer support for the hypothesis of a latent theory of natural right.

(c) Finally, can justice be vouchsafed by abundance? The notion of abundance can itself assume different meanings, depending on whether it is relative to an absolute minimum, a flexible and unlimited conception of needs, or a system of reasonable (and self-regulated) needs. Geras retains the last meaning. There, the very notion of justice is transformed, yet it does not disappear with juridical institutions. It passes from the domain of formal equality (the juridical formalism inherent in the very notion of right) to the assumption of the real inequality that governs the needs principle. Because he did not draw all the consequences of this logic, which is operative in the *Critique of the Gotha Programme* in particular, Marx, victim of his own 'impatience with the language of norms and values', allowed the confusion attaching to the 'abolition' of freedom or justice proclaimed by the *Communist Manifesto* to set in.[10]

Thus Geras seeks to reconcile the irreconcilable. In so far as the very notion of justice is alien to the sphere of production, discussing the unjust character of exploitation, in effect, makes no sense. Nothing obliges us to treat justice and theft as logically connected categories: the capitalist can perfectly well rob the worker without thereby deviating from his own idea of justice. In the last instance, Geras's synthesis rests upon the right to inconsistency: if Marx did not think what he believed he thought, the strategy pays off! Pushed into a corner, Geras aims to demonstrate that 'Marx did condemn capitalism as unjust in the light of transhistorical norms, albeit inconsistently with his own emphatic disavowals'.[11] Marx's theory thus condemned capitalist society on the basis of criteria that are by no means relative. Although it appears to develop a relativist conception of justice, it is shot through with another notion of justice (in the broad sense), irreducible to the juridical institution. While the formal antinomy between a relativist conception and a transhistorical conception of justice can result only in an impasse, there is in reality movement and mediation, a progressive development of justice. As with the slave or the feudal system in their day, capitalism and its specific representation of justice are open to condemnation in the name of a superior system. The whole problem then consists in determining how this superiority is defined, and who decides it. Here the theory of justice connects up with the theory of history according to G.A. Cohen. For him, the succession of modes of production is not an arbitrary sequence of incommensurable social systems. It implies a common normative measure rendering socialism not a simple preference, but an 'objective tendency' or 'necessity'.

If no theory of justice makes it possible to adjudicate, why should capital so often be accused of robbery? 'The description of exploitation as an unequal exchange already says it is a kind of theft,' observes Geras. Why should Marx have so frequently reverted to this theft? 'Marx need not have written like this. But he did.'[12] If the notion of justice is deemed dubious, even bourgeois, why not that of exploitation, which is connected with it? In 'buying' labour-power on the market, capital violates no principle of equity. But in consuming it as a commodity, it divests labourers not only of their time, but also of their humanity.

Despite the subtleties of interpretation, the controversy seems to have reached an impasse. By dint of privileging philological analysis over the logic of *Capital*, one ends up taking refuge in the convenient argument of inconsistency, or in a psychoanalysis of the work: 'He [Marx] was ... confused. His explicit concept of justice contradicted, and was contradicted by, the broader concept of justice implicit in his work.'[13] To dispel this confusion, it would suffice to acknowledge the ethical content of Marxism, to conceive it as a protest throughout – as, quite simply, a refusal to accept the unacceptable.

Much ado about virtually nothing? Were so much effort and so many detours required to discover a dual meaning to the idea of justice in Marx (a dual notion of justice in both broad and narrow senses, at once transhistorical and relative to the specific mode of production), just as there is a dual meaning to the notions of social classes or productive labour? In the strict or specific sense, there is nothing surprising about the fact that formal justice, based on actual inequality and duress, proves to be as limited and illusory as the contractual freedom of wage-labourers *compelled* to sell their labour-power to survive. It is no more surprising to note the contradictory unity of justice and injustice in the relation of exploitation: the unity of the formal justice of the purchase of labour-power and the actual injustice of its exploitation as a commodity. This double-dealing accords with the general duplicity of the reign of the commodity. It prolongs and reproduces the split between use-value and exchange-value, concrete labour and abstract labour, production and circulation. The internal logic of *Capital* dispels the apparent textual inconsistency.

It likewise clarifies the paradoxical ('mildly shocking', according to Geras) recourse to the universality of natural law, on condition that we understand – as does Geras when he refers to 'tendential' universality – that what is involved is not some original abstract universality, but a process of real universalization. Against a class justice, partial in all senses, is thus affirmed the development of a concrete justice that can surmount distributive formalism and tackle particular inequalities and conditions. The transition to the limit-point foreshadowed by the *Critique of the Gotha Programme* may be reckoned as illusory as the recourse to abundance to evoke the horizon of communism. They are nevertheless at the heart of Marx's problematic, and are opposed to the idea that the only kind of justice is distributive.

The vigour of the debate indicates its contemporary significance. Faced with the débâcle of bureaucratic planning, apologias for 'market socialism' resort to the contributions of game theory and a principle of justice to rectify the excesses of liberal deregulation. After a fruitless search for proof of the historical superiority of Marxism in its proclaimed scientific-ity, it is now a question of modestly rehabilitating its ethical and humanist dimension. This oscillation between a coldly economistic discourse and a fervent profession of moral faith perpetuates the questionable dissociation between facts and values, science and ethics, theory and practice.

Ellen Meiksins Wood clearly perceives what is at stake in what she calls 'rational choice Marxism', for which societies are composed of individuals endowed with different resources and seeking to employ them in the most rational fashion.[14] Following the collapse of bureaucratic collectivism, this line of argument was supposed to make it possible to construct a norma-tive theory combining market socialism, distributive justice, and individu-alist ethics. In sum, it involved a modernizing initiative, based on the Rawlsian theory of justice and communicative action, aiming to reinvigor-ate a consensual path to socialism with a human face. The enterprise is explicitly revisionist. The distributive theory of exploitation (in accor-dance with methodological individualism) is opposed to the theory of surplus-value. The relation of exploitation is effectively reduced to an allocation of comparative advantages. 'Rational choice Marxism' is thus led to consider market constraints as already given, and to treat economic motivations as deriving strictly from individual rational choices. In reality, 'the individual "properties" which motivate the "rational choice" must . . . be deduced from the "macro-economic processes" which are to be explained'.[15]

In fact, methodological individualism defends the paradoxical idea that class membership is a matter of individual choice on the basis of determi-nate endowments. Developing this conception of 'chosen' classes, Adam Przeworski counterposes to any sociological determinism the concept of contingent classes. Meiksins Wood responds with a very sensible question: do people choose their class in the same way as they choose their party or union? The exchange relation always assumes a constraining relation of production, which it simultaneously reveals and conceals. If this ABC is abandoned, it is, to say the least, inappropriate to carry on referring to 'Marxism', even of an 'analytic' variety. 'Rational choice' Marxism's claim to reconcile the logic of the structure and the return of the (inter-individual) subject culminates in the utopia of abstractly sovereign micro-subjects, reduced to embodying a ventriloquistic structure. As for the 'choice', in this bizarre wedding of liberal individualism and a rather archaic utopian socialism, there is no longer anything to choose. The model operates in a vacuum with human motivations.

Finite and Infinite Games

After a meticulous inventory of its occurrences, Jon Elster comes to the following conclusion on the notion of exploitation:

> Altogether these passages mention some fifteen groups that appear as classes in the various modes of production: bureaucrats and theocrats in the Asiatic mode of production; slaves, plebeians and patricians under slavery; lord, serf, guild-master and journeyman under feudalism; industrial capitalists, financial capitalists, landlords, peasants, petty bourgeoisie and wage labourers under capitalism. The task is to construct an intensional definition consistent both with this enumeration and with the theoretical constraints on the notion. In particular, classes must be defined so as to be at least potential collective actors. Also, the interests they have as collective actors must somehow emerge out of their economic situation. These are broad constraints, but serve to rule out of court at least some proposals. Income groups are not classes, nor are groupings defined by ethnic, religious or linguistic criteria.[16]

Elster considers the property (or non-property) relation in the means of production, as well as the distribution of classes exclusively according to the relation of exploitation, too crude: 'if we want classes to be relevant for social struggle and collective action, they should not be defined in terms of exploitation, since no one knows exactly where the dividing line between exploiters and exploited is to be drawn'. Conversely, the 'definition of class in terms of domination and subordination is too behavioural and insufficiently structural'.[17]

Accordingly, Elster proposes a general definition of classes in terms of endowments and behaviour:

> The endowments include tangible property, intangible skills and more subtle cultural traits. The behaviours include working vs. not working, selling vs. buying labour-power, lending vs. borrowing capital, renting vs. hiring land, giving vs. receiving commands in the management of corporate property. These enumerations are intended as exhaustive. *A class is a group of people who by virtue of what they possess are compelled to engage in the same activities if they want to make the best use of their endowments.* Although I believe this definition is quite satisfactory both from the extensional and the theoretical point of view, it is somewhat defective on the methodological side. The admission of variable objective functions is one weakness, the admission of non-tangible endowments another. Also, of course, it may turn out that the notion thus constructed is less useful in explaining social conflict than Marx expected it to be.[18]

This definition of classes obeys the rational constraint of the optimal employment of endowments. Elster recognizes that reducing class struggle to a game in which the cards are distributed at the outset according to 'non-tangible endowments' is open to question. It would have been prudent to clarify the analogy: is it a finite or an infinite game? A finite game has a precise beginning and end. It is played according to contractual rules within specified limits of time and space. It finishes with a decisive move, crowned with victory or a title. An infinite game, in contrast, has neither beginning nor end. It knows no limits of space or number. Each of its rounds 'opens to players a new horizon of time'.[19] Its rules can vary over the course of the game. It does not end in victory or defeat, but springs to life again in a perpetual process of birth and renewal that establishes a new field of possibilities. The difference is significant.

The finite game can serve as a model for discourses on the end of history. Destined to conclude, it makes it possible to rationalize the past according to the present, to 'look backward and see how the sequence of moves . . . could have resulted only in this outcome'. It thus celebrates the triumph of the past over the future. Strategic foresight is reduced to explanation by anticipation, invalidating all subsequent research. Contrariwise, infinite games escape the verdict of the outcome, and preserve an open future. Their players 'play in complete openness', and 'continue their play in the expectation of being surprised'. With each surprise, the past discloses a new beginning: 'Inasmuch as the future is always surprising, the past is always changing.' It is no longer a question of training for the repetition and mastery of a familiar pattern, but of being alert to the invention that replays an unfinished past in the future. Stretching towards this receding horizon, the infinite player 'does not consume time but generates it'. Each moment is 'the beginning of an event', 'moving toward a future which itself has a future'. Whereas the player of the finite game is content to recap the knowledge that the same causes will produce the same effects, players of the infinite give themselves over to the narrative that invites them to reconsider what they thought they knew.[20]

The class struggle pertains more to the infinite game: there is no beginning, no limit, no endgame. Nor is there any referee to blow the whistle and send someone off, to ensure that the rules are observed, and to anoint the victor. The last word is never spoken. Like the show, the game must go on. Memories become weighed down with the experience of the losing and winning moves of previous rounds, to the point of exhaustion, in the mists of the horizon, when an improbable messianic irruption will re-establish the provisional meaning of the distance that has been travelled.

How can we preserve all our finite games in an infinite game? How are we to resist indifference both to the derisory winning of the round and to the no less derisory illusion of its victory? How should we struggle – not to confirm the course of history, but to alter its possibilities by continually pushing back the limits of the game? The answer probably lies in politics, 'the art of the possible' – not in the sense prosaically given it by Bismarck, but as a strategy of awakening that can interrupt the catastrophic sequence of mechanical time.

Like an infinite game, the class struggle knows only provisional victories (and compromises). But the comparison has its limits. Game theory has as its principle that 'no one can play if compelled to play', and that 'anyone who must play cannot play'. Elster takes account of the problem when he apologizes for including 'variable objective functions and non-tangible endowments'. Individually, one can always seek to change games, and alter the situation, by switching from one class to another. In modern societies, social mobility permits such transfers and promotions. Within certain limits, the individual can thus entertain the illusion of choosing his or her class, situation and place at the conference table. Exemplary success stories perpetuate the myth of this freedom. Collectively, roles are nevertheless securely distributed and maintained by social reproduction.

The struggle is not a game: it is a conflict. In it, the oppressed are condemned to resist on pain of being purely and simply crushed. The obligation to struggle precludes any model in terms of games. Without beginning or end, this conflict is a pitiless, close-quarters battle, whose rules vary with the strength of the protagonists.

This and That Side of Justice

Roemer and Elster are perfectly justified in establishing a general theory of exploitation that subordinates class theory to a theory of justice. But to the extent that they claim to be inspired by Marx, they are obliged explicitly to situate their initiative with respect to the hard core of his theory, that is, exploitation. In the event, they do so obliquely, through an individualization of exploitation, in accordance with the theory of justice.[21] In order to identify its premises, Elster returns to the numerous denunciations of exploitation as daylight robbery: 'I shall argue that despite many statements by Marx to the contrary, both the theory of exploitation in *Capital* and the theory of communism in the *Critique of the*

Gotha Program embody principles of justice.'[22] Here we recognize one of the positions expounded by Norman Geras. However, the fact that the 'word "exploitation" is highly value-laden, with overtones of moral wrongness and unfairness', is insufficient to permit the conclusion that the notions of social justice or injustice *ipso facto* imply a distributive theory of justice. The *Critique of the Gotha Programme* in its entirety is, in fact, opposed to the temptation to define a 'fair wage' or a 'normal working day'. In so far as exploitation is a class relation, not an individual injustice, its negation consists neither in just distribution nor in outright abolition of surplus labour, but in democratic control over the social surplus product and its allocation.

Moreover, Elster cites numerous texts of Marx's that are manifestly foreign to any theory of justice. In *The German Ideology*, communism is not defined as a state of justice to be attained: 'Communism is not for us a *state of affairs* which is to be established, an *ideal* to which reality [will] have to adjust itself. We call communism the *real* movement which abolishes the present state of things.'[23] The labour of the negative does not amount to developing a principle of fair allocation: 'The working class . . . have no ideals to realize, but to set free the elements of the new society with which old collapsing bourgeois society itself is pregnant.'[24] In line with the same logic, Volume Three of *Capital* firmly rejects the notion of natural fairness as absurd:

> The justice of transactions between agents of production consists in the fact that these transactions arise from the relations of production as their natural consequence. The legal forms in which these economic transactions appear as voluntary actions of the participants, as the expression of their common will and as contracts that can be enforced on the parties concerned by the power of the state, are mere forms that cannot themselves determine this content. They simply express it. The content is just so long as it corresponds to the mode of production and is adequate to it. It is unjust as soon as it contradicts it.[25]

It is impossible to be more explicit. In Marx there is no general, ahistorical definition of justice. The concept of justice is immanent in social relations. Each mode of production has its own. It makes no sense to pronounce exploitation 'unjust' without further explanation: from the standpoint of capital, exploitation is regarded as compensation for the risk, initiative or responsibility of the entrepreneur. It seems fair so long as it partakes of the famous 'correspondence' between the juridical sphere and the mode of production. When it is challenged, it is not in the name of justice set against injustice, of pure right against absolute non-right. That would be too simple. In reality, two representations of right clash, in the name of formally antagonistic juridical arguments: there is an antinomy, right against right. The sequel is familiar: between two equal rights, force is the arbiter. For it is indeed the case that right, while it is not reducible to force, is never wholly foreign to it, even in the initial establishment of its legitimacy.

Some critics of Marx spot a dangerous lacuna here. In the name of some far-off withering away of law, the absence of a positive theory of justice allegedly leaves a vacuum that is all too conducive to bureaucratic fiat. Even so, it is scarcely legitimate to misinterpret Marx's position on the basis of a few scattered pages on 'daylight robbery'. The formulations of *Wages, Price and Profit* are unequivocal:

> To clamour for *equal or even equitable retribution* on the basis of the wages system is the same as to clamour for *freedom* on the basis of the slavery system. What you think just or equitable is out of the question. The question is: What is necessary and unavoidable with a given system of production?[26]

Thus what is at stake is not a theory of justice, but a different idea of justice, which assumes the overthrow of the existing order. Having himself noted these unequivocal lines, Elster dismisses them with a terse comment: 'Marx in these passages does not assert that capitalist exploitation *is* just, only that it appears to be so.'[27] It is obviously difficult for him to relinquish his general idea of justice.

Thus, Marx does not regard capitalist exploitation as just or unjust. He merely observes that it cannot be deemed unjust from the standpoint of the capitalist mode of production, its logic and ideological values. Any judgement about justice involves a partisan stance. Elster, for his part, seeks a compromise. Denying the transhistorical justice of capitalist transactions, Marx merely 'denied the "transhistorical" not the "justice" part. This . . . is the only unstrained interpretation of the passages cited. These passages offer no *argument* for the relative nature of rights and justice.'[28] This interpretation is, precisely, highly strained. The critique of juridical formalism and equality based on equal amounts for all is a constant of the Marxian problematic. Allen Wood vigorously reasserts this against the theses of 'analytical Marxism':

> Marx rejects the idea of equality because he views it in practice as a pretext for class oppression . . . A system of equal rights might lead to a very unequal distribution of wealth . . . We ought to distinguish Marx's attitude towards equality as a right from his attitude towards equality as a goal . . . Marx's attitude towards the ideal of equal rights is highly critical. One of the main reasons Marx attacks the notion of equality is its close association in people's minds

with the notions of right and justice . . . Marx does believe that capital exploits and oppresses the workers, but he does not attack exploitation or oppression on the grounds of right or justice.[29]

Right and justice are themselves to be established according to a self-referential loop. To take sides is thus, indissociably, to establish right by giving it force, and to legitimate force promoted to the dignity of right. Marx thus considered that equality was always essentially a political notion of bourgeois provenance.

In *Anti-Dühring*, Engels notes that the demand for equality always has a dual significance. On the one hand, it represents an instinctive revolutionary response to social inequality; on the other, it represents a response to the bourgeois demand for equality: 'In both cases the real content of the proletarian demand for equality is the demand for the *abolition of classes*.'[30] Ignoring the consistency of this approach, Elster allows himself to attribute a general theory of justice to Marx (and Engels): 'Marx's theory of exploitation, and notably the frequent characterization of profit as theft, only make sense if we impute to him a theory of distributive justice.'[31] This loan is unduly generous! A review of the problematic of transition sketched in the *Critique of the Gotha Programme* will supply the evidence. Philippe Van Parijs concedes that the two principles stated by Marx there ('to each according to his labour' and 'to each according to his needs') make any comparison between Rawls and Marx difficult. The first principle is situated 'short of' distributive justice, while the second is 'beyond' it: an elegant way of saying that Marx never situated himself on the terrain of distributive justice.

Three interlinked issues illustrate this decisive point.

1. *The problem of 'just distribution'* is tackled head-on in the *Critique of the Gotha Programme*. '[G]iven the present mode of production,' Marx inquires, 'is not [the present system of distribution], in fact, the only "just" system of distribution?' The very notion is a 'hollow phrase', setting in motion an ideological machinery whose every component poses a new enigma: what is the social product? To whom does it belong? How is it to be divided? Marx never succumbs to the illusion of an egalitarian distribution between producers. Social reproduction obviously cannot be reduced to individual consumption. In any complex society, a surplus product is required. The key to the mystery lies in the political arbitrations that make it possible to establish a consumption fund and an accumulation fund, according to priorities and needs that always remain open to

discussion. The theme of just distribution, on the other hand, risks demagogically encouraging a simplistic egalitarianism:

> If we start by taking 'proceeds of labour' to mean the product of labour, then the cooperative proceeds of labour are the *total* social product. From this the following must be deducted:
> *Firstly*: cover to replace the means of production used up.
> *Secondly*: an additional portion for the expansion of production.
> *Thirdly*: a reserve or insurance fund in case of accidents, disruption caused by natural calamities, etc.[32]

Marx makes it clear that these deductions can on no account be calculated by 'reference to justice'.

Once these deductions have been made, there remains the portion of the total product allocated to consumption:

> But before this is distributed to individuals the following further deductions must be made:
> *Firstly: the general costs of all administration not directly appertaining to production.* . . .
> *Secondly: the amount set aside for needs communally satisfied,* such as schools, health services, etc. . . .
> *Thirdly: a fund for people unable to work,* etc., in short, for what today comes under so-called official poor relief.

Individual shares thus enter the picture only in the context of this social distribution: 'The "undiminished proceeds of labour" have meanwhile already been quietly "diminished", although as a member of society the producer still receives, directly or indirectly, what is withheld from him as a private individual.'[33] The problematic of allocation is thus symmetrical with that of exploitation. Overall reproduction takes precedence over individual distribution. The major decisions about resource allocation are first of all a matter of political choice.

2. *The question of 'equal right'* is dealt with in a frequently quoted and discussed passage from the *Critique of the Gotha Programme*:

> *equal right* is here still – in principle – a *bourgeois right,* although principle and practice are no longer at loggerheads, while the exchange of equivalents in commodity exchange only exists *on the average* and not in the individual case. In spite of such progress this *equal right* still constantly suffers a bourgeois limitation. The right of the producers is *proportional* to the labour they do; the equality consists in the fact that measurement is *by the same standard,* labour.

Yet real individuals and concrete labour are unequal. Equal right thus goes together with the abstraction inherent in general commodity production and the abstraction of labour in particular. As for the anonymous labourer, or the man without qualities, stripped of individual gifts and tastes, it remains 'an unequal right for unequal labour'. Accordingly, Marx stresses, '*in its content [it is] one of inequality, like any other right*'. Juridical formalism assumes the equality of that which is not equal. The reduction of human beings to their abstract labour-power, a temporal shell, allows it to do so. This formal equality can constitute progress (though this is not the issue, since it is also the case that '[r]ight can never rise above the economic structure of a society and its contingent cultural development'); it nevertheless remains indissociable from real inequality. A concrete right, taking actual differences into account, 'would have to be unequal rather than equal'.[34]

3. Finally, *the question of labour certificates*, already broached in *The Poverty of Philosophy* and *A Contribution to the Critique of Political Economy*, is further developed in the *Critique of the Gotha Programme*. If it became richer in the course of these various polemics, the line of argument scarcely altered in its essentials. Elster misjudges the significance of a controversy that is decisive for the theory of justice with which he wants to credit Marx at all costs. Three texts clarify the debate perfectly.

In *The Poverty of Philosophy*, Marx polemicizes against Proudhon's pretension to apply an 'equalitarian' formula for distribution 'by transforming all men into immediate workers exchanging equal amounts of labour'.[35] This idea, he says, draws inspiration from an old English socialist tradition. Thus, Mr Bray, author of *Labour's Wrongs and Labour's Remedy*, proposed a direct exchange between producers on the basis of certificates representing hours of labour. The consequence of such a fantasy is immediately apparent. If Peter possesses twelve hours, while Paul works only six, Peter will have the option of consuming the product of his own labour, or enjoying the wasted hours of the right to be lazy exercised by Paul: 'Everyone will want to be Paul, there will be a competition to occupy Paul's position, a competition in idleness.' This absurd hypothesis is not unrelated to the reality of bureaucratic chaos and negligence. To decree the abolition pure and simple of the law of value, as opposed to ensuring the real conditions for its gradual disappearance, leads straight to general irrationality:

> Well, then! What has the exchange of equal quantities of labour brought us? Overproduction, depreciation, excess of labour followed by unemployment; in short, economic relations such as we see in present-day society, minus the competition of labour ... Thus, if all the members of society are supposed to

be immediate workers, the exchange of equal quantities of hours of labour is possible only on condition that the number of hours to be spent on material production is agreed on beforehand. But such an agreement negates individual exchange.[36]

This is the essential thing. Production and distribution are social practices. Direct exchange (not socially mediated) of labour between the direct producers is a bad Robinsonnade. Exchange assumes a common measure. If it is not the market that determines it, it can be an agreement. But in that case, individual exchange is no longer the means of distribution, and distributive justice can operate only if it is subordinated to the general agreement:

> What is today the result of capital and the competition of workers among themselves will be tomorrow, if you sever the relation between labour and capital, an actual agreement based upon the relation between the sum of productive forces and the sum of existing needs. But such an agreement is a condemnation of individual exchange, and we are back again at our first conclusion!

In reality, the mode of exchange of products is organically linked to their mode of production. Thus, individual exchange is inscribed straight away in a relation of production characterized by exploitation: 'no individual exchange without class antagonism'. Distributive justice cannot escape this primary antagonism. The illusion of individual exchange typically derives from an ideological representation sealed by commodity fetishism:

> Mr. Bray turns the *illusion* of the respectable bourgeois into an *ideal* he would like to attain. In a purified individual exchange, freed from all the elements of antagonism he finds in it, he sees an *'equalitarian'* relation which he would like society to adopt. Mr. Bray does not see that this equalitarian relation, this *corrective ideal* that he would like to apply to the world, is itself nothing but the reflection of the actual world; and that therefore it is totally impossible to reconstitute society on the basis of what is merely an embellished shadow of it.

If it is conceded that the system of labour certificates is ultimately a naive variant of distributive justice, Marx delivers a categorical response to the theory of justice here: it is to be attributed to the 'corrective ideal' and the ideological 'illusion' whereby the 'embellished shadow' of this vale of tears prefigures paradise regained.[37]

Ten years later, the *Contribution to the Critique of Political Economy* takes as its target John Gray's proposals.[38] In exchange for the commodity, the producer was to receive a certificate testifying to the quantity of labour contained in it. He would thus possess bank notes for a week, a day, or an hour of labour, serving as certificates for purchasing the commodities stocked in the general stores of the bank. This solution derives from simplistic reasoning. Observing that time is the immanent measure of values, Gray asks why another – external – monetary measure should be added to it. This amounts to asking why exchange-value is expressed in prices and pretending to abolish this logical metamorphosis, whose mediation is ensured by circulation and competition. Instead of resolving this complex question, Gray 'assumed that commodities could be directly compared with one another as products of social labour'. This is to want to revert to a barter economy, and get shot of the mystery and mystical character of commodities: they 'are the direct product of isolated, independent individual kinds of labour, and through their alienation in the course of individual exchange they must prove that that they are general social labour'. On the basis of commodity production, labour thus becomes social labour only 'as a result of the universal alienation of individual kinds of labour'. Money partakes of this necessary transition via universal alienation, without which forms of private labour would remain incommensurable and mutually indifferent. Gray's error thus consists in positing the labour-time contained in commodities as '*immediately social*' – that is to say, as 'communal labour-time or labour-time of directly associated individuals'. He harbours the illusion of being able to organize non-commodity distribution on the basis of commodity production: '*goods are to be produced as commodities but not exchanged as commodities.* Gray entrusts the realisation of this pious wish to a national bank.' Yet '[t]he dogma that a commodity is immediately money or that the particular labour of a private individual contained in it is immediately social labour, does not of course become true because a bank believes in it and conducts its operations in accordance with this dogma'.[39]

Finally, in the *Critique of the Gotha Programme*, the problem of labour certificates is tackled from another angle – no longer as a justifiable improvement in the framework of commodity production, but in communist society 'just as it *emerges* from capitalist society . . . still stamped with the birth-marks of the old society'. Marx examines the idea that the individual producer should receive back 'from society' (once the necessary general deductions have been made for collective funds for insurance, accumulation, administration, etc.) 'exactly what he has given it'. He could then exchange a certificate made out in labour-time against objects representing an equivalent quantity of social labour: 'The same amount of labour he has given to society in one form, he receives back in another.'

The objection raised by Marx no longer bears on the illusory character of the measure, since the socialization of production now renders it conceivable, but on the very principle of equity involved in it. This formally equal exchange in fact contains the 'birth-marks' of the old society from which the new society has the greatest difficulty in emerging:

> Clearly, the same principle is at work here as that which regulates the exchange of commodities as far as this is an exchange of equal values. Content and form have changed because under the new conditions no one can contribute anything except his labour and conversely nothing can pass into the ownership of individuals except individual means of consumption. The latter's distribution among individual producers, however, is governed by the same principle as the exchange of commodity equivalents: a given amount of labour in one form is exchanged for the same amount in another.[40]

Thus, the critique of the system of labour certificates changes terrain here. In the context of a transition to communism, it deepens into a more fundamental critique of 'equal right'.

The whole polemic on labour certificates can be summarized thus: 'If value is divided into value and price, the same labour time appears at once as equal and unequal to itself – something that is not possible on the basis of labour certificates.'[41] The money form is the precise form of this division.

Farewell Value, Abstract Labour . . .

The individualist postulate of analytical Marxism reduces exploitation to an inter-individual relationship, and assimilates class struggle to game theory. The so-called 'prisoner's dilemma' illustrates the contradiction between collective and individual interest in this respect. Various legends have it that Marx naively ignored this antagonism in the name of class consciousness. On the contrary, he describes its mechanism with great precision:

> In practical life we find not only competition, monopoly and the antagonism between them, but also the synthesis of the two, which is not a formula, but a movement. Monopoly produces competition, competition produces monopoly. Monopolists compete among themselves; competitors become monopolists. If the monopolists restrict their mutual competition by means of partial associations, competition increases among the workers; and the more the mass of proletarians grows as against the monopolists of one nation, the more desperate competition becomes between the monopolists of different nations.[42]

Just as competition between capitalists is incessant, so it is between proletarians, whose common interest in the face of capitalism is undermined by competition on the labour market.

Elster concludes that an objective interest cannot in any eventuality constitute a goal: such a thing is expressed only if it coincides, or can be made to coincide, with the interests of the relevant individuals. Objective interest traces a horizon of possibilities in which the intentionality of choice is inscribed.[43] Game theory concludes that in such a case, if the game is played only once, collective action is bound to misfire. Yet the class struggle unfolds incessantly and over time. It involves memorizing and transmitting experiences. Once again, to struggle is not to play.

The 'free-rider' problem is often used to illustrate the idea that it can be individually advantageous to abstain from collective action and avoid a dispute. If rational individuals do co-operate, the converse problem arises: what now has to be explained is why the members of a class co-operate when their individual interests, properly understood, prompt them to act as free-riders.

Numerous parameters of real conflict (history, tradition, culture) elude modelling in game-theoretical terms. Thus, every actual strike demonstrates that the free-rider's interest in playing the role of strike-breaker (he benefits from the collective gain in case of victory, and earns managerial respect in the event of defeat) comes into contradiction with the more or less open reprisals he will suffer at the hands of his comrades long after the struggle is over. In the same way, the most sophisticated computer simulations have the greatest difficulty predicting the medium-term consequences of the effects of memory. Yet in actual conflicts, the individual and collective memory of earlier experiences is an essential dimension of strategic behaviour.

Every trade-union militant has experienced this contradiction. Those who strike risk their wages and sanctions if the strike fails. If it succeeds, non-strikers will benefit from the gains secured without having taken the slightest risk. The non-striking free-rider believes he can wager on both outcomes and win every time: if the strike fails, he loses nothing; if it wins, he benefits like everyone else. The calculation whereby individual agents are logically tempted to play the free-rider is, however, limited to the horizon of a finite, amnesiac game.

Elster concludes that a mature working class should be capable of biding its time, avoiding the free-riding tendencies of both the yellows (egotistical calculation) and the reds (vanguardist impatience). In modernized form, this represents the return of the old Kautskyist dream of being precisely 'on time': the socialist movement is no longer a school of struggle, subject to the rhythms and risks of the conflict, but a school of patience and discipline where the proletariat learns to march at the same pace, and to foil untimely provocations. Social contradictions, all too real, are resolved neither by education nor by theory. They are inherent in the general process of division characteristic of capitalist society: concrete labour/abstract labour, man/citizen, private/public, producer/consumer ... Thus, each capitalist has an interest in his competitor's workers consuming more and his own less: each capitalist wants his own workers to save, because he deals with them solely as workers, but not other workers, because he relates to them as consumers. Investigations of behaviour generally estimate that collective action is less likely the more important the group is. To the extent that the loss from each agent through abstention diminishes, the advantage of the 'free-rider' increases with the size of the group. Adopting these arguments, analytical Marxism, while putting its finger on some genuine problems, reduces class struggle to an abstraction. This struggle, which is never a sum of rational calculations, partakes of the event and the logic of 'fused groups'.[44]

According to Elster, Marx's attachment to the centrality of class conflict 'is increasingly seen as an implausible proposition': it evinces a total lack of 'intellectual discipline'.[45] This snap judgement betrays above all a failure of understanding. For Marx, the centrality of class conflict does not result from a phenomenal description of antagonisms. Inherent in the relations of production and exchange, it expresses the very structure of the mode of production articulated with other forms of conflictuality. Therefore it cannot be a question of grasping a society sometimes according to class relations, and sometimes according to collective actors engaged in diverse conflicts. In the capitalist mode of production, the class relation constitutes the key that makes it possible to decipher the conflictual dynamic of history.

Must we conclude with Elster that for Marx, '[o]bjectively defined classes tend to acquire class consciousness, or else to disappear', while '[n]on-class collective actors become increasingly marginal over time'?[46] Several of Marx's texts identify the 'historical party', or 'the party in the broad sense', with the multiform movement of class organization. The transient party, or party in the narrow sense, is then reduced to an occasional organization called upon to perform a limited function in a given conjuncture. For a long time, this vision underlay the conception of the party in the Second International, whose flagship was German social democracy: a party that encompasses, and has overall responsibility for, the set of trade-union, co-operative and associational forms with which the working class equips itself. In this perspective, it is possible to imagine 'collective actors' or 'social movements' being summoned to merge into the vast movement that constitutes the class as a 'historical party'. It is also possible to envisage the existence of 'non-contemporaneous' forms of conflict (inasmuch as the dominance of a mode of production is insufficient to synchronize and homogenize the contradictions of a particular social formation). These are not parallel and indifferent to one another, but transverse to class relations, whether they be antagonisms of sex, nationality, or ecological issues. Thus, a politics of women's liberation is not reducible to its anti-capitalist dimension; on the other hand, it cannot identify the root of the oppression except on the basis of the way in which the commodification of bodies and the division of labour have reshaped this oppression. Similarly, while abolishing the blind law of the market does not suffice to resolve the major ecological challenges, radical ecology is inconceivable unless market logic and the reign of private interest are challenged.

Elster entertains 'a broader historical perspective', in which class struggle is decisive solely for '*epochal transformations*', but only to reject it: 'One might fully accept, that is, the pervasive presence throughout history of social conflicts that cannot be reduced to class struggle in any of the proposed ways, and yet argue that these play no role in the setting-up of new relations of production.'[47] This would be a tactical response, aiming to rescue the centrality of class conflict by distinguishing between economic and non-economic conflicts, while conceding on a secondary point. In reality, from Marx's viewpoint, there is no difficulty acknowledging the existence of conflicts that are not immediately reducible to class struggle. His political or concrete historical analyses are replete with these antagonisms, which are indirectly related to the basic classes. Once this relative autonomy is granted, the real problem consists in elucidating the mediations and specific articulation of the different contradictions. Such work cannot end up at the level of abstraction to which the relations of production in general belong. It operates in the nub of the social formation, in concrete struggles – in a word, in the interplay of displacements and condensations in which the conflict finds its particular political expression. At this level, not only class relations, but also the state, the institutional network, and religious and juridical representations come into play.

In criticizing Marx for an economistic reduction of class conflict, Elster is on the wrong track. It is true that vulgar Marxism readily identifies the economy with the gravity of matter in contrast to a deracinated politics and the ephemera of ideology, which melts into air. As soon as they are translated into deeds, political and juridical decisions possess their own material weight and density. As it actually unfolds, the class struggle does not boil down to an economic opposition.

Conflating vulgar Marxism with Marx's theory, methodological individualism ends up abandoning certain of its pillars, starting with the law of value, the concept of abstract labour, and the labour theory of value: 'When labour is heterogeneous, the contributions cannot be measured on a common scale.'[48] But this is precisely where what is at stake in the 'critique of political economy' is to be found: by what miracle, what alchemy of exchange, do heterogeneous products and labours become commensurable? Methodological individualism cannot understand it. Once value is assumed to be quantifiable on the basis of individual needs and consumption, social determination disintegrates. The worker's freedom of choice as a consumer is 'quite incompatible with the assumption of "fixed coefficients of consumption" underlying the notion of the value of labour-power in *Capital*'.[49] A cruder error can scarcely be imagined. Marx never claimed to quantify the social labour-time embodied in the commodity on the basis of 'fixed coefficients of consumption'. Its determination occurs a posteriori, according to the verdict of the market, the historical development of recognized needs, and hence class struggle and the balance of forces. That is why it is fluid and fluctuating.

Elster's enormous blunder derives from a failure to understand the general logic of *Capital* and a confusion between value, prices and wages, between social needs and effective consumption. Marx supposedly clung to the labour theory of value because accounting in value made it easier to reveal and condemn the essence of the capitalist system, whereas price movements did not go beyond appearances. Prices are precisely not a mere appearance, but the expression and determinate manifestation of their essence: irreducible to value, they are nevertheless not immaterial to it. The mysteries of capital are played out in this hieroglyphic relation of simultaneous revelation and dissimulation.

There are reasons for Elster's blindness. They invariably derive from the same methodological postulate: 'individual behaviour can never be explained by reference to values, which, being invisible, have no place in the purposive explanation of action'.[50] In truth, this is a curious method. No doubt 'individual behaviour' cannot be deduced from the occult law of value. Yet notwithstanding the good sense it advertises, Elster's formulation is saturated with ideological presuppositions. Why cannot something that is 'invisible' enter into the explanation of action? The critique of political economy and psychoanalysis both recognize the particular efficacy of causes that are not only 'invisible', but 'absent' (the lack of the penis in the aetiology of neuroses). Elster is careful to specify that he is referring to the 'purposive' explanation of action. Purposive explanation or purposive action? As required by rational choice, he claims to be accounting for the motives and motivations for action of a subject endowed with reasons that are transparent to his own deliberation. This represents a major metaphysical wager, on subject and reason alike!

Finally, it will be objected, Elster is dealing with individual behaviour. There is nothing to prevent us thinking that collective behaviour might have some relation with the invisible universe of essences. Certainly, but such a hypothesis would dispatch us straight to the inferno of methodological collectivism! Methodological individualism, by contrast, requires that we adhere strictly to the primacy of individual behaviour, and therefore replace the critique of political economy with social psychology.

This is certainly an 'analytical' approach. But in what sense is it 'Marxist'?

Once abstract labour has been abandoned, value theory rejected, and classes dissolved into games, what remains of what Georges Sorel once called 'Marx's Marxism' (which might today be designated 'critical Marxism', without worrying about the pleonasm)? All that survives are some incoherent scraps of his deconstructed thought: 'surely it was Marx's intention that labour values of commodities should be definable in terms of labour expenditure only, and not be sensitive to changes in the reward of labour'.[51] In the logic of *Capital*, this sentence is meaningless. How could the labour values of commodities be defined exclusively in terms of labour expenditure? From the outset, this labour is time and labour-power socially determined by competition, by the tendential equalization of the profit rate, and by the needs historically taken into account in reproduction. Social recognition of these needs takes effect through incessant struggle over labour-time, social protection and remuneration. The expenditure of labour-time in the sphere of production is an abstraction. It presupposes the overall process of reproduction that socially determines labour-time. The beginning always presupposes the end.

Elster, for his part, persists in repeating that 'Marx never explains . . . how more and less intensive labour can be reduced to a common standard of labour time'; and that 'the presence of genuinely and irreducibly heterogeneous labour is a major stumbling-block for Marxist economics'.[52] Not only for Marxist economics: it is precisely the problem of the capitalist economy. Marx responds to it by making out, behind the overly biblical simplicity of the commodity, its 'theological subtleties', its division into use-value and exchange-value, and of labour into concrete labour and abstract labour.[53]

In the strict sense, methodological individualism and the logic of *Capital* are incompatible.[54] Criticizing 'the interpretative error that consists in saying that value is expressed in abstract labour and measured in labour-time', Tran Hai Hac dots the i's:

> On the contrary, it is abstract labour that is expressed in the form of value, and the measure of labour-time in the form of magnitude of value . . . The value of a commodity cannot be expressed in labour-time since it is *impossible to measure the quantity of labour directly* . . . For the only time that is directly measurable in labour units is the time of concrete labour, not the time of abstract labour . . . This amounts to saying that value can only be grasped in its price form, and that there is thus no measure of value other than by its form.[55]

Thus abstract labour is a form of social labour. That is why methodological individualism ignores it. At this point, the whole edifice of the Marxian critique crumbles. For 'it is not labour in itself that creates value, but only labour in as much as it expresses the determinate social conditions of production, abstract labour'. Even so, the problem of the notion of abstract labour is certainly not resolved. For some, as general labour, it is simply a logical abstraction, a hypothesis of commensurability assuming the homogeneity of labours that are patently not homogeneous. For others, in contrast, it is a physiological reality, an expenditure of energy that is present in any labour activity regardless of its concrete forms. In the event, it is neither the one nor the other: 'The form refers, on the one hand, to the social relation that constitutes its internal determination, but also, on the other hand, to the material medium that is its external determination.'[56]

Concrete labour does not disappear into abstract labour any more than use-value is abolished in value. In social labour, their unity is always strained, conflictual. The reduction of the diversity of practical knowledge, skills, and competence to a homogeneous and empty time is always an act of violence. Measuring all wealth, and dictating the relations between beings, according to the exclusive imperative of labour-time does not eradicate this ever more acute and painful contradiction. Non-quantifiable, irreducible to a standard temporal measure, the work of art (or of creation in general) challenges this formal equalization by denying its own character as labour. In the *Grundrisse*, Marx clearly foresaw that the historical tendency of labour to enrich itself with intellectual labour and become more complex would render this measure increasingly 'miserable'.

Its antinomic quantification carries its own limit within it. The temporal abstraction that denies the particular in the universal, intensity in homogeneous duration, is that of capital as a social relation:

> Labour time itself exists as such only subjectively, only in the form of activity. In so far as it is exchangeable (itself a commodity) as such, it is defined and differentiated not only quantitatively but also qualitatively, and is by no means general, self-equivalent labour time; rather, labour time as subject corresponds as little to the general labour time which determines exchange values as the particular commodities and products correspond to it as object.[57]

Thus, the same time is opposed to itself in so far as it forms use-value and determines exchange-value.

The reduction of complex labour to simple labour occurs every day in the process of exchange. Effective labour-time must be translated into a time of average intensity. Once a regulative principle intervenes to make the link between producer and consumer, seller and buyer, this mediator is not money but, more fundamentally, abstract labour. It does not make it possible to respond to a simple problem, which at first sight is insoluble: commensurability. The contrary relationship between use-value and value refers more profoundly to a 'clash of temporalities': abstract/general labour-time cannot exist without the concrete/particular labour-time whose negation it represents. *Qua* universality that transcends and incorporates particular acts of labour, abstract labour is not an empirical reality. Nor is it the mere average of the labour of different individuals, but a social abstraction of which actually working human beings become the 'simple organs'. Thus, the relation of exploitation such as it appears in the sphere of production always presupposes social relations as a whole (or reproduction):

> The value of a commodity would therefore remain constant, if the labour-time required for its production also remained constant. But the latter changes with every variation in the productivity of labour. This is determined by a wide range of circumstances; it is determined amongst other things by the workers' average degree of skill, the level of development of science and its technological application, the social organization of the process of production, the extent and effectiveness of the means of production, and the conditions found in the natural environment.[58]

The Ambiguities of Fairness

The shadow of Rawls looms large in attempts to reconcile class theory and the theory of justice. Circumspect about methodological individualism,

Rawls does not conceive the social contract as a sum of isolated transactions, but in its social dimension from the outset. The 'basic structure of society' is presented as 'the way in which the major social institutions fit together into one system, and how they assign fundamental rights and duties and shape the division of advantages that arise through social cooperation'.[59] Moreover, Rawls acknowledges the difficulty of calculating positional advantages at the individual level.

His political theory of justice as fairness rests, however, on two decidedly hypothetical operations: the pacification of social conflict and the elimination of ideological effects. In the course of discussions and clarifications, it is affirmed as a theory of consensus. Starting from the observation that modern democracies are characterized by the coexistence of irreconcilable comprehensive doctrines (philosophical or religious), Rawls considers that the 'fact of pluralism' dictates 'remov[ing] from the political agenda the most divisive issues, serious contention about which must undermine the bases of social cooperation'. Governed by the virtues of tolerance, moderation and fairness, the sphere of the political is thus restricted, by a sort of consensual asceticism, to disputes deemed rationally and peacefully surmountable. This 'overlapping consensus' supposedly permits an agreement on a political conception of justice and 'the preservation of a balanced social unity'. The two pillars of the reasoning consist in 'primary goods' and 'principles of justice'.[60] In good formal logic, the conclusions are thus directly contained in the premises and definitions.

The 'primary goods' comprise everything 'rational beings' might be thought to desire, whatever their other desires. This statement assumes that a shared definition of rationality, and of the desires (needs) related to the individual behaviour of human beings in society, has been reached. These imputed desires form the framework for assessing the justice of a distribution of primary goods – that is, the 'basic rights and liberties' (of thought and expression), 'freedom of movement and free choice of occupation', the 'powers and prerogatives of office', 'income and wealth' in the broad sense, and lastly, the 'social bases of self-respect'.[61]

As for the 'first principles', they boil down to two imperatives:

(a) Each person has an equal claim to a fully adequate scheme of equal basic rights and liberties, which scheme is compatible with the same scheme for all . . .

(b) Social and economic inequalities are to satisfy two conditions: first, they are to be attached to positions and offices open to all under conditions of fair equality of opportunity; and second, they are to be to the greatest benefit of the least advantaged members of society.[62]

Inequalities are therefore legitimate to the extent that they make a functional contribution to the expectations of the least advantaged. This hypothesis pertains to an ideology of growth commonly illustrated by 'shares of the cake': so long as the cake gets bigger, the smallest share likewise continues to grow, even if the largest grows more quickly and the difference between them increases. The theory of justice thus appears as the consistent ethico-juridical complement of a well-tempered social liberalism. Faced with the effects of crisis, deregulation, and the attenuation of social security policies, its current success assumes a tonality that is at once nostalgic and unreal: in what way are flourishing social inequalities to the greatest advantage of the worst-off? How can it be argued that offices and positions are open to the excluded? And how can it be claimed that equality of opportunity exists for those without rights? Unless it serves as a pretext for a 'novel approach to social conflict', for so-called strategies of 'mutual advantage', and methods of negotiation that make it possible to 'leave behind old models of the balance of forces' – in other words, for the transition from struggle to resignation; from resistance to collaboration.

The brutality of the crisis exposes the contradiction between 'first principles' and actually existing inequality. The theory of justice can escape it only by excluding social conflict, which is supposed to be politically controllable. Social liberalism accepts 'the plurality of conceptions of the good as a fact of modern life, provided, of course, these conceptions respect the limits specified by the appropriate principles of justice'. The vicious circle closes in a giddy round. Agreement postulates a social community that is no longer founded on a 'conception of the good', but on 'a shared public conception of justice appropriate to the conception of citizens in a democratic state as free and equal persons'.[63] All in all, agreement presupposes . . . agreement (on rules and limits), while the real struggle carries on inventing its own rules and extending its boundaries.

Thus the emergence of an 'overlapping consensus', veritable cornerstone of the edifice, demands of political philosophy that it 'must be, so far as possible, suitably independent of other parts of philosophy, especially from philosophy's long-standing problems and controversies'. A stable frontier supposedly separates eternal (undecidable) philosophical problems from many temporal (decidable) political problems about what is just. Overlapping consensus thus does not come down to a simple *modus vivendi*, or a compromise according to the balance of forces. It exists when a political conception of justice regulating the basic institutional structure of society is endorsed by each of the 'reasonable but opposing comprehensive doctrines', understood as general doctrines 'cover[ing] all recognized values and virtues within one rather precisely articulated system'.[64] By the same token as religious beliefs, these doctrines are thus repressed to the rank of private convictions. It is not a question of giving up ethical speculation about the good life, but of admitting – with Rawls and Habermas – that, unlike a 'just society', it is not amenable to rational discussion.

The operation consists in bracketing social conflict, conceived not as the basis, but as a consequence, of confrontation between irreconcilable comprehensive doctrines; and reducing politics to a disembodied consensus in a process of levitation. In the same way, the role of force is conjured away by juridical relations. Finally, the state is assigned an idealized mission as educator, guarantor of the neutrality of the public juridical space *vis-à-vis* comprehensive doctrines and their thirst for the absolute. This neutrality consists in three injunctions:

(a) that the state is to ensure for all citizens equal opportunity to advance any conception of the good they freely affirm;

(b) that the state is not to do anything intended to favor or promote any particular comprehensive doctrine rather than another, or to give greater assistance to those who pursue it;

(c) that the state is no longer to do anything that makes it more likely that individuals accept any particular conception rather than another unless steps are taken to cancel, or to compensate for, the effects of policies that do this.

Disembodied arbiter and guardian of the consensus, this phantom state bears little relation to the real state, its anti-strike or anti-immigrant laws, its role in the reproduction of social relations, its ideological apparatuses, its apparatuses of coercion, and the exercise of a monopoly of force. It is scarcely surprising, then, that Rawls should rediscover in his conclusions the political harmony he introduced into the premises: 'The other reason political values normally win out is that severe conflicts with other values are much reduced. This is because when an overlapping consensus supports the political conception, this conception is not viewed as incompatible with basic religious, philosophical and moral values.'[65] QED. . . .

The eclipse of social conflict proceeds in tandem with the dissolution of ideological opacity in consensual transparency. According to Rawls, the social contract assumes 'normal and fully cooperating members of society': 'The capacity for a conception of the good is the capacity to form, to revise, and rationally to pursue . . . a conception of what we regard as a worthwhile human life'.[66] The formal presuppositions of justice are thus granted a priori: normal human beings, a shared conception of the good, rational behaviour. This society capable of abstracting from beliefs and convictions is composed wholly of reasonable, sovereign subjects. Despite the existence of contradictory conceptions, there thus exists no obstacle to the existence of an overlapping consensus. For this, it suffices to accept that ideology can be dispelled by the grip of good will. More precisely, it would seem that for Rawls, ideology does not exist, or is limited to a smokescreen. It is without origin, without materiality, without any efficacy of its own. Adherence to comprehensive doctrines expresses neither social relations nor social interests. It derives from a pure choice of conscience, whether free or merely capricious. It is then easy to bracket beliefs and convictions in favour of consensus.

The transparent rationality of justice is combined quite naturally with the equally transparent rationality of communication. The theory of speech acts involves statements without ambiguity and awareness of the total context. Similarly, for Habermas, any communication postulates an ideal understanding based on the requisite homogeneous vocabulary. It thus tends to a procedural sovereignty, disseminated in forms of communication without a subject. A public space of discussion and argument permitting all interested parties to establish intersubjectively the legitimacy of the decisions taken by the public power, this communicative reason, which is irreducible to a unified, homogeneous subject, in effect grounds legitimacy in an intersubjective dissolution of the popular will. It is thus thought to achieve the disembodiment of power (dissolution of the royal or political 'body'), and assemble the conditions for a political secularization whose practical translation would be pure 'constitutional patriotism'.

Doubtless the aim is laudable. Yet abandonment of some exhaustive recapitulation of the meaning of universal History from the viewpoint of a last judgement renders the operation illusory. The field of meanings is open, and words are never reliable. The repetition of the sign on the social battle front makes meaning vacillate, rather than fixing it. If scientists also think with words, scientific controversy gains in fertility to the extent that the participants at least agree on the formulation of the problems requiring resolution. Political controversy, on the other hand, is characterized by a primary disagreement as to the terms of the formulation: it does not avoid confrontation between interests and their inscription, which is immediately ideological, in the horizon of fetishism. People do not think falsely because they 'come up' with false ideas, or because they undergo indoctrination: they think falsely because they live in the positively phantasmagorical world of commodity fetishism. Communication is not on the side of understanding and appeasement, but always in-between, in the minefield between peace and war, reasonable agreement and dictated compromise. Its distortion by the conflictual practices of strategic action is therefore unavoidable.

To the abstract and crippled universalization of capital, to the tyrannical eruption of fragmented divinities and fetishes, communicative rationality offers a response that is immediately ensnared in ideology. With a view to establishing an organic link between socialism and democracy, Habermas thus dissolves class interests into those of humanity constituting itself as a species, in purely imaginary fashion. The production paradigm is erased in favour of the communication paradigm. Social relations become relations of communication.

Moral consciousness thus withdraws from individual practical reason to take refuge in the social process of communication. The universal conditions of mutual understanding are thought to dictate a sort of immanent ethical normativity. Just as, depending on the occasion, the vague invocation of the right or duty to intervene mixes sales blurb, moral imperative and legal norm, so law and ethics tend to merge in the concept of justice.

Pluralized, the supra-individual reason of the Enlightenment would then be salvaged. This salvation, however, assumes an identity between practical intersubjectivity and supra-individual reason that cannot be demonstrated. Uprooted from the relations of production (and reproduction) and domination, this intersubjectivity is as abstract and formal as that of the Rawlsian theory of justice. Whereas the reality is one of inequality and violence (even in the communicative relation and the cruelty of words), it postulates a peaceful general reciprocity.

If a method is to be judged on its results, Rawls's scarcely stands the test of the practical dilemmas of freedom, equality, and property. For him, the basic freedoms are exclusively political: 'freedom of thought and liberty of conscience; the political liberties and freedom of association, as well as the freedoms specified by the liberty and integrity of the person; and finally, the rights and liberties covered by the rule of law'. It is important 'to limit the basic liberties to those that are truly essential'. Their status requires severe restriction of any list, for '[w]henever we enlarge the list of basic liberties we risk weakening the protection of the most essential ones and recreating within the scheme of liberties the indeterminate and unguided balancing problems we had hoped to avoid by a suitably circumscribed notion of priority'. This system of liberties holds up only on condition that it is never confronted with the demand for social freedoms, immediately and exclusively expressible in terms of rights: to employment, housing, education, health. In sum, the theory of justice claims to silence the antinomy exposed by the French Revolution between strictly political liberties (including the right to property) and the freedoms summed up since 1793 by the assertion of the right to existence. To the accusations of formalism traditionally made by 'many' ('radical democrats and socialists'), Rawls replies by basing himself on the 'second principle' (the 'difference principle'). It allows him to seal his theory, in such a way that it must be accepted or refused *en bloc*: 'the all-purpose means available to the least advantaged members of society to achieve their ends would be even less were social and economic inequalities, as measured by the index of primary goods, different from what they are'. But how can such a claim be proved if, as a matter of principle, any hypothetical comparison with another mode of social regulation is refused ('[n]either our situation in other societies, nor in a state of nature, have any role in assessing conceptions of justice')?[67]

The model thus functions on condition that its premisses are accepted unconditionally. Once the restrictive list of basic liberties has been accepted, the rest follows. Defined as a symmetrical relation between partners (as a result of which they are supposedly equal), political equality becomes indifferent to social inequality. Likewise, to remain compatible with the basic liberties, the right to property deliberately sets aside rights to possess the means of production and natural resources, and to participate in control over them. It signifies merely the right to obtain, and have exclusive control over, private property – a sufficient material basis for personal independence. Just as class relations are dissolved into a network of inter-individual juridical relations, property relations disappear behind the personal right to limited appropriation.

Rawls accepts without reservations the formal character of a 'well-ordered society' as a closed system: 'Since membership in their society is given, there is no question of the parties comparing the attractions of other societies.'[68] The rules of the game are fixed once and for all, and 'knowing whether our conclusions are equally valid in a broader context is another matter'. Condemned to circulate in the iron cage of reality, we are precluded from measuring the real against the possible. The theory thus becomes subtly apologetic. In the absence of being able to present the universe of capital and the despotism of the market as the best of economic worlds, it is tempting to promote it to the status of best possible juridical world. But this assumes preliminary agreement that the principles of justice selected at the outset are the most reasonable for all concerned. Obviously, this is conceivable only in the name of a Reason imposing itself without violence on contrary reasons, which is supposedly the thing most widely shared between the free and equal citizens of a well-ordered society. The theory goes round in circles. In its conclusion, it rediscovers its own premisses: 'the aim of a theory of justice as fairness is to develop a conception of political and social justice that accords with the most settled convictions and traditions of a modern democratic state'.[69] In reality, the 'veil of ignorance', by virtue of which each citizen to this contract is supposed to be unaware of the lot and place reserved for him or her, modestly veils the 'invisible hand' of the market. For the hand to remain invisible, the eye must be blind.

Marx criticized vulgar socialism, which in this respect was the legatee of bourgeois economists, for evading the problem of production by insisting one-sidedly on distribution. He stressed that the allocation of objects of consumption was simply a consequence of the way in which the conditions of production were themselves distributed. In offering a declining welfare state the reinforcement of his theory of justice, Rawls flirts with this old tradition.

As for Philippe Van Parijs, he dodges the objection by proposing to construe distribution in a way that is not limited to income distribution: 'Ownership of the means of production, control over investments, power in the workplace, and access to a job are no less important distribuenda than purchasing power.'[70] Indeed. But step by step, power in the workplace, control over investment, and ownership of the means of production assume nothing less than a revolution in the relations of production. Regarded as a fully fledged right, access to employment would in fact abolish the commodity character of labour-power.

On another level, Van Parijs declines to play the trump card of abundance, too often deployed to evade the real problems of distribution. The development of the ecological crisis has supposedly ended up destroying faith in this *deus ex machina* . . . Because of the failure to clarify the issues, the debate thus characterized becomes extremely confused. Either the theoreticians of justice claim to intervene in the sphere of distribution without disrupting the relations of production; and then Marx's criticisms of vulgar socialism remain pertinent: how can the question of unemployment be posed in terms of distributive justice without going to the root of the law of value? Or the theory of justice presents itself as a pedagogy of subversion, conducive to challenging the ownership of the means of production. Doubtless this interpretation is not dominant, and it would be preferable to clarify positions. The collapse of the bureaucratically managed economies and the questions involved

in the ecological crisis oblige us to conceptualize the transition to socialism (including its juridical dimension) in more precise terms than Marx.
When principle and practice are no longer at loggerheads, a critical
theory of justice could be a precious contribution in this context. For
the 'narrow horizon of bourgeois right' can be positively transcended
only at the end of a protracted process.

Determinism on the Rebound

According to G.A. Cohen, a class can prevail historically when it corresponds to the development of the productive forces and, in emancipating
itself, satisfies the interests of all humanity. This thesis raises all sorts of
problems. From the standpoint of 'methodological individualism', the
interests of humanity are even more indefinable than those of a group or
class. The coincidence between class interest and productive forces
assumes a single and unique path of development for the productive
forces. If optimal development and maximal development are no longer
identical, optimality involves a value judgement. Because it cannot determine the 'objective' optimum, 'analytical Marxism' is forced into the great
leap to the ethical imperative.

How are the ideas of historical progress and the combinatory of justice
to be reconciled? Why are social relations transformed? Why should it be
absolutely for the better, and not sometimes for the worse? Philippe Van
Parijs endeavours to harmonize the hypothesis of progress and the
Rawlsian difference principle. The question of transition – the transition
from 'non-progressiveness' to replacement – seems to him to be an
especially obscure point in the Marxist conception of history. When a
mode of production ceases to be progressive, its intrinsic inequalities
(deriving from capitalist exploitation) stop satisfying the 'difference principle', according to which equality of income and power must always be
preferred unless inequalities permit everyone to receive more income or
power than they would in a condition of equality. This rather tautological
law of change presupposes the notion of capitalist exploitation as an
'interaction' of individual relations.

Yet no one can withdraw from the class struggle. On the one hand, it
is historically impossible to compare the lot of the worst-off group in
different systems and then, in full possession of the facts, repudiate the
system whose output is decreasing. More consistent on this point, Rawls
indicates that there can be no question of the partners comparing their
'advantages' with those offered by other societies. Comparisons remain

internal to the logic of the system, or are conceivable only between 'really existing' systems.

On the other hand, the idea of historical development governed by the 'difference principle' leads to deeming a society just solely by virtue of the quantity of primary goods that fall to the worst-off. It would involve maximizing the minimal well-being of society's rejects by regarding those inequalities that are liable to improve the lot of the worst-off as fair. This amounts to displacing the front of the social conflict over exploitation towards exclusion, as if the latter were not the consequence and corollary of the former.[71]

As long as the variable sum of the 'game' increases and allows for a relative improvement in the condition of the worst-off, the theory of justice legitimates exploitation. Injustice begins only when exploitation contributes to increasing inequalities to the detriment of the weakest. Van Parijs adopts for his own purposes the general definition of exploitation given by John Roemer, according to which a group is capitalistically exploited if, and only if, it would be better off were it to withdraw from society with its proportionate share of the means of production. To be completely clear: exploitation as it operates under capitalism can be unjust, without thereby being unjust in itself. So what is this *exploitation in itself*? Practically, historically, it always involves determinate exploitation – slave, feudal, capitalist, or bureaucratic exploitation. Capitalist exploitation is unjust from the standpoint of the class that suffers it. There is thus no theory of justice in itself, only a justice relative to the mode of production that it proposes to improve and temper, sharing the old and false commonsensical view that it is pointless to redistribute the wealth of the rich, as opposed to helping them perform their wealth-creating role better, with a view to increasing the size of the common cake!

For Van Parijs, methodological individualism leads to pulverizing class relations into a network of inter-individual relations. The result is a significant alteration in the notion of exploitation. Rather than characterizing a social relation, it now designates a game of statuses: 'One can . . . define a *job exploiter* (a *job exploited*) as someone who would be worse off (better off) if job assets were equally distributed, with the distribution of skills remaining unchanged and all efficiency effects being assumed away.'[72] Shifts in terminology have their importance. Exploitation does not concern labour-power, but the situation, the job or job assets: sources, in some sense, of a new form of rent. Van Parijs conceives this notion of 'job exploiter' (assuming an employment capital) in the manner of Bourdieu's multiplication of capitalisms at the expense of any overall regulation, referring to a cultural capital or an organizational capital alongside economic capital proper.[73]

The conclusions he draws are eloquent. The front line in the conflict no longer runs between exploiters and exploited, but between the exploited themselves: 'Should one then expect the central class struggle under welfare-state capitalism to be one between those with a stable, decently paid job and those deprived of access to such a job'?[74] Here is something to confirm the dominant discourse, incriminating those waged workers with a more or less stable job as 'affluent'. Poles apart from collective solidarity in defence of common rights to employment and income, the inevitable consequence is obviously a sharing out of shortage (not of employment, but of unemployment and wage income, while sparing non-wage incomes). Thus, the unemployed would gain a lot more 'from a redistribution of employment than a redistribution of wealth'.

The alternative is socially and economically absurd: it is impossible to have the one without the other. The very idea of redistributing employment assumes a stable and indisputable volume of labour, when precisely what we have to know is which needs to satisfy, and how to recycle the productivity gains facilitated by technological development in socially useful jobs. Correlated with the determination of social needs and their prioritization, the distribution of employment necessarily brings into question the distribution of wealth. And this in two respects: as an allocation of production goods (control and orientation of investment); and as disposable income at the level of final consumption, making it possible to complete the cycle of reproduction positively.

Having made 'job exploitation' one form of exploitation among others, Van Parijs goes further. His approach, in effect, ends up making this very particular mode of exploitation the dominant spring in social conflict. Allegedly more significant than class division, 'job division' is now the 'central component' of class structure. Rather than mounting a class front between workers, the unemployed and the excluded against unemployment and insecurity, what we have compounds one division by another, proposing as a priority (and under the guise of depoliticized ethical urgency, as dictated by the theory of justice!) a movement of those suffering poverty of employment.[75]

At a time of crisis, when virtually the only thing that remains to be shared is shortage, does the 'difference principle' continue to operate in favour of the worst-off (as claimed by supporters of lower taxes, wage- and job-sharing, and charitable campaigns)? Or does it vanish in an unprincipled stampede? The theorem of social change according to Van Parijs concludes with some sombre prophecies as to the immediate future of capitalism: 'With the difference principle no longer being satisfied, the members (dominated and dominant) of the society in question soon stop regarding these inequalities as legitimate or fair. The revolt of the dominated grows in strength; the resistance of the dominant weakens. The time is then ripe for a change of mode of production.'[76] Paradoxically, the law of Rawls–Van Parijs thus lapses back into a determinist, mechanistic vision of historical mutations. The results are worth as much as the method.

The formal circularity of a system dictates a choice: to enter into it or not. Key figure of a muscular neoliberalism, Robert Nozick reckons that political philosophers after Rawls will have to work in the framework of his theory, or explain why they are not doing so. There are certainly various ways of not doing so. Attempts to temper the critique of Marx with a theory of justice amount to a mixture of chalk and cheese. Theories of justice and the critique of political economy are irreconcilable. Conceived as the protection of the private sphere, liberal politics seals the holy alliance between the nightwatchman state and the market of opinions in which individual interests are supposed to be harmonized. Marx's critique is poles apart. Volume One of *Capital*, especially the chapters on co-operation and the division of labour (in the part devoted to the 'production of relative surplus-value'), establishes the impossibility of allocating the collective productivity of social labour individually. Whereas the theory of justice rests on the atomism of contractual procedures, and on the formalist fiction of mutual agreement (whereby individuals become partners in a co-operative adventure for their mutual advantage), social relations of exploitation are irreducible to intersubjective relations.

Notes

1. See especially G.A. Cohen, *Karl Marx's Theory of History: A Defence*, Clarendon Press, Oxford 1978; Jon Elster, *Making Sense of Marx*, Cambridge University Press, Cambridge/ Éditions de la Maison des Sciences de l'Homme, Cambridge and Paris 1985; John Roemer, *A General Theory of Exploitation and Class*, Harvard University Press, Cambridge, MA 1982, and Roemer, ed., *Analytical Marxism*, Cambridge University Press/Éditions de la Maison des Sciences de l'Homme, Cambridge and Paris 1986. See also Philippe Van Parijs, *Qu'est-ce qu'une société juste?*, Seuil, Paris 1992, and *Actuel Marx*, no. 7, 'Le marxisme analytique anglo-saxon', Presses Universitaires de France, Paris 1990.
2. Elster, *Making Sense of Marx*, p. 5; emphasis added.
3. Ibid. p. 38.
4. Ibid., p. 39.
5. In particular, in the pages of *New Left Review*: see Norman Geras, 'The Controversy about Marx and Justice', *New Left Review*, no. 150, March/April 1985; Ellen Meiksins Wood,

'Rational Choice Marxism: Is the Game Worth the Candle?', *New Left Review*, no. 177, September/October 1989; Joseph McCarney, 'Marx and Justice Again', and Norman Geras, 'Bringing Marx to Justice: An Addendum and Rejoinder', *New Left Review*, no. 195, September/October 1992.

6. Geras, 'The Controversy about Marx and Justice', p. 58.
7. Ibid., p. 60.
8. Ibid., p. 70.
9. Ibid., p. 77.
10. Ibid., p. 85.
11. Geras, 'Bringing Marx to Justice', p. 37.
12. Ibid., pp. 53, 56.
13. Ibid., p. 65.
14. Alan Carling situates in the current of 'rational choice Marxism' authors such as Jon Elster, John Roemer and Adam Przeworski, as well as Robert Brenner and G.A. Cohen, whose methodological position is distinctly different. Norman Geras occupies an original position, and is said to maintain his distance with respect to the hard core of this rational choice Marxism, i.e. the combination of game theory and methodological individualism, or 'Cohen's theory of history plus Roemer's theory of exploitation' ('Rational Choice Marxism', *New Left Review*, no. 160, November/December 1986).
15. Wood, 'Rational Choice Marxism', p. 49.
16. Elster, *Making Sense of Marx*, pp. 321–2. Elster believes that '[i]t is not possible today, morally or intellectually, to be a Marxist in the traditional sense' (p. 531). The sentence is too peremptory not to be a snare. If by 'Marxist in the traditional sense' is meant the political and theoretical stance of the parties of 'orthodox Marxism', whether social-democratic or Stalinist, I readily agree that it is no longer possible, morally or intellectually, to be a Marxist of this stamp. However, I challenge the notion that this impossibility dates only from 'today' or yesterday. What was for a long time impossible has simply become inexpressible. Elster's *current* renunciation of traditional Marxism suggests an alternative, non-traditional Marxism: an 'analytical Marxism'. In reality, it involves a liquidation of Marx's theory that is no less systematic for being oblique.
17. Ibid., pp. 328, 330.
18. Ibid., pp. 330–31.
19 James P. Carse, *Finite Games and Infinite Games*, Penguin, Harmondsworth 1987, p. 7.
20. Ibid., pp. 17–18, 94. Published in 1944, von Neumann and Morgenstern's founding text (*Theory of Games and Economic Behaviour*) brought out the analogical relationship between the economic situations of competition and negotiation, on the one hand, and games mingling chance and the skill of the protagonists, on the other. Most of the cases studied related to zero-sum games. An infatuation with game theory has since spread to all branches of economic analysis, with an attempt to envisage dynamic situations as the effects of memory and repetition between successive rounds.
21. See John Rawls, *A Theory of Justice*, Oxford University Press, Oxford 1971; the collective volume *Individu et justice sociale*, Seuil, Paris 1988; and Van Parijs, *Qu'est-ce qu'une société juste?*.
22. Elster, *Making Sense of Marx*, p. 216.
23. Karl Marx and Frederick Engels, 'The German Ideology', in Marx and Engels, *Collected Works*, vol. 5, Lawrence & Wishart, London 1976, p. 49.
24. Karl Marx, 'The Civil War in France', in Marx, *The First International and After*, Penguin/NLR, Harmondsworth 1974, p. 213.
25. Karl Marx, *Capital*, vol. 3, trans. David Fernbach, Penguin/NLR, Harmondsworth 1981, pp. 460–61.
26. Karl Marx, *Wages, Price and Profit*, Foreign Languages Press, Peking 1975, p. 46.
27. Elster, *Making Sense of Marx*, p. 220.
28. Ibid.
29. Allen Wood, 'Marx and Equality', in Roemer, ed., *Analytical Marxism*, pp. 284–5.

30. Frederick Engels, *Anti-Dühring*, trans. Emile Burns, Progress Publishers, Moscow 1947, p. 132.
31. Elster, *Making Sense of Marx*, p. 516.
32. Karl Marx, 'Critique of the Gotha Programme', in Marx, *The First International and After*, p. 344.
33. Ibid., p. 345.
34. Ibid., pp. 346–7.
35. Karl Marx, 'The Poverty of Philosophy', in Marx and Engels, *Collected Works*, vol. 6, Lawrence & Wishart, London 1976, p. 138.
36. Ibid., pp. 142–3.
37. Ibid., pp. 143–4.
38. John Gray, *The Social System: A Treatise on the Principle of Exchange*, London 1831.
39. Karl Marx, *A Contribution to the Critique of Political Economy*, trans. S.W. Ryazanskaya, Lawrence & Wishart, London 1971, pp. 84–6.
40. Marx, 'Critique of the Gotha Programme', p. 346.
41. Stavros Tombazos, *Les Catégories du temps dans l'analyse économique*, Cahiers des saisons, Paris 1994, p. 221.
42. Marx, 'The Poverty of Philosophy', p. 195.
43. This assumes an individual subject endowed with a psychology that is simply a modernized version of the old psychology of faculties.
44. In the discussion about the coherence of a collective class interest, what is really at stake is whether the concept of class refers to a thought-concrete (a constructed set of determinations) or to a positive empirical reality. Schumpeter compares class to a bus that is always full, but full of different people. Conversely, for E.P. Thompson, class-in-itself is not a thing, but an event, a 'happening'. Finally, for G.A. Cohen, adept of a tempered structuralism, classes undergo a process of cultural and political formation, but are not reducible to it: the process itself is based on the permanence of the structure. For the most part, these discussions betray a misunderstanding of the concept of class in Marx. For him, the radical disjunction between the thought-concrete and effective reality, between collective interest and individual interest, scarcely has any meaning. Since classes are not things but relations, they exist and manifest themselves in the conflict that fashions them.
45. Elster, *Making Sense of Marx*, p. 390.
46. Ibid., p. 391.
47. Ibid., p. 393.
48. Ibid., p. 516.
49. Ibid., p. 12.
50. Ibid., p. 515.
51. Ibid., p. 130.
52. Ibid., pp. 192, 131.
53. As Marc Fleurbaey notes in connection with John Roemer, '[i]t is truly paradoxical to reject the labour theory of value without referring to the very concept that defines it, i.e. abstract labour' ('Exploitation et inégalité: du côté du marxisme analytique', *Actuel Marx*, no. 7, p. 120).
54. In the footsteps of Roemer, Philippe Van Parijs clearly emphasizes this contradiction:

Assessing the contribution of each worker in terms of labour-value is a very tricky business. Not only because skilled labour is supposed to create more value than unskilled labour, and hence an adequate procedure for reducing complex labour to simple labour is presupposed. But even more because the quantity of value created by a worker at a given moment depends upon his relative productivity, compared with that of other workers producing the same good. Yet if this productivity can in principle be assessed in the case of workers individually producing identifiable products, it cannot be – even in principle – in the general case where goods are the joint product of many operations carried out by a multiplicity of workers. As a result, it is generally impossible to determine whether the socially necessary labour supplied by a particular worker (or group of workers) is lesser or greater than the number of hours actually worked or, *a fortiori*, than the value embodied in the goods he consumes. (*Qu-est-ce qu'une société juste?*, p. 104)

Here Van Parijs restricts himself to registering the limitations of the analytical approach when faced with co-operative, complex and composite labour. However, the impasse is more fundamental. In a society of general commodity production, the commodity is the necessary mediation of the whole social relation. Labour is from the outset a social relation. The labour-powers consumed in production are commensurable only as abstract social labour – something Van Parijs, proceeding from an elementary theoretical pitfall to a more essential stumbling block, recalls: 'If labour is relevant to determining what a worker is entitled to, it must be labour that has actually been supplied, and not the labour that would have been necessary for an averagely endowed individual to produce the same goods in average technical conditions' (ibid., p. 105).

55. Pierre Salama and Tran Hai Hac, *Une Introduction à l'économie politique*, Maspero, Paris 1973, p. 15.

56. Ibid., p. 26. Following the same logic, Tran Hai Hac tackles the so-called 'transformation problem' in precisely the right fashion:

Thus, from whatever angle one approaches things, it turns out to be impossible to conceive a concrete process, economic or historical, of transformation of exchange-value into price of production. This is because there is no exchange at the value to which exchange at the price of production would succeed. Exchange-value precedes the price of production only from a logical, conceptual viewpoint: the transition from one to the other is only the development of the law of value from the level of capital in general to the level of capital in competition. In other words, the concepts of exchange-value and price of production refer to one and the same economic and historical reality, but grasped at two different levels of abstraction. (p. 62)

57. Karl Marx, *Grundrisse*, trans. Martin Nicolaus, Penguin/NLR, Harmondsworth 1973, p. 171.

58. Karl Marx, *Capital*, vol. 1, trans. Ben Fowkes, Penguin/NLR, Harmondsworth 1976, p. 130.

59. John Rawls, *Political Liberalism*, Columbia University Press, New York 1993, p. 258.

60. Ibid., p. 157.

61. Ibid., p. 181.

62. Ibid., pp. 5–6.

63. Ibid., p. 304.

64. Ibid., pp. 171–2, 13–15.

65. Ibid., pp. 192–3, 157.

66. Ibid., pp. 178, 302.

67. Ibid., pp. 291, 296, 325–6, 279.

68. Ibid., p. 276.

69. See ibid., pp. 11–15.

70. Van Parijs, *Qu'est-ce qu'une société juste?*, p. 263.

71. The 'Minc Report' (*La France de l'an 2000*, Odile Jacob, Paris 1994) is a perfect illustration of the standard liberal use of equity as a charger against equality and solidarity: 'The perspective of positive discrimination can result in reviewing the principle of free public services in some instances. The latter most often operate to the advantage of the best-off categories. Hitherto, free services have been part and parcel of the French conception of equality . . . In practice, positively discriminating in favour of some people means interfering with free services for others' (p. 93).

72. Philippe Van Parijs, 'A Revolution in Class Theory', in *Marxism Recycled*, Cambridge University Press/Éditions de la Maison des Sciences de l'Homme, Cambridge and Paris 1993, p. 126.

73. Unlike methodological individualism, the Bourdieusian sociology of the 'weight of the world' nevertheless bears on the totality of social relations. It tackles the causal series *en route*, while stopping 'at the threshold of exploitation'. Henri Maler detects here the sign of a sociology unreconciled to no longer thinking social change, but confronting a conjuncture in which such change seems to be blocked. Caught in a pincer movement between prophetic and bureaucratic demands, it takes refuge in requirements of scientificity that can only evade social demands. The autonomy it claims is thus paid for by an 'insurmountable solitude': those who have an interest in understanding cannot, and those who can are not interested (Henri Maler, 'Politique de la sociologie', *Futur antérieur*, nos 19–20, 1993).

74. Van Parijs, 'A Revolution in Class Theory', p. 128.

75. What is actually taking shape is movements of the unemployed and excluded ('Agir ensemble contre le chômage', 'Droits devant'), which strive to maintain contacts between the unemployed, those with insecure jobs, and stable wage-earners.

76 Van Parijs, *Qu'est-ce qu'une société juste?*, p. 94. Van Parijs specifies that this scenario for transition is 'inspired by Roemer'.

6

Whatever Happened to Class?

Assessment of the historical role of class struggle fluctuates with the struggle itself. After the Paris Commune, nascent sociology countered the notion of social class with a vocabulary foregrounding social groups: elites, 'intermediate', 'ruling' or 'middle' classes.[1] May 1968, the Italian 'Hot Autumn', and the Portuguese Revolution suddenly restored class struggle to prominence. The dominant discourse of the 1980s once again insisted on categories and classifications. The concept of class was widely redefined as a 'predominantly classificatory concept', or an 'information filter' making it possible to bring some order to social heterogeneity and establish 'formally adequate classifications'.[2] This is how things stand today.

At a time when economic crisis and neoliberal policies translate into a fiercer struggle over the division between profits and wages, over labour legislation and the organization of work, and over generalized flexibility, this ideological offensive is at once understandable and paradoxical. Exclusion does not replace exploitation; rather, it is its necessary consequence and reverse side. Relegation from the productive process in fact deprives the 'excluded' of any possible reappropriation of the means and ends of production. Their disarray then finds expression in sporadic explosions against the mirages of consumption, which are simultaneously symbols of their frustrated ambitions and the reigning scale of values. This rebellion is rooted in the depths of the relations of exploitation, which make social labour-time the measure of all wealth, and periodically eject the 'losers'.

As for the fashionable infatuation with 'urban policy', it expresses a concern to urbanize escalating conflicts through a mixture of security and vote-catching measures aimed at the new 'dangerous classes'.

A General Theory of Exploitation

Two main questions underlie the challenge to the historical role of social classes: the enigma of the social relations in the countries of so-called 'real socialism'; and the socio-strategic puzzle of the 'middle classes'. John Roemer and Erik Olin Wright offer two systematic attempts to respond to these questions from an 'analytical Marxist' standpoint.[3]

Following the Indochinese crisis and the Sino–Vietnamese confrontation, Roemer sought to understand the politics of the bureaucratic regimes from a theoretical perspective, by identifying the 'laws of motion' of socialism. To this end he offers a 'general theory of exploitation and classes', of which capitalist exploitation is only a particular case.

According to his 'correspondence principle' between exploitation and class, any producer who buys labour-power is an exploiter, and any producer who sells it figures among the exploited. This principle is not a self-evident truth, but a 'theorem'. Class status and exploitation status emerge within the system as a consequence of optimizing behaviour. According to Roemer, individual optimization determines class structure: if a labour market is introduced, classes form and class membership corresponds to the relation of exploitation. The next thing is to know whether the correspondence principle is valid solely for a particular mode of production, that is, the capitalist mode of production. Since the labour-time embodied in a commodity cannot be known before equilibrium prices are known, labour value depends on the market. Roemer concludes that the extortion of surplus labour is not the determining characteristic of the relation of exploitation, and proposes to redefine it quite independently of the labour theory of value. This renunciation is in fact the precondition of a 'general theory' applicable to various modes of production.

The major institutional innovation of capitalism consists in making the contractual exchange of labour non-coercive. If no hierarchical bond of personal dependence any longer compels the 'free worker' to furnish labour gratis, how is the appropriation and accumulation of the surplus product to be explained? The labour theory of value offers a response to this mystery. Roemer opposes to it a definition of exploitation corrected by the theory of justice, according to which an individual or a coalition is exploited if a more advantageous alternative than the existing system of distribution is available to it. The Marxist theory of exploitation based on surplus labour thus emerges as a specific instance of the general theory, which, in addition to the capitalist relation of exploitation, also applies to slave, feudal or 'socialist' exploitation.[4]

This theory proposes an elaborate modelling of the social relation: 'exploitation, in the Marxian sense, can exist even when there is no institution of labor exchange, no surplus produced, and no accumulation of wealth in the economy'. It is mediated through the exchange of produced commodities, and is a matter of 'unequal exchange'. The appearance of exploitation and class has its origin in the institution of private property and market competition, rather than in the direct process of expropriation of labour: 'The fundamental feature of capitalist exploitation is not what happens in the labour process, but the differential ownership of productive assets.'[5] Thus construed, exploitation can result from the unequal exchange of goods, and classes can crystallize as a result of a credit market in the absence of any labour market. This hypothesis is illustrated by the comparison between two imaginary islands, one of which has a labour market but no credit market, while the other has a credit market but no labour market. Both see the same class division develop. Roemer deduces that the main form of coercion is aimed at maintaining the property relation, while the coercion exercised in the enterprise to extract surplus labour is of secondary significance in understanding exploitation and class.

This line of reasoning establishes a firm distinction between exploitation and alienation, essential for *A General Theory*. Exploitation could in fact be eliminated in its specifically capitalist form, without the relations of authority and alienation in the labour process thereby being eliminated. The possibility of a 'socialist exploitation' would then be inscribed in the celebrated formula of the *Critique of the Gotha Programme* ('to each according to his labour'), which in no way excludes inequalities based on skills and qualifications. Communism ('to each according to his needs') has for its specific historical task the suppression of this 'socialist exploitation'.

The theoretical generalizations of analytical Marxism attain a degree of abstraction here in which the critical substance of *Capital* disappears: the labour theory of value, the conceptualization of abstract labour, and so on. Let us review the stations of this expiatory calvary.

1. Arguing that the labour-time embodied in the commodity cannot be known before equilibrium prices are known, Roemer concludes 'heretically' (his term) that labour value depends upon the market. This heresy is more minor than he thinks. Inasmuch as the labour-time embodied in the commodity is 'socially necessary', the value that it determines retrospectively or a posteriori via reproduction as a whole does indeed depend

on the market. Hence the logical circularity of *Capital*. Up to this point, Roemer is not so far from Marx as he imagines. The revision consists, rather, in the dissociation of production and exchange. While vulgar Marxism reduces exploitation to the production relation, Roemer reduces it to property and exchange relations, claiming: 'not only is a labor market unnecessary to produce Marxian exploitation, it is also unnecessary to produce Marxian classes'.[6]

2. The compulsion exercised in the labour process then becomes a 'secondary' feature of exploitation compared with the maintenance of property relations. For Marx, by contrast, production and exchange mutually determine one another, in such a way that capital revolutionizes the labour process and shapes the organization of labour. The development of machinery and the corresponding mode of labour are not subsidiary: they are the substance of the relation of exploitation. Factory despotism encapsulates the social relation. Obviously, Roemer's reservations about the cult of labour that haunts the socialist movement are understandable, as is his mistrust of any reduction of class struggle to the confrontation between capital and labour at the point of production. But he goes a lot further. His relativization of the concrete relation of exploitation is wholly consistent with his rejection of value theory: 'although *production* of surplus value may occur at the point of production, *appropriation* of surplus value . . . can occur at the point of exchange'.[7] Reverting to classical economics, he thus travels the path of *Capital* in reverse, separating the spheres (of production and exchange) articulated by Marx within a *mode of production and exchange*. For the latter, the relation of exploitation is a relation of reproduction as a whole, whose innermost secret is unveiled by the labour theory of value and surplus-value.

3. Despite the self-proclaimed rigour, abandonment of the labour theory of value leads to some rather confused formulations. Capitalist exploitation is thus defined as the appropriation of the labour of one class by another, without any mention of labour-time and labour-power. It is reduced to an unequal market exchange based on the shrewdness or naivety of the partners. Labour is said to be exploited when the bundle of commodities bought by the wage-earner contains less time than she has worked. The highly peculiar capacity of the commodity that is labour-power to function beyond the time socially necessary for its reproduction disappears in such formulations. In contrast to the quest for a fair exchange between wage and goods bundle, the labour theory of value

inscribes in the production process as a whole the specific moment of the production of surplus-value in which the relation of exploitation originates, without being reducible to it.

The return to the vocabulary of classical economics marks the explicit renunciation by Roemer of the labour theory of value and the concept of abstract labour, confused with the idea (which is in fact chimerical) of a genuinely homogeneous labour. The irreducible heterogeneity of labour renders the terms of exchange incommensurable, and exploitation itself tendentially indefinable.[8]

4. Roemer proposes to abandon the labour theory of value in favour of a general theory of exploitation, derived from game theory, which assumes an alternative allocation to the existing allocation as a reference point. Comparison between the two makes it possible to distinguish different types of exploitation. According to game theory, withdrawal from the game constitutes the decisive test of exploitation in a given system. Thus, serfs are exploited in feudal society because they would be better off if they withdrew from the game with their plot of land and means of self-subsistence without being obliged to perform the corvée. Whatever the prospective interest of these formal exercises, they run up against the fact that history is not a game. In quitting the feudal 'game', serfs might be shot of the corvée, but would they not by the same token have to ensure their own military protection, hitherto undertaken by their lord, risk their lives, and so on? They could thus suffer the torments of primitive accumulation, become unemployed and of no fixed abode, at the end of a process of proletarianization in the capitalist 'game'. The ludic hypothesis of withdrawal does not correspond to the harsh constraints of real struggle. Conceived as social relations, and not as a product of 'individual optimization', class relations offer little hope of escaping one's fate. Certainly, everyone is formally free to escape their proletarian condition. But the precondition for this is that not everyone attempts it: the individual freedom of the free worker has as its obverse the collective unfreedom of the class! One does not escape *en masse* from the proletariat.[9] That is why, under the rod of capital, the contractual exchange of labour is not as institutionally 'non-coercive' as Roemer claims.

5. *A General Theory of Exploitation and Class* rests not on the extortion of surplus-value, but on a model of unequal exchange operating in time and space:

this 'unequal exchange' and international division of labor occur even when all countries have the same technological capabilities and labor forces of even skill. We observe, systematically, the operation of labor intensive sectors in poor countries and capital intensive sectors in rich ones, but that is a consequence of optimizing behavior given the capital constraint, not lack of technological knowledge. There is no extra-economic imperialism necessary to generate this unequal exchange either; that is, the terms of trade need not be politically enforced, as they are the competitive solution to a regime of free trade, given the optimizing behavior of the countries and their differential wealths.[10]

Having rejected the labour theory of value, Roemer notes that exchange is naturally unequal in a given society, as at the international level. In the absence of the 'abstract labour' that would make it possible to establish a common social measure between heterogeneous labours and products, these remain irrevocably incommensurable. In what, then, does the unequal character of the exchange consist? In the fact that the optimization of natural resources (of an individual or a country) takes more or less time? This is doubtless why such unequal exchange can dispense with 'extra-economic imperialism'! The uneven and combined development of the really existing world market is, however, clearly structured by a hierarchy of domination and dependence that is simultaneously economic and monetary, political and military, educational and cultural. To the extent that commodity production remains peripheral, unequal exchange can initially result from the brute exercise of force (plundering for the purposes of extravagant consumption). Market regulation of production and exchange is established by imposing a socially necessary abstract time on production. Inequality of exchange derives not from a natural temporality of products, but from the unequal social productivity of labour. In the absence of a globally unified labour market, the transfer of wealth to the richest operates on an international scale through deteriorating terms of exchange (not unequal exchange), through the impetus of competition between unequally productive labour forces.[11]

6. In seeking to reconcile Marx's theory with game theory, Roemer gets bogged down in inconsistencies that attach in large part to his failure to understand the double determination of classes. *In the broad historical sense*, class and exploitation can refer to highly diverse realities and modes of extraction of surplus labour, which are irreducible to capitalist exploitation of wage-labour: the relations of domination and exploitation are imbricated differently in a slave or feudal society and in a society of general commodity production. *In the narrow sense*, the 'critique of political economy' is directed at the capitalist relation of exploitation and the class

relations that it determines. Obscuring a conceptual understanding of this reality, *A General Theory* loses in precision what it claims to gain in extension, without thereby facilitating a convincing historical periodization. Elster's extrapolations exacerbate these inconsistencies. The question is whether classes play an equally decisive role in explaining collective action in different societies. Considering the opposition between ownership and non-ownership too vague to characterize the notion of class, he proposes a general definition: '*A class is a group of people who by virtue of what they possess are compelled to engage in the same activities if they want to make the best use of their endowments.*'[12] These endowments include alienable property as well as inalienable skills and cultural goods. Exploitation is then no longer based upon the consumption of labour-power beyond the time required for its own reproduction, but, as in Roemer, on unequal exchange: (1) 'all commodities are exploited under capitalism, not only labour-power, and so the exploitation of labour does not explain profits'; (2) domination is not simply the reverse side of exploitation; (3) measuring differential alienation in terms of surplus-value is possible, but not of much interest; (4) inequality with respect to the means of production is not measurable in terms of exploitation. Roemer's conclusion is that 'exploitation theory is a domicile that we need no longer maintain: it has provided a home for raising a vigorous family, who must now move on'.[13] This verdict is scarcely a cause for surprise: renunciation of the labour theory of value logically leads to abandonment of the theory of exploitation. By virtue of the correspondence principle, abandonment of the theory of exploitation should lead next to renunciation of the concept of classes, in favour of a micro-sociology of groups, agents and actors.[14]

Roemer acknowledges the abstract character of his model, stressing that it does not claim to discuss real history. History definitely does nothing; yet it so happens that it strikes back. The *General Theory* was supposed to facilitate an (economic) analysis of 'real socialism' at the moment of the Sino–Vietnamese conflict and Brezhnevite stagnation. Capitalist exploitation and socialist exploitation, it was claimed, represent two variants of exploitation in general. 'Real socialism' was in fact understood as a combination of socialist (skills) exploitation and hierarchical (or status) exploitation, without any extortion of surplus-value; socialist exploitation took the form of material incentives to professional qualifications. If suppression of these incentives led to a deterioration in the situation of the worst-off through a general fall in productivity, this specific exploitation could, in accordance with the theory of justice, be regarded as socially necessary for a given period.

According to Roemer, socialist exploitation is inscribed in the distributive formula 'to each according to his labour', inasmuch as it precisely implies these inequalities in qualifications, degrees, skills, capacities. Socialism can begin to combat alienation in work relations, but only communism and distribution 'according to needs' can put paid to socialist exploitation. Two questions then arise:

 (i) Is status exploitation socially necessary?
(ii) Would the workers be better off in a capitalist system?

If the response to the second question is 'no', the answer to the first is 'yes'. Conversely, if the answer to the second is affirmative, then the answer to the first is negative. In real history, these questions are not decidable in terms of models. Action unfolds in a space–time governed by the law of uneven and combined development, in which the response to both questions can be unequivocally 'no'. Parasitic bureaucratic exploitation and the privileges of the nomenklatura can be adjudged wholly unnecessary in the Soviet Union, China and elsewhere, without simultaneously concluding that the workers would definitely have been better off under capitalism. After the fall of the Berlin Wall, this binary alternative fed many illusions about the promised land of the market. The choice between a before and an after, a here and a there, is always simplistic. Bureaucratic exploitation (or spoliation) was intolerable – not by comparison with capitalism in its global reality, or with an as yet nonexistent democratic socialism, but as a result of the irrationality and suffering it inflicted on the oppressed. For the populations concerned, the restoration of capitalism and the dictatorship of the market were nevertheless not guaranteed to be an improvement. They were hoping for Swedish or French living standards. With their insertion into a global relation of domination and dependence, their actual fate is instead that of a new 'third-and-a-half world'. Speculations about collective destinies according to the theoretical principle of withdrawal underestimate the fact that, in these upheavals, there is no homogeneous social trajectory. The 'player' (in the event, the labouring class and the nationalities) is divided: in the general redistribution of the cards, there are always a few winners and many losers.

In 1982, Roemer considered the dream of an egalitarian, classless socialist society utopian. According to him, socialist revolution was restricted to the elimination of a specifically capitalist form of exploitation, not every form of exploitation. The crucial question was then whether 'socialist exploitation' was 'socially necessary' to this step, in the sense that an exploitation can be considered socially necessary if its elimination would worsen the lot of the exploited: 'My claim is that at this stage, socialist exploitation is socially necessary in existing socialist societies'[15] – just as capitalist exploitation was originally socially necessary and progressive in Marx's view. Explicitly inspired by the 'maximin' of the Rawlsian theory of justice, this line of thought results in the same apologetic conclusions about bureaucratic socialism as those of Rawls on a temperate liberalism. If socialist exploitation had boiled down exclusively to the exploitation of skills by means of material incentives, without the intervention of status exploitation (through privileges), these societies could 'unreservedly' have been regarded as socialist. As it was, according to Roemer, history was more complex because of the presence of other forms of inequality, whose distribution had nothing random about it.

It might also be thought that status exploitation is socially necessary (and not parasitic), in so far as privileges contribute to the optimal development of the productive forces at a given moment. This, in various forms, was often the self-serving argument of the ruling bureaucracy. Roemer is well aware that he is in danger of indulging the bureaucratic order. But he is the prisoner of his own theory. Socialist exploitation would obtain if the workers would be better off withdrawing from the game. But to go where? To fall back into capitalist exploitation, or to move towards a self-managing socialism whose potential efficiency cannot be demonstrated. The consequence is obvious: 'If status exploitation is socially necessary and randomly distributed', in the name of what is really existing socialism to be criticized? In Rawlsian terminology, such a regime would be deemed 'just'.[16] Having fixed as his goal a 'theory of economic exploitation under socialism', Roemer then plays his trump card by introducing the idea of a subjective appraisal of 'social necessity'. Distinct from justice, assessment of this necessity would in part be a matter for adjudication by a collective consciousness. Like Marx when he was faced with the results of early capitalism, one could thus acknowledge the social necessity of a form of exploitation, without endorsing it or being resigned to it: 'although early capitalism was progressive, and its exploitation was socially necessary, it was unjust. A concept of justice will permit the existence of a necessary evil.'[17] The degree of revolt and rebelliousness would then become one of the dynamic criteria of non-necessity – were it not for the fact that for Marx, rebellion derives not from the fate reserved, in another hypothetical game, for the worst-off player of the current game, but from the implacable logic of conflict, which is immanent in the relation of exploitation itself.

A General Theory renders most characterizations of 'real socialism' unsatisfactory: state capitalism, the power of a managerial class, capitalism without capitalists. More inspired and serious than French ideologues in the same period, Roemer stresses the structural differences between a capitalist society, whose overall regulation is market-led, and where exploitation takes the form of the appropriation of extorted surplus-value, and a society bureaucratically regulated by the plan. In the second case, the rich are less rich than the capitalists; there is no real market in labour-power; and economic privileges derive from the monopoly of political power. These differences have been verified *a contrario* since the dismemberment of the Soviet Union. A shortage of productive capital is not the least of the difficulties on the road to restoring market regulation.

For Roemer, the privileged position of the bureaucracy derives from status exploitation rather than capitalist exploitation. Its control over property proceeds from its domination, not vice versa. As soon as it is combined with the re-establishment of market criteria, socialist exploitation generates the rebirth of a specifically capitalist exploitation. Reverting from models to history, class struggle reasserts its rights over the game.

Concerned to preserve a law of progress, Roemer combines his general theory of exploitation with Cohen's theory of history, suggesting that history necessarily eliminates the various forms of exploitation in a specific order. The difference between vulgar bourgeois economics and the critique of political economy consists in the fact that the latter can adjudge capitalist exploitation progressive at a given stage, without hesitating to call it by its name, whereas the former goes to great lengths to mask this social relation. Similarly, revolutionary communists can contest the privileges and crimes of bureaucratic despotism while understanding its historical determinants, whereas the Thermidorian bureaucracy refused to be designated by its name, and adamantly denied the reality of bureaucratic exploitation. From the perspective of historical materialism according to Roemer, 'history progresses by the successive elimination of forms of exploitation which are socially unnecessary in the dynamic sense'.[18] The exploited do not find themselves better off from one day to the next: it is a question of rhythms and transitions. This problematic has the advantage of uncoupling justice from history: 'although early capitalism was progressive, and its exploitation was socially necessary, it was unjust. A concept of justice will permit the existence of a necessary evil.'[19] But if the principle of justice is not respected, in what sense is such exploitation socially necessary?

In eliminating the labour theory of value (of socially, and hence historically, necessary labour-time), *A General Theory* evacuates historicity, just as the game eliminates the struggle. The abstract logic of formalization prevails.

The Puzzle of the Middle Classes

In *Theories of Surplus-Value*, Marx criticizes Ricardo for neglecting the numerical growth in the middle classes. A similar remark appears in the unfinished chapter of *Capital*. This insistence contradicts the mechanistic vision of the inevitable disappearance of intermediate classes frequently attributed to him. In Marx's view, endlessly new forms of social differentiation only make it more necessary to understand the fundamental relations between classes, for that is the only way to preserve the intelligibility of historical development.

Where Roemer's *General Theory* aims to elucidate the question of 'socialist exploitation', the works of Erik Olin Wright attack that of the middle classes.[20] Wright intends to endow the general concept of class with its full 'complexity', in order to achieve a better grasp of the contradictory reality of intermediate classes. His search for 'micro-foundations' responds to the siren calls of sociology and game theory.

However, Wright challenges the idea that micro-sociological analysis inevitably involves rallying to methodological individualism: 'I have never argued that class structures are *reducible* to the properties of individuals, which is an essential claim of methodological individualism', or that 'all of the causal processes in class theory can be adequately represented at the level of individuals and their interactions'.[21]

Reviewing his successive essays and experiments, Wright has explored two types of response. A first problematic attempted to resolve the question of the middle classes by combining status criteria of domination and economic criteria of exploitation. Introducing the dynamic of networks and trajectories, it sought to elaborate 'a coherent concept of class structure',[22] precondition of any satisfactory understanding of the relations between class structure, class formation and class struggle. Guided by a strategic concern for enduring alliances between the working class and certain sections of the middle classes, he thus arrived at the notion of 'contradictory class locations'. This first problematic defines exploitation as 'appropriation of the surplus'. This general formula once again finesses the labour theory of value. Just as one finds dominant exploited and dominated exploiters in Bourdieu, 'contradictory locations' in Wright can pertain simultaneously to several classes. Exploited as wage-earners, and dominant by virtue of their hierarchical function, managers find themselves in a capitalist location from the standpoint of control, and in a proletarian location from the standpoint of property relations.

Following Poulantzas's distinction between mode of production and social formation, this approach based on the difference between class structure and class formation contains two major weaknesses. On the one hand, it tends to privilege the notion of domination at the expense of the relation of exploitation; on the other, it makes it very difficult to tackle the question of classes within the state apparatus in general and bureaucratic societies in particular. In *Classes*, Wright shares his disquiet at seeing his mixture of criteria reduce class struggle to one conflictual relation among others, and dissolve the notion of class into a fragmented sociology of interest and power groups. Insistence on relations of authority and domination in fact suits forms of conflict that are specific to bureaucratic societies, but the eclectic compromise between exploitation and domination represents a convenient tool for grading at the price of theoretical laxity. Accordingly, a decision is required either to privilege criteria of domination (at the risk of endless fragmentation of groups and categories), or to revert to the primacy of exploitation.

Wright's initial endeavour thus leads to a curious alternative. A combination of relations of exploitation and domination is conceivable at the level of reproduction as a whole and political conflict, where the class configuration comes into play in the last instance. In certain social formations, hierarchical relations, sealed by political or religious authority, could be dominant. In the capitalist mode of production, by contrast, the economy, in becoming autonomous of the political, determines the structuration of social relations. This is why the relation of exploitation occupies the dominant position.[23]

Reverting to the primacy of exploitation, Wright's second problematic is inspired by Roemer's multiple exploitations. Rather than restricting the notion of exploitation to capitalist society proper, and referring to other inegalitarian forms of social relations as domination, Roemer distinguishes between capitalist exploitation (based on ownership of the means of production) and feudal exploitation (based on status), or 'socialist' exploitation (based on control of organizational goods). This is not simply a matter of terminological convenience. In each instance, the term 'exploitation' refers to a distribution of assets and wealth that reproduces inequality, not to a subjective sense of subordination or oppression. Wright, for his part, identifies four types of resources whose unequal appropriation is the foundation of various modes of exploitation: (a) labour-power goods, whose direct exploitation is feudal; (b) capital goods, whose exploitation is capitalist; (c) organizational goods, whose exploitation is statist; and

(d) skills goods (titles, degrees, qualifications), whose exploitation is socialist. This typology would define exploited and exploiting classes corresponding to the different modes of production, accounting for a historical sequence of 'successive eliminations' (feudalism–capitalism–statism–socialism) – at the risk of succumbing to a sadly linear historical determinism!

Wright candidly recognizes the problems with this second solution. Why say that someone who possesses a degree is an exploiter of less skilled or unskilled labour, as opposed to saying that she herself is simply less exploited? Here, once again, we encounter the old problem of the unobtainable 'fair wage', which would define a degree zero of exploitation thanks to a *fair exchange* of social labour-time against goods and services representing an equivalent social labour-time. There is nothing surprising about the fact that the enigma of the 'middle classes' leads to this massive 'grey area' without exploiters or exploited. However, there is no simple means of tracing these dividing lines between advantages: 'Thus, credentials are a relatively ambiguous basis for defining a *class* relation, at least if we want the concept of class to be built around relations of exploitation.'[24] Inequality in qualifications becomes relevant to the analysis of class relations only once it intervenes directly in the access to power or property. If managers are exploited (as labour-power) and exploiters (as possessors of organizational capital), they should have an objective interest in the elimination of capitalist exploitation, and in a society based exclusively on organizational exploitation. Yet in practice, this is not the case.

The successive solutions envisaged by Olin Wright thus prove unsatisfactory in his own eyes.[25] By virtue of the problematic of 'contradictory locations', the middle class is simultaneously situated in the working class and the capitalist class. Secondary exploitation (of skill and organization) determines various intermediate statuses and temporal trajectories within classes. Relations of exploitation without domination, and vice versa (gaoler/prisoner, children/parents), are thus not class relations: 'the capitalist labour-process is to be understood as a relational structure in which capitalists possess the capacity to dominate workers'. As Wright himself so pertinently puts it, '[t]he question . . . is whether this repertoire of new complexities actually enriches the theory or simply adds confusion'.[26]

Roemer defines exploitation in purely economic terms. On the other hand, his concept of class is specifically political. In characterizing class relations as a combination of relations of appropriation and domination,

Wright is closer to Marx's theory. The skilled do not 'dominate' the unskilled, and a relatively privileged layer does not *ipso facto* constitute a different class. Conversely: '[i]f domination is ignored or made marginal, as it is in some of Roemer's analysis, the concept of class loses much of its power in explaining social conflict and historical transformation'. Wright therefore proposes to shift from a crude belief in the primacy of classes to an open approach to the causal role of classes.[27]

The strategic stakes of the controversy are twofold.

1. While it does not necessarily endorse the established order, putting different inegalitarian modes of appropriation on a par, without a central regulative relation, leads to a multiplication of the battle lines and a fragmentation of class struggle. Anti-capitalism is diluted into anti-capitalisms. Abandoning unifying programmes and the strategic issue of power, this approach provides a theoretical foundation for the practice of single-issue coalitions, pressure groups, and shifting alliances. It is certainly wholly legitimate to conceive social actors not as given realities, but as 'constructs'. But it is not enough to ponder whether classes still exist: it must also be determined whether this form of conflict develops a logic of emancipation that is superior to other – religious or community-based – forms of confrontation. If such a choice is not to be a matter of sheer voluntarism or pious hopes, there must be a relationship between reality and construct. In other words, the unification of plural forms of conflict around a structuring conflict must correspond to the centralizing role of overall market regulation and the political power that secures it. If this is not the case, no political strategy is possible on the fragmented front of scattered exploitations and the rebellions they generate, merely a spectrum of *ad hoc* lobbies.

2. The other consequence is that a general theory of exploitation based on market access (not on the extraction and appropriation of surplus-value) strengthens 'market socialism'. In their various ways, Roemer and Van Parijs have exerted themselves to this end. Roemer has imagined a duality of monetary forms (for consumption and for stock), as if distribution could in practice govern production. Conscious of the difficulty, Van Parijs concedes that distribution also concerns the means of production, which simply returns us to the starting point. In 'A Capitalist Road to Communism', Van Parijs, who is not going to quibble over a contradiction, proposes an individual right to universal income permitting everyone to live in morally acceptable conditions. In the absence of any link between being deprived of the means of production

and being deprived of the means of subsistence, there would in fact no longer be any social compulsion to sell labour-power.[28] Without such compulsion, there would be no labour market, reserve army of labour, or devalorization of labour-power. Yet the labour theory of value sends its kind regards to liberal-communist ingénus. The unconditional right to existence is as incompatible with really existing capitalism as participatory democracy was with 'really existing socialism'. In the profane world, universal income takes the form of a minimum income and state-aided exclusion. Thus Van Parijs's elucubrations do not even possess the merit of setting us dreaming. They veer towards the reactionary utopia of a market communism based on mixed ownership, without it being known who decides to invest, with what priorities, and according to which labour process.

Who Exploits Whom?

In the 1950s, Alan Touraine's sociology of labour accorded greater importance to group consciousness than to class consciousness. The fashionable theme of the day was social integration. With individuals no longer expressing their demands as producers but as 'consumers', the notion of class was becoming obsolete. In *La nouvelle classe ouvrière*, Serge Mallet, who never regarded the working class as a 'sociological community', criticized Touraine for confusing the condition of the working class as a sociological notion with the working class as a politico-historical concept. He highlighted the internal mutations in the working class (massification of unskilled workers, expansion of white-collar wage-earners), as opposed to its extinction. These recurrent polemics correspond to real social changes and more directly ideological developments (the promotion of individualism and apologias for competition go together with the disintegration or repression of class solidarities), obliging us to update the analysis of social movements.

If we must hit upon a definition of classes at any price, we should search (and search hard) for it in Lenin, rather than Marx:

Classes are large groups of people differing from each other by the place they occupy in a historically determined system of social production, by their relation (in most cases fixed and formulated in law) to the means of production, by their role in the social organisation of labour, and, consequently, by the dimensions of the share of social income of which they dispose and the mode of acquiring it.[29]

This didactic definition, certainly the least bad of those available, articulates three criteria:

(a) position *vis-à-vis* the means of production (into which Lenin introduces the juridical definition of property – *laws*);
(b) location in the division and organization of labour;
(c) the nature (wage or otherwise), but also the size (amount), of income.

The fact that class involves 'large groups of people' should, moreover, cut short sterile sociological exercises on borderline cases or individual cases. The dynamic of class relations is not a principle of sectional classification.

Subjecting the empirical data of the official statistics to a critical interpretation in class terms makes it possible to test its conceptual relevance. According to the French census of 1975, nearly 83 per cent of the active population were at the time wage-earners (compared with 76 per cent in 1968). In the context of a general expansion of the wage-earning class, senior and middle managers and white-collar workers experienced the highest growth rates, together with significant changes in these same categories. From 1968 to 1975, the number of manual workers increased by 510,000 overall, and that of senior managers by 464,000, that of 'middle managers' by 759,000, and that of employees by 944,000. These crude statistics do not, however, allow a direct interpretation in class terms: for example, foremen are counted as workers, and technicians as middle managers. On the other hand, they do allow us to register an overall progression in workers and employees greater than that of senior and middle managers. Out of the total active population, the proportion of workers in the strict sense went from 33 per cent (in 1954) to 37.8 per cent in 1968, and then 37.7 per cent in 1975, while their numbers increased by half a million in this period.

With a total of 3,100,000, the category of office workers increased more rapidly than that of business employees, but it contains the staff of a number of public or nationalized enterprises, including 77,000 postal workers. Business employees account for 737,000 wage-earners, a majority of them women. According to Lenin's problematic, the overwhelming majority of these employees: (a) are not owners of their own instruments of labour; (b) occupy a subaltern position in the division of labour, exercise no authority and, in a significant number of cases, perform manual labour; and (c) have a wage income inferior to that of skilled workers. Accordingly, once we abandon the symbolic and ideologically charged image of a class identified, depending on the epoch, with the profile of the miner, railwayman or steelworker, they belong in their great majority to the proletariat.

'Middle managers' experienced a rapid growth after 1954: from 6 per cent to 14 per cent in 1975, with 2.8 million wage-earners. The statistical rubric they come under groups four basic categories: 'teachers and artistic professions'; technicians, who differ from middle administrative managers by virtue of the fact that their role is invariably a productive one, and they receive a wage close to that of skilled workers; 'medical and social intermediaries'; and, finally, 'middle administrative managers', who perform an organizational function, directing and supervising employees in administration, banks and business (their organizational role is attested by a sizeable gap of around 20 per cent between their average salary and that of the totality of the category 'middle managers').

Analysis of the socioprofessional census of 1975 allows us to draw the following conclusions:

1. The bourgeoisie proper represents around 5 per cent of the active population (industrialists, large shopkeepers, a fraction of farmers and the liberal professions, the clerical and military hierarchy, the largest portion of 'senior administrative managers').
2. The traditional petty bourgeoisie (self-employed farmers, artisans, small shopkeepers, liberal and artistic professions) still represents about 15 per cent of the active population.
3. The 'new petty bourgeoisie' represents between 8 and 12 per cent, depending upon whether, in addition to a proportion of senior and middle administrative managers, we include journalists and advertising agents, liberal professions that have become salaried, higher and secondary education teachers, and primary-school teachers (which, incidentally, is highly debatable).

At all events, the proletariat (industrial workers and employees in business, banking and insurance, public services, and agricultural wage-earners) constitutes two-thirds (65–70 per cent) of the active population (from which the census excludes 'housewives' and young people still in education).

The 1982 census registers the initial general effects of the crisis. Comparison with earlier censuses is, however, complicated by alterations of nomenclature. Nevertheless, it is clear that the overall share of the wage-earning class in the active population continued to grow, reaching 84.9 per cent as against 82.7 in 1975 and 71.8 in 1962. The proportion of industrial workers, which had begun to decline from 1975 (35.7 against

35.9 per cent in 1968), fell to 33.1 per cent. In absolute terms, this category still progressed by 0.5 per cent between 1975 and 1982, and its rate of growth settled at an average of 10.2 per cent between 1962 and 1982. This average masks a deep disparity between skilled workers, whose number continued to augment (+ 10.2 per cent), and that of unskilled or semi-skilled workers, which declined (− 11.6 per cent). The rate of growth in the category of 'employees' during the seven-year period 1975–82 was 21 per cent (95 per cent since 1962). In absolute terms, they totalled 4.6 million (compared with 7.8 million workers). But the socioprofessional breakdown suppresses the effects of unemployment: a net loss of 700,000 industrial jobs and an actual drop in the number of active workers. At the other pole, the share of middle and senior managers in the active population went up from 8.7 per cent in 1954 to 21.5 in 1982. However, in line with our interpretation of the 1975 census, they cannot be said to constitute a homogeneous class under the catch-all term 'petty bourgeoisie'. In fact, a portion belongs to the higher layers of the proletariat, and another to the bourgeoisie, with the remainder constituting a new petty bourgeoisie or 'service petty bourgeoisie', whose expansion since 1975 has not amounted to an explosion.

So what we are witnessing is a relative erosion of the proletariat and decline in industrial workers in favour of the new petty bourgeoisie, without this as yet amounting to a qualitative mutation. On the other hand, processes of differentiation within the proletariat are impairing solidarity and clouding class consciousness. They result from a decentralization of production units, a flexible reorganization of labour, and an increased individualization of social relations, accompanied by growing social mobility for a section of skilled workers. At the level of reproduction, the halt in urban growth (from the 1982 census, towns with fewer than twenty thousand inhabitants are undergoing above-average growth), exclusion from production and extended education, the privatization and consumption of leisure – these are undermining class identification among the new generations. Are we witnessing the end of the 'culture of exclusion'? The rate of unionization has fallen spectacularly, but the phenomenon is too uneven on a European scale not to be attributable to nationally specific factors. The percentage of those stating that they felt they belonged to a social class fell from 66 per cent in 1976 to 56 per cent in 1987: among workers, the sense of belonging to the world of labour went from 76 per cent in 1976 to 50 per cent in 1987; among the young, the decline is even more pronounced. Explicable by the growing weight of unemployment, a non-linear decline in strike activity was evident from 1976 to 1977, with a recovery in 1986–89 and a new recovery in 1993.

The problem is not a sociological one. What we must instead attend to is the question of the political reversibility of these tendencies – in other words, the relation between social changes, struggles, and effects at the level of consciousness.

Whereas Marx starts from production in order to ground reproduction, most sociological analyses attempt to determine classes through consumption and distribution groups. As a result of status and wage differentials, workers would thus themselves tend to become exploiters. At whose expense? This line of reasoning inevitably leads to tackling the subject of classes from the preferential angle of income, and to investigating *who exploits whom* among waged workers. Baudelot and Establet have pushed this logic to its furthest extent.[30]

In *La Petite Bourgeoisie en France*,[31] they observed (together with Jacques Malemort) that the wage scale disclosed poles and points of crystallization (between a pole inferior to x and a pole superior to $3x$, with a trough between the two). They revealed the inequality between the rate of growth in the wages of the first group, the foremost beneficiary of the growth in the national product; in particular, they discovered that managerial wages did not fluctuate as the wage-earner aged, and that junior managers were gaining access to shareholding. They concluded that the wage of engineers, technicians and managers represented not only the time socially necessary for the reproduction of their own labour-power, but also a share of surplus-value ceded by the bosses in exchange for their loyal service organizing labour. They thus ended up with a calculation of what a fair wage, corresponding to the reproduction of labour-power, might be. Forgetting that value continues to conceal itself behind price fluctuations, they assessed the 'fair price of labour-power' at $x + x/10$ francs, and drew the logical conclusion that the 40 per cent of wage-earners receiving in excess of that were benefiting from a retrocession of surplus-value, and belonged to a new petty bourgeoisie, subdivided into public servants, engineers-technicians and managers in the private sector, the former tied to state hierarchy and the latter to factory despotism.

This approach was scientifically debatable inasmuch as it assumed the legitimacy of quantification in price terms (wage) of the average value of labour-power and individual calculation of the rate of exploitation. In *Qui travaille pour qui?*, Baudelot and Establet refined their proposals by introducing the method of the 'labour equivalent' – in other words, calculation of the quantity of labour embodied in a product, an identical monetary value embodying a different quantity of labour depending on the productivity of the branches concerned. They thus identified three major consumers: households, firms and the state. Households consume consumption goods and accumulate property. Firms consume raw material and accumulate capital. The state consumes raw material and accumulates capital.

In the structure of household consumption, expenditure on food by the different social categories (except the liberal professions) is equivalent. More generally, if social needs were the same, budgets would be comparable. Yet the structure of consumption varies, the most divergent budget headings being those of culture, holidays, domestic equipment, and housing.[32] There are thus dividing lines between lifestyles, as a result of the level of resources (culture really represents a budget heading only among the wealthy classes), and the division between mental and manual labour (manual workers seeking relaxation more). The family remains the privileged site of arbitration between these consumer choices. Hence its transformation and reinforcement. With days off and modern forms of leisure, socialization was allegedly decreasing in all social milieux, and the loosening of social solidarities would give birth to an 'atomized population of families'.

What were the consequences of these tendencies from the standpoint of class?

> Either relations of production are understood as the totality of components that characterize someone's labour in the overall system of production. At base, obviously, there is the fundamental relation (the extraction of surplus-value, the capitalist form of human exploitation). But all the other relations that result from this, and make it possible, form part of them: the amount of resources, the way in which income is obtained, the status that is threatened or developed by capitalism, the material or intellectual nature of the work. If the concept of relations of production is used in this way, it is clear that only it can explain visible lifestyles and budgets. But a major consequence follows: there are as many social classes as there are budgets and relations of production – that is to say, so many groups with definite needs and distinct material interests. Alternatively, we can preserve the old distinction between owner of the means of production and owners of labour-power, with an evident gain in simplicity (two classes), Manicheanism and political simplicity. But we are obliged to deny the collective interest, evident in budgets as in work, of thousands of people who are neither bourgeois nor proletarian.[33]

Where, our authors ask, is the dividing line between what is necessary (simple renewal of labour-power) and what is superfluous located? In their summarizing table, everyone, with the exception of the industrial worker and the agricultural wage-labourer, 'overconsumes'.[34] They thus end up with four sociological 'clumps':

(a) industrialists, well-off inactive population, small shopkeepers, fairly wealthy non-workers;
(b) salaried middle strata (managers and employees);
(c) proletarians (unskilled and semi-skilled workers, skilled workers, agricultural wage-labourers, poor non-workers);
(d) self-employed farmers (who approximate to (c) as regards consumption and (a) as regards property).

Abandoning critical class theory for a descriptive sociology of consumption ends up blurring the lines of force, in favour of a mosaic of infinitely divisible groups.

Farewell to the Red Proletariat?

In his *Farewell to the Working Class*, André Gorz attributes the 'crisis of Marxism' not to some ideological collapse, but to changes in the working class: at issue, in the first instance, is a crisis of the working-class movement itself. From the Crash to the war, capitalism survived – not unscathed, but it survived. Why? Because the development of the productive forces, subject to its own norms and needs, is increasingly incompatible with the socialist transformation for which it was supposed to lay the foundations. The contradiction between the daily lot of a proletariat maimed by labour and its emancipatory vocation is resolved by registering its impotence. Capitalism has supposedly ended up 'produc[ing] a working class which, on the whole, is unable to take command of the means of production', so that 'its transcendence in the name of a different rationality can only come from areas of society which embody or prefigure the dissolution of all social classes, including the working class itself'.[35]

We are back with the old contradiction: how, being nothing, to become everything? By taking this nothingness to a conclusion, replies Gorz.

For this, we must take our leave of the great subject of the revolutionary epic according to Saint Marx. The concept of class in his work was generated not by the experience of a militant, but out of an abstract historical imperative: 'only [consciousness of their class] mission will make it possible to discover the true being of the proletarians'. What flesh-and-blood proletarians happen to imagine or believe is of little consequence. The only thing that counts is their ontological fate: become what you are! In short, the being of the proletariat transcends the proletarians.[36] This philosophical hypostasis resulted from a dubious mixture of Christianity, Hegelianism and scientism. It allowed a self-proclaimed vanguard to play

the intermediary between what the class was and what it should be. Since
no one is in a position to settle the questions that divide it (especially not
the actual proletariat, alienated and crippled as it is by work), the last
word was reserved for a ventriloquist history, invested with the power to
condemn or acquit.

For Marx, labour is at the heart of the emancipatory process. General
abstract labour uproots the artisan or the independent small producer
from their narrow individuality and projects them into the universal.
Appropriating everything through collective labour would make it possible to 'become everything' – except that appropriation and development
do not necessarily coincide. Just as the vanguard usurped the being of a
scattered, mute class, so the bureaucracy presented itself as the embodiment of Prometheus unbound. These delegations and substitutions
might have derived from the development of a capitalism that was still
too weak to allow the working class to display its full potential. Unfortunately, notes Gorz, contrary to the hopes formerly invested in the 'new
working class', technological progress leads not to the formation of an
overwhelmingly skilled and cultivated proletariat, but to new forms of
differentiation and polarization that recompose the mass of those who
are unskilled, excluded and insecure in various respects: the ascendancy
of professional workers was a mere 'parenthesis'. If the weight of the
proletariat in society has increased in accordance with Marx's forecasts,
it has not released proletarians from their impotence as individuals and
as a group: the collective worker has remained external to actual proletarians. Finally, remarks Gorz, Marxist theory has never clarified who
exactly performs collective appropriation; what it consists in; who exercises the emancipatory power conquered by the working class, and
where; which political mediations might guarantee the voluntary character of social co-operation; and what the relationship is between individual
workers and the collective worker, proletarians and the proletariat. The
result is confusion between the statist institutionalization of the collective
worker and the collective appropriation of the means of production by
the associated producers.

Gorz passes without due caution from these legitimate queries to the
critique of an imaginary militancy. The militant spirit, according to him,
consists in a specifically religious belief in the great reversal of nothing
into everything, enjoining workers to lose themselves as individuals to find
themselves again as a class: 'The class as a unit is the imaginary subject
who performs the reappropriation of the system; but it is a subject external
and transcendent to any individual and all existing proletarians.'[37] That
the class became a robotic fetish of this sort, in whose name the bureauc-

racies demanded pious allegiance, is a fact. To impute it to Marx, who consistently denounced society-as-person, history-as-person, and all mythical personifications and incarnations – in other words, any transcendence in which irreducible inter-individuality vanishes – is unserious. Carried away by his own momentum, Gorz ends up condemning the 'power of the proletariat [as] the symmetrical inverse of the power of capital': the bourgeois is alienated by 'his' capital and the proletarian by the proletariat.[38] The confiscation of power by the bureaucracy, however, constitutes a social and historical *coup de force* attested by the Stalinist counter-revolution's millions of victims.

The whole ambiguity of *Farewell to the Working Class* lies here. It raises real problems about the emancipatory capacities of the working class, in the concrete conditions of its alienation. But it constantly mixes this examination with an ideological overinterpretation that is one-sided, to say the least. We no longer really know which has contributed more to the blossoming of dictatorships in the name of the proletariat: the social conditions of exploitation or the genealogy of the concept.

The consummate proletarian, says Gorz, is a pure supplier of abstract general labour. Everything he consumes is bought; everything he produces is sold. The absence of any visible link between consumption and production has as its inevitable consequence an indifference towards concrete labour. And the worker becomes the spectator of a labour he no longer performs. The prophetic conclusion of Volume One of *Capital* evaporates in this stupor: 'The negation of capital's negation of the worker has not taken place.'[39] Yet the controversial chapter does not promise emancipation exclusively in the sphere of production. Breaking the iron logic of capital, says Marx, involves not the formal dialectic of oppression and emancipation through labour, but a political irruption.

The critique then proceeds to strategy, and from Marx to Lenin. Gorz anticipates this change of terrain. He clearly hears this summons of the political. But he conceives it solely in familiar statist forms: 'The project of popular or socialist power is confused with a political project in which the state is everything and society nothing.' This, in its Stalinist and social-democratic modalities, was indeed the response of the majority working-class movement throughout the century. And if it is not the only conceivable one, it derives from the very evolution of capitalism. With the establishment of clientelistic relations to the parties, the attenuation of political mediations, and the growing autonomy of the state, 'the line separating state monopoly capitalism from state capitalism [is] narrow'.[40] Unable to demonstrate its practical cultural capacity, Marx endowed the proletariat with an imaginary ontological capacity to negate its own oppression.

In his *Critique of Economic Reason*, Gorz returns to the transformation of the proletariat and its social practice. The segmentation and disintegration of the working class, insecurity, deskilling, and job insecurity prevail over reprofessionalization:

> At the very point when a privileged fraction of the working class seems to be in a position to acquire multiple skills, to achieve workplace autonomy and continually widen their capacities for action – all of which are things that were ideals of the worker self-management currents within the labour movement – the meaning of this ideal is thus radically altered by the conditions in which it seems destined to be fulfilled. It is not *the working class* which is achieving these possibilities of self-organization and increasing technological power; it is a small core of privileged workers who are integrating into new-style enterprises at the expense of a mass of people who are marginalized and whose job security is destroyed . . .[41]

Stimulated by the crisis, competition rages among workers, and disrupts solidarity. Work's loss of material substance deprives them of the promised reappropriation of their confiscated creativity. In short, work has changed; and so have the workers.

In thirty years, observes Gorz, the annual individual duration of full-time work has decreased by 23 per cent. Work is no longer the main source of social identity and class membership: 'We are leaving the work-based society behind, but we are exiting backwards from it and walking backwards into a civilization of free time.' The conclusion dictates itself:

> It no longer makes sense to expect the pressure of needs engendered by work to lead to a socialist transformation of society, or for such a transformation to be effected by the working class alone. The class antagonism between labour and capital still exists, but it now has superimposed upon it antagonisms which are not of the order of workplace struggles and relations of exploitation, and thus are not covered by traditional class analysis. It is not through identification with their work and their work role that modern wage-earners feel themselves justified in making demands for power which have the potential to change society. It is as citizens, residents, parents, teachers, students or as unemployed; it is their experience outside work that leads them to call capitalism into question.[42]

Since the late 1970s, the number of the industrial working class has undergone an absolute decline. But this decrease appears to be an overall erosion of the proletariat as a result of an optical illusion (not without a whiff of workerism), which reduces the working class to the active, symbolic core workers of a given epoch. The proletariat has neither the same composition, nor the same image, as in 1848 (apart from the Silesian weavers, the proletarians evoked in the *Communist Manifesto* are predominantly artisans or craft workers from small Parisian workshops[43]); under the Commune (following the boom and industrialization of the Second Empire); in June 1936; or May 1968. It is successively represented by craft workers, miners and railwaymen (from Zola to Nizan), steelworkers (Renoir, Vaillant, Visconti), and so on. And history does not stop there. But the destruction of the iron and steel industry or shipbuilding does not signify the disappearance of the proletariat. Rather, it heralds new mutations.

The weakening of workers' identification with work poses a real problem. But Gorz risks an excessive generalization from various types of service or supervisory work that lack any intelligent grasp on the material and its transformation. From this he draws the falsely innovative conclusion that contestation of capitalist exploitation has now been relocated outside of the enterprise, as if it had hitherto been confined there. If the relation of exploitation is rooted in production, the whole logic of *Capital* demonstrates that it is not reducible to it. It structures the field of reproduction in its entirety. The working-class movement did not first of all constitute itself as a movement within the enterprise (if only because it was legally excluded from it by divine right), but as a social, civic, urban and cultural movement. Its confinement to the workplace and the restriction of trade-union practice to negotiations over labour-power were the result of a protracted and conflictual process, the establishment of the welfare state, the growing dissociation between politico-electoral representation and the institutionalization of union rights in the enterprise. The crisis of the nation-state and the representative system's loss of legitimacy contribute just as much as the metamorphoses of the wage relation to weakening trade-union practices, and prompting the relocation of conflict on to the territorial (urban), civic (immigration), ecological, or cultural levels.

Insisting on the proletariat's loss of subversive charge, Gorz adopts certain arguments that he contested at the beginning of the 1960s. At the time, the critical potential of the class had been wrecked – in the view of numerous sociologists – by relative affluence, social integration, and a fascination with 'things'. Now the same is supposedly true by virtue of deprivation and exclusion. Discussion of the obstacles to the development of bonds of solidarity and a critical collective consciousness is doubtless required. But we must beware linear extrapolations that are too quickly shot of political events and their unforeseen advent. A year before May '68, France was allegedly 'bored'. . . .

Gorz rejects the postulate according to which the contradiction between the emancipatory power of the proletariat and its crippling subservience to work is automatically overcome by growing social polarization, with numerical development, concentration, and raised consciousness proceeding in tandem. According to this optimistic perspective, controlling production and recapturing a sense of purpose in work would restore the alienated workers to themselves. The divisions provoked and maintained by competition in the ranks of the class might counter this tendency, but not cancel it.

Ernest Mandel resolves the problem by invoking the asymmetrical destinies of the exploiting and exploited classes:

> In spite of all the inherent segmentations of the working class – all the constantly recurring phenomena of division along craft, national, sex, generational, etc. lines – there are no inbuilt structural obstacles to the overall class solidarity of workers under capitalism. There are only different levels of consciousness which make the conquest of that overall class solidarity more or less difficult, more or less uneven in time and space. The same is not true of bourgeois class solidarity. In periods of prosperity when their struggles are essentially for larger or smaller shares of an increasing mass of profits, class solidarity easily asserts itself among capitalists. In periods of crisis, however, competition has to take a much more savage form, since for each individual capitalist it is no longer a question of getting more or less profit, but one of his survival as a capitalist. . . . Of course, what I have just said applies to inter-capitalist competition, not to the class struggle between Capital and Labour as such, in which, by contrast, the graver the socio-political crisis, the more sharply ruling-class solidarity will assert itself. But the fundamental asymmetry of economic class solidarity within, respectively, the capital-owning and the wage-earning class has to be stressed. . . . Competition among wage-earners . . . is imposed upon them from outside, not structurally inherent in the very nature of that class. On the contrary, wage-earners normally and instinctively strive towards collective cooperation and solidarity.[44]

If this tendency does indeed recurrently manifest itself, the counter-tendency to fragmentation is equally constant. The asymmetry invoked by Mandel attaches to natural competition between capitalists, and artificial competition between wage-earners ('imposed from outside'). This is to underestimate the coherence of the mode of production in which capital, as a living fetish, imposes its law on the whole of society, and inseparably maintains competition between owners and wage-earners thrown on to the labour market. Reducing sometimes antagonistic social differences to mere 'uneven levels of consciousness' disposes of the difficulty. Mandel thus ends up trusting in time, the great restorer and leveller in the face of eternity, to iron out these inequalities, imposing solidarity in conformity with the postulated ontology of the proletariat.

Gorz queries the bases of this triumphant march of the historical subject. Taylorism, the division and scientific organization of labour, has supposedly irrevocably done away with workers conscious of their practical sovereignty. The idea of the class and the associated producers as subjects was, according to him, merely a projection of the specific consciousness of craft workers, possessed of a culture, an ethic and a tradition. The working class that then aspired to power was not a deracinated, ignorant mass of poor wretches, but a potentially hegemonic stratum in society. Syndicalism was the advanced expression of this working class, demanding the mine for the miners and the factory for the workers, confident of its own ability to manage production as well as society. The point of production was consequently perceived as the privileged site for constructing the new power, the factory being no mere economic unit dissociated from the centres of decision-making.

Conversely, in gigantic factories the very idea of the workers' council has become a kind of anachronism. Employers' hierarchy has replaced working-class hierarchy. The only conceivable counter-power (of control or veto) has been reduced to subsidiary issues: hence the assimilation of the velleities of self-organization and self-management by trade-union structures that are themselves institutionalized and subordinate. The acknowledged material impossibility of working-class power creates the space for a trade-union power that has been integrated, a mere social replica of parliamentary delegation. Bureaucracy has become the central figure of society, privileged instrument and component of a subjectless power. The era of unskilled workers and fragmented labour sounds the death knell of the working-class culture and humanism of labour that were the great utopia of the socialist and revolutionary-syndicalist movement in the early twentieth century. Work has lost its meaning as creative activity, shaping matter and mastering nature, acquired in the course of the nineteenth century. Dematerialized, it no longer constitutes the activity via which human beings realize their being by exercising power over matter.

Hence the need 'to find a new utopia'[45] – abandoning the basic presuppositions of the 'industrialist utopia' according to which the inflexibility and social constraints of the machine could be abolished, with autonomous personal activity and social labour converging to the point where they became one. Promethean legacy of the Enlightenment, the Marxist utopia was 'the consummate form of rationalization: the total triumph of Reason and the triumph of total Reason; scientific domination of Nature and reflexive scientific mastery of the process of this domination'. Henceforth, 'the dualization of society will be checked, and then reversed, not by the unattainable utopia of an all-absorbing, full-time job for everyone, but by formulae for redistributing work which will reduce the amount of work *everyone* does, without for all that de-skilling or compartmentalizing it'.[46] Gorz concludes from this that hopes of emancipation through and in work are obsolete. If the labour of production is now disjoined from sensory experience, and restricted to a declining minority, '*who* is there who can transform work into a fulfilling *poiesis*? Surely not the immense majority of the wage-earning classes.' There will be an exit from the vicious circle only when we give up conceiving work as the essential socializing factor, and consider it as one simple factor among numerous others. The conclusion follows naturally: 'The aspiration to all-round personal development in autonomous activities does not, therefore, *presuppose* a prior transformation of work . . . *the old notion of work is no longer valid, the subject assumes a critical distance not only from the product of his work but from that work itself.*'[47]

This candid break with Marx's problematic leads into a search for new emancipatory subjects and new strategies. What is now at issue is not so much emancipating ourselves in work as liberating ourselves from work, beginning by reconquering the sphere of free time. According to Gorz:

> The central conflict over the extent and limits of economic rationality . . . used to be conducted, culturally and politically, at the level of workplace struggles; it has gradually spread to other areas of social life . . . The question as to the 'subject' that will decide the central conflict, and in practice carry out the socialist transformation, cannot, consequently, be answered by means of traditional class analysis.

This new subject (for Gorz's approach does not avoid the old problematic of the subject) nevertheless has difficulty escaping limbo. It is evoked as 'a multidimensional social movement that can no longer be defined in terms of class antagonism. . . . This movement is essentially a struggle for collective and individual rights to self-determination.'[48]

As for its strategic consequences, radical innovation leads, via novel paths, to some old tunes. Incapable of taking on the state and controlling work, this polymorphous and rhizomatic subject is summoned to develop its counter-culture, with a hegemonic vocation, in free time. In *Farewell to the Working Class*, Gorz had argued that power could be taken only by a class that was already *de facto* dominant. Such is indeed the strategic enigma of the proletarian revolution. Whereas the conquest of economic and cultural power precedes the conquest of political power for the bourgeoisie, for the proletariat the conquest of political power would have to initiate social and cultural transformation.

This is an obsessive leitmotiv: how, being nothing, to become at least something? In the 1960s, Lucien Goldmann responded with a 'revolutionary reformism' of Austro-Marxist inspiration. Still insurmountable because of the minority status of the proletariat, the contradiction would be resolved by historical development itself. A socially majoritarian and increasingly cultivated proletariat could progressively extend its self-managerial counter-powers, and establish its hegemony prior to the conquest of political power proper. As the political majority caught up with the social majority, this last act could be peaceful and electoral. The intervening thirty years have scarcely confirmed such optimism. The social homogenization and cultural autonomy heralded by the affluent postwar years have not withstood the effects of the crisis. How can we imagine emancipation in leisure when work remains alienated and alienating? How can a collective, creative culture develop when the cultural sphere itself is increasingly subject to commodity production? How can state domination be escaped when the dominant ideology is imposed mainly through the fantastical universe of general commodity production? If querying the emancipatory capacities of the proletariat is (to say the least) current, how can we have credence in those of the 'non-class' formed by the deprived and excluded?

To claim that this new, post-industrial proletariat does 'not find any source of potential power in social labour' is to attribute to marginality virtues that it does not possess. After the encirclement of the towns by the countryside, that of the sphere of production by the fluctuating world of precariousness? Defining this new proletariat as a 'non-force' dedicated to conquering not 'power', which is inherently corrupting, but increasing 'areas of autonomy', is to make impotence a virtue and seek to surpass productivism (which is certainly open to criticism) in a troubling 'free subjectivity'. 'Only the non-class of non-producers is capable of such [a constitutive] act,' writes Gorz, '[f]or it alone embodies what lies beyond productivism: the rejection of the accumulation ethic and the dissolution of all classes.'[49]

In 1980, before the crisis had produced its social and moral effects, Gorz could still retain the illusions of the previous period. A decade later, it was no longer possible to believe in the emancipatory virtues of this forced exclusion that would make the *déclassés* or 'underclass' the new champions of a better world. Under the pretext of embracing the cause of the worst-off, this ideology of non-work, centred on the primacy of individual sovereignty, is actually the new guise of a utopia of the distraught middle classes (reviving the 'thought of a revolutionary bourgeoisie'), for whom 'real life' begins outside work. Gorz went so far as to accuse women's movements of reinforcing capitalist rationality by seeking to 'free women from non-economically oriented activities'.[50] For him, the real objective is not to liberate women from non-market domestic activities, but to extend the non-economic rationality of such activities beyond the home. Blithely ignoring the fact that these domestic activities, which are themselves alienated, are the reverse side and complement of alienated wage-labour, this proposal anticipated propositions on community business and new personalized services, which are set to become props of insecurity.

In another respect, well before the dismemberment of the bureaucratic dictatorships, Gorz rightly put his finger on the fact that the individual could not wholly coincide with his or her social being. To suppose that individual existence is 'integrally' socializable is to set in motion the repressive machinery of 'socialist morality' as a universal passion for order: 'In this context [the totalitarian states], individual consciousness reveals itself sub rosa as the sole possible foundation of morality. Moral consciousness always arises through an act of rebellion ... a revolt against ... "objective morality".'[51] Yet the solution does not consist in planning some peaceful cohabitation between an autonomous society and an untouchable state, between a liberated sphere of free time and an alienated sphere of work, whose impossibility has been demonstrated by all historical experience, often with bloody results. Instead, it consists in the refusal of any artificially decreed assimilation of society and state, individual and class.

Marx and Lenin referred to the withering away or extinction – not the abolition – of the state. This withering away is conceivable only as a process, the time in which nothing, in effect, becomes everything (if it ever does). As long as relative scarcity and the division of labour persist, the state will inevitably re-enter through the back window. Its positive disappearance cannot be decreed. It involves a form of dual power prolonging the revolutionary event in a process of extinction–construction, in which society would control the state and progressively appropriate the functions that no longer need to be delegated. Such an approach invites us to consider the institutional architecture of power and the relative autonomy of the sphere of law, rather than assuming that both would naturally ensue from might dictating right (courtesy of the 'dictatorship of the proletariat').

Rather than embarking on this path, Gorz registers the impossibility of abolishing necessity. The extension of free time would thus coexist with a compulsory, alienated labour that would still have to be performed. The sphere of necessity would include the activities required to produce what is socially necessary. Hence the untranscendable function of the political:

> A disjuncture between the sphere of necessity and the area of autonomy, an objectification of the operational necessities of communal life in the form of laws, prohibitions and obligations, the existence of a system of law distinct from mere usage and of a state distinct from society – these are the very preconditions of a sphere in which autonomous individuals may freely cooperate for their own ends.[52]

Thus formulated, the indicated disjuncture is simply the exact obverse of some fantastic restoration of the unity between the public and the private. Outside any historical dynamic, it works out an armed peace between the heteronomy of the state and the autonomy of civil society. Resigned to suffering the antinomy between freedom and necessity, it is content to demand a clearly defined and codified necessity. Having been proudly invited to change utopias, we are reduced to a tepid utopia (prosaically juridical and statist) – a tattered utopia for times of crisis, refuge of a new, salaried and consumerist petty bourgeoisie, trapped between the bureaucratic hammer and the liberal anvil.

Gorz criticizes Marx for building his theory on sand – on a *philosophical* conception of the proletariat lacking any solid relation with its reality. This criticism is not unfounded. Seeking to transcend German philosophy, which was powerless to transform reality, the young Marx initially sought a solution in a speculative alliance between philosophy and the proletariat, between suffering humanity and thinking humanity. The proletarian class was then in the process of being formed. According to Marx, it was a class that possessed a 'universal character' ('a class of civil society which is not a class of civil society'); was the victim of injustice pure and simple, not of some particular injustice; and was the vehicle of both a dissolution of capitalist society and a total recovery of humanity.[53] What this involves is indeed a philosophical presentation of the proletariat, predating the 'critique of political economy'. The following year, the revolt of the Silesian weavers was likewise presented by Marx as the material manifestation of the proletarian essence.

Following Engels's investigations of the actual proletariat (the working classes in England), the critique of political economy worked out the concrete configuration of the proletariat (as commodified labour-power) in its overall relations to capital. Rather than meticulously retracing this path, if only to demarcate himself from it, Gorz inopportunely takes the quickest route. He summons to the rescue the 'non-class of non-producers' whose mission, *qua* negation of the negation, is closely akin to that of the young Marx's 'philosophical' proletariat! Who better than those excluded and deprived of everything, including their own labour, could today represent a nascent class that is universal in character, the victim of utter injustice, and the vehicle of a reconquest of humanity through the dissolution of society? Summoned to explode a programmed, one-dimensional society, this new subject is, rather, the symptom of a mythical regression compared with the patient determination of classes in and through the reproduction of capital.

The relation of exploitation is at the heart of class relations. For Marx, the concepts of necessary labour and surplus labour are retrospectively determined by the metabolism of competition and the process as a whole. Analytical Marxist authors *individualize exploitation* by relating it to the consumption of each actor. For Jon Elster, '[b]eing exploited means, fundamentally, working more hours than are needed to produce the goods one consumes'. For Andrès de Francisco, individuals enter into class relations to maximize their private interests: 'I shall refer to classes as a precise set of relations between individuals ... I am proposing an individualist theory of classes as preliminary to a classist theory of society.'[54]

For Marx, by contrast, the relation of exploitation is – and cannot but be – from the outset a *social relation*, not an individual relation. The rate of exploitation (s/v) expresses a class relation illustrated by the analysis of co-operation and the division of labour: co-operation gives rise to an economy of time due to the spatial simultaneity of productive tasks; one day of one hundred hours from ten workers is more productive than ten successive days of ten hours; the combined productive power is superior to the sum of individual powers. The bar of the relation (s/v) represents the mobile front line between necessary labour and surplus labour around which conflict is structured. This relation of exploitation presupposes the process of reproduction as a whole, and hence the class struggle. Outside the global determination of the labour-time socially necessary for the reproduction of labour-power, the notion of individual exploitation is theoretically flimsy.

In *The German Ideology*, Marx condemns the reduction of individuals to the status of serial exemplars of a formal class, and philosophical representations of classes as preceding the individuals who comprise them. In the *Grundrisse*, he symmetrically rejects the Robinsonnades of classical political economy and the reduction of classes to a sum of individual relations: 'The individual and isolated hunter and fisherman, with whom Smith and Ricardo begin, belongs among the unimaginative conceits of the eighteenth-century Robinsonades.'[55] Finally, in the three volumes of *Capital*, the reciprocal determination of individuals and classes is understood according to the dynamic totality of social relations. The struggle to limit the working day sets the 'global capitalist' (that is, the class of capitalists) and the 'global worker' (or labouring class) against one another. As soon as the worker is separated from the means of production, 'this [class] relation does ... exist, because the conditions for the realization of labour-power, i.e. means of subsistence and means of production, are separated, as the property of another, from the possessor of labour-power'.[56] Finally, 'each individual capitalist, just like the totality of all capitalists in each particular sphere of production, participates in the *exploitation of the entire working class by capital as a whole*', and 'the average rate of profit depends on the level of exploitation of labour as a whole by capital as a whole'.[57] That is why – the competition that divides it notwithstanding – the bourgeoisie constitutes a veritable 'freemasonry' *vis-à-vis* the 'working class as a whole'.

Exploitation through the extortion of surplus-value involves the splitting of the commodity into use-value and exchange-value, as well as the splitting of labour into concrete labour and abstract labour:

The *common factor* in the exchange relation, or in the exchange-value of the commodity, is therefore its value ... A use-value, or useful article, therefore, has value only because abstract human labour is objectified or materialized in it. How, then, is the magnitude of this value to be measured? By means of the quantity of the 'value-forming substance', the labour, contained in the article. This quantity is measured by its duration, and the labour-time is itself measured on the particular scale of hours, days etc. It might seem that if the value of a commodity is determined by the quantity of labour expended to produce it, it would be the more valuable the more unskilful and lazy the worker who produced it, because he would need more time to complete the article. However, the labour that forms the substance of value is *equal human labour, the expenditure of identical human labour-power*. *The total labour-power of society*, which is manifested in the values of the world of commodities, counts here as *one homogeneous mass of human labour-power*, although composed of innumerable individual units of labour-power. Each of these units is *the same as any other*, to the extent that it has the *character of a socially average unit of labour-power* and acts as such, i.e. only needs, in order to produce a commodity, the *labour time* which is necessary on average, or in other words is *socially necessary*.[58]

Without this concept of abstract labour, the labour theory of value would result in the absurdity that time wasted dawdling and idling creates value. The expenditure of labour-power is not individual in the first instance. It presupposes 'average' labour-power, 'identical' labour-power, 'socially necessary' labour. This average is not established exclusively in the sphere of production. It in turn presupposes the metabolism of competition, the establishment of an average profit rate, and the historical recognition of needs imposed by class struggle (which are not restricted to immediate consumption needs, but extend to reproduction needs, including factors of education, culture and environment common to several generations).

Abstract labour is thus historically determined by the system of needs – in other words, by the universality of lack. The equality of different kinds of labour assumes abstraction from their actual inequality. Their reduction to their common character as 'expenditure of labour-power' is a consequence of exchange. Marx insists on this in Part 2, Chapter 6:

> natural needs, such as food, clothing, fuel and housing vary according to the climatic and other physical peculiarities of [a] country. On the other hand, the number and extent of . . . so-called necessary requirements, as also the manner in which they are satisfied, are themselves products of history, and depend therefore to a great extent on the level of civilization attained by a country; in particular they depend on the conditions in which, and consequently on the habits and expectations with which, the class of free workers has been formed. In contrast, therefore, with the case of other commodities, the determination of the value of labour-power contains a historical and moral element. Nevertheless, in a given country at a given period, the average amount of the means of subsistence necessary for the worker is a known *datum* . . . the sum of means of subsistence necessary for the production of labour-power must include the means necessary for the worker's replacements, i.e. his children, in order that this race of peculiar commodity-owners may perpetuate its presence on the market.[59]

If labour-power 'contains a historical and moral element', and if its reproduction includes generational succession, the determination of the labour-time that is socially necessary for this reproduction presupposes . . . the class struggle!

Capital, a social relation, is thus the unity of a relation of domination and a relation of competition. At the level of production, the rate of surplus-value s/v expresses the class relation independently of the relation of competition. At the level of (re)production as a whole, the rate of profit (s/c+v) expresses the relation of exploitation mediated by the relation of competition. Pierre Salama and Tran Hai Hac emphasize the conceptual difference between surplus-value and profit, which is often misconstrued in the so-called 'transformation' controversy:

> Thus, just as the level of the class relation is structured by the existence of the rate of exploitation, the inter-capitalist relation is structured by the formation of the general rate of profit, which is the form in which the rate of exploitation is imposed on individual capitalists in competition. In this sense, the general profit rate is a transformed form of exchange-value previously defined at the level of capital-in-general. The development of exchange-value from the level of capital-in-general to the level of competing capitals is known as the transformation of exchange-value into production price. This is nothing other than the transition from the analysis of capital at one level of abstraction to another. Transformation signifies that the struggle for profit engaged in by capitalists is restricted to the sum of surplus-value extracted from the class of workers: the capitalists cannot share more than has been extracted in the class relation. In other words, the transformation of exchange-value into production price expresses the division of the surplus-value extracted at the level of capital-in-general between competing capitals.[60]

The sum and forms of redistribution of surplus-value are subordinate to its extraction. Accordingly, exploitation cannot be determined by the individual allocation of consumption goods compared with individual labour-time.

Notes

1. Vilfredo Pareto insisted on social mobility and the 'circulation of elites' capable of eliminating cultural barriers between classes. Roberto Michels defended his iron law of oligarchy. Karl Renner deduced from unproductive labour the idea of a 'service class'. At the same time, Talcott Parsons developed an analytical theory of social stratification. The very use of the word 'class' varies, with peaks of frequency before 1914, between the wars (1924–28, 1933–34, 1938–39), or after the Second World War (1953–58, 1970–72). Contrariwise, the expression 'middle classes' was particularly prized on the eve of the Second World War, in the 1950s, and again after 1981. See Hélène Desbrousses, 'Définition des classes et rapports d'hégémonie', in *Classes et catégories sociales*, Érides, Paris 1985. See also Larry Portis, *Les Classes sociales en France*, Éditions ouvrières, Paris 1988.
2. See Andrès de Francisco, 'Que hay de teorico en la "teoria" marxista de las clases', *Zona Abierta*, nos 59/60, Madrid 1992.
3. John Roemer, *A General Theory of Exploitation and Class*, Harvard University Press, Cambridge, MA 1982; Roemer, ed., *Analytical Marxism*, Cambridge University Press/ Éditions de la Maison des Sciences de l'Homme, Cambridge and Paris 1986; Erik Olin Wright, *Class, Crisis and the State*, New Left Books, London 1978; *Classes*, Verso, London 1985; and *Interrogating Inequality*, Verso, London and New York 1994.

4. Roemer, *A General Theory of Exploitation and Class*, p. 192.
5. Ibid., pp. 28, 94–5.
6. Ibid., p. 16.
7. Ibid., p. 39.
8. Ibid., p. 179. Detecting in Marx a 'quasi-homogenization' of the producers by means of proletarianization, Roemer confirms his incomprehension of the importance of abstract labour and the logical relation between conditions of production and the generalization of commodity production.
9. See G.A. Cohen, 'The Structure of Proletarian Unfreedom', in Roemer, ed., *Analytical Marxism.*
10. Roemer, *A General Theory of Exploitation and Class*, p. 60.
11. See Thomas Coutrot and Michel Husson, *Les Destins du tiers monde*, Nathan, Paris 1993.
12. Jon Elster, *Making Sense of Marx*, Cambridge University Press/Éditions de la Maison des Sciences de l'Homme, Cambridge and Paris 1985, p. 331.
13. John Roemer, 'Should Marxists be Interested in Exploitation?', in Roemer, ed., *Analytical Marxism*, p. 262.
14. At the cost of some conceptual acrobatics: what does the *exploitation* of commodities or the *exploitation* of things mean? As for the idea of measuring alienation *individually*, by the surplus-value extracted from each person, it derives from a mania for measuring.
15. Roemer, *A General Theory of Exploitation and Class*, p. 241.
16. Ibid., p. 248.
17. Ibid., p. 276. For Roemer, the theory of exploitation based on labour-values applies exclusively to capitalism, and presents only one facet of historical materialism. Left to one side, the other facet consists in the mechanism through which historical materialism proposes to fulfil its determinist prediction, i.e. class struggle. Thus, '[i]t is the sociology of injustice which must provide the link between these two facets of the Marxian theory of history' (p. 289).
18. Ibid., p. 273.
19. Ibid., p. 276.
20. See Erik Olin Wright, 'What is Middle about the Middle Class?', in Roemer, ed., *Analytical Marxism*, and 'Rethinking Once Again the Concept of Class Structure', in Wright *et al.*, *The Debate on Classes*, Verso, London and New York 1989.
21. Wright, 'Rethinking Once Again the Concept of Class Structure', p. 276. In the same text, Wright nevertheless cannot avoid sliding in this direction: 'as an individual, to be a capitalist means that economic welfare depends upon extraction of surplus labor from workers . . . as an individual, to be a worker means that economic welfare depends upon successfully selling one's labor power to a capitalist' (ibid., pp. 286–7). Describing the members of a class as individuals who share material interests suggests that they have the same dilemmas in common when it comes to collective action and the individual search for economic well-being and power. Similarly, Andrès de Francisco, for whom the concept of class is 'primarily a classificatory concept', writes that a theory of classes 'will therefore start from a classification of individuals' ('Que hay de teorico . . .?').
22. Wright, 'Rethinking Once Again the Concept of Class Structure', p. 271.
23. In his extensive application of the double criterion of exploitation and domination to the determination of classes, Anthony Giddens, in contrast, restricts the primacy of the first to the capitalist mode of production. There, private ownership of the means of production is supposedly the source in and of itself of overall social power, whereas under feudalism and in all other class societies, control over the means of authority is determinant. Thus, Giddens distinguishes between class society (i.e. capitalist society, where division into classes is the central principle of social organization) and class-divided society (i.e. societies in which classes do not constitute the determinant structural principle). Such a distinction might seem like sheer artifice. Resistance to reducing the whole history of humanity to the class struggle such as it specifically develops under capitalism assumes, however, another significance when Giddens contests the 'reduction'

of social conflict to class conflict in bourgeois society. For him, coercive appropriation and possession constitute as important a criterion as property and exploitation. Therewith, the primacy of domination is established surreptitiously, and class theory is effaced in favour of a Weberian sociology of groups.

24. Wright, 'Rethinking Once Again the Concept of Class Structure', p. 310.
25. For Weberian sociology, the undertaking is more straightforward. Since stratification operates directly in the relation to the market, there is in fact no need for the concept of class to be associated with a particular mode of production; nor does it rest upon a central antagonistic polarization, but licenses an indeterminate fragmentation of groups and classes.
26. Wright, 'Rethinking Once Again the Concept of Class Structure', p. 348.
27. Wright, *Interrogating Inequality*, pp. 71, 247.
28. Philippe Van Parijs, 'A Capitalist Road to Communism', in Van Parijs, *Marxism Recycled*, Cambridge University Press/Éditions de la Maison des Sciences de l'Homme, Cambridge and Paris 1993. See also 'Les paradigmes de la démocratie', *Actuel Marx*, Presses Universitaires de France, Paris 1994.
29. V.I. Lenin, 'A Great Beginning', in Lenin, *Collected Works*, vol. XXIX, Progress Publishers, Moscow 1965, p. 421.
30. See Christian Baudelot, Roger Establet, Jacques Toisier and P.-O. Flavigny, *Qui travaille pour qui?*, Maspero, Paris 1979.
31. Christian Baudelot, Roger Establet and Jacques Malemort, *La Petite Bourgeoisie en France*, Maspero, Paris 1974.
32. Baudelot *et al.*, *Qui travaille pour qui?*, p. 76.
33. Ibid., pp. 121–2.
34. Ibid., p. 135.
35. André Gorz, *Farewell to the Working Class*, trans. Michael Sonenscher, Pluto Press, London 1982, p. 15.
36. Ibid., p. 16. Erik Olin Wright similarly considers that the constitutive position of the working class in classical Marxism includes a set of material interests, common lived experiences, and capacities for collective struggle that are supposed to converge naturally. In his view, however, these three factors no longer coincide.
37. Ibid., p. 37.
38. Ibid.
39. Ibid., p. 39.
40. Ibid., pp. 40, 43.
41. André Gorz, *Critique of Economic Reason*, trans. Gillian Handyside and Chris Turner, Verso, London and New York 1990, p. 70.
42. André Gorz, *Capitalism, Socialism, Ecology*, trans. Chris Turner, Verso, London and New York 1994, pp. 45, 42.
43. See the sociology of the Communist League in Michaël Löwy, *La Théorie de la révolution chez le jeune Marx*, Maspero, Paris 1970.
44. Ernest Mandel, Introduction to Karl Marx, *Capital*, vol. 3, trans. David Fernbach, Penguin/NLR, Harmondsworth 1981, pp. 76–7.
45. Gorz,, *Critique of Economic Reason*, p. 8.
46. Ibid., p. 71.
47. Gorz, *Capitalism, Socialism, Ecology*, pp. 58–9.
48. Ibid., pp. 69, 89–90.
49. Gorz, *Farewell to the Working Class*, pp. 71–4.
50. Ibid., p. 84.
51. Ibid., p. 93.
52. Ibid., p. 111.
53. See Karl Marx, 'A Contribution to the Critique of Hegel's Philosophy of Right. Introduction', in Marx, *Early Writings*, trans. Gregor Benton and Rodney Livingstone, Penguin/NLR, Harmondsworth 1975, pp. 243–57. See, in this connection, Georges Labica,

200   STRUGGLE AND NECESSITY

Marxism and the Status of Philosophy, trans. Kate Soper and Martin Ryle, Harvester, Brighton 1980.

54. Elster, *Making Sense of Marx*, p. 167; de Francisco, 'Que hay de teorico en la "teoria" marxista de las clases?' and 'Théorie classiste de la société ou théorie individualiste des classes', *Viento Sur*, no. 12, December 1993. In the same issue of *Zona Abierta* (nos 59/60, 1992), Val Burris offers an extensive definition of exploitation ('the ability of an individual or a class to appropriate the labour of another'). But the class relation is reduced to economic exploitation, with relations of domination being considered secondary. The idea that 'the appropriation of surplus-value occurs exclusively in the production process' is a misinterpretation of the role of the process as a whole: the extraction of surplus-value in production is not yet appropriation, which presupposes the market and reproduction as a whole.

55. Karl Marx, *Grundrisse*, trans. Martin Nicolaus, Penguin/NLR, Harmondsworth 1973, p. 83.

56. Karl Marx, *Capital*, vol. 2, trans. David Fernbach, Penguin/NLR, Harmondsworth 1978, p. 115.

57. Marx, *Capital*, vol. 3, pp. 298–9; emphasis added. Suzanne de Brunhoff is wholly faithful to this approach when she writes: 'The notion of class refers to a conflictual economic and social relation . . . The surplus-labour supplied by the worker does not manifest itself directly and individually . . . The notion of class is not an instrument of economic analysis that starts out from individuals and their rational choices' ('Ce que disent les économistes', *Politis*, no. 4, 1993).

58. Karl Marx, *Capital*, vol. 1, trans. Ben Fowkes, Penguin/NLR, Harmondsworth 1976, pp. 128–9.

59. Ibid., p. 275.

60. Pierre Salama and Tran Hai Hac, *Introduction à l'économie de Marx*, La Découverte, Paris 1992, p. 55.

PART III

The Order of Disorder
Marx's Critique of Scientific Positivism

> . . . nowhere in the universe can be
> A final edge, and no escape be found
> From the endless possibility of flight.
>
> Lucretius, *On the Nature of the Universe*

7

Doing Science Differently

Marx is subject to two quite opposite types of critique. Sometimes he is criticized for economic determinism; sometimes for departing from the requirements of causality and predictability without which there would be nothing but 'pseudo-science', cunningly disguised as scientificity. Each criticism contains its share of truth, but both miss the essential point.

Fascinated by the success of the natural sciences, Marx was unquestionably seduced by the 'will to do science' animating them. The preface to the first edition of *Capital* evokes the community of 'all sciences'. It takes them as a model for the critique of political economy: the 'commodity form' presents itself as 'the economic cell-form'; the 'natural laws' of capitalist production generate social antagonisms; society attempts to discover 'the natural laws of its movement'. These laws are expressed with 'iron necessity'. To register an irreducible singularity, this necessity is immediately rectified, assuming the less rigid shape of 'tendencies'.[1]

Charmed by the metallic accents of English science, Marx seems to be restrained by the bonds of 'German science' and the whispers of a history in which the voices of Leibniz and Goethe, Fichte and Hegel, mingle. This unresolved dilemma was to prove fruitful. Situated between the development of philosophy into science and of science into politics, between English science and German science, Marx's thought, balanced on the knife edge of critique, beckons towards the 'organic mechanism' and the 'science of borders' or 'plena' whose spectres haunt our instrumental reason.

Science in the German Sense

Marx's relation to science is disconcerting for many readers in thrall to an epistemology that reduces 'genuine' science to its physical model. In the idea of 'German science', in contrast, what we find is an encounter between an apparently archaic representation of science, still bound up

with philosophy, and the anticipation of a new science that has sur-
mounted the *Krise* of the European sciences. As if with regret, Schumpeter
registers this disquieting novelty:

> Marx's mixture is a chemical one: that is to say, he introduced [the facts of
> economic history] into the very argument that produces the results. He was the
> first economist of top rank to see and to teach systematically how economic
> theory may be turned into historical analysis and how the historical narrative
> may be turned into *histoire raisonnée*.

Sensitive to the 'access of vitality' thereby imparted to the analysis – '[t]he
ghostly concepts of economic theory begin to breathe. The bloodless
theorem descends into *agmen, pulverem et clamorem*' – Schumpeter nevertheless rejects this heterodox 'mixture' of concepts and propositions, at
once economic and sociological, which defies the organized academic
division of intellectual labour: 'The trait peculiar to the Marxian system is
that it subjects those historical events and social institutions themselves to
the explanatory process of economic analysis or, to use the technical
lingo, that it treats them not as data but as variables.'[2]

A disconcerting 'science', this science of Marx's. In a breathless quest
for the living organism, where conceptual order constantly comes undone
in carnal disorder, it continually mingles synchrony and diachrony, the
universality of the structure and the singularity of history.

For a long time, positive science and speculative philosophy coexisted
on the basis of a mutually beneficial pact. If science did not 'think',
philosophers could retain the vast domain of thought that was not
susceptible of proof, while in exchange scientists were assigned exclusive
rights to definitive truth. Transformations of the hard sciences, challenges
to their purpose, and the proliferation of scientific practices incompatible
with the restrictive criteria in force, ruptured this compromise. It is now
agreed that science thinks and, consequently, that it thinks with words. In
the absence of a system of univocal and transparent words, arbitrating
disagreements over meaning, these words are not reliable. Indeed, they
are less reliable than ever.

The concepts of classical physics are 'figurative concepts'. But according to Niels Bohr, we must abandon the need for intuitive representations
with which our language is saturated.[3] Where are we to find the terms
capable of conveying situations so bizarre that they set a thousand fancies,
seductive or disquieting, dancing on the thread of our imaginary? It is
possible to have understood a certain state of affairs and yet appreciate
that it can be evoked only by images and parables. At the furthermost
bounds of worlds where familiar representations fail us, the only alterna-

tives are to be silent or to listen to language tremble. Where dictionaries, classifications and nomenclatures are unavailing, it has proved necessary to revive the fecundity of metaphors and poems. Time's arrow, black holes, double helix, big bang and big crunch, strange attractors, fractals, memory of water: this is where we are. There is no longer some absolute elsewhere than science, inseparable from its double, ignorance – only a relative other: *its* other. In turn, this relation of alterity must be known, and so on, in a boundless flight towards the inaudible last word of a metascience, or a universal *Caractéristique* as vainly dreamt of by Leibniz.

The metaphorical style of *Capital* has attracted much sarcasm. It allegedly attests to obvious imposture. It evinces an inability to submit to the rigours of scientific formalization. It displays the indelible stamp of a speculative – or, worse still, literary – nostalgia. A number of readers are discouraged by a lack of univocal, reliable definitions, by so many terminological variations and inconsistencies! Marx's writing does indeed wrestle with the uncertainties of the language. Many misinterpretations can result.

Engels grew irritated with the inflexibility of the French language: 'It is becoming increasingly impossible to think originally in the strait-jacket of modern French.' 'Marx would never have written in German in that way'![4] The German language embraces the movement of ideas and the reciprocal relations between form and content. Marx thus invokes 'German science', or the 'German dialectical manner', as if conceptual inadequacies could be corrected by the memory of a culture. *Wissenschaft*, which includes all theoretical knowledge, is not burdened with the heavily positive connotations of 'Science' in the French sense. Its specifically 'German' character evokes a rich philosophical heritage. The issue goes far beyond problems of translation and dictionaries. It raises questions of language, style and composition that find a fragile response in the unity of an *œuvre* whose aesthetic dimension signals a different rationality and another form of knowledge: '*Whatever shortcomings they may have*, the advantage of my writings is that they are an artistic whole.'[5] This assertion is not to be taken lightly, as the *amour propre* of a frustrated novelist. Marx's metaphorical creativity discloses the need for a knowledge that is simultaneously analytical and synthetic, scientific and critical, theoretical and practical. Sometimes a short cut, sometimes a detour, it expresses defiance of formalized language as much as it expresses a regret for its absence. Karl Korsch, for whom metaphorical thought performed an irreplaceable heuristic function in phases of theoretical gestation, clearly understood it thus.

There is no question of countering the scientistic Marx of superficial detractors with a Marx who pioneered future scientific revolutions. But under the influence of 'English science', he thought within the constraints of a strange object – capital – an intimate understanding of which required another causality, different laws, another temporality – in short, a different mode of scientificity. 'German science' marks the spot. This is where we must dig – read, discuss and interpret – rather than accepting the slapdash accusations that sometimes make Marx into a vulgar economist (despite his declared concern for the 'artistic whole'), and sometimes a tragic poet of history. If he was obviously unable to foresee the epistemological upheavals which confront us today, his partial responses to the theological niceties of the commodity transcend the scientific horizon of his century. His thought hardly seems out of place in contemporary controversies.

In an article written in 1980, Manuel Sacristan demonstrated how the 'crisis of Marxism' had impacted differently on the various readings of Marx. The scientistic reading of the 1960s was directly affected by the repercussions of the decomposition of Stalinism, but also by challenges to any rationalism (under the influence of a dubious fad for 'zero growth'). In the political field, the Solzhenitsyn effect was amplified and combined with the effects of the Brezhnevite stagnation, disenchantment with the Chinese Cultural Revolution, Indochinese dissensions, and the ambiguities of the 'Iranian revolution'. Under the impact of these, some, like Colletti, rediscovered a dual concept of science in Marx, contrary to what they were claiming but a short while before: a 'normal' concept of positive science, corresponding to the dominant image of scientific discourse; and a concept of *Wissenschaft*, which does not repudiate a knowledge of essences.

Sacristan marvels ironically at so belated a discovery. To avoid imputing a positivist scientism to Marx, he observes, it would have sufficed to attend to his vocabulary, to the difference between Anglo-French science and *deutschen Wissenschaft*. A careful reading would at least have disclosed a double temptation: a positive scientific model that attracts Marx, but which is immediately countered by a concern for knowledge of the totality and singularity. Enrique Dussel aptly writes: 'Were we to judge Marx according to the meaning attributed to normal science, science in its current – e.g. Popperian – sense, we would no longer be able to understand anything of the practice of scientific rationality in Marx.'[6]

Several letters evoke the kind of science that Marx intended to engage in: 'economics as a science in the German sense of the word [*im deutschen Sinn*] has yet to be tackled . . . in a work such as mine, there are bound to be many *shortcomings* in the detail. But the *composition*, the structure is a triumph of German scholarship [*deutschen Wissenschaft*]'.[7] A critique of appearances and fetishism, this science is directed towards the 'inner relations' underlying phenomenal forms. *Deutschen Wissenschaft* betokens no theoretical chauvinism. Marx is far too admiring and respectful of the results of the positive (or English) sciences to spurn them. They are a necessary moment in the movement of knowledge – on condition that we do not stop there.

According to Sacristan, the Hegelian legacy served as a vehicle for a hybrid representation of science that prevented Marx 'clarifying the epistemological status of his intellectual work'. Closer to critique than the 'absolute science' whose excessive claims are condemned in a letter to Ruge as early as 1843, his 'German science' forms part of an intellectual tradition to which English empiricism and French rationalism have proved obstinately recalcitrant.[8] The point at issue is not abandoning the totality under the pretext of elucidating each of its parts, but rediscovering the universal in the singular. Such a science is liable to grant itself excessive liberties. It must avoid sterile disdain for normal science (the 'crude' or 'Baconian' English science of Darwin), and Hegelian scorn for the 'thing that is learnt'. This 'thing' is a necessary moment in scientific development:

> Science in the current sense, not as a wisdom reserved for idealist Titans, does exist, when one works with things that can be learnt and taught, and whose use can consequently be challenged by any colleague. What cannot be verified through things that can be taught (transmitted) might be of greater interest than any kind of science, but will precisely not be a science.[9]

Pondering the protocols for elaborating its own categories, critique undertakes to reply to an established science. That is why Marx consistently conceived his task as the 'critique of political economy'.[10]

Deutschen Wissenschaft: 'German' science? What does this Germanness consist in? In Germany's celebrated political 'backwardness': the political delay in German unity and state construction; the economic backwardness of a fragmented society held back by its squirearchy; and technological and scientific backwardness. While England and France were the first to enter the age of competitive capitalism, Germany was still ruminating on the myth of the rendezvous it had missed. Hence, probably, the Romantic defiance of the emergence of instrumental reason, anticipating the violent blood-wedding between this cold reason and the warm-blooded mysteries of soil and roots.

In the uneven and combined development of the world, in the discordance of temporalities and non-contemporaneity of contradictions, backwardness is also the condition for an 'advance'. Marx was fully conscious of the fact: 'We [Germans] have shared the restorations of modern nations without ever having shared their revolutions.'[11] The political revolution in France was followed by a philosophical revolution in Germany, whose backwardness yielded a specific advantage:

> Just as ancient peoples lived their previous history in the imagination, in *mythology*, so we Germans have lived our future history in thought, in *philosophy*. We are the *philosophical* contemporaries of the present without being its *historical* contemporaries. German philosophy is the *ideal prolongation* of German history . . . What for advanced nations is a *practical* quarrel with modern political questions is for Germany, where such conditions do not yet exist, a *critical* quarrel with their reflection in philosophy.[12]

The non-synchronization of social development and philosophical development is no cause for surprise. Political backwardness is converted into social 'advance'; the 'backwardness' of the bourgeoisie into the 'advance' of the proletariat. Thus, the 'Silesian [weavers'] rebellion *starts* where the French and English workers' *finish*, namely with an understanding of the nature of the proletariat'.[13] The dialectic of German anachronism transforms practical backwardness into theoretical advance, political backwardness into social advance.

The sources of German science

Following in Hegel's footsteps, Marx resists the exclusive claim to rationality of positive science. Whereas the English sciences turn their back on the totality, plunging into the practical positivity of fragmentary results, 'German science' turns the critical gaze of knowledge on itself. It is not some refractory archaism, nostalgic for 'gay sciences' in the face of new disciplinary exigencies. Instead, it discloses the presence of a detotalized, negative and dissatisfied totality, which recollects itself in the aporias of technology.[14]

In an age when the rupture between science and philosophy had not yet been consummated, the *Phenomenology*, the *Encyclopaedia* and the *Logic* represent a desperate attempt at a universal science. Whereas the understanding operative in the exact sciences can end up only formulating the mechanical laws of an inert material world, 'German science' perpetuates the ambition of an absolute knowledge.[15]

Demanded in the face of the unilateral mathematization of a bitter modernity, this 'other knowledge' has its antecedents. The quest for a non-instrumental rationality inevitably revives Spinoza, without whom philosophy vanishes. Together with Hegel's *Logic*, this was indeed the first source of science according to Marx. As early as 1841, he transcribed long passages from the *Theological-Political Treatise* in a notebook with the astonishing title:

> *Spinoza*
> *Theological-Political Treatise*
> *by*
> *Karl Heinrich Marx, Berlin, 1841*[16]

Marx's interest in this *Treatise* is consistent with his political and juridical preoccupations of the moment. Spinoza wanted to shield philosophy from theological tutelage – philosophy, not science. At the time, the crucial boundary passed between theology and philosophy, which encompassed not only analytical and discursive knowledge (the only knowledge considered scientific today), but also 'synoptic and intuitive' knowledge. Knowing the world was insufficient; the aim of such knowledge must be the supreme ethical goal of salvation. Refusing to dissociate two forms of rationality, 'discursive and intuitive, fragmentary and synoptic, emotionally dull and emotionally explosive', Spinoza proposed an exercise of reason combining science and ethics.[17]

This new alliance defined 'knowledge of the third kind'. Knowledge by 'vague experience' or 'hearsay', knowledge of the first type (or kind) is partial and inadequate, predominantly characterized by the ambiguous signs in which it is shrouded. Rational knowledge by means of causes, knowledge of the second kind yields the general common notions that do not yet provide access to the knowledge of particular essences. Intuitive and mystical for some, rational and superior for others, knowledge of the third type, which is simultaneously intuitive and rational, is the intellectual love of God. It attains to essences and assembles adequate ideas of ourselves, God, and other things. The quest for singularity distinguishes it from knowledge of the second type. To produce this knowledge is to glimpse the truth as subject and self-development: 'Knowledge of the third kind will itself only be perfected when we have genetically reconstructed the combination of motion and rest that characterizes our particular essence.'[18]

Proceeding from an adequate idea of God's attributes to a knowledge of things, it synoptically gathers in a multiplicity of determinations, such that the object and the mode of its knowledge are conjointly transformed. If this intuitive science expresses a higher form of rationality, it cannot short-circuit the ordinary form of reason, for it is necessary to begin by explaining the object extrinsically in order for intuition then to be able to recover the causal information in a new synthesis. For Spinoza, the jubilation of knowledge is generated by knowledge of the third kind, which presupposes and supersedes the second kind. Fascinated by the expansion of the positive sciences, Spinoza nevertheless preventively repudiates the scientistic ideology hatched by their success.

Knowledge of the first type remains at the level of the imagination and representations. That of the second type provides only a partial aspect of reality, still lacking a grasp of things in their particular essence. Knowledge of the third type preserves the critical unity of mathematical and narrative approaches: the intuitive moment in it crowns the process of scientific objectification. God no longer appears as abstract concept, but as concrete totality and singularity. The philosopher can finally 'penetrate into nature's interior design whereas formerly he had its external facet only'.[19]

With the pleasure attendant upon grasping the thing itself, rational knowledge is no longer separated from aesthetic pleasure. Acknowledging his debt to Spinoza, Hegel nevertheless criticizes him for a conception of the totality that is inert and unilateral, since it lacks mediations and negation. Founding a new knowledge, the Spinozist philosophy of immanence does not yet posit the mediation of historicity that makes humanity its own creator.

Correcting Spinoza by Hegel, and vice versa, Marx makes labour the relation with nature through which humanity contemplates itself in a world of its own creation. That is why, pioneer of the 'North-West passage', he considers the division of science into natural and human sciences as a phase destined to be replaced – not by decree, but as a result of a real historical process – by a single science: that of humanized nature and naturalized humanity.[20] A *scienza nuova*, as it were.

Capital deciphers the dynamic of emancipation inscribed in the immanent laws of tendency of social reality. As a negative science, the 'critique of political economy' is no longer a regional science established alongside others in the divisions and classifications of academic knowledge. Strictly speaking, it becomes the moment that makes it possible to recapture the totalizing dynamic of knowledge in a specific – capitalist – society, where the economic determines the totality. In it, judgements of fact and of value coincide, as they do in 'knowledge of the third type'.[21]

Historical emancipation cannot proceed from a moral imperative external to its object. The struggle obeys neither the mirages of utopia nor the impatience of the will. It can achieve liberation only through a conscious recognition of constraints and the deployment of a conditioned effort. Although he grasps this emancipatory dialectic of immanence perfectly, Yovel declines to follow Marx's radical Spinozism to its logical conclusion. He accuses it of lapsing back into the snare of a badly outmoded transcendence:

> because he historicizes redemption and sees the entire human race as its subject, Marx must indulge in some sort of secular eschatology. Redemption can no longer be predicted by a calculus of deterministic probability, and the shadow of illicit teleology again looms on the horizon. All that Marx can logically do is affirm that, as a matter of historical fact, we are nearing the goal, grounding his claim in a dialectical analysis of the rise of capitalism and its inherent conflicts, in which a new era seems to be incipient.[22]

The historicization of Spinozist substance seems to be closely akin to a historical teleology modelled on Kantian natural teleology: '*All the natural capacities of a creature are destined sooner or later to be developed completely and in conformity with their end*' – with this opening proposition from the 'Idea for a Universal History', the specular circle would be rigorously closed, were it not for the fact that Kant immediately raises the issue of the 'freedom of the will' without which any political space or action is inconceivable. How are the determination of the universal laws of nature, and this human ability to decide, to be combined? The design of nature is embodied neither in individuals, nor even in generations. It is inscribed in the sequence of generations and the cumulative transmission of knowledge that takes the form of progress. Hypothetical knowledge of a plan of nature now no longer cancels freedom of the will. On the contrary, it gives it its full meaning. Were history to be the accumulation and piling-up of chaotic facts, the very idea of a rational choice would lose any sense. To the extent that there exists an anticipation, a straining towards the end, the 'goal of man's aspirations' sustains a determinate freedom.[23]

For Marx, too, the antinomy of necessity and freedom is resolved in the aleatory process of the struggle.

The polemical allocation of science to a historically situated culture, and the invocation of 'German science', draw attention to the sources of a scientificity to which the positivist tradition has remained obstinately resistant. The reasons for the degree of ignorance, hostility and misinterpretation that Spinoza, Hegel and Marx have suffered in France often have common roots.[24]

If the role of Spinoza in Marx's formation has been the subject of many studies, that of Leibniz is less well known. Yet the Spinozist track leads to the philosopher who – in search of a logic of probability and a metaphysic of possibility, an accord between faith and reason, necessity and contingency, grace and freedom – declared himself 'nothing less than Cartesian'. Leibniz counterposed to Cartesian mechanics, set in motion by an original flick, the irreducible contingency of what happens: the random is not an illusion of our ignorance, and nothing escapes the reality of possibilities.[25]

Unlike the Cartesian analytic, the primacy of the totality leads from universal Harmony to fragments. The *Monadology* reconstructs the viewpoint of God, who sees all things in both their individuality and their unity. To do this, it requires a logic that proceeds from the general to the particular, from the possible to the real; a 'mathematics of concepts' approximating to the 'contingent truths' inaccessible to the mathematics of numbers, but without attaining them (since intuitive synthetic knowledge pertains exclusively to God).

Like Spinoza, Leibniz resists the idea of an exclusive science of generality. The general is abstract; the concrete is always particular. In the movement from matter to life, each individual being expresses the entire universe from a certain point of view. In it, universality and individuality are reconciled. The monad, a living unity, escapes the formal combinatory and is immersed in a history punctuated by the particularities of 'effective time'. This transition institutes a mode of historical truth allocated to a 'determinate time and place': such truth no longer bears on possibilities, but on events.[26] What is possible *sub ratione generalitatis* (governed by sheer necessity) is distinguished from what is possible *sub specie individuorum* (governed by hypothetical necessity). All possible worlds are contingent, and each type of possibility is the object of a specific knowledge: for simple possibilities, the 'science of simple understanding'; for actual events, the 'science of vision'; for conditional events (which might occur under certain conditions), a 'median science', which is not that of conditional futures, but that of 'contingent possibilities in general'. Whereas the science of 'simple understanding' applies to possible and necessary truths, and the science of 'vision' to contingent and actual truths, the 'median science' is directed towards possible and contingent truths.[27]

This distinction between sheer (or absolute) necessity and hypothetical necessity, between *müssen* and *sollen*, helps to obviate frequent misinterpretations of the notion of necessity in Hegel and Marx. In Leibniz, there is always a cause of the will to be found, but this will, which makes us human beings, does not escape strict logical necessity. History knows only particularities and existential truths that escape brute necessity. Everything that is given and truly exists presupposes a choice and a will, a moral necessity irreducible to the abstraction of numbers. God is a synthesis of the understanding and the will. His choices are simultaneously necessary and possible.[28]

Whereas Descartes separates understanding and divine will, wisdom and goodness, Leibnizian theology thus combines science and faith, to crown the hierarchy of logical and mechanical causes in God. Such, in fact, is the ambition of this 'German science': the application of mathematics to finite, contingent things, and the creation of an alliance between ethics and science, determination and freedom. On the horizon of this science, analytical knowledge of the universal merges into the intuitive vision of the particular, which is peculiar to God. 'The Knowledge of finite magnitudes', algebra explores simply the approach to a science of the infinite, which would be 'the higher part of the knowledge of magnitude'.[29]

In his essay on the 'Difference between the Systems of Fichte and Schelling', Hegel lays the foundations of what, in the *Encyclopaedia*, was to become the Science of the sciences. The so-called human sciences are superior to those of nature. History is their crowning achievement, for nothing is valid for humanity unless it is the object of its self-consciousness. The knowledge that the mind achieves of itself and by itself, through knowledge of the world, is the ultimate goal of science.

The Hegelian idea of a philosophy of nature and knowledge of life is opposed to the dismemberment and indifferent cohabitation of various forms of knowledge. It reduces neither to the Romantic aestheticization nor to the mania for classification that haunt the century. Against the compartmentalization of scientific discourses, it strives to establish a cross-disciplinary circulation, and to recapture the universalizing movement of knowledge: 'The Spirit that, so developed, knows itself as Spirit, is *Science*; Science is its actuality and the realm which it builds for itself in its own element . . . It is this coming-to-be of *Science as such* or of *knowledge*, that is described in this *Phenomenology* of Spirit.'[30]

Thus 'mathematical truths' cannot be science's last word, merely one of its moments. For '[t]he movement of mathematical proof does not belong to the object, but rather is an activity external to the matter in hand'. The positive sciences partake of 'philosophical cognition', where 'the way in which the [*outer*] *existence qua* existence of a thing comes about, is distinct from the way in which its *essence* or inner nature comes to be'. Furthermore, it unites these two particular processes: 'The movement is the twofold process and the genesis of the whole, in such wise that each side simultaneously posits the other, and each therefore has both perspectives within itself; together they thus constitute the whole by dissolving themselves, and by making themselves into its moments.'[31]

The arrogance of the positive sciences towards philosophy is thus unfounded. They take pride in a flawed knowledge, which is 'defective' in its poverty of purpose 'as well as in its material'. In fact, the aim of mathematics can be nothing other than 'magnitude' as a 'relationship that is unessential, lacking the Notion'. What is involved is a process of knowledge that 'proceeds on the surface' and 'does not touch the thing itself', since '[t]he *actual* is not something spatial, as it is regarded in mathematics'. This is why it only ever attains 'a [non-actual] truth', and makes do with 'rigid, dead propositions': 'it is the Notion which divides space into its dimensions and determines the connections between and within them'.[32]

Hence 'the necessity of a different kind of knowledge' – a philosophical knowledge concerned with 'a determination in so far as it is essential':

> [Philosophy] is the process which begets and traverses its own moments, and this whole movement constitutes what is positive [in it] and its truth. This truth therefore includes the negative also, what would be called the false, if it could be regarded as something from which one might abstract. The evanescent itself must, on the contrary, be regarded as essential, not as something fixed, cut off from the True, and left lying who knows where outside it, any more than the True is to be regarded as something on the other side, positive and dead.[33]

Hence the transformation of the relationship between the 'English' positive sciences and 'German science' (or philosophy), in accordance with the initial project of the *Phenomenology*: 'To help bring philosophy closer to the form of Science, to the goal where it can lay aside the title "*love* of knowing" and be *actual* knowing – this is what I have set myself to do.'[34]

This ambitious objective conveys a refusal to abandon the history of philosophy to the infernal realm of pre-science. To save philosophy by subjecting it to the formal constraint of science is, by the same token, to save the sciences from the empty formalism that lies in wait for them:

> Philosophy is frequently taken to be a purely formal kind of knowledge, void of content, and the insight is sadly lacking that, whatever truth there may be in the content of any discipline or science, it can only deserve the name if such truth has been engendered by philosophy. Let the other sciences try to argue as much as they like without philosophy – without it they can have in them neither life, Spirit, nor truth.[35]

Hegel returns to the point in the *Logic*:

> Philosophy, if it would be a science, cannot . . . borrow its method from a subordinate science like mathematics . . . To establish or explain the Notion of science ratiocinatively can at most achieve this, that a general idea of the Notion is present to our thinking and a historical knowledge of it is produced; but a definition of science – or more precisely of logic – has its proof solely in the already mentioned necessity of its emergence in consciousness. The definition with which any science makes an absolute beginning cannot contain anything other than the precise and correct expression of what is imagined to be the accepted and familiar subject matter and aim of the science. That precisely *this* is what is imagined is an historical asseveration . . .[36]

Truth and certainty, subject and object, concept and reality, tend, historically and asymptotically, to merge. This tendential process generates relations of truth.

Hegel is not content to situate non-knowledge. He introduces time into logic. He temporalizes it, without thereby yielding to relativism. In point of fact, the historicity of knowledge does away with its relativity. The science of a constantly evolving totality, the concept of speculative science thus radicalizes Kant's Copernican revolution, for which humanity's self-knowledge determines not only its own conduct, but also the other modes of knowledge.

Just as the essence is, according to Hegel, 'the truth of being', so value is the truth of capital, its 'non-temporal past', over and above its metamorphoses. A negation of particular use-values, the value form is a desubstantialized essence, which is nevertheless irreducible to a 'pure relation' indifferent to the actual exchange of material goods. As a relation, it determines its own measurable content. Just as the essence is phenomenalized in existence, so value is phenomenalized in capital. But the phenomenal world is the inverted image of the world in itself: 'The north pole in the world of Appearance is *in and for itself* the south pole, and conversely.'[37] Reality, finally, is the unity of essence and existence, the unity of value and capital. This is the relation science must elucidate.

But which science? In *Capital*, the movement of knowledge follows the 'vast syllogism' of Hegelian logic. It starts from the mechanical relations of exploitation and the linear time underlying them (Volume One), proceeds to the chemical relations of the cyclical permutations of circulation (Volume Two), and ends up with the relations and organic time of reproduction (Volume Three).

> This is what constitutes the character of *mechanism*, namely, that whatever relation obtains between the things combined, this relation is one *extraneous* to them that does not concern their nature at all . . . A *mechanical style of thinking, a mechanical memory, habit, a mechanical way of acting*, signify that the peculiar pervasion and presence of spirit is lacking in what spirit apprehends or does.[38]

Whereas the mechanical object is a totality indifferent to any 'determinateness', determinateness and, consequently, 'the *relation to other* and the kind and manner of this relation' are part of the very nature of the chemical object: 'Chemism itself is *the first negation of indifferent* objectivity and of the *externality* of *determinateness*.' In chemical combinations, the progressive variation of proportions and mixtures gives rise to 'qualitative nodes and leaps': 'at certain points in the scale of mixtures, two substances form products exhibiting certain qualities'.[39] The notion of elective affinities originates in these chemical relations. With these 'nodes' and 'leaps', the time of chemism is no longer the linear homogeneous time of mechanism.

However, chemism still participates in the steep ascent of abstraction towards the concrete synthesis of the living being: 'The Idea of Life is concerned with a subject matter so concrete, and if you will so real, that with it we may seem to have overstepped the domain of logic as it is commonly conceived.'[40] And yet, the real is living! Capital likewise.

To overcome the antinomy of Logic and Life, what is therefore required is a logic that goes beyond the current conception. A logic of the living being: 'the self-determination of the living being is its judgement or its self-limitation, whereby it relates itself to the external as to a *presupposed* objectivity and is in reciprocal *activity* with it'.[41] The living being is in fact 'the individual', irreducible singularity.

In *Capital* as in the *Logic*, it is only with *reproduction* that 'life is *concrete* and is vitality; in it as in its truth, life for the first time has also feeling and the power of resistance'. 'In every other science', specifies the introduction to the *Logic*, subject matter and method are distinct. By contrast, the very notion of science constitutes the subject matter and final result of logic. It is therefore 'the science of thinking in general', overcoming the separation of form and content, truth and certainty, at work in 'ordinary consciousness':

> The truth is rather that the insubstantial nature of logical forms originates solely in the way in which they are considered and dealt with. When they are taken as fixed determinations and consequently in their separation from each other and not as held together in an organic unity, then they are dead forms and the spirit which is their living, concrete unity does not dwell in them . . .

But logical reason itself is the substantial or real being which holds together within itself every abstract determination and is their substantial, absolutely concrete unity.[42]

Conceived thus, logic is no longer 'a merely abstract universal and reveals itself as the universal which embraces within itself the wealth of the particular'.[43] The greater *Logic* is divided into two parts: the doctrine of Being and the doctrine of Essence are both contrasted with 'subjective logic or the doctrine of the notion'. Every being occurs as 'motility' between being-in-itself and being-there, essence and existence, interior and exterior, possibility and actuality. *Qua* totality, Life is the light that 'discloses being in its truth', and abolishes the antinomy between nature and history. The result is a conception of knowledge as 'thinking movement'. Where ordinary empirical logic produces only an 'irrational knowledge of the rational', the *Logic*, according to Marcuse, constitutes 'the basis of a theory of historicity'.[44] In abolishing the separation between Nature and History, humanity accomplishes its 'greatest leap'.

Thus, Hegel opens the way:

> The complete, abstract indifference of developed measure, i.e. the *laws* of measure, can only be manifested in the sphere of *mechanics* in which the concrete bodily factor is itself only *abstract* matter; the qualitative differences of such matter are essentially quantitatively determined ... On the other hand, such quantitative determinateness of abstract matter is deranged simply by the plurality of conflicting qualities in the inorganic sphere and still more even in the organic world. But here there is involved not merely a conflict of qualities, for measure here is subordinated to higher relationships ... Natural science is still far from possessing an insight into the connection between such quantities and the organic functions on which they wholly depend. But the readiest example of the reduction of an immanent measure to a merely externally determined magnitude is *motion* ... And in the reality of spirit there is still less to be found a characteristic, free development of measure. It is quite evident, for example, that a republican constitution like that of Athens, or an aristocratic constitution tempered by democracy, is suitable only for States of a certain size, and that in a developed civil society the numbers of individuals belonging to different occupations stand in a certain ratio to one another; but all this yields neither laws of measure nor characteristic forms of it. In the spiritual sphere as such there occur differences of *intensity* ... [45]

Marx received this message loud and clear. He embarked upon a way of practising science in which the calculating virtues of the understanding are exhausted.

The chapter devoted to measurement in the *Logic* ends with an invitation to cross the security zone of the understanding (instrumental reason) to plunge into the search for a knowledge that cannot be reduced to measuring, estimating, describing and calculating relations. This German – or philosophical – science 'is not meant to be a narration of happenings but a cognition of what is true in them, and further, on the basis of this cognition, is to *comprehend* that which, in the narrative, appears a mere happening'.[46]

What is true in happenings? Event and truth are intimately bound up with one another.

Knowledge is the elaboration of the differences that happen. Sciences of the finite, after the fashion of geometry (whose space is abstraction and the void), the analytical (positive) sciences essentially proceed by comparing magnitudes. Synthetic knowledge realizes the unity of diverse determinations. Thus, in the 'circle of circles' of science ('the end being wound back into the beginning ... by the mediation'), the '[l]inks of this chain are the individual sciences, each of which has an *antecedent* and a *successor*'. But these links coincide in the Absolute Idea. Just as capital reverts to the simple unity of the commodity, which is its logical starting point, the Idea reverts to 'the pure immediacy of being in which at first every determination appears to be extinguished or removed by abstraction'.[47] A concrete totality, capital is likewise the consummate being of the commodity.

The science of the concept conceiving itself, Logic is 'the *beginning of another sphere and science*'.[48] A new science? A metascience? A science of the third type, said Spinoza. A science of the contingent, specified Leibniz. A speculative science, added Hegel. Or, in Marx's summary: 'German science'.

Its novelty is akin to 'one of those ancient sciences that have been most misunderstood in the metaphysics of the moderns'. Dialectic: the word is out. Alas, '[d]ialectic has often been regarded as an *art*, as though it rested on a subjective *talent* and did not belong to the objectivity of the Notion'. Quite the reverse: the fact that the dialectic 'is once more recognized as necessary to reason' should be regarded as inordinately important.[49] The triumphant positive spirit and scientism were not ready to pardon Hegel for this challenge. His dialectic risked once again blurring the boundaries between science and fiction, truth and error. It incited rebellion against the pact between knowledge and power.

Our century is still confronting this challenge, 'deinsulating' and 'peninsulating' the concept of science, registering the imprecision of its border with philosophy or criticism, discovering unsuspected sociological debts in scientific disinterestedness, and exploring via comparative ethnology and anthropology other modes of thought, to which it would be presumptuous to deny all scientificity. It has become clear that for a long time we have lived off the proceeds of a historically dated scientific paradigm.

In the process, Hegel's dialectical logic has been rehabilitated. With him, what we have is a novel concept of treating things scientifically, in which the laws of thinking are not external to the object being thought, and the movement of thought does not derive from an external process. There are no rules of thinking outside their actual implementation, no method external to its object. This logic is indeed the basis for a theory of historicity. But how can Marx conserve its logical core and, at the same time, reject the philosophy of history that is its reverse side? By overturning the system. With a radically immanent theory of history punctuated by conflict, the logic of the thing is modified in return. The theory of historicity becomes its foundation.

What remains is the impulse to do science differently.[50] Against the current of Enlightenment rationalization, Hegel scarcely changed his opinion on this point. His inaugural lecture of October 1818 advanced the idea that the German nation, which had just salvaged its nationality, found itself projected by its backwardness to the vanguard of the philosophical front: the science of Philosophy had taken refuge with the Germans, and was now alive exclusively in Germany. At a moment when forms of knowledge were lapsing into the realm of opinion or mere conviction, he maintained his course for the truth: 'The scientific cognition of truth is what I have laboured upon, and still do labour upon always, in all of my philosophical endeavours.'[51] There was no such thing as 'philosophical opinions'.

In this aspiration to truth, it is appropriate to single out the *empirical sciences*, which propose and furnish laws, general ideas and propositions about what exists. *Speculative science* does not dispense with their empirical content. It acknowledges and uses their general element. It retains the same categories, the same forms of thought, the same objects, but transforms them in order to resolve the paradoxes generated by the abstractness of the understanding. It is 'the *immanent* transcending, in which the one-sidedness and restrictions of the determination of the understanding displays itself as what it is, i.e., as their negation. That is what everything finite is: its own sublation': 'The *speculative* or *positively rational* apprehends the unity of the determinations in their opposition.'[52]

Hence we have empirical, positive, or 'English' sciences; and 'speculative', 'philosophical', or 'German' science.

For Hegel, the whole of philosophy constitutes a single science, which can also be regarded as a set of particular sciences. In his view, this is what distinguishes a philosophical encyclopaedia from an ordinary encyclopaedia (a mere aggregate, he says, of sciences collected contingently).

What is at stake in this distinction is crucial for Hegel: nothing less than resisting the disenchantment of modernity. With its 'formal and abstract thinking', the Enlightenment period has emptied religion of any content – in particular, the thirst for truth that it could harbour. Henceforth, 'the lifeless water of the understanding, with its generalities and its abstract rationalism, cannot tolerate the specificity of an inwardly determinate, expressly formed Christian concept and doctrinal content'.[53] Foreshadowing the ambivalence of the nascent Romanticism, the tradition protests against the arbitrariness of geometrical reason. The lifeless water of the understanding, with its generalities and its abstract rationalism? The century would not be short of that.

At moments of the deepest uncertainty and all-pervasive doubt, Marx and Lenin found new intellectual inspiration in the greater *Logic*: Marx in 1858, when he wrote the rough drafts of the *Grundrisse* amid the stimulus of the new American crisis; and Lenin after August 1914, when his mental universe threatened to collapse with the Second International. A chance rereading of the *Logic* furnished Marx with the keys to *Capital*. For Lenin, the notebooks on the *Logic* represented a spiritual exercise preparatory to the audacious strategic stroke of October.

The idea of a 'philosophical science' that does not yield before the sacred positive sciences: that is Hegel's inaudible thunderclap, echoed by Marx. How can we not have heard this 'other *thinking of knowledge*' which, without excluding science, 'overturns and overflows its received idea'?[54] How has this deafening thunder been so obstinately misheard and misconstrued?

> *Capital* is an essentially subversive work. It is so less because it leads, by way of scientific objectivity, to the necessary consequence of revolution than because it includes, without formulating it too explicitly, a mode of theoretical thinking that overturns the very idea of science. Actually, neither science nor thought emerges from Marx's work intact. This must be taken in the strongest sense, insofar as science designates itself there as a radical transformation of itself, as a theory of mutation always in play in practice, just as in this practice the mutation is always theoretical.

Although, by a misunderstanding, it has won him the recognition of the established representatives of knowledge, according to Blanchot this scientific 'third voice' of Marx thus remains bound up with his political 'second voice', 'brief and direct', which calls for a violent 'decision of 'rupture', recommending 'permanent revolution' as 'ever-present demand'.[55]

The Consistencies of Critique

From Spinoza, Leibniz and Hegel, Marx received an idea of science that was irreducible to the mere sum of the positive sciences. The dividing line was, however, displaced. With the upsurge of the modern sciences, the issue was no longer merely to disentangle philosophy from theology. The fracture now ran through the core of philosophy itself: between speculative philosophy (treated as early as *The German Ideology* as ideology squared) and the philosophy of praxis (which moves towards an 'exit from philosophy'). If it is certainly no longer a question *solely* of interpreting the world, the exit from philosophy does not boil down to an opposition between science and ideology. Plunged into history, knowledge of the third type becomes critical theory and strategic thought.

Manuel Sacristan identifies a threefold idea of science in Marx:

- Science (positive or English);
- Critique (young Hegelian in inspiration, according to him);
- *deutschen Wissenschaft.*

Having become revolutionary theory, science according to Marx articulates these three dimensions in the 'Critique of Political Economy':[56]

> While it is not our intention here to consider the way in which the immanent laws of capitalist production manifest themselves in the external movement of the individual capitals, assert themselves as the coercive laws of competition, and therefore enter into the consciousness of the individual capitalist as the motives which drive him forward, this much is clear: a scientific analysis of capital is possible only if we can grasp the inner nature of capital . . .[57]

From the Paris *Manuscripts* to *Capital*, theory remains 'critical' throughout.

Projected as early as 1845, and conducted with exemplary tenacity, the critique of political economy remains its red thread. It betrays not a trace of residual philosophical nostalgia as it approaches the *terra firma* of economic science. Despite the consistency of the term, its concept varies – from a critical form of philosophy to a critical form of science; or from critique as theoretical practice of philosophy to critique as theoretical practice of communism. Laid claim to in early correspondence, the '*ruthless criticism of the existing order*'[58] also has its constants – notably, the unity of theory and practice in opposition to all speculative or dogmatic knowledge. The critical turn of philosophy leads towards practice, in order to combine the arm of critique with the critique of arms. For on the conceptual battlefield, critique is a double-edged weapon, deployed against the scientistic illusion of attaining reality via the facts, and against the idealist illusion of absorbing reality into its symbolic representation.

Henceforth it will be a question of 'ruthless criticism', rather than 'excommunicating'.[59]

The concept of critique came to Marx by way of Feuerbach.

In the article on 'Critique' in the *Encyclopédie*, Marmontel writes:

> What must critique do? Observe the known facts; determine the relations and distance between them; correct faulty observations – in a word, convince the human mind of its frailty so as to make it employ profitably the little strength that it expends in vain, and thus confront whoever would bend experience to his ideas. Its vocation is to interrogate nature, not to make it speak.

Safeguard of secularized reason, critique fixes limits to the power mania of the compartmentalized sciences, which are tempted to extend their specific domain illegitimately. 'Art of judging and distinguishing', according to Bayle's *Dictionary*, it traces a line of demarcation between the prerogatives of reason and what escapes it. Error and truth have meaning only under its jurisdiction. Beyond it begin the disquieting lands of physical and mental monsters. 'Science of borders', critique announced itself very early on as the bad conscience of the instrumental sciences.[60]

With Feuerbach, the traditional critical question of conditions of possibility is formulated as questioning the incarnation of the universal in the particular, the species in the individual. Critique receives its new mission: crossing the crepuscular horizon of historical closure:

> Here is precisely what engendered the critical attitude: a recognition that Hegelian Absolute Knowledge had not extinguished all the lights of history, that the sun of the Spirit had not absorbed all the light of the world. That it was still daylight in the world, that there still was a world after the speculative sun had shone – this was the veritable death of the Sun! At the death of Hegel, Critique dawned in a world astonished not to have been dissolved in the realization of the Idea ... Critique will thus be the night light of a world that has lost its speculative torch and to which there remains nothing but ... night lights![61]

Critique tests the beginning, the better to loosen the buckle of the system. It shatters the conceptual circle of the greater *Logic*, which is too neatly closed. It slices through its desperately smooth totality, in order to half-open the field of possibilities. It is not so much a new doctrine as a 'theoretical stance', a polemical relation to history, which refuses to fix the intelligibility of the real in the hypostasis of science. Having become critique of political economy, it will be a sort of negative science, irreducible to dogmatic and doctrinaire formulas. Refusing itself the slightest repose, it knows that it will never have the last word, and that it is at best a matter of leading thought to the threshold of the struggle, where it takes strategic wing.

This form of critique acts as a link between the necessary moment of the positive sciences and the detotalized totality of German science. It mediates their relation by precluding the insulation of a new system, which would be the worst of ideologies. Aware of this role of impediment, Sacristan fails to draw out all its consequences for 'normal science'. The latter often appears in Marx with the invocation of its royal disciplines (chemistry, physics, astronomy) as reference points. How valid is the extension of these models to the economy or history? What way of doing science is represented by the theoretical triangle whose apex is occupied by 'German science'? What are the relations of complementarity or antagonism, inclusion and domination, between critique and German science, between normal science and German science, between critique and normal science? Does critique play a spoiling role, constantly recalling normal science to its modest limits? Are the normal sciences fragments of a 'German science' that encompasses and surpasses them? Does 'German science' restrict the horizon of critique, reduced to mediating between compartmentalized forms of knowledge?

A revolving door at breakneck speed! Refusing the crippling antinomies of part and whole, subject and object, absolute and relative, singular and universal, theory and practice, critique is, as it were, the Holy Ghost of a dialectical rationality, prey to the swaggering spectres of instrumental rationality, rather than the poor relative of a scientific holy trinity.

These articulations determine the concept of scientific knowledge, without ever defining it positively. They confer on the distinction between classical science and vulgar science a content that is precisely that of the critique of political economy. If only positive or normal (analytical) science existed, there would be no possible third way between rigorously demarcated camps of truth and error, good science and bad ideology. Were there only German (synthetic) science, all the sciences, classical or vulgar, would have to be inducted into its system. In opposition to the repetitive sterility of vulgar apologetics, classical fecundity consists in the critical tension of an open totalization. The critique of classical economics, its truths as well as its revealing slips, is on the agenda when the generalization of commodity production imparts to the scientific abstractions of *Capital* their content. An understanding of the present then commands an understanding of the past. The developed form discloses the secrets of the embryonic forms, of which it is nevertheless not the sole and inevitable destiny.

If the present governs knowledge of the past, is 'German science' a sort of crepuscular wisdom announcing the culmination of history in a totality transparent to itself? Critique averts this menacing end. The present is not content to dominate the rough drafts of the past from its summits. It scans the flickerings of reality and watches out, on the crests of the future, for the shimmering of unfulfilled possibilities.

Marx's 'accidental' reunion with Hegelian logic (his 1858 rereading) did not foreshadow a speculative relapse. It made possible the elaboration of a 'proper scientific conception'. 'German science' does not renounce a knowledge of essences. In so far as it preserves the aspiration to a science of the particular, its 'metaphysics was productive for Marx's science': 'This superb pre-critical programme marks the success and the failure of Marx's contribution to social science and revolutionary knowledge.'[62]

What does this mixture of success and failure consist in? Wresting Marx from his Hegelian roots to install him in the normality of modern science is a nonsense. His 'scientific' practice, disconcerting in many respects, makes him the 'original metaphysical author of his own positive science', 'a scientist who evinces the unusual peculiarity of being the author of his own metaphysics, a general and explicit vision of reality'.[63] Marx's initial internal rupture with the dominant image of science – his characterization of political economy as 'infamy' in 1844 – would have remained sterile without the Hegelian rejuvenation of 1858.

Contrary to what Sacristan claims, this 'return' does not, for all that, signify a definitive transcendence of 'critique' in the direction of 'German science', a variety of general epistemology or rationalized metaphysics. Its preservation in the subtitle of *Capital* bears witness to an unresolved theoretical tension. Marx remained torn between the fecundity of positive science and the persistent dissatisfaction of dialectical knowledge. 'Critique' makes it possible to reconcile the two. Was this a bad compromise, or healthy resistance restraining instrumental reason on the slope of its own fetishization?

A labour of demystification and defetishization attuned to the discourse of capital, the mission of critique (of political economy) is not to speak the truth on the truth. In the first two volumes of *Capital*, it rips apart the appearances, tears off the masks, unveils the two-faced being of the commodity and labour, penetrates the mysteries of production, and elucidates the metamorphoses of circulation. In the third volume, it finally launches an assault on the mysticism of capital.

'[E]conomy in the use of means of production', Marx writes,

> this method of attaining a certain result ... appears as a power inherent in capital and a method specific to and characteristic of the capitalist mode of production. This way of conceiving things [*Vorstellungweise*] is all the less surprising in that it corresponds to the semblance [*der Schein*] of the matter and that the capital relation actually does conceal the inner connection [*innern Zusammenhang*] in the state of complete indifference, externality and alienation [*Ausserlichkeit/Entfremdung*] in which it places the worker *vis-à-vis* the conditions of realization of his own labour.

The worker cannot but feel indifference towards means of production that rebound on him as means of exploitation. Towards the social character of labour (the labour of others) he conducts himself as towards 'a power that is alien to him' [*als zu einer fremden Macht*]. But 'there is more to this than the alienation and indifference that the worker, as the bearer of living labour, has towards the economical, i.e. rational and frugal use of his conditions of labour': 'the squandering of the life and health of the worker' and 'the depression of his conditions of existence' become the condition for an increase in the rate of profit.[64] Capital thus increasingly appears as a 'social power' whose functionary is the capitalist – 'a power that no longer stands in any kind of possible relationship to what the work of one individual can create, but an alienated social power which has gained an autonomous position and confronts society as a thing, and as the power that the capitalist has through this thing'.[65] The contradiction between the social power of capital and the private power of industrial capitalists becomes ever more blatant. The identification of capital with profit, ground with rent, labour with wages – such is the 'trinity formula' containing 'all the mysteries of the social process of production'. As a material form, money interest conjures away profit and surplus-value, which are 'specific to and characteristic of the capitalist mode of production'.

The marvel of the increase M-M', money generating money, then emerges as the 'most estranged and peculiar form' of the capital fetish. In interest-bearing capital, the idea of the capitalist fetish is consummated, attributing to the accumulated product of labour, fixed in the form of money, the fabulous capacity to produce more surplus-value thanks to 'some innate quality and in a geometrical progression'.[66]

The setting in motion of these 'occult qualities' explains the false consciousness of the economists, the incredible but nevertheless real mystification that transforms 'social relations ... into properties of ... things themselves ... still more explicitly transforming the relation of production itself into a thing'.[67] Critique is thus the incessant labour of consciousness against its own religious representations in a historically determinate society. The capitalist process is itself the determinate form of the social process of production in the framework of specific relations of production. It produces and *reproduces* these relations of production and their agents, capital and wage-labour. From the angle of its economic structure, society is constituted by the totality of relations of social agents with one another and with nature. The material conditions are the supports [*Träger*] of social relations into which individuals are inserted.

The dynamism of capital prepares the conditions for an effective socialization of the means of production and labour. It thus creates the material means and the 'germ of a situation' which, in a differently organized society, would allow a closer correlation between labour and surplus-labour – in other words, a greater liberation of socially available time and a reorientation of its use according to a logic of accumulation that is not necessarily quantitative. The real wealth of society does not in fact depend on the amount of time devoted to labour, but on its productivity: 'The realm of freedom really begins only where labour determined by necessity and external expediency ends.'[68] Not beyond the sphere of production, but in the fixed necessity of reproduction as a whole; not beyond necessity, but in the very dialectic of necessity and freedom.

On the misleading surface of circulation, capital thus appears as *Kapitalfetisch* (the capitalist fetish of fetishized capital). In the form of interest-bearing capital, it assumes its most alienated characteristic form in production as a whole. Finally, in rent, landed property gives rise to alienation and 'reciprocal ossification'. The result is the height of mystification, a general reification [*Verdinglichung*] of social relations, an imbrication of material relations and sociohistorical determination. Where Max Weber would see a disenchanted world, Marx is filled with wonder by the marvels of an enchanted world, turned upside-down. This is a world where the fetishes of money, the state, science and art rise up in all their stony immobility, like the statues on Easter Island; where beings walk on their heads; where Monsieur le Capital and Madame la Terre, simultaneously social characters and mere things, uncannily dance their macabre round. The agents of production feel at home in the 'illusory forms' in which they move every day. This is the reign of the personification of things and the reification of persons.[69] This is the diabolical religiosity of everyday life in the modern world.

The reification of social relations and triumphant commodity fetishism determine the role and the limits of critique:

> In presenting the reification of the relations of production and the autonomy they acquire *vis-à-vis* the agents of production, we shall not go into the form and manner in which these connections appear to them as overwhelming natural laws, governing them irrespective of their will, in the form that the world market and its conjunctures, the movement of market prices, the cycles of industry and trade and alternation of prosperity and crisis prevails on them as blind necessity. This is because the actual movement of competition lies outside our plan, and we are only out to present the internal organization of production, its ideal average, as it were.[70]

Fetishism is not simple misrepresentation. If it were, an ordinary science would suffice to divest it of its disguises and unveil its hidden truth. If it were only a bad image of the real, a good pair of spectacles would suffice to rectify it and exhibit the object as it really is. But the representation of fetishism operates constantly in the mutual illusion of subject and object, which are inextricably linked in the distorting mirror of their relationship. So there is no question of founding the science that would dispel false consciousness once and for all, and establish the lucid sovereignty of a subject who is master and possessor of his object. False consciousness does not occur in the head. It results from the very conditions of its self-production. As long as the relations generating it survive, alienation can only be contested, not abolished. In a world prey to general commodity fetishism, there is no triumphal exit from ideology through the arch of science. Critique is aware of its own incapacity to possess the truth and speak the truth on the truth. Its endlessly renewed struggle against the invading undergrowth of madness and myth can never end. It can only lead to the fleeting glades where political events can supervene.

Critique is thus never done with ideology.[71] It cannot do more than demystify, resist, and formulate the conditions for positive dis-illusionment.

The sequel is played out in the struggle, where the arm of critique can no longer dispense with the critique of arms; where theory becomes practice, and thought becomes strategy.

Aiming in the first instance to undo the spells of the commodity, the 'science of capital' cannot begin with a discourse on method. This would still be to search in vain for 'the science *before* science', and remain in thrall to appearances.[72] In the game of hide-and-seek between *Schein* and *Wesen*, the essence, which makes things what they are, is contradictorily opposed to their phenomenal existence. It governs the play of appearances from within: rather than the world of phenomena being that of laws, the determination of the content binds together the phenomena with their law, prices with value. The manifestation of the essence thus forms part of the appearance, and every science involves a theory of appearance without it being the case that the essence, which Hegel sometimes calls a 'desert', is richer than the appearance.

Over and above measurable magnitudes, science presents itself as traversed by appearances, for 'all science would be superfluous if the form of appearance of things directly coincided with their essence':

• '[A] scientific analysis of competition is possible only if we grasp the inner nature of capital, just as the apparent motions of the heavenly bodies are intelligible only to someone who is acquainted with their real motions, which are not perceptible to the senses.'

• 'The phenomena under investigation in this chapter assume for their full development the credit system and competition on the world market, the latter being the very basis and living atmosphere of the capitalist mode of production. These concrete forms of capitalist production, however, can be comprehensively depicted only after the general nature of capital is understood.'

• 'There it will be seen how the philistine's and vulgar economist's *way of looking at things* arises, namely, because it is only the immediate phenomenal *form* of these relations that is reflected in their brains and not their *inner connection*. Incidentally, if the latter were the case what need would there be of *science*?'

• 'Science consists precisely in demonstrating *how* the law of value asserts itself. So that if one wanted at the very beginning to "explain" all the phenomena which seemingly contradict the law, one would have to present the science *before* science. It is precisely Ricardo's mistake that in his first chapter on value he takes *as given* a variety of categories that have not yet been explained in order to prove their conformity with the law of value ... Since the reasoning process itself proceeds from the existing conditions, and is itself a *natural process*, intelligent thinking must always be the same, and can vary only gradually, according to the degree of development, including the development of the organ by which the thinking is done. Everything else is drivel ... the vulgar economist thinks he has made a great discovery when, in face of the disclosure of intrinsic interconnection, he proudly states that on the surface things look different. In fact, he boasts that he sticks to appearance, and takes it for the ultimate. Why, then, have any science at all?'[73]

These passages and letters bring out some constants in the contradictory relationship between phenomenon and essence, appearance and reality. Immediate empirical knowledge remains at the level of 'sense perception', 'phenomena', 'appearances', the 'visible motion', 'the immediate phenomenal form', 'an appearance', and so on. Scientific knowledge bears on the 'inner nature', 'real motion', 'essence', 'inner real motion', 'inner connection', 'law', 'intrinsic interconnection', and so on.

The couples 'surface/depth', 'illusion/reality', and 'fragments/structure' are so many approximate expressions. Between sense perception and inner structure, phenomena and real motion, appearance and essence, visible motion and inner connection, aspect and law, there operates the labour of the concept – science as production and transition (the production of its object, not the revelation of a hidden essence). This labour of thought on the real seems to repeat the confusion of which Althusser exclusively accuses Engels: scientific labour uncovers a problematic relation between the concrete-in-thought and the real-concrete, subjected to the critique of appearances, but none the less real. The real movement is indeed that of the planets, not their equations.

Criticizing Ricardo for wanting to provide 'the science before science', Marx accuses him of being oblivious of scientific labour as production and exploration, poles apart from the confusion between thought and reality. But thought remains a component part of reality, in a process of 'gradual differentiation'.[74] This close differentiation of the object, this gestation of the subject in the object, avoids the specular trap of tautological reflection. Through the mediation of practice, theory can 'truly apprehend things', rather than embracing their conceptual phantom.

Marx thus counterposes appearance and essence; form and content; illusion and reality; phenomenon and concealed substratum; manifestation and inner connection. These antinomies ground the necessity and possibility of scientific knowledge. Access to the 'inner connection' passes via a deconstruction of appearances.

When human relations assume the 'fantastic form of a relation between things',[75] and their social action takes the form of objects governing their producers rather than being governed by them, the fact that fetishism carries within it not only mystification, but domination as well, can no longer be ignored. Unlike the personal domination of pre-capitalist societies, reified domination becomes impersonal. An effect of fetishism,

alienation becomes a historical, and no longer an anthropological, concept. In Volume One, fetishism explicitly designates 'the *fantastic form* of a
relation between things'. It directly involves the alienation of labour and
of the worker: 'the process of production has mastery over man, instead
of the opposite'.[76] In Volume Three, this relation between fetishism and
alienation (or 'estrangement') is recalled on several occasions: 'Capital
shows itself more and more to be a social power ... It becomes an
autonomous, alienated social power, standing over against society like an
object.'[77]

There is nothing imaginary about these fetishized and alienated relations. Value and values are not abstractions, but realities – the actual,
specific form of capitalist social relations. In these relations between form
and content, appearance and essence, the first term is never synonymous
with illusion. The scientific toil of critique is thus not reduced to a journey
from fiction to reality, in the course of which eyes are opened or
innocence is lost. It involves elucidating reality itself. Thus the value-form
is not dispelled like a mirage, but penetrated like a secret (Volume One).

Mystification consists above all in the transformation of social facts into
natural facts. If it merely involved illusions, a good theory of knowledge
would be enough to dispel them: the sovereign consciousness, Cartesian
self-evidence, divine revelation, the liberal contract, or Hegelian reappropriation would do away with them. But unlike the corvée, the wage-form,
the classic example of appearance, conceals unpaid labour-time behind
the putative payment of labour in full. Similarly, while performing its own
necessary function, the circulation process conjures away the mystery of
production. In overall reproduction, the division of capital into various
different fractions, into a multiplicity of capitals, masks the circuit of
capital in its entirety, blurs the evidence of the original crime of primitive
expropriation and the extortion of surplus-value, and consequently reinforces money fetishism.

It is only when commodity production is generalized, when productive
capital subjugates mercantile and finance capital, that it becomes possible
to change terrain, penetrate the secret laboratory of capitalist alchemy,
and triumph over its mystery. It does not follow that this knowledge is
mechanically subject to sociological determination; it still requires constant confrontation, both critical and reflexive, with the political horizon
of its own scientific practice.

How did Marx assess his own 'discoveries'? And what was their relation
with the notion of 'German science'?

In his letter to Engels of 24 August 1867, Marx writes:

The best points in my book are: 1) the *two-fold character of labour*, according to whether it is expressed in use value or exchange value . . . 2) the treatment of *surplus value independently of its particular* forms as profit, interest, rent, etc. This will be seen especially in the second volume. The treatment of the particular forms by classical economy, which always mixes them up with the general form, is a regular hash.[78]

In his letter to Engels of 8 January 1868, he insists:

1) That in contrast to *all* former political economy, which *from the very outset* treats the different fragments of surplus value with their fixed forms of rent, profit, and interest as already given, I first deal with the *general form of surplus value*, in which all these fragments are still undifferentiated – in solution, as it were. 2) That the economists, without exception, have missed the simple point that if the commodity has a double character – use value and exchange value – then the *labour* represented by the commodity must also have a *two-fold character*, while the mere analysis of labour as such, as in Smith, Ricardo, etc., is bound to come up everywhere against inexplicable problems. This is, in fact, the whole secret of the critical conception. 3) That for the first time *wages* are presented as an *irrational manifestation of a relation concealed behind them*, and that this is scrupulously demonstrated with regard to the two forms of wages – time rates and piece rates.[79]

Finally, in some marginal notes from 1880, he emphasizes:

in the analysis of the commodity I do not stop at the double manner in which it is represented, but immediately go on to say that in this double being of the commodity is represented the two-fold *character* of the *labour* whose product it is: *useful* labour, i.e. the concrete modes of the labours which create use-values, and abstract *labour, labour as expenditure of labour-power*, irrespective of whatever 'useful' way it is expended . . .; that in the development of the *value form of the commodity*, in the last instance of its money form and hence of *money*, the *value* of a commodity is represented in the *use-value* of the other, i.e., in the natural form of the other commodity; that *surplus value* itself is derived from a 'specific' *use-value of labour-power* exclusively pertaining to the latter, etc., etc., that thus for me use-value plays a far more important part than it has in economics hitherto, NB however, that it is only ever taken into account where this springs from the analysis of given economic constellations . . ., not from arguing backwards and forwards about the concepts or words 'use-value' and 'value'.[80]

Thus, according to Marx, his own scientific discoveries consist in:

- revelation of the general forms (still undifferentiated) of surplus-value;
- revelation of the dual character of labour;
- an understanding of capital (and its corollary, wages) as a social relation;

- an appreciation that use-value is not simply abolished in exchange-value, but retains a specific importance.

Furthermore, they clearly reveal the status:

- of general forms compared with empirical chaos ('a regular hash');
- of the dialectical division of the commodity and of labour;
- of the social relation inscribed in the totality of the movement.

These discoveries assume their full significance in the light of 'German science', which aims for a synthetic knowledge of the concrete, like the particularity of the historical moment, or the pathological cases of the analytic cure.

The bright light shed on the part by the whole determines an epoch's maximum possible scientific self-consciousness. Smith and Ricardo glimpsed order under the seeming disorder of the economic universe. They understood that, far from obeying some higher will, this order derived from exchanges and transactions between individuals seeking to maximize their own gains. A species of strange attractor imposing an immanent regularity on the irregular movements of the market, the law of value expresses this 'order in disorder'.

The 'critique of political economy' thus inaugurates a different way of doing science. It is reducible neither to the foundation of a positive science of the economy, nor to a speculative return to German science, nor to the negativity of critique. A revolutionary theory, it confronts the mirages of fetishism without being able to defeat its spells.

Denouncing the ambiguity of the natural sciences promoted to the rank of 'sciences *par excellence*' or 'fetish sciences', Gramsci grasped this originality. Persuaded that there is no such thing as science in itself, any more than there is method in itself, that the hypostasis of an abstract scientificity is one more trick of fetishism, Gramsci fought the illusion of a scientific Esperanto or Volapuk, reducing the diversity of knowledge to a single language. For the same reasons, he was indignant to find in Bukharin's *Historical Materialism* a positivist concept of science 'taken root and branch from the natural sciences'.[81] Yielding to the perverse mania for precision, the quest for regularity, normality, uniformity had been substituted for the 'historical dialectic'. Only the fact of struggle could be forecast 'scientifically', not its moments or outcomes.

Only struggle can be forecast! Associating Marx's theory with Freud's in his attack on 'pseudo-sciences', in one sense Popper's aim was accurate. These forms of knowledge have conflict for their object (class struggle in the one instance; struggle between desires in the other), and permanently altered its formulation solely by virtue of conceptualizing it.[82] Similarly, for Clausewitz, knowledge of war could be conceived neither as a science nor as an art. For want of anything better, it would be a theory destined to become strategy: military strategy, analytical strategy, political strategy.

'Marx's science' definitely cannot be laid securely on the epistemological plinth of his age. Constrained by its object (the social relations and economic rhythms of capital), by the non-linear logic of its temporalities, by disconcerting 'laws' that contradict themselves, it aspires to a different rationality.

'Prophetic science'? 'Knowledge of a third type'? 'Mathematics of concepts' and the 'necessity of a different knowledge'? All these formulas resonate with an appeal to another knowledge, which is receptive to the reasons for unreason: a knowledge deploying a strategic thought for which an 'obscure', 'non-obvious' theory, more attentive to what is hidden than what is disclosed, remains to be invented.[83]

Notes

1. Karl Marx, 'Preface to the First Edition', in *Capital*, vol. 1, trans. Ben Fowkes, Penguin/ NLR, Harmondsworth 1976, pp. 89–93.
2. Joseph A. Schumpeter, *Capitalism, Socialism and Democracy*, Routledge, London 1992, pp. 44–7.
3. See Niels Bohr, *Atomic Physics and Human Knowledge*, Wiley and Sons, New York 1958.
4. Frederick Engels, letter to Marx of 29 November 1873, in Marx and Engels, *Collected Works*, vol. 44, Lawrence & Wishart, London 1989, pp. 540–41; letter to Friedrich Adolph Sorge of 29 June 1883, in Marx and Engels, *Collected Works*, vol. 47, Lawrence & Wishart, London 1993, p. 42.
5. Karl Marx, letter to Engels of 31 July 1865, in Marx and Engels, *Collected Works*, vol. 42, Lawrence & Wishart, London 1982, p. 173.
6. Enrique Dussel, *Hacia un Marx desconocido*, Siglo XXI, Mexico 1988, p. 285.
7. Karl Marx, letter to Lassalle of 12 November 1858, in Marx and Engels, *Collected Works*, vol. 40, Lawrence & Wishart, London 1983, p. 355; letter to Engels of 20 February 1866, in Marx and Engels, *Collected Works*, vol. 42, p. 232.
8. Via Hegel, it inherits the influence of Master Eckhardt or Jakob Böhme. We might also detect in it the obscure filiation of Jewish mysticism, for which what is called philosophical science is simply an initiation into a superior 'prophetic science', just as 'combinatory science' is superior to formal logic. See Abraham Aboulafia, *Épître des sept voies*, Éditions de l'Éclair, Paris 1985.
9. Manuel Sacristan, 'El trabajo científico de Marx y su nocio de cencia' (1980), reprinted in the collection *Sobre Marx y marxismo*, Edicion Icaria, Barcelona 1984, p. 317. The date is important: enthusiasm for Popper was then at its height, and 'Marx's science', so prestigious but a few years before, was relegated to the infernal regions of 'pseudo-science'.
10. Sacristan notes that the manner of citation in Volume One of *Capital* still contains traces of this Young-Hegelian philosophy of science. Its subtitle ('A Critique of Political

Economy') also attests to it, although the final plan of the whole work, according to Sacristan, succeeded in dissociating the strictly critical part (entitled *Theories of Surplus-Value*) from the systematic part of the first three volumes. Here Sacristan would seem to be guilty of a misinterpretation. The 'critique' is not reserved for the historical exposition of economic doctrines, but runs through Marx's conceptual labour in its entirety: *Capital* fully merits its subtitle.

11. Karl Marx, 'A Contribution to the Critique of Hegel's Philosophy of Right. Introduction', in Marx, *Early Writings*, trans. Rodney Livingstone and Gregor Benton, Penguin/NLR 1975, p. 245. Engels was to return to this idea nearly forty years later, in his 1882 preface to the first German edition of *Socialism: Utopian and Scientific*: 'Scientific socialism is after all an essentially German product and could arise only in that nation whose classical philosophy had kept alive the tradition of conscious dialectics: among Germans. . . . Only by the subjection of the economic and political conditions produced in England and France to German dialectical criticism could a real result be achieved' (Marx and Engels, *Collected Works*, vol. 24, Lawrence & Wishart, London 1983, pp.458–9).

12. Marx, 'Critique of Hegel's Philosophy of Right. Introduction', p. 249.

13. Karl Marx, 'Critical Notes on the Article "The King of Prussia and Social Reform. By a Prussian"', in Marx, *Early Writings*, p. 415.

14. See Georges Labica, *Marxism and the Status of Philosophy*, trans. Kate Soper and Martin Ryle, Harvester, Brighton 1980, p. 36: 'The desire for a "scientific" alliance between theory and practice, which we have already met with, there finds its most concrete expression. But it introduces a new problematic, which calls in question the concept of philosophy itself, since it must now ask itself under what conditions it becomes possible for philosophy to find its *way out*.' See also the works of Theodor Shanin on the late Marx and Russia.

15. This philosophical science, which is sought for its own sake, unlike a knowledge unconcerned with the 'why' of things, seeks the truth of constantly changing things. In Aristotle, this philosopher's science is the science of being *qua* being, while physics and mathematics are simply regions of philosophy.

16. Yirmiyahu Yovel notes the unusual character of this title: '*By* Karl Marx? If so, this was a perfect case of plagiarism. There is not a single sentence in this notebook which Marx had not copied from Spinoza. But this may be an act of philosophical appropriation. For indeed, Spinoza's thought . . . remained at the foundation of Marx's later thinking . . . Spinoza was above all a counterbalance and corrective to Hegel, restoring the concept of nature and man as a concrete, natural being for what had seemed to Marx his immersion in the lofty and semireligious heights of Hegelian *Geist*' (*Spinoza and Other Heretics*, vol. 2, Princeton University Press, Princeton, NJ 1989, p. 78).

17. Yirmiyahu Yovel, *Spinoza and Other Heretics*, vol. 1, Princeton University Press, Princeton, NJ 1989, p. 154.

18. André Tosel, *Du matéralisme, de Spinoza*, Éditions Kimé, Paris 1994, p. 53. For commentary on knowledge of the third kind, see also Gilles Deleuze, *Spinoza: Practical Philosophy*, trans. Robert Hurley, City Lights Books, San Francisco 1988; and Étienne Balibar, *Spinoza and Politics*, trans. Peter Snowdon, Verso, London and New York 1998.

19. Yovel, *Spinoza and Other Heretics*, vol. 1, p. 166.

20. Michel Serres naturally invokes Leibniz as regards this 'North-West passage': 'At the beginning of the classical age already, the sciences were divided or classified by comparison with separate continents. This is the image Leibniz derided, claiming that for the purposes of classifying the sciences it was preferable to take the metaphor of the sea, which, he said, is readily divisible into oceans or lakes with the aid of a sword' (*Le Passage du Nord-Ouest*, Éditions du Minuit, Paris 1986, p. 165). Leibniz, Marx, *même combat?*

21. For Yovel, *Capital* is clearly 'Marx's own way, following Spinoza, of discussing ethical vision and powerful human aspirations as if they were points, lines, and bodies' (*Spinoza*

and Other Heretics, vol. 2, p. 98). Following the geometry of passions, what we have is a dynamic geometry of social conflicts.

22. Ibid., p. 100.
23. Immanuel Kant, 'Idea for a Universal History with a Cosmopolitan Purpose', in Kant, *Political Writings*, trans. H.B. Nisbet, Cambridge University Press, Cambridge 1991, pp. 42–3. In Husserl, we again encounter a teleological conception of history in the sense of a 'process of finality', infinite and open, implying neither mechanical fatality nor inevitable historical progress.
24. The history of the French reception of Spinoza is in large part a protracted failure to understand him, inaugurated by Malebranche's hostility to the 'wretched Spinoza', continued by the diatribes of Massillon and the coarse rhymes of Voltaire against the 'little Jew with the long nose and the pallid complexion'. From the Bishop d'Avranches to Bayle, seventeenth-century believers and eighteenth-century non-believers had equal difficulty understanding this distinct system of thought (see Paul Janet, 'Le spinozisme en France', *Revue philosophique*, February 1882). When he was not accepted on the basis of a misunderstanding, Hegel met with similar incomprehension. In the tradition established by Quinet, Kant was the constitutent and legislative philosopher of the Third Republic whose educational system bore the stamp of a virtuous moralism, while the Hegelian system was happily reduced to a 'logicist apologia for the facts'.
25. See Georges Friedmann, *Leibniz et Spinoza*, Gallimard, Paris 1975; Yvon Belaval, *Leibniz, initiation à sa philosophie*, Vrin, Paris 1969; Émile Boutroux, *La Philosophie allemande au xviiᵉ siècle*, Vrin, Paris 1948. Michel Vadée, who judiciously expands upon the contribution of Aristotle in *Marx penseur du possible*, barely lingers over the Leibnizian metaphysic of possibility. However, in a note he indicates that Nikolai Hartmann regarded Leibniz and Hegel as the only two great Aristotelians since the Middle Ages. He also recalls that, in order to prepare his thesis defence, Marx, on the advice of Bruno Bauer, worked in particular on Aristotle, Spinoza and Leibniz. If he does not develop this path, Vadée does not neglect it either: Marx 'belongs with those philosophers who, like Leibniz and Hegel among the moderns, or Aristotle and Heraclitus among the Ancients, rejected the mechanistic conception of nature' (*Marx penseur du possible*, Klincksieck, Paris 1992, p. 265). Perceptively, Lenin was one of those who stressed the importance of Leibniz for Marx (despite his 'pieties' and 'Lassallean' – conciliatory – side in politics!).
26. See Michel Fichant's Postface to *De l'horizon de la doctrine humaine*, Vrin, Paris 1993.
27. See G.W. Leibniz, *Theodicy*, trans. E.M. Huggard, Open Court, New York 1985.
28.

> To sum up, if we take only the divine understanding, Leibniz's thesis could be summarized thus: only individuals can exist; there are no two identical individuals; consequently, even for God, existential truths cannot be resolved into identicals. Existential truths thus elude brute necessity. How? Through the choice sanctioned by their contingency. God distinguishes them from absolutely necessary truths like the elective from the ineluctable ... Choosing between an infinity of possible worlds, God has thereby chosen between 'an infinity of laws, some appropriate to one, others to another'. (Belaval, *Leibniz*, p. 162)

29. Leibniz, letter of 24 January 1694 to J.-P. Bignon.
30. G.W.F. Hegel, *Phenomenology of Spirit*, trans. A.V. Miller, Oxford University Press, Oxford and New York 1977, pp. 14–15. The relation of philosophy to science is fully developed in the *Phenomenology*: 'Science is not that idealism which replaced the dogmatism of assertion with a dogmatism of assurance, or a dogmatism of self-certainty ... This nature of scientific method, which consists partly in not being separate from the content, and partly in spontaneously determining the rhythm of its movement, has ... its proper exposition in speculative philosophy' (ibid., pp. 33, 35). On the classification of knowledge in the nineteenth century, see Patrick Tort, *La Raison classificatoire*, Aubier, Paris 1989. In his writings on the sciences, Engels, for his part, seems torn between a mania

for classification and nostalgia for the German grand synthesis. For him, the transition of the sciences to 'theory' still characterizes the domain of German science:

> Empirical natural science has accumulated such a tremendous mass of positive material for knowledge that the necessity of classifying it in each separate field of investigation systematically and in accordance with its inner inter-connection has become absolutely imperative. It is becoming equally imperative to bring the individual spheres of knowledge into the correct connection with one another. In doing so, however, natural science enters the field of theory and here the methods of empiricism will not work, here only theoretical thinking can be of assistance. But theoretical thinking is an innate quality only as regards natural capacity. This natural capacity must be developed, improved, and for its improvement there is as yet no other means than the study of previous philosophy. (Frederick Engels, *Dialectics of Nature*, trans. Clemens Dutt, Progress Publishers, Moscow 1976, pp. 42–3)

31. Hegel, *Phenomenology of Spirit*, pp. 24–5.
32. Ibid., pp. 25–7.
33. Ibid., p. 27.
34. Ibid., p. 3.
35. Ibid., p. 41.
36. G.W.F. Hegel, *Science of Logic*, trans. A.V. Miller, Allen & Unwin, London 1969, pp. 27, 48–9.
37. Ibid., p. 509.
38. Ibid., p. 711.
39. Ibid., pp. 727, 731.
40. Ibid., p. 761.
41. Ibid., pp. 768–9.
42. Ibid., pp. 43–4, 48.
43. Ibid., p. 58. Logic is formal to the extent that it confines itself to a science of form and reduces a process to a static state. The mutual exteriority of its elements reduces logic, which should be the science of thinking, to mere 'calculating'. Hegel's *Logic*, on the contrary, exhibits the development of the Concept from the abstract to the concrete and this, surmounting the dualism essence/existence like the exteriority of the concept to the object, to attain the logic of the thing. Thus, the object of logic is thinking, but it cannot be given in advance. It can only be thought thinking itself. This is precisely the role of critique with respect to capital: not a science as thought given in advance, but an object that abolishes itself in the process of thinking itself.
44. Herbert Marcuse, *Hegel's Ontology and the Theory of Historicity*, trans. Seyla Benhabib, MIT Press, Cambridge, MA and London 1987, p. 195. Similarly, for Ludovico Geymonat as for Vico, it is history that compels us to acknowledge a different type of rationality.
45. Hegel, *Science of Logic*, pp. 331–2.
46. Ibid., p. 588.
47. Ibid., p. 842.
48. Ibid., p. 843.
49. Ibid., p. 831.
50. As Catherine Colliot-Thélène writes, the second part of the *Logic* (the doctrine of Essence) 'tests the substance of the basic categories of ordinary scientific disciplines in the fire of speculative philosophy: thing, law, force, necessity, causality, reciprocal action. This test reveals not the lack of validity of these forms of knowledge, but the limited character of the intelligibility offered by them … In other words, it is not the finite knowledge of the ordinary sciences whose validity is questioned by Hegelian speculation, but scientific ideology' (*Le Désenchantement de l'État*, Éditions de Minuit, Paris 1992, p. 38).
51. G.W.F. Hegel, *The Encyclopaedia Logic*, trans. T.F. Geraets, W.A. Suchting and H.S. Harris, Hackett Publishing Company, Indianapolis and Cambridge 1991, p. 4.
52. Ibid., pp. 128, 131.

53. Ibid., p. 21.
54. Jacques Derrida, *Specters of Marx*, trans. Peggy Kamuf, Routledge, New York and London 1994, p. 34. See also Tony Smith, *The Logic of Marx's 'Capital'*, State University of New York Press, New York 1990, and *Dialectical Social Theory and its Critics*, State University of New York Press, New York 1994. See also Roy Bhaskar, *Dialectic: The Pulse of Freedom*, Verso, London and New York 1993.
55. Maurice Blanchot, 'Marx's Three Voices', in Blanchot, *Friendship*, trans. Elizabeth Rottenberg, Stanford University Press, Stanford, CA 1997, p. 99.
56. Lucien Sebag suggests another version of this theoretical triad: 'revolutionary theory appears simultaneously as utopia, as science, and as quotidian disclosure of the content of the praxis that is ours' (*Marxisme et structuralisme*, Payot, Paris 1964, p. 68). Here we once again have science (English) and critique (as disclosure), but German science disappears in favour of utopia as anticipatory knowledge. Adhering to this problematic, Henri Maler offers a stimulating reading of the uncontrolled return of an unguided utopia in Marx, and its effects on his whole theoretical apparatus (*Congédier l'utopie*, L'Harmattan, Paris 1994 and *Convoiter l'impossible*, Albin Michel, Paris 1995).
57. Marx, *Capital*, vol. 1, p. 433.
58. Karl Marx, letter to Arnold Ruge of September 1843, in Marx, *Early Writings*, p. 207. On the variations in the concept of critique, see Maler, *Congédier l'utopie*, pp. 34–42.
59. See Marx's letter to Annenkov of 28 December 1846, in Marx and Engels, *Selected Correspondence*, Progress Publishers, Moscow 1975, p. 38.
60. 'Critique is indeed a science of borders': Serres, *Le Passage du Nord-Ouest*, p. 59.
61. Paul-Laurent Assoun and Gérard Raulet, *Marxisme et théorie critique*, Payot, Paris 1978, p. 36.
62. Sacristan, *Sobre Marx y marxismo*, p. 364.
63. Ibid.
64. Karl Marx, *Capital*, vol. 3, trans. David Fernbach, Penguin/NLR, Harmondsworth 1981, pp. 178–9.
65. Ibid., p. 373.
66. Ibid., p. 968.
67. Ibid., p. 965.
68. Ibid., pp. 958–9.
69. *The Enchanted World* is the title of a comparative analysis of ancient pre-Christian religions and the religions of 'savages' published in 1691 by the Dutchman Balthazar Becker. See Alfonso Iacono, *Le Fétichisme: histoire d'un concept*, Presses Universitaires de France, Paris 1992.
70. Marx, *Capital*, vol. 3, pp. 969–70.
71. See Georges Labica, *Le Paradigme du Grand Hornu*, La Brèche, Paris 1988; and Patrick Tort, *Marx et le problème de l'idéologie*, Presses Universitaires de France, Paris 1988:

> At best, then, even when it involves a scientific enterprise, demystifying serves only to produce the truth of a relation in the domain of specialists, theoreticians and ideologues, not in the sphere of producers, who are prisoners of the veil because, through their activity, they live and continue to live in the non-reflexive element of illusion, indefinitely subject to its undeniable power. By virtue of a necessity that now no longer appears paradoxical, those who live and act closest to reality are thus the first and most numerous victims of appearances. (p. 96)

72. In *Que faire du Capital?* (Klincksieck, Paris 1984), Jacques Bidet undertakes to demonstrate the articulation of the theory of fetishism with the social relations that define the concept of value. The evolution from the German version of *Capital* to the French version, following a process of 'theoretical maturation', tends towards eliminating certain philosophical categories like 'singular/particular/universal' or 'subject/object'. Hence three interpretations of fetishism as the 'structural category of the ideology of commodity production':

(a) as reification;
(b) as value-form;
(c) 'structural' interpretation.

Fetishism as reification represents both the 'inverted being' and 'the inverted represen-tation of being'. This interpretation is regressive, in the sense that it relapses into a classical problematic of the subject/object relationship. The merit of *Capital*, in contrast, is to 'break up this globalized category of the subject', in favour of the bearer [*Träger*] or agent of a system of social relations – in other words, Althusser's famous 'process without a subject'. Interpretation by value-form gets bogged down in the discrepancy between the logic of behaviour and the consciousness of agents. According to the structural interpretation, finally, the producers enter into contact with one another solely as exchangers, and precisely not as producers.

In Volume One, Marx imagines four instances of transparency in which the social relation discloses itself without the mask of value. The real is then an immediate datum of consciousness, of which it is no longer necessary to produce the science. Yet false consciousness is not mere bad faith, but distorted vision, which only a scientific approach, operating beyond appearances, can rectify. Why does this law in fact remain unknown to the producers? Because its terms of reference extend beyond the field of experience of the private producer. Fetishism in the strong sense of the term thus exists, in so far as the law of value that governs the market, and presides over exchanges of labour, necessarily remains unknown to the producers.

73. Marx, *Capital*, vol. 3, p. 956; *Capital*, vol. 1, p. 433; *Capital*, vol. 3, p. 205; letter of 27 June 1867 to Engels, in Marx and Engels, *Selected Correspondence*, p. 179; letter of 11 July 1868 to Kugelmann, in ibid., pp. 196–7.

74. Such is indeed the materialist postulate reaffirmed in the letter to Kugelmann of 11 July 1868, or after the publication of Volume One of *Capital*, in terms recalling those of the 1844 *Manuscripts*.

75. Marx, *Capital*, vol. 1, p. 165.

76. Ibid., p. 175.

77. Marx, *Capital*, vol. 3, p. 373,

78. Marx and Engels, *Selected Correspondence*, p. 180.

79. Ibid., pp. 186–7.

80. Karl Marx, 'Marginal Notes on Adolph Wagner's *Lehrbuch der politischen Ökonomie*', *Theoretical Practice*, no. 5, Spring 1972, pp. 51–2.

81. Antonio Gramsci, *Selections from the Prison Notebooks*, ed. and trans. Quintin Hoare and Geoffrey Nowell Smith, Lawrence & Wishart, London 1971, p. 438.

82. In a text of January 1964 on 'Freud and Lacan', Louis Althusser emphasized this kinship:

Psychoanalysis, in its sole survivors, is concerned with a different struggle, in the sole war without memoirs or memorials, which humanity pretends never to have fought, the one it thinks it has always won in advance, quite simply because its very existence is a function of having survived it, of living and giving birth to itself as culture within human nature. This is a war that, at every instant, is waged in each of its offspring, who, projected, deformed, rejected, each for himself, in solitude and against death, have to undertake the long forced march that turns mammalian larvae into human children, that is, *subjects*. (Althusser, *Writings on Psychoanalysis: Freud and Lacan*, trans. Jeffrey Mehlman, Columbia University Press, New York 1996, pp. 22–3)

83. 'We should invent a theory of obscure, confused, dark, nonevident knowledge – a theory of "adelo-knowledge"': Michel Serres with Bruno Latour, *Conversations on Science, Culture, and Time*, trans. Roxanne Lapidus, University of Michigan Press, Ann Arbor 1995, p. 148.

8

A New Immanence

Marx sometimes presents his notebooks and drafts as 'scientific *essays*', passageways and paths, rather than as moments of appropriation of a truth that can be possessed like a simple object. For:

> Science consists precisely in demonstrating *how* the law of value asserts itself. So that if one wanted at the very beginning to 'explain' all the phenomena which seemingly contradict that law, one would have to present the science *before* science . . . the vulgar economist thinks he has made a great discovery when, in face of the disclosure of intricate interconnection, he proudly states that on the surface things look different. In fact, he boasts that he sticks to appearance, and takes it for the ultimate. Why, then, have any science at all?[1]

Poles apart from the major illusions of empiricism, science does not disclose itself in appearances. It is produced in a polemical relationship with the false obviousness of the facts. Wanting to expound 'the science *before* science': that is the real trap.

In fact, the 'intricate interconnection' discloses a dynamic of necessary determinations in the logical order that is distinct from the superficial, crudely causal sequence of phenomena. Thus, in Volume One of *Capital* scientific labour appears as the elucidation of a mystery. The determination of value by labour-time is 'a *secret hidden* under the apparent movements'. It presupposes the 'full development' of commodity production, such that 'scientific conviction' can emerge. This is why 'scientific analysis . . . takes a course directly opposite to [the] real development'. It begins '*post festum*, and therefore with the results of the process of development ready to hand'.[2]

Under the lash of money, the world becomes frenzied. To understand these marvels, we must, says Marx at the end of Part Two, abandon the din of the market, that 'noisy sphere, where everything takes place on the surface', and descend into 'the *hidden abode* of production', surprise and lay bare the 'secret' of modern society: the production of surplus-value.[3] The critique of a phantasmagoria, in which the animated idol of money seems to cause the circulation of commodities, science strips away the 'false appearances' of exchange.

This is why, according to Marx, the bourgeois science of economics, although it has only just been born, has already become impossible 'among us' (in Germany):

> The peculiar historical development of German society therefore excluded any original development of 'bourgeois' economics there, but did not exclude its critique. In so far as such a critique represents a class, it can only represent the class whose historical task is the overthrow of the capitalist mode of production and the final abolition of all classes – the proletariat.[4]

Perceiving even in the false consciousness of the proletariat an aspiration to the truth of capitalist society, Lukács pushed this social determination to an extreme. The image of a class represented by the critique of political economy in fact raises more problems than it resolves.

The class standpoint constitutes the internal obstacle, the innermost negative limit of classical science. It limits its horizons and dictates its relativity: 'The profound and correct explanation that [Smith] himself offered elsewhere did not prevail, whereas this blunder did.'[5] In the brains of the vulgar economists, 'only the immediate phenomenal *form* of [the] relations . . . is reflected . . . and not their *inner connection*'. Moreover, 'if the latter were the case, what need would there be of *science?*'[6]

To trace a stable frontier between science and non-science, Althusser drew upon the Preface to Volume Two of *Capital*, in which Engels compares surplus-value in the classical economists with oxygen in Lavoisier and Priestley: both had produced it, 'but they were unaware of what they had laid their hands on'.[7] To produce is not to discover. Where people hastened to see a solution, Marx still detected a problem. Because they did not distinguish between labour and labour-power, Smith and Ricardo never knew what they had laid their hands on.

Does the concept of surplus-value betoken a Copernican revolution or an epistemological break? Towards the end of his life, Engels counterposed an evolutionary, cumulative conception of the history of science to this way of dividing it up: 'The history of science is the history of the gradual clearing away of this nonsense or rather of its replacement by fresh and less absurd nonsense.' A less triumphalist image of science? A Sisyphean labour of critique, in which the decreasing order of absurdity, while not completely freeing itself of recurrent idiocy, makes it possible, with the modesty of Pascal, to say the opposite of the ancients without contradicting them? The discovery of surplus-value does not signify that Hegel or Spinoza is done with: 'What all these gentlemen lack is dialectics.

They always see only cause here, effect there … As far as they are concerned, Hegel never existed.'[8]

Open Totality and Contradiction

Marx's debt to Hegel has often been questioned, as if this compromising flirtation meant a metaphysical relapse. On 14 January 1858, while frantically engaged in writing the *Grundrisse*, Marx wrote to Engels that he had just 'again glanced through Hegel's *Logik*': 'If there should ever be time for such work again, I should very much like to make accessible to the ordinary human intelligence – in two or three printer's sheets – what is *rational* in the method which Hegel discovered but at the same time enveloped in mysticism.'[9] Alas, Marx never found time.

Yet Lenin was not mistaken. After 4 August 1914, confronted with one of the great turning points in human history, he too returned to Hegel's *Logic*. His conclusion was as peremptory as it was provocative: those who believed it possible to proceed directly to Marx, bypassing Hegel, could understand nothing of him.

Imitating classical physics, positive science proceeds by reductions. Elusive in its perfect circularity, and flawless, the totality then appears as a pre-scientific category *par excellence*, suspected of Romanticism and lyrical fascination with the mysteries of life. In Marx's theory, the 'different logic' amounts to a determinate, differentiated totality exhibiting the articulation [*Gliederung*] of its moments. In the Preface to the *Phenomenology*, Hegel stresses the conceptual significance of these *mediations*, which inspire 'abhorrence' in the analytical understanding, 'as if absolute cognition were being surrendered when more is made of mediation than in simply saying that it is nothing absolute, and is completely absent in the Absolute'. This abhorrence 'in fact stems from ignorance of the nature of mediation, and of absolute cognition itself. For mediation is nothing beyond self-moving selfsameness, or is reflection into self, the moment of the "I" which is for itself pure negativity or, when reduced to its pure abstraction, *simple becoming*.'[10] In abolishing by decree the difference between private and public, the separation of economic and political, and the distinction between law and force, abstract, identitarian totalization unilaterally subjects the part to the whole. Similarly, in identifying class, people, party and state, it veers towards totalitarian diktat.[11]

For Hegel, concrete totalization is articulated and mediated. Unlike the system, whose unity rests upon violence, the whole is the set of its moments. For Marx, it proceeds from laws of tendency and an organic causality. The great open circle of *Capital* reproduces this 'self-moving selfsameness' through its own differentiation and contradictions. Anyone who mentions mediation must then conceptualize law, morality, institutions, a reciprocity of differences, a logic of conflicts and oppositions, and not some formally declared reconciliation.

This detotalized totality breaks with current notions of identity, causality and time, borrowed from the mechanistic model. It pertains to a logic of relations in which the determinate elements of the totality are in turn reciprocally co-determined. This 'circular knowledge' partakes of the infinite movement which, 'were it even possible to know everything, and everything about everything, would still ensure the eternal renewal of knowledge'.[12]

This open totalization is necessarily and essentially pluralistic: a question of relations and mediations.

Where does a totality begin? Which end should it be taken from? Where can we find the entry point that makes it possible to pierce its opacity and illuminate it from within? Where is its smooth, spiralling surface to be crossed? How can we interrupt the infernal circle of exchange, shatter the cycle of metamorphoses of the commodity, arrest the sequence of production, circulation and reproduction, suspend the diabolical permutation of the roles of capital – sometimes money, sometimes machines and labour-power, and then finally commodity and money once again – while other fractions of the same capital operate the same mechanism of transfiguration and transubstantiation in reverse?

Where do we begin? For Marx, Hegel and Proust, it is the same haunting question. The totality inhabits each link, each fragment, each detail of the chain. Yet there is one that encapsulates and discloses the whole: being, Proust's madeleine, the commodity. Banal and innocent, quite simple, the fractured commodity opens out like a kind of magic nut from which use-value and exchange-value, abstract labour and concrete labour, surplus-value and profit escape, just as Swann's way and the Guermantes way are summoned up by sucking the madeleine. The categories of the commodity or memory that flow from these wounds unveil the marvellous totality of a constantly changing world.[13]

'[T]he True ... is the process of its own becoming, the circle that presupposes its end as its goal', writes Hegel in the *Phenomenology*.[14] In the *Logic*, he is more explicit:

> Thoroughness seems to require that the beginning, as the foundation on which everything is built, should be examined before anything else ... This thorough-

ness at the same time has the advantage of guaranteeing that the labour of thinking shall be reduced to a minimum; it has before it, enclosed in this germ, the entire development and reckons that it has settled the whole business when it has disposed of the beginning . . .

It is only in our own times, he observes, that account has been taken of 'the difficulty of finding a beginning in philosophy'.[15] The beginning is 'pure being', but, in the movement of the totality, pure being immediately summons its other: nothingness. The lacerated totality is then set in motion, in a desperate quest for its lost unity.

Without value disappearing into price, or surplus-value into profit, capital constitutes the concrete development of the commodity. For 'the *progress* from that which forms the beginning is to be regarded as only a further determination of it, hence that which forms the starting point of the development remains at the base of all that follows and does not vanish for it'. Through this progress:

> the beginning loses the onesidedness which attaches to it as something simply immediate and abstract; it becomes something mediated, and hence the line of the scientific advance becomes a *circle*. It also follows that because that which forms the beginning is still undeveloped, devoid of content, it is not truly known in the beginning; it is the science of logic in its whole compass which first constitutes the completed knowledge of it with its developed content and first truly grounds that knowledge.

To discover the path of the concrete, a mutilated, unilateral beginning, an absolute and imperfect beginning, was required. It was necessary to begin with a knowledge devoid of content, a misunderstanding, to discover the path of comprehension and content. 'Comprehensive' knowledge, unveiled in the plenitude of its moments, is not a matter of the mechanical addition of knowledge, but an activity of knowledge such that 'the end is the beginning, the consequent the ground, the effect the cause, . . . it is a becoming of what has become . . . in it only what already exists comes into existence'.[16] Thus, it is in the light of the end, in the dialectic of positing and presupposing, that the beginning emerges from obscurity to initiate a new circle of circles, without ever encountering its absolute starting point. All becoming is a beginning and an end, stresses Lenin, such that each advance in determinations, in so far as it moves further away from the beginning, is also a return towards it.[17]

At the beginning of *Capital* was the commodity. In the circulation process, it moves away from its initial abstraction before reappearing concretely, at the end of the 'process as a whole', in the organic life of capital. We need to have been mistaken about the beginning in order to reach the end that delivers the key to it. This beginning, then, is in no sense an inaugural foundation. It is transformed in the course of its own development, since it is also the case that 'the origin is the end'.

Under the impetus of its own contradictions, the totality develops:

> the exchange of commodities implies contradictory and mutually exclusive conditions. The further development of the commodity does not abolish these contradictions, but rather provides the form within which they have room to move. This is, in general, the way in which real contradictions are resolved. For instance, it is a contradiction to depict one body as constantly falling towards another and at the same time constantly flying away from it. The ellipse is a form of motion within which this contradiction is both realized and resolved.[18]

A 'superior rational process', thanks to which apparently separate terms pass over into one another, just as being and nothingness manifest their unity and truth in development, the motion of capital then appears to its full extent: the division of the commodity, a real contradiction, its antagonistic development, and its actual resolution through formal development. Stretched towards the horizon of crisis as towards the end that might also be a new beginning for it, the fracture of the totality is its very principle.

Often interchangeable in Marx's terminology, contradiction [*Widerspruch*], antagonism [*Gegensatz*], and conflict [*Konflikt*] articulate dialectical logic and history, without conflating them. At once logical and historical, contradiction is thus incorporated into the concept of law. As 'necessary inner connection', law 'reconnects' what 'contradiction separates'. The commodity presents itself as a contradictory unity, and the laws of commodity exchange are those of the inner contradiction of its form. From Volume One onwards, Marx notes 'contradictory tendencies' (between maximum possible surplus-value and maximum reduction of variable capital). Breaking the barrier that separates the totality from the phenomenal and the rational, contradiction makes possible a process of conceptualization. Hence the need to distinguish between two orders of contradictions, which are no more one another's reflection than the rational totality is the reflection of the phenomenal totality: that of the real-concrete and the concrete-in-thought.[19]

In *Capital*, the term 'contradiction' sometimes designates the conflict of interests between capitalists; sometimes the conflict between capitalists and workers; sometimes the conflict between production and consumption (production and realization of surplus-value), or between relations and forces of production; and sometimes, finally, the conflict between capital and feudal survivals. These diverse occurrences indicate a distinction between contradictions that are internal to the capitalist mode of production, and contradictions between this system and the remains of previous systems. The former are specific to it, and are expressed in the class struggle. But are they thereby the fundamental contradiction? Maurice Godelier thinks not: the principal contradiction between the development and socialization of the productive forces, on the one hand, and private ownership of the means of production, on the other, is not immediately visible. It constitutes not a contradiction internal to the structure, but a contradiction between two rival structures (and logics), of which crises reveal only a 'general idea'. Unintentional, structural contradiction expresses the internal limits – 'immanent' and 'insuperable' – of the capitalist mode of production and relations based on private ownership. Thus, the capitalist mode of production in its entirety 'is precisely only a relative mode of production, whose limits, while not absolute, have, on its own basis, an absolute value for it'. This is manifest at a certain stage of development of the productive forces, when 'capital itself' become the real barrier to capitalist production.[20]

Internal to the relations of production, the first contradiction does not contain within it all the conditions required for its own solution. It is externalized in class struggle. Marx, in fact, declines to resort to the identity of opposites as the kind of 'magical operator' exploited by Hegel to build his palace of ideas. Capital is not a totality ossified into a thing, but a living, mobile social relation. Fissured, rent, wounded, the totality is prey to real contradictions, irreducible to the appeasement of identity.[21]

Determination as Focusing

Whether in the case of value, classes or capital, handy, reassuring definitions are not to be found in Marx. The imperfect beginning of a totality that starts over and over again, without ever finishing, precludes an illusory inventory of exhaustive criteria. The return of the whole into its parts proceeds not by one-sided abstractions destined to be consumed on the spot, but by determinate abstractions that approximate to the concrete. Like the relation between rhythm and arrhythmia in the Sophists, Hegelian determination involves disclosure by contrast against the background of totality:

> Pure light and pure darkness are two voids which are the same thing. Something can be distinguished only in determinate light or darkness (light is

determined by darkness and so is darkened light, and darkness is determined by light, is illuminated darkness), and for this reason, that it is only darkened light and illuminated darkness which have within themselves the moment of difference and are, therefore, *determinate* being.

Hegelian discourse is thus conceived as a process that 'must let the inherently living determinations take their own course'.[22]

A prisoner of its own positivity, definition is a category of being and determination a category of becoming: 'Determinateness is negation posited as affirmative.' What is at stake in this opposition is crucial: nothing less than avoiding the unknowable thing-in-itself: 'Things are called "in themselves" in so far as abstraction is made from all being-for-other, which means simply, in so far as they are thought devoid of all determination, as nothings. In this sense, it is of course impossible to know *what* the *thing-in-itself* is.' Abstract definition always lets an elusive world escape. It wrests the phenomenality of being from its essential obscurity. The uninterrupted movement of determination, on the other hand, tends to reunite being and its double:

> the definitions of metaphysics, like its presuppositions, distinctions and conclusions, seek to assert and produce only what comes under the category of *being*, and that, too, of *being-in-itself. Being-for-other* is, in the unity of the something with itself, identical with its *in-itself*; the being-for-other is thus present *in* the something. The determinateness thus reflected into itself is, therefore, again in the simple form of *being*, and hence is again a quality: *determination*.[23]

Determination is not a matter of convention or dictionaries. It is enriched by the multiplication and differentiation of its relations with the other. Thus, value is never defined, but always determined by socially necessary labour-time, which is itself historically determined by class struggle, in such a way that the beginning (the commodity, value, surplus-value) always presupposes the end (capital, profit, class struggle). As a necessary inner connection, the law of value designates the determination of value by labour-time:

> Value is labour. This internal relation forms part of its concept and is inseparable from its nature. Hence its absolute necessity with respect to any external determination, whose action is asserted only through a multitude of other factors and therewith assumes a contingent character. When I write: value is labour and its measure is provided by that of labour-time, this determination in fact proves to be in no way different from the statement of the very concept of value.[24]

Marx explicitly lays claim to this dynamic logic of determination, as opposed to the static, classificatory logic of definitions: 'What is at issue here is not a set of *definitions under which things are to be subsumed.* It is rather *definite functions* that are expressed in specific categories.'[25] To dispel the 'misunderstanding' (the search for definition at any price) which misleads readers of Marx, like Conrad Schmidt, who are not dialecticians, Engels's Preface to Volume Three drives the point home. Schmidt's remarks:

> rest on the misunderstanding to the effect that Marx seeks to *define* where he only *explains,* and that one can generally look in Marx for fixed, cut-and-dried definitions that are valid for all time. It should go without saying that where things and their mutual relations are conceived not as fixed but rather as changing, their mental images, too, i.e. concepts, are also subject to change and reformulation; that *they are not to be encapsulated in rigid definitions, but rather developed in their process of historical or logical formation.*[26]

Concepts originate in the totality. Depending on whether they refer to modes of production in general, or the capitalist mode of production in particular, those of 'class' or 'productive labour' thus correspond to a general determination, or a particular determination, and assume a broad or narrow sense.[27] The reciprocal determination of a concept (use-value/ exchange-value) expresses a double reference, logical and historical, contradictorily present in reality. It refers to the dual universality, histori- cal and systemic, of the categories employed. Thus, the concept of productive labour specific to capitalist production relations contains no reference to the content of this labour, and remains at the level of abstract labour. Contrary to the common confusion, as specific productive labour it requires us to distinguish between the utility and productivity of labour.

The production of material wealth, the second determination [*Nebend- stimmung*] does not disappear in the search for abstract wealth (or profit). The extortion of surplus-value (crystallized social labour-time) indepen- dently of the purpose of the labour, the first determination is articulated with it as the 'decisive characteristic' or 'specific difference' of the capitalist mode of production.[28] Unproductive exclusively from the stand- point of production, commercial labour becomes 'indirectly productive' from the angle of circulation and reproduction as a whole, in that it allows commercial capital to appropriate a portion of the surplus-value produced in the sphere of production. Its determination refers to the division of capital into fractions, to the distribution of its functions, and to the consequent social division of labour.

The relation of the abstract to the concrete proceeds directly from determination. Unlike one-sided abstraction (speculative), determinate abstraction makes possible a historical focusing of the categories by their inner organic connexion.[29] Affirmative, rapid definitions satisfy a thirst for immediate positivity. In the patient labour of the negative, determination occurs by 'absenting' or suppression of lack.[30]

Contradiction originates in division. The division of the commodity into commodity and money enters the picture from the beginning of Volume One. Then the commodity, in turn, 'becomes double'. Similarly, circulation splits into sale and purchase. But division is not some indifferent separation. Its terms are interdependent. Thus, the commodity cannot possess value unless it is first an object of utility. Exchange-value implies and presupposes use-value as its own condition. In other words, utility is indispensable to value, even though use-value and exchange-value, combined in the commodity, belong to two distinct logical totalities. As exchange-value, the commodity represents a certain volume of embodied social labour. As use-value, it must also correspond to a solvent social need. The mediation of competition enables it to be simultaneously the one and the other. Thus, supply and demand reflect the innermost necessities of the commodity.

Inherent in this division of the commodity, its contradiction is resolved in circulation and reproduction. The principles of this process are formulated as early as Volume One: 'every social process of production is at the same time a process of reproduction. The conditions of production are at the same time the conditions of reproduction.'[31] What is at issue here, however, is still simple reproduction. In Volume Two, this simple reproduction emerges as the moment of necessary abstraction *en route* to reproduction on an expanded scale; and the cyclical process in the course of which 'the circuits of individual capitals are interlinked, . . . presuppose one another and condition one another, and . . . precisely by being interlinked in this way . . . constitute the movement of the total social capital'.[32]

Hence the relation between the plan of *Capital* and its object.

The circularity of knowledge reproduces the circularity of its object. From metamorphoses to permutations, the commodity abandons one cast-off immediately to slip into another, in such a way that each moment appears as a starting point, an intermediate point, a return to the starting point. The open circle of reproduction on an expanded scale makes it possible to transcend doleful repetition in the aleatory event.

This development is not the dismal 'progressiveness', sheer increase or magnification, characterized by Hegel as 'merely immaterial change'.

Combining quality and quantity, it is transformation, sublation, revolution. Non-immaterial change, it preserves as much as it transforms. For every revolutionary dream directed towards the future contains its share of preservation and redemption: 'What is sublated is not thereby reduced to nothing. Nothing is *immediate*; what is sublated, on the other hand, is the result of *mediation* . . . Thus what is sublated is at the same time preserved.'[33] Thus, the negation of the negation 'does not re-establish private property, but it does indeed establish individual property on the basis of the achievements of the capitalist era: namely co-operation and the possession in common of the land and the means of production produced by labour itself'.[34]

A Science of the Concrete Particular

Hegel's severity towards mathematical arrogance, and the 'defective cognition' in which it takes pride, is well known. The goal of such knowledge is magnitude. Whereas the concept divides space into its dimensions and determines relations, magnitude is an 'inessential' difference. Whereas the process in its totality, which engenders and runs through its moments, constitutes the concrete and the truth of the concrete, the determinations of quantity are those of mutual exteriority. In simple calculation, logic tends to be invalidated to the detriment of thinking.

Quantity, however, is conceivable only starting from the quality by which being emerges from initial indeterminacy. Quality ushers in change. Quantity arises from the indifferent development of qualitative differences. However, denying itself, it tends to re-establish quality.[35] Quantity thus first of all appears to be in opposition with quality, but in reality, 'the truth of quality is just this, to be quantity, immediate determinateness as sublated': 'At first, then, quantity as such appears in opposition to quality; but quantity is itself *a* quality, a purely self-related determinateness distinct from the determinateness of its other, from quality as such.'[36] Quantity, then, is the truth of quality. Thus, in *Capital*, the abstraction of labour, which has become indifferent to concrete labours, is the condition of its quantification. For Marx, as for Hegel, it is a question of conceiving the quantitative as displacement and explication, but also as a negation/subsumption of the qualitative.

The *Logic* follows being determined from within. All the processes and determinations by which it is reflected remain enclosed in the sphere of being according to determinateness as such (quality), the absence of determinateness (quantity), and as qualitatively defined quantity: measure.

Quantity, then, no longer falls outside of quality. It is simply quality that has become negative, or a determinateness that has become indifferent to being. In the same way, exchange-value does not abolish use-value, or abstract labour concrete labour. Exchange-value is use-value that has become negative, just as abstract labour is concrete labour become negative. Quantity in the pure state is distinguished by its indifference both towards the qualities it has to do with and towards itself. Any actual magnitude, by contrast, is a unity of quantity and quality, where quantity is the means by which one approaches quality in order to modify it. For measurement does not amount to one-sided quantification. It is a dialectic of quantity and quality. Hence the commonplace, obstinate lack of understanding on the part of econometricians (who are very unHegelian), obsessed as they are by the one-sided quantification (how much?) of qualitatively indeterminate value.

In the theory of measurement, magnitude has a double determination, extensive and intensive. In Marx, this duality refers to the problem of laws and their different meanings. Over and above quantitative laws, which bear on causal relations, Marx introduces a 'qualitative law' bearing on structural relations; and thus is verified the law that surplus-value originates not in the labour-power that the capitalist replaces with machines, but in the labour-power he employs.[37] Accordingly, the rate of exploitation can perfectly well increase quantitatively, while the rate of profit falls structurally. Political economy precisely aims to quantify quality by homogenizing an irreducibly heterogeneous economic space. It succeeds thanks to a 'common measure': time. Marx seems to subscribe to this reduction, considering 'time as the measure of labour'.[38] A curious formula. Why should labour be measurable by time? And what is time as a measure of labour? Would it not be more accurate to say that the measure of labour is labour-time, at the risk of avoiding incommensurability only to lapse into tautology? Adam Smith reduces the value of the commodity to the quantity of labour, abstracting from the different qualities (of difficulty or skill) deployed by this labour. In measuring the value of labour-power (and not labour *tout court*) by the labour-time socially necessary for its reproduction (and not time *tout court*), Marx changes register. Time is no longer a sort of supposedly uniform standard of reference, but a social relation that is determined in production, exchange and conflict. Competition and the market see to it that concrete labour is reduced to abstract labour. There is then no longer any question of quality: 'Quantity alone decides everything.'[39]

Everything? Concrete labour and use-value have not disappeared. They rebound in crises. If he cursorily characterizes time as 'the measure of labour', Marx does not forget that the measure concerns not a quantity indifferent to quality, but being as 'qualitatively determinate quantity'. In measurement, 'quality becomes quantity'. As such, 'measure is only an *immediate* unity of quality and quantity'. This is why the analysis of measurement, beginning with immediate, external measurement:

> should, on the one hand, go on to develop the abstract determination of the *quantitative* aspects of natural objects (a mathematics of nature), and on the other hand, to indicate the connection between this determination of measure and the *qualities* of natural objects, at least in general; for the specific proof, derived from the Notion of the concrete object, of the *connection* between its qualitative and quantitative aspects, belongs to the special science of the concrete.[40]

This 'special science of the concrete' heralds the critique of political economy as a knowledge of capital, or psychoanalysis as the interpretation of dreams. The metabolism of the living being, as of capital, requires a specific mode of measurement, different from the one that is valid for mechanism or chemism:

> The complete, abstract indifference of developed measure, i.e. the *laws* of measure, can only be manifested in the sphere of *mechanics* in which the concrete bodily factor is itself only *abstract* matter . . . On the other hand, such quantitative determinateness of abstract matter is deranged simply by the plurality of conflicting qualities in the inorganic sphere and still more even in the organic world.[41]

From the mechanical via the chemical to the organic, the plan of *Capital* runs through the moments of Hegelian logic. Authors who exhaust themselves on the transformation of value into price, by persisting in reducing the idea of measurement to abstract quantification, would avoid much misinterpretation were they to attend to the third part of the *Logic*. Just as formal necessity and possibility become actual in order to be resolved in absolute necessity, so formal measurement (or specific quantity) becomes real measurement in order to lead from the being to the 'becoming of essence'. If measurement in general is 'intended to represent a relation between measures that establish the quality of diverse, independent things', formal measurement corresponds to 'abstract qualities such as space and time', whereas 'real measurement' applies to 'determinations of material existence' (specific weight, chemical properties), of which time and space become the moments. At the end of measuring process, being 'will have completed the cycle of its metamorphoses'. Its immediacy will be erased in the becoming of essence.[42]

The measurement that determines itself as qualitatively defined quantity is immanent to the object that it determines. By many a subtlety, this circular logic pertains to the aporia of humanity as the measure of all things and of itself.

Logical Order and Historical Order

Historical and logical instances constantly overlap in Marx. Time, operator of change, is thus inscribed at the very heart of development. *Capital* temporalizes logic and logicizes economic rhythms.

Determination thus connects back up with measurement. For values initially require a common measure that is itself invariant, an invariant general commodity equivalent. Yet as commodities, all values are social magnitudes that vary with the class struggle. The measure determined by its object constantly changes with it. This is why qualities seem to manifest themselves in time, whereas, in reality, it is time that is the nascent new quality. This is also why phenomena, including natural phenomena, can never be reduced to a single measure. The mensuration conducted by the understanding recognizes only what is measurable as real, whereas genuine measurement consists in knowing what, within bodies, determines their simultaneously specific and measurable character. Just as motion is measured by the most rapid possible uniform movement, the measure is always of the same kind as the thing it measures: 'a magnitude that measures magnitudes'.

This reflexivity of measurement is precisely Marx's problem when it comes to analyzing the commodity. What is the value that measures other values, and how can social labour (-time) measure the labour (-time) embodied in the value-form? Labour-time quantifies the process, but the labour used up is itself a component part of this process. In exchange, use-values are substituted for one another in the manner of bodies 'that are combined in certain quantitative relations when forming chemical equivalents'.[43]

The distinction between what the object has become and the history of the object pertains to that between logic and history. According to Jindrich Zeleny, the first chapter of Volume One of *Capital* has as its object the commodity structure, while the second reverts to the historical development of the commodity. But the opposition between developed object and development of the object oversimplifies the relation between logical structure and historical development. This relation, incompatible with the ontological representations of Galilean–Cartesian science, once again recalls Marx's debt to Spinoza, Leibniz and Hegel. The genesis of a form is not the same as its historical genesis. It is only the 'ideal expression' of it. To this distinction corresponds that between 'evolutionary lawfulness' (immanent law) and external causality (transitive cause). The complementary nature of the two approaches is illustrated in the historical-materialist analysis of money.[44]

Marx first of all applied himself to uncovering the invisible real structures. His theory of structure provided him with the key to genesis and evolution. The developed form (the anatomy of man) unveils the secret of the less developed forms (the anatomy of the ape). But the ideal genesis, thus reconstituted, is as distinct from real history as a concrete social formation is from the mode of production. Whereas empirical economics starts out systematically from surface phenomena without elucidating the invisible structure, the transformation of the rate of surplus-value into profit rate commands the process of understanding, not vice versa. The logical relation between categories is *also* chronological. The theory is an 'ideal genesis' that divides the concept of origin into a structural concept and a historical concept. In it, structure presupposes history. The free worker is thus the 'résumé' of a prior historical evolution. Capitalist production starts from the presupposition that 'living labour capacity [is found] on the market, in circulation'. Likewise, the commodity is to be found there as 'a universal elementary form of wealth'. Vice versa, in making circulation the theoretical (logical) presupposition of the formulation of capitalism and starting with money, analysis reconnects with the historical process. The 'confrontation [between money and labour capacity as a commodity] is conditioned by a definite historical process which narrows down the worker to pure labour capacity'.[45]

The inversion of the relation between logical order and historical order is explicit in *Capital*: 'In the course of our investigation, we shall find that both merchants' capital and interest-bearing capital are derivative forms, and at the same time it will become clear why, historically, these two forms appear before the modern primary form of capital.'[46] In the capitalist mode of production once it has reached maturity, the structure seems to reproduce itself autonomously. In the ordinary course of things, the worker thus appears to be abandoned to the action of natural laws, to dependency on capital maintained and perpetuated by the very mechanism of capital. It is different during the historical genesis of capitalist production, when the relation of exploitation is established thanks to brutal state intervention. As developed (structural) relations and connections, the ordinary course of things thus clearly contrasts with the real development of the historical genesis.

In Volume Three, Marx discharges the commitment made in Volume One. The structural order is enriched by new determinations in proceeding from the abstract to the concrete, the general to the particular, following the process of mediation by which the universal is particularized. Foiling what Hegel calls 'fondness for the empirical universe', thinking begins to be practised in abstraction as a one-sided manifestation of the negative. In its development towards the concept, no longer immediate and empirical but conceptualized and determinate, the abstract nevertheless subsists as a condition of its conceptualization. One-sided, economic categories are 'merely abstractions' from real relations.[47] As a unity (not a mere external, mechanical combination) of multiple determinations, immanent synthesis (unity-in-itself of differences) brings out the 'non-truth' of these abstractions. This is what Volume Three accomplishes, therewith ruining vain attempts to construct a theory of classes starting from the extortion of surplus-value discovered in Volume One, or a theory of crises starting from the reproduction schemas of Volume Two.

'In the course of scientific analysis', writes Marx, the formation of the general rate of profit seems to derive from competition between industrial capitals, 'being only later rectified, supplemented and modified by the intervention of commercial capital'. 'In the course of historical development', however, 'the situation is exactly the reverse'![48] Real history is an inversion of the structure, and vice versa. Historically, commercial capital determined the price of commodities, and the general rate of profit was constituted in the sphere of circulation. But in the developed capitalist mode of production, the transformation of surplus-value into profit and profit into average profit proceeds logically from the structure of the commodity – from production, via the circulation process, to reproduction as a whole.[49]

This inverse articulation of historical order and structural order appears in striking fashion in Chapter 20 of Volume Three ('Historical Material on Merchant's Capital'). Commercial capital is the oldest independent mode of existence of capital. In previous social formations, it appears as 'the function of capital *par excellence*'. Conversely, in the framework of production that has become specifically capitalist, it is 'demoted from its earlier separate existence, to become a particular moment of capital investment in general'. Now it 'functions simply as the agent of productive capital'.[50] Before coming, in accordance with the logical-structural order, to 'dominate its extremes' – the different spheres of production that circulation interconnects – capital has first of all emerged from the circulation process according to the chronological-historical order. This is

why, through this inversion of the two orders, '[t]he genuine science of
modern economics begins only when the theoretical discussion moves
from the circulation process to the production process'. It is also why 'the
method of presentation must differ in form from that of inquiry'.[51]

The non-coincidence of the logical order and the historical order is
stressed as early as the 1857 Introduction. In *Capital*:

> In the course of the scientific analysis, the formation of the general rate of profit
> appears to proceed from industrial capitals and the competition between them,
> being only later rectified, supplemented and modified by the intervention of
> commercial capital. In the course of historical development, the situation
> is exactly the reverse. It is commercial capital which first fixes the prices
> of commodities more or less according to their values, and it is the sphere of
> circulation that mediates the production process in which a general rate of profit
> is first formed. Commercial profit originally determines industrial profit.[52]

Up to Chapter 20 of Volume Three, Marx considers 'merchant's capital
from the standpoint of the capitalist mode of production and within its
limits', according to its logical (or structural) determination, although
trade and commercial capital are historically prior to the capitalist mode
of production. The structure holds the key to its own genesis. Whereas
commercial capital appears in earlier modes of production as 'the function *par excellence* of capital', with production remaining direct production
of the means of subsistence for the producers themselves, once 'capital
has seized hold of production itself' (the peculiarity of capitalist production), it is no more than a capital endowed with a particular function. It
thus appears as a 'historical form' of capital well before capital has
'subjugated production itself'.

In the pre-capitalist economy, the product becomes a commodity in
trade, and capital emerges in the circulation process. It must crystallize
there before it can 'dominate the extremes', the different spheres of
production that circulation interconnects. The initial relative autonomy
of the circulation process has a double significance. First of all, it indicates
that capital does not directly subjugate production. The production
process incorporates circulation as a simple phase as a result of a dialectical inversion. Circulation then becomes an interim phase of production,
the realization of the product created as a commodity and the replacement of its elements of production produced as a commodity; and
commercial capital becomes one of the forms taken by capital when it
undergoes the circuit of its reproduction.

At the first stage of capitalist society, commerce dominates industry.
Then their relation is reversed. But it is commerce that begins to subject

production to the reign of exchange-value, by breaking up the old conditions, increasing the circulation of money, and gradually encroaching on production itself. The efficacy and rhythm of this dissolvent action obviously depend upon the resistance of the economies concerned. The autonomous development of commercial capital is thus in inverse ratio to the development of specifically capitalist production. Among the Venetians, Genoans and Dutch, profit remained the profit of middlemen, not exporters. Commercial capital appears 'pure' there, separated from the extremes of production. Monopoly on the commerce of commission was the source of its formation. Conversely, it collapsed with the economic development of the peoples whom it brought into contact. In effect, the quantitative exchange relation is initially wholly fortuitous, in so far as there exists no commercial space unified by a socially necessary labour for the production of commodities. Products take the form of commodities to the extent that they can be exchanged and expressed in a similar third term. Thus, continuous exchange and more regular reproduction with a view to exchange increasingly abolish chance.

The same applies to interest-bearing (or usurer's) capital: it 'belongs together with its twin brother, merchant's capital, to the antediluvian forms of capital which long precede the capitalist mode of production'. It 'requires nothing more for its existence than that at least a portion of the products is transformed into commodities and that money in its various functions develops concurrently with trade in commodities'. In periods prior to the capitalist mode of production, usurer's capital thus exists in two 'characteristic' forms that will cease to exist in the specifically capitalist economy: '*firstly*, usury by lending money to extravagant magnates ... [and] *secondly*, usury by lending money to small producers who possess their own conditions of labour'. These two forms lead to 'the formation and concentration of large money capitals' by ruining debtors.[53] As the characteristic form of interest-bearing capital, usurer's capital thus corresponds to the predominance of petty production. The bank is esteemed and the usurer hated because the former lends to the rich and the latter to the poor. In the capitalist mode of production, usury can no longer perform this function of separating labour-power from the means of production.

In interest-bearing capital or usury, an old form of capitalism *par excellence* in popular eyes, the production of surplus-value thus remains an 'occult quality' of the economy. It reveals itself to the light of day only when capitalist forms of production are fully developed.

We can see how erroneous it would be to imagine that the present uncovers the secrets of the past simply by making it possible to follow the thread of a determinist sequence. The present dispels the necessary misrecognition of the inner structure of the mode of production at the price of a spectacular inversion, by which capital dominates and redefines its various initial forms. A negation of scientific fetishism, the critique of political economy is rooted in this inaugural present: 'The genuine science of modern economics begins only when theoretical discussion moves from the circulation process to the production process.'[54] Just as it could not survive it, this curious, modestly temporal science could not precede its object.

Notes

1. Karl Marx, letter of 11 July 1868 to Ludwig Kugelmann, in Marx and Engels, *Selected Correspondence*, Progress Publishers, Moscow 1975, pp. 196–7. See also Marx's letter of 27 June 1867 to Engels, in ibid., p. 179.
2. Karl Marx, *Capital*, vol. 1, trans. Ben Fowkes, Penguin/NLR, Harmondsworth 1976, p. 168; my emphasis added.
3. Ibid., p. 279.
4. Ibid., p. 98.
5. Karl Marx, *Capital*, vol. 2, trans. David Fernbach, Penguin/NLR, Harmondsworth 1978, p. 292.
6. Karl Marx, letter of 27 June 1867 to Engels, in *Selected Correspondence*, p. 179.
7. Frederick Engels, Preface to *Capital*, vol. 2, p. 98; see also Louis Althusser and Étienne Balibar, *Reading Capital*, trans. Ben Brewster, New Left Books, London 1970, pp. 150–57.
8. Frederick Engels, letter of 27 October 1890 to Conrad Schmidt, in Marx and Engels, *Selected Correspondence*, pp. 401–2.
9. Karl Marx, letter of 14 January 1858 to Engels, in ibid., p. 93.
10. G.W.F. Hegel, *Phenomenology of Spirit*, trans. A.V. Miller, Oxford University Press, Oxford and New York 1977, p. 11.
11. Adorno rightly rejects this pacified totality of a world reduced to an unproblematic system of moral and aesthetic values. Against it, he pits the labour of the negative, the detail and the fragment. In opposition to bad totalizations without mediations, Sartre speaks of a 'detotalized totality' and Henri Lefebvre of 'open totality'.
12. Maurice Blanchot, 'The Time of Encyclopedias', in Blanchot, *Friendship*, trans. Elizabeth Rottenberg, Stanford University Press, Stanford, CA 1997, p. 50. To the question of Hölderlin, keen to know whether the whole or the detail was predominant, Sartre replied: 'But if the Whole existed, there would be no more struggle, for the details would necessarily be included within it. And if there were just a sum of units, details would be units in turn and the question would not arise. There can be a struggle only if the Whole is never the synthetic total unity (it is never completely the Whole) and if the details are never completely isolated (there are never just details)' (Jean-Paul Sartre, *Notebooks for an Ethics*, trans. David Pellauer, University of Chicago Press, Chicago and London 1992, pp. 85–6). For Roy Bhaskar, the closed totality or bad totality is characteristic of speculative philosophy. He likewise adopts the idea of an open systemic totality.
13. In *Introduction à la lecture de la science de la logique de Hegel* (Aubier, Paris 1987), J. Biard and his fellow authors assert that '[i]t is because modern philosophy is supposed to be built on the category of the subject' that beginnings are difficult. According to them, the question of the beginning touches on the systematicity of philosophies of the subject:

'Thus, the difficulty of the choice of starting-point derives from the fact that its content cannot possess value independently of the systematic sequence that it is supposed to found.' This problem remains insurmountable prior to clarification of the relations between being and knowing, which pertains to the doctrine of the concept. However, we do not share their opinion that 'the difficulties that arise in analysis of the beginning consist in the fact that it is arbitrary as such'. At the least what is involved is a determinate arbitrariness, and not all arbitrary beginnings are equally valid. Thus, *Capital* could not begin with money or prices. Marx spent a long time deciding to begin with the commodity. Elsewhere, the authors of the *Introduction* correct this idea of arbitrariness by successively proposing the hypothesis of the 'beginning as grounded' and that of the 'beginning in its absolute immediacy'. According to the former, the 'circularity of the logical process imparts to the beginning its genuine status, clears up the aporias of its unilateral determination, and exhibits its necessity. It is, if one likes, that of the abstract universe in which the development of concrete determinations originates; and at the same time, the concrete universality of the result endows the abstract universal with its meaning and confers its necessity on it.' According to the second hypothesis, 'the beginning as such is contradictory, since it necessarily displays the two characteristics of immediacy and mediation' (pp. 27–41).

14. Hegel, *Phenomenology of Spirit*, p. 10.
15. G.W.F. Hegel, *Science of Logic*, trans. A.V. Miller, Allen & Unwin, London 1969, pp. 41, 67.
16. Ibid., pp. 71–2, 748.
17. See V.I. Lenin, 'Conspectus of Hegel's Book *The Science of Logic*', in *Collected Works*, vol. 38, Progress Publishers, Moscow 1961.
18. Marx, *Capital*, vol. 1, p. 198. On the dialectic, see Hegel, *Science of Logic*, pp. 105, 831.
19. See Gérard Duménil, *Le Concept de loi économique dans le Capital*, Maspero, Paris 1978, pp. 361–2.
20. Ibid., p. 269.
21. Contrary to the claims of Karl Popper and Lucio Colletti, who perceive here strict logical oppositions and not real oppositions. According to Colletti, logical opposition pertains to the idealist tradition (from Plato to Hegel) and endlessly repeats the opposition between being and non-being. For Popper, Marx excludes himself from the scientific community by mixing the two types of contradiction. For Jean-Pierre Potier, in contrast, the theory of value, the theory of fetishism, and the theory of dialectical contradiction in the Hegelian manner form a whole. Ruy Fausto judiciously inquires whether a contradictory response is necessarily a bad response. His question is addressed to Castoriadis, for whom Marx made the mistake of oscillating between two contradictory theses: that value existed before capitalism, and that it emerged only with capitalism. Castoriadis stumbles over the traditional prejudice of non-contradictory discourse.
22. Hegel, *Science of Logic*, p. 93; *The Encyclopedia Logic*, trans. T.F. Geraets, W.A. Suchting and H.S. Harris, Hackett Publishing Company, Indianapolis and Cambridge 1991, p. 59.
23. Hegel, *Science of Logic*, pp. 113, 121–2: '*Determination is negation* – is the absolute principle of Spinoza's philosophy'; this true and simple insight establishes the absolute unity of substance. But Spinoza stops short at *negation as determinateness* or quality; he does not advance to a cognition of negation as absolute, that is *self-negating, negation*' (ibid., p. 536). Marcuse insists on the relation established here between logic and philosophy of history:

> The category of 'determination' characterizes being as change and as in the process of changing. It concretizes the meaning of 'in-itselfness'. The latter is no longer defined as restfulness but as permanent movement in relation to other beings. The fullness of being is now understood as the ever new 'filling of in-itselfness with determinateness' ... This filling is not only one that always becomes but also one that is never fulfilled. Determination is once again 'an *ought* ...'. (Herbert Marcuse, *Hegel's Ontology and the Theory of Historicity*, trans. Seyla Benhabib, MIT Press, Cambridge, MA and London 1987, p. 53)

24. Duménil, *Le Concept de loi économique dans le Capital*, pp. 44–5.
25. Marx, *Capital*, vol. 2, p. 303; emphasis added.
26. Marx, *Capital*, vol. 3, p. 103; emphasis added.
27. See on this Maurice Godelier, *The Mental and the Material*, trans. Martin Thom, Verso, London 1986. If Aristotle was unable to discover the secret of value in labour-power, it was because a social homogeneity of value, measurable by an abstract social labour-time, did not yet exist.
28. Jacques Bidet interprets the relations between the two determinations as the relations between structure and tendency (*Que faire du Capital?*, Klincksieck, Paris 1984, p. 102).
29. See Galvano Della Volpe, *Logic as a Positive Science*, trans. Jon Rothschild, New Left Books, London 1980, Chapter 2.
30. Roy Bhaskar brilliantly develops this dialectic of 'absenting', insisting on the search for '*the negative in the positive*, the absent in the present, the ground in the figure, the periphery in the centre, the content obscured by the form, the living masked by the dead'. Absence thus connotes the hidden, the void, desire, lack and need (*Dialectic: The Pulse of Freedom*, Verso, London and New York 1993, p. 241).
31. Marx, *Capital*, vol. 1, p. 711.
32. Marx, *Capital*, vol. 2, p. 429.
33. Hegel, *Science of Logic*, p. 107.
34. Marx, *Capital*, vol. 1, p. 929.
35. 'Quite generally: quantum is sublated quality; but quantum is infinite, goes beyond itself, is the negation of itself. Thus its passage beyond itself is, therefore, *in itself* the negation of the negated quality, the restoration of it': Hegel, *Science of Logic*, p. 240.
36. Ibid., pp. 322–3. See also Biard *et al.*, *Introduction à la lecture de la Science de la logique de Hegel*, vol. 3, pp. 45, 80, 123, 160.
37. Gérard Duménil emphasizes that '[t]he frequent uses of the term "law" in connection with the qualitative dimension of the structure permits of no ambiguity. Marx quite obviously considered such relations to be laws.' He insists: 'We have most often referred to two structures, a qualitative structure and a quantitative structure. The union of the two types of determination is characteristic of the conceptual character of the totality. Within the concept, they are inseparable, but the existence of the quantitative determination does not presuppose the existence of the qualitative determination' (*Le Concept de loi économique dans le Capital*, pp. 57, 59).
38. Marx, letter of 2 April 1858 to Engels, in *Selected Correspondence*, p. 98.
39. Karl Marx, 'The Poverty of Philosophy', in Marx and Frederick Engels, *Collected Works*, vol. 6, Lawrence & Wishart, London 1976, p. 127.
40. Hegel, *Science of Logic*, p. 331.
41. Ibid.
42. Biard *et al.*, *Introduction à la lecture de la Science de la logique de Hegel*, p. 231. The authors quite rightly stress: 'As regards the category of measurement as deployed and expounded in the *Science of Logic*, one would thus be led to expect that Hegel intended to examine and explain the mode of authentic, i.e. dialectical and conceptual, relation between the qualitative and the quantitative – in short, to disregard what Husserl regarded as the implicit presupposition of the Galilean mathematization of nature' (p. 233).
43. Jacques d'Hondt, *La Logique de Marx*, Presses Universitaires de France, Paris 1974, p. 101. See also Eugène Fleischmann, *La Science universelle ou la logique de Hegel*, Plon, Paris 1968, p. 120.
44. The structural reading of Marx in the 1960s was conducted against the trend of the then dominant historicism. Even so, we should not succumb to the very French illusion that Althusser represented a total innovation. A movement of research had already begun in the early 1950s, with the works of Otto Morf and B. A. Grousine. The latter particularly stressed the dual approach of *Capital* and the articulation between 'historical relations and connections' and 'developed [structural] relations and connections'. See Morf, *Rapports entre histoire et théorie économique chez Marx*, Berne 1951; Grousine, *Logique et*

historique dans le Capital de Marx, Moscow 1955; Evgeny Ilienkov, *Dialectics of the Abstract and the Concrete in Capital*, Moscow 1960; Karel Kosik, *Dialectics of the Concrete* (1963), D. Reidel, Dordrecht 1976. The first edition of Jindrich Zeleny's *The Logic of Marx* (trans. Terrell Carver, Basil Blackwell, Oxford 1980) appeared in Czech in 1962, and a German edition in 1968.

45. Karl Marx, 1861–63 Manuscripts, in Marx and Engels, *Collected Works*, vol. 30, Lawrence & Wishart, London 1988, pp. 37, 39, 86–7.

46. Marx, *Capital*, vol. 1, p. 267,

47. See Marx's letter of 28 December 1846 to Pavel Annenkov: 'owing to a mystical inversion', Proudhon, by contrast, sees in the real relations merely 'reifications of these abstractions' (Marx and Engels, *Selected Correspondence*, p. 34).

48. Marx, *Capital*, vol. 3, p. 400.

49. 'How is the value of a commodity transformed into its price of production? . . . Answering this question presupposes: I. That the transformation of, for example, the value of a day's labour power into wages, or the price of a day's labour has been explained . . . II. That the transformation of surplus value into profit, and profit into average profit, etc., has been explained. This presupposes that the circulation process of capital has been previously explained, since the turnover of capital, etc., plays a role here' (letter of 27 June 1867 from Marx to Engels, in *Selected Correspondence*, p. 179). In another letter (30 April 1868), Marx explains the formation of prices, which distributes social surplus-value between the different masses of capital. He concludes:

> At last we have arrived at the *phenomena* which serve as the *starting point* for the vulgar economist: rent originating from the land, profit (interest) from capital, wages from labour. But from our point of view the thing now looks differently. The apparent movement is explained . . . Finally, since these three (wages, rent, profit (interest)) constitute the respective sources of income of the three classes of landowners, capitalists, and wage labourers, we have, in conclusion, the *class struggle* into which the movement and the analysis of the whole business resolves itself. (ibid., p. 195)

50. Marx, *Capital*, vol. 3, p. 444. In a letter to Engels of 11 August 1894, Antonio Labriola distinguished between the 'abstract genesis' of the commodity, which is in some sense structural, and the 'concrete genesis' (history of English accumulation).

51. Marx, *Capital*, vol. 3, p. 455; Postface to the Second Edition, *Capital*, vol. 1, p. 102. See also Pierre Macherey, 'A propos du processus d'exposition du *Capital*', in Louis Althusser *et al.*, *Lire le Capital*, Presses Universitaires de France, Paris 1996.

52. Marx, *Capital*, vol. 3, pp. 400–01.

53. Ibid., pp. 728–9.

54. Ibid., p. 455.

9

The Distress of Historical Logic

Marx's novel response to the problem that haunts the 'human sciences' in general, and history in particular, became inaudible almost immediately. From the moment the Second International was founded, the working class movement harboured a majority orthodoxy as far removed from his problematic as vulgar Darwinism was from the paths opened up by Darwin. At the same time, the subversive import of his critique was repressed by the academic *Methodenstreit* and the growing influence of a sociology attuned to the historic compromises of Bismarckian Germany.

The 'quarrel over methods' erupted in 1883, the year of Marx's death and the publication by Dilthey of *Introduction to the Sciences of Spirit*. With the expansion of psychology, sociology and economics, promoted to the rank of academic disciplines, a distinction was asserted between two objects and two modes of knowledge: the explanatory sciences of nature and the interpretative sciences of spirit (Dilthey); nomothetic sciences and idiographic sciences (Windelband); natural sciences and cultural sciences (Rickert). The former were thought to formalize relations of regularity (laws); the latter were directed towards the 'individual concept'.

To avoid history becoming ensnared in the paradoxes of a science of the particular, some historians then tried to reduce historical knowledge to the massive, the typical, the measurable, to the exclusion of the accidental, concrete figures, and insignificant events. Others accepted the biographical character of their discipline, 'the specific task of history being to explain a historical event'.[1] Defending an intermediate position, Eduard Meyer distinguished between immanent teleological chance and relative chance resulting from a factor extrinsic to causal relations. This methodological distinction aimed to establish a notion of causality specific to history.

Historical Causality and Objective Possibility

In the view of Max Weber, this credence in a way of handling the concept of causation peculiar to history was utterly illusory. Meyer's principle of teleological dependency, according to which effects disclose the historical meaning of causes, in reality betrayed a confused understanding of historical effectivity. If the only thing with a legitimate place in historical discourse was what exercises influence, the question as to which end-state served as a reference point for the reconstruction of historical development became unavoidable. The significance of the event in fact depended upon the temporal scale on which it was located.

Weber borrowed the notion of 'objective possibility' from the physiologist Von Kries. The Battle of Marathon decided between several possibilities – a theocratic-religious culture or the Hellenic spirit – just as those of Waterloo or Gettysburg decided between several possible futures. The outcome of a battle is determined, not fatal. The struggle decides between two objective possibilities inscribed in the causal sequence. In making out ordered relations of causality, the historian confronts the same difficulties as justice when defining criminal responsibility. The causes of death are not the same for the doctor who draws up the death certificate, for the judge who determines individual responsibilities, and for the political leader who deals with the social factors involved. Drawing upon the works of Von Kries and jurists, Weber proposed to retain the notion of 'adequate causation' to designate 'those cases in which the relationship of certain complexes of "conditions" is synthesized into a unity by historical reflection', as opposed to the notion of 'chance causation', referring to an arbitrary (insufficient) relation between a complex of conditions and the event produced.[2] The category of objective or historical possibility rendered the 'rules of development' intelligible.

The rules of a contingent evolution? The laws of random events? Weber appreciated the difficulties inherent in the very notion of law: 'it depends on the breadth or narrowness of one's definition of "law" as to whether one will also include regularities which because they are not quantifiable are not subject to numerical analysis'. Historical phenomena never came under ' "laws" in the narrower exact natural science sense, but with *adequate* causal relationships expressed in rules and with the application of the category of "objective possibility" '.[3] And yet scientific work seems to have no other goal but the discovery of laws.

It was necessary to agree on the content of the concept. As the formulation of causal relations, scientific laws work by simplifying complex material, in such a way, wrote Georg Simmel, that a law connecting correlated states 'is only valid for one case'. The currently recognized synonymy between law and causation was in no way self-evident. Distinguishing between them made it possible to dispel the confusion between a relation of universal causation in the natural realm and a relation of singular causation in spiritual domains. Simmel thus imagined a complex world in which, rather than being followed by an identical effect, a cause could be succeeded by variable effects, without the causal relation thereby disappearing to make way for random succession. Accordingly, he applied the notion of 'individual' causation to a unique, incomparable event.[4]

In the absence of nomological regularities, the expression 'laws of history' necessarily possessed an analogical, relative sense, and should be compared with 'philosophical speculations'. Stripped of their pretension to supply the universal rules of complex totalities, they should confine themselves to sorting out the chaos of singular realities. Human history did not constitute an autonomous chapter in the evolution of the world. In so far as the 'intrinsic import of the concept of the historical is not quantitatively rich enough to fulfil the conditions that the concept of a law requires', it was annulled in the development of partial but precise knowledge, since '[i]t is impossible to establish whether [the historical law] really has the sort of validity that distinguishes it, as a law, from a mere sequence of matters of fact'.[5]

Either 'historical laws' represented the embryonic form, still in their infancy, of scientific laws that remained to be discovered; or they expressed the rational intelligibility of historical particularities. It became tempting to elevate them into a model of interpretative knowledge, which interprets messages as opposed to weighing up relations – on condition that the disparate sum of events permits attribution of a meaning to them. In fact, the unity of history appeared as a point receding to infinity, as inaccessible as the Last Judgement. It was thus possible to imagine a grand historical design being discovered a posteriori. It was also possible to reject the hypothesis of a history directed towards any end. If the teleological vision animated the construct of history itself, it remained difficult to attribute any efficacy of its own to an end without a subject that posits it. The singular as singular and the individual as individual thus did indeed constitute the heart of the enigma.

Simmel's approach involves a critique of the idea of progress, which, as then understood, assumed an estimation of the forward march towards an end-state. For the liberal optimist, all change is equivalent to progress, which is at worst frustrated by 'delays' and 'slow-downs'. A 'subterranean connection' must then ensure the continuity of the movement towards the future, despite temporary stagnation and regression. In other words, 'the belief in historical progress' and its religious cult crush contingency in a rigorous determinism. Laden with metaphysical presuppositions, this inevitable progress further assumes 'that the entity to which [it] is ascribed has the status of a homogeneous substance', and is not uneven, articulated, shot through with discordant rhythms and non-contemporaneous contradictions.[6]

When he sets about historical materialism (its allegedly a priori idea of the unity of history), and denounces the mechanicism of 'a kind of parthenogenesis of the economy', Simmel is in fact aiming at the orthodox social-democratic vulgate of the period. '[N]ot much better than an explanation ... by reference to the "force of time"', he ripostes triumphantly to historical materialism. He seems to be unaware of the fact that, eighty years earlier, Engels had already observed that 'history does nothing', initiating a conceptual revolution in time whose significance was suspected by neither Weber nor Simmel.

Often subtle and full of ingenious coinages, the discussion that was pursued from Meyer to Weber, Dilthey to Simmel, problematizes the relationship between historical knowledge and the dominant rationality of the epoch. Yet it is striking to note just how inaudible the thunderclap of *Capital* remained to these authors – in part because of their simple ignorance of the texts, in part out of ideological deafness. Their intuitions, suggestions and refinements have an academic whiff about them. At issue between them was a methodological controversy over the comparative relationship between disciplines and their rules of investigation. That is why their critique of historical reason never gets to the root of things. Indeed, how can the 'poor condition of the logical analysis of history' (Weber), with its categories of necessity, causality and accident, be tackled without going back to the temporal structure of the rhythms, continuities and ruptures of social relations?

Weber's pioneering exploration in this regard had led Marx to the threshold of a different rationality, in which history is bound up with politics and knowledge becomes strategic.

Rejection of speculative philosophy of history in fact demands a new conceptualization of temporality and causality. *Capital* claims to discover 'the natural laws of [social] development', similar to the 'iron necessity' established by the physical sciences.[7] Yet political economy is not readily reducible to the model of mechanical causality. Upon contact with it, laws become 'deep tendencies' pertaining to a causality of essence that is at once both structural and accidental.

The natural law of evolution invoked by Marx is a homage to Darwin, whose work Marx read with enthusiasm. Yet Darwinian theory does not establish general relations of causality. It develops by introducing ever greater complexity into the reasons for evolution. In the case of the 'laws' of evolution, the well-nigh infinite number and diversity of the deviations of structure transmissible by heredity creates difficulties that are comparable to those of political economy. Faced with the indeterminacy of the universal laws that were supposed to govern heredity, Darwin invoked the vigour of hereditary 'tendencies'. Engels registers the originality of the law of evolution which, like all 'historical laws', pertains to an anti-empiricist and anti-positivist concept. The infinite accidental differences of evolution prevail over necessity. The impossibility of proving evolution by inductive reasoning thus relativizes the notions of class, genus and species.

The epistolary polemic of 1866 between Marx and Engels (in the middle of the composition of *Capital*) over Pierre Trémaux's book *Origine et transformations de l'homme et des autres êtres* (Paris 1865) captures the determinist inclinations of the former, and the latter's sensitivity to the tentative emergence of a different form of causality. Marx expressed his keen interest in Trémaux's theses. The ideological reasons for this enthusiasm are evident – salvaging the idea of progress, which was threatened by the uncertainties of Darwinian evolution: 'Progress, which Darwin regards as purely accidental, is essential [in Trémaux]'. Engels's response was stinging. Trémaux's theory was worthless, 'because he knows nothing of geology, and is incapable of even the most common-or-garden literary-historical critique'. It involved a vulgar determinism one-sidedly revolving around the influence of the soil. When the author 'declare[s] that the effect of the soil's greater or lesser age, modified by crossing, is the *sole* cause of change in organic species or races, I see absolutely no reason to go along with the man thus far.' Darwin, by contrast, made the connection between necessity and contingency. After a hint of resistance, Marx beat a prudent retreat.[8]

Even so, the question of progress and the *tendential* laws of evolution had not been resolved. Neither evolution, nor political economy, nor the unconscious functions like a machine. The Freudian aetiology of the neuroses was to explore the specific efficacy of absent causes or symbolic structures, irreducible to Galilean causality and its linear time.

Intransitive Cause and Free Necessity

For Aristotle, a cause is 'the essence of the thing that makes it what it is' – the matter, or the origin of the movement, or, finally, the goal for which a thing is made. Since Galileo, it has been 'that which is such that, when it is posited, the effect follows; and when it is removed, the effect is removed'. This functional relation assumes a continuous, homogeneous temporality (between what is posited and what follows), as well as correspondence between commensurable magnitudes. Abandoning reasons (why?) to study relations (laws), Galilean causality established the framework of a new rationality and a new representation of motion. Henceforth, something is rationally known when its cause is known. The putative Newtonian refusal of hypotheses radicalizes this explanatory model of modern science, at the expense of Aristotelian metaphysics. The reduction of scientific objects to mathematizable correlations, however, involves a restrictive delimitation of scientific knowledge.

Challenging a mechanical model that was unable to express the specific productivity of relations, Spinoza and Leibniz emerge as precocious 'dissidents' from the new rationality.[9] For Spinoza, the *causa sui* is no mere correlation, but production. The representation of God as 'intransitive cause' shatters the conceptual framework of Cartesianism. Whereas transitive causality, which is finite and formal, external to things, is trapped in tautology, the totality unfolds in an immanent, reciprocal relationship, both causing and caused, where each term is at once both cause and effect. For Leibniz, 'expression' (expressive causality) constitutes an original mode of causality. The world is not a machine: everything in it is force, life, desire. Far from 'causing an intolerable inevitability', the connection of causes and effects furnishes the means of emancipation from it. Intermediate between power and action, a unity of contrary properties, the notion of 'tendency' becomes the governing idea.

Via Hegelian logic, Marx inherited this dissidence. For Hegel, the notion of causality is in fact as 'highly questionable, as regards the physical world already, but much more so when it comes to the world of the spirit, to which the economy belongs as an aspect of objective spirit'.[10] In the theory of essence, Hegel takes up the Leibnizian distinction between sufficient reason and 'causality in the strict sense', as 'mechanical mode of action'. Law is 'free necessity', and only 'the free mechanism is subject to a law'. In other words, by its own law, mechanism becomes 'free mechanism'. Here Hegel follows Spinoza: substance does not behave according to natural necessity. Conscious action changes necessity into freedom. The (tendential) law that knows it is a law is distinguished from the natural or mechanical law. The transition from mechanical causality to teleology underscores this difference:

> Teleology is especially contrasted with *mechanism*, in which the determinateness posited in the object, being external, is essentially one in which no *self-determination* is manifested. The opposition between *causae efficientes* and *causae finales*, between merely efficient and final causes, relates to this distinction; and this distinction, taken in a concrete form, is also made the criterion for deciding whether the absolute essence of the world is to be conceived as blind natural mechanism or as an intelligence that determines itself in accordance with ends. The antinomy between *fatalism*, along with *determinism* and *freedom*, is likewise concerned with the opposition of mechanism and teleology; for the free is the Notion in its existence.[11]

The relation of causality 'is, in the first instance, merely this *relation* of *cause* and *effect*, as such, it is the *formal* relation of causality': 'cause is nothing but this determination, to have an effect'. If it stopped producing effects, it would by the same token cease to be a cause. Whereas this relation of immediate causality is tautological, with a 'remote' (or mediated) cause: 'The change of form suffered by the basic fact in this passage through a number of intermediate terms conceals the identity which it retains in this passage.' The example of 'remote causality' clearly pertains to 'historical logic'. At issue is whether a young man's talent, revealed after the death of his father killed in battle by a bullet, is the effect of the bullet or of other circumstances, which are many and remote. The shot is thus considered 'not cause at all but only a single moment which belonged to the *circumstances of the possibility*'.[12]

Having underlined the lacunae of formal causality in physical relations, Hegel elaborates his position:

> we must note the *inadmissible application* of the relation of causality to relations of *physico-organic* and spiritual life. Here, what is called cause certainly reveals itself as having a different content from the effect; but the reason is that that which acts on a living being is independently determined, changed and transmuted by it, because the living thing does not let the cause come to its effect, that is, it sublates it as cause.

Through an extraordinary inversion of necessity into chance, '[t]he reverse rather is true, namely, that such a petty and contingent circumstance is the occasion of the event *only* because the latter has determined it to be such'! Such inversion marks the limits of formal causality, which is 'extinguished in the effect'. It is different with the relation of determinate causality, where the cause is reborn in its effect, just as the effect, vanishing into the cause, 'equally *becomes* again in it'.[13]

In mechanism, causality is strictly external. The 'reciprocal' action or causality of 'presupposed substances', conditioning one another, is of a different order. But since each substance is thus simultaneously passive and active alike, 'any distinction between them has already been sublated', so that reciprocity is 'only an empty mode of representing this'. This void is overcome when a cause coincides with itself as cause in the effect, when, negating itself, it 'essentially converts itself into *effect* and precisely through this is cause': '*Reciprocity* is, therefore, only causality itself; cause not only *has* an effect, but in the effect it stands, as *cause*, in relation to itself. Causality has hereby returned to *its absolute Notion*.'[14] It is 'inner identity' and real necessity. Necessity and causality vanish in reciprocal action, while awaiting the subjective logic of the concept, where accident becomes freedom.

In the logic of essence, law occurs before causality. The latter determines reality; the former determines the phenomenon: 'Law is the *reflection* of Appearance into identity-with-self', 'appearance's reflection-into-itself', 'negative unity'. Law is thus not found outside or beyond the phenomenon. It is directly immanent to it – or, rather, '[a]ppearance and law form a totality'. Law, which 'is *essential relation*' ('[t]he truth of the unessential world is, at first, a world in and for itself and *other to it*'), will reappear in the subjective logic of the concept, under the heading of 'mechanism' (reciprocal causality occurs under the heading of 'chemism' and complex metabolism under the title of 'teleology'), as 'in its own self the imperishable source of self-kindling movement' or as '*free necessity*'.[15]

Law and causality, which belong to objective logic, manifest themselves as fate or destiny, in so far as they are a matter of blind 'mechanism' (in that it is not recognized in its specificity by the subject). Finality, on the other hand, belongs exclusively to subjective logic. Hegelian teleology is thus opposed to mechanism, as self-determination is to purely external determination: 'The antinomy between *fatalism*, along with *determinism* and *freedom*, is likewise concerned with the opposition of mechanism and teleology; for the free is the Notion in its existence.'[16] The determination of teleological activity is thus related to the category of totality, in which the end constitutes the beginning, the consequent the premiss, and the effect the cause, 'the becoming of what has become'.

Mechanical Necessity and Permissive Necessity

In the *Phenomenology*, Hegel stresses that the notions of subject and predicate, being and thought, finite and infinite, designate what they are 'outside of their unity'. Yet 'the use of an instrument on a thing certainly does not let it be what it is for itself, but rather sets out to reshape and alter it'.[17] Knowledge that is conscious of itself, science conceiving itself as science as against opinion, ideology or fiction, consciousness is essentially ambivalent: on the one hand, consciousness of the object; on the other, self-consciousness. Science is thus not some absolute other, indifferent to opinion or fiction, but *their* relative other, inscribed in this relationship of difference. Far from resting in positive self-sufficiency, it is determined by its own negativity.

Through this process, consciousness produces its object as an object of knowledge. This object is not a chimera of reason. It 'is', and the relation of knowledge to the object is resolved in the absolute as subject–object. 'Substance is subject.' The interior is exterior. The end is the means. The subject is a non-subject. This mediated identity of opposites deconstructs sovereign subjectivity. We find it once again in Marx, in the relation between the reified character of social relations (individuals being the supports – *Träger* – of the structure) and the subjective will to change the world. Neglect of this contradictory unity results in abstract, unilateral interpretations, structuralist-objectivist on the one hand (the radical elimination of the subject is consummated in the contemplation of structural machinery); humanist-voluntarist on the other (reducing the crisis of humanity to a 'crisis of revolutionary leadership').

Yet, as Marx writes very clearly, '[t]he same elements of capital which, from the point of view of the labour process, can be distinguished respectively as the objective and subjective factors, as means of production and labour-power, can be distinguished, from the point of view of the valorization process, as constant and variable capital.'[18] If means of production and labour-power can be distinguished as objective and subjective factors of production, they remain united in the reality of the production process, by the same token as use-value and exchange-value are united in the commodity, and constant capital and variable capital in the valorization process of capital. Capital itself is the differentiated unity of this objectivity and subjectivity.[19] Without this immanent inclusion of the subject in the object, structures would be hopelessly immobile. Without the warmth of speech, the language system would become glacial. Without the action of classes, parties and individuals, without conflict and struggle, social formations would be condemned to the systemic repetition of irresolvable crises.

If, ultimately, the masses make history, this 'making' sits ill with the way in which will and consciousness are ordinarily represented. Is a class a subject? Maybe, but an unruly, contradictory, schizoid subject. Is the party as imagined by Lukács a subject? Perhaps, but subject to lunacies, lapses, terrifying nightmares. For a long time, the Marxist vulgate contrasted the blind mechanism of the market with the controlled future of planning, conceived as the expected advent of consciousness in history, the long-sought transition from prehistoric chaos to historical harmony. A pitiless century has subjected this edifying vision to a severe scientific and political ordeal.

An ideal stripped of any divine omniscience, objectivity has become a modest 'objectivity for us' in the light of our history. Conversely, the subject is no longer the divine master and possessor of its object, but, more humbly, the subject of its labour and product. Hence a fallible subject. And that is still a lot. Despite their stated intention to treat social facts as things, history, economics and sociology never succeed in discounting the subject or, more precisely, the struggle. Conscious of the extent to which a knowledge (topographic, logistical, strategic) of war can alter its course, Clausewitz preferred the notion of theory to that of science. Based on the interaction between theory and practical experimentation, experimental dialogue also brings into play a 'veritable strategy'.

Historical facts are neither objective nor subjective. A historical fact ends up lapsing into a simulacrum of objectivity only 'as soon as it no longer does anything'.[20] But history cools down (very) slowly.

Its time is no longer the absolute referent of Newtonianism. Deconstructed and reconstructed, it is multiplied and fractured, at the risk of a 'cognitive collapse' were it to be the case that concepts presuppose the continuity of phenomena. The law is temporalized. Plunged into the haze of history, its contingent necessity varies like the surfaces of a labyrinth that constantly alters on contact. Subject to the broken and discordant times of relations of exchange, exploitation and domination, history appears as a 'process of rhythmical determination', constantly inventing new harmonies and disharmonies. Irregular sequences, aperiodic forms, unpredictable recurrences, fractal motifs, magnificent shapes of determinate complexity, a marvellous galaxy of 'topologies, choreographies and genealogies' – these herald an 'authentically multidimensional and dynamic new logic'.[21]

Each individual is thus engaged in a multiplicity of *durées*: a biographical narrative, organic, economic and ecological cycles, long-range climatic, geological and demographic tendencies. Things, societies and beings change, and any notion of time that goes beyond these articulated changes is open to question. Selection, evolution, history are temporal concepts from the outset, realized in the time that they engender. The dynamic temporalization of their complexity is the system's adaptation to the irreversibility of time.

In shattering the alliance between linear time and causality, have we escaped the trap of mechanical determinism, only at once to succumb to that of teleology? No, so long as teleology is rid of its religious connotations and seen, not as subordination to an external order, but as an 'internal finality' and an immanent thrust. The opposition between Hegelian teleology and Spinozist immanence is then resolved in the invention of temporal relations without first or final causes, and in the gravitational necessities of social conflict.

These tentative steps are clarified in the light of contemporary scientific developments. Newton's universe is determinist, its time homogeneous and reversible. Its science speaks of certainties. In the second half of the nineteenth century, three major innovations disturbed its bewitching harmony: Darwinian biology, the thermodynamic laws of Carnot and Clausius, and Marx's critique of political economy. 'Sciences' of evolution and transformation, they confronted instability and disequilibrium, tendential or probabilistic laws, the arrow of time and temporal asymmetries. They no longer speak of certainty, but of uncertainty and determinate choices. They thus herald a radical upheaval in the epistemological base.

This major transition from clocks to clouds, and towards representations with shattered symmetry, is still not complete. We know only that there are realms where classical laws no longer operate, and where we find outlined – as Ilya Prigogine puts it – 'a new rationality in which probability is not ignorance and science no longer rhymes with certainty'. With evolution, the notions of event and creativity 'make their entry into the basic laws of nature'.[22] In painful gestation, lying somewhere between rigorous research and the effects of fashion, this new rationality demands that the smooth mirror of uniform temporality be shattered. Time rediscovers its rhythms and catastrophes, its nodes and antinodes.

Clinamen saturated with novelties, and *kairos* full of opportunities. Mechanical causes and probabilistic contingencies intersect and combine, without excluding one another: 'At the point of bifurcation, prediction has a probabilistic character, while between the points of bifurcation we may speak of determinist laws.'[23]

For all that, mechanical causality is not abolished. Mediated by rhythms, it is attached to complex (tendential) laws, and fitted into holistic structures (involving reciprocal determination of whole and parts). These open, systemic causalities are no longer amenable to decisive experiments, capable of sealing history and eliminating contradiction. These systems, which generate their own causality, can no longer be explained causally. *Causa sui*, like Spinozist substance, they presuppose themselves indefinitely as production of their self-production. A radically immanent conception of causality thus illuminates the antinomies of 'historical necessity'.

The ambiguity of the term 'necessity' is largely attributable to the fact that some philosophers, tautologically considering possible what actually happens, end up thinking that everything is absolutely necessary. Leibniz, in contrast, distinguishes absolute or geometrical necessity [*müssen*] from hypothetical or moral necessity [*sollen*]. What is absolutely necessary cannot be otherwise; what is hypothetically necessary assumes a choice. The opposition between blind necessity (absolute) and moral necessity (hypothetical) makes it possible to salvage the justice that reforms and punishes. Intermediate between blind necessity and geometrical necessity, divine action is in fact governed by moral necessity. We are thus not necessitated, but only 'predisposed'. This crucial difference sanctions 'conditional events', between 'certain futures' and 'necessary futures'. The middle term between destiny and indifference, the freedom that 'predisposes without necessity' thus founds specifically historical 'futurability'.[24]

The uncertainty of historical necessity is attested by the contingency of the event, which 'has nothing in it to render it necessary and to suggest that no other thing might have happened in its stead'.[25] It is not impossible for what has been foreseen *not* to occur. Strongly 'predisposed', 'conditional necessity' is no longer contrasted with contingency. Each thing is contingent to the extent that it requires another thing in order to exist. In their unity and mutual preservation, the real and the possible form a contingent being. The necessity of particular beings can consist only in their relation to the totality. Thus, chance exists only in the borderline case of 'indifference of equipoise', exemplified by the mortal paradox of Buridan. The future of the conditional necessity is simultaneously determined and contingent. In fact, Leibniz refuses any confusion between certain and determined, certainty and necessity, metaphysical necessity, which leaves no room for choice, and moral necessity, 'which obliges the wisest to choose the best'.

Necessity and contingency refer to what is possible. What is possible involves no contradictions; what is geometrically (absolutely) necessary is something the opposite of which is impossible. Accordingly, not everything is geometrically necessary in creation. Descartes was wrong to confine himself exclusively to absolute necessity, and Spinoza, although he mellowed on the issue of necessity, wrong to deduce everything from a first cause 'by a wholly geometrical necessity'. Moral necessity inclines without compelling, for God's will is not *causal*, but *permissive*, and his reason is the root of the possible: 'the predestination I admit is such as always to predispose, but never to necessitate.'[26] God has opted for the most perfect of possible worlds, the best that could be chosen, understanding by world 'the whole series and collection of existing things', in order to prevent it being said that other worlds can exist in different times and places. Leibniz responds thus to the theological problem of sin and evil, punishment and salvation. But the closed totality of the best of possible worlds or the universal *Caractéristique* never coincides with the open combinatory of an infinite game. The result is that the mathematics of the possible remains insufficient faced with the singularity of the real.

The possible is governed by hypothetical necessity, and vice versa. In their singularity, possible worlds are essentially contingent. In so far as their contingency requires choices, only non-identical individuals and existential truths escaping absolute necessity can exist.[27] *De l'horizon de la doctrine humaine* and *La Restitution universelle* take their reasoning to the ultimate extreme. From the finite number of possible truths and falsities, it inevitably follows that were the human race to survive, it would not be possible to utter what has not already been uttered, word for word. Starting from a finite number of elements, the combinations of language are inevitably exhausted, so that in the last analysis it is not possible to construct a 'romance' that has not already been constructed by someone else. In an infinite statement composed of elements that are finite and self-identical, repetitions are logically unavoidable, and 'reiterations' appear to be novelties solely by virtue of the major time intervals separating them. This picture of reiteration is, however, conditioned by an invariance of elements. It assumes the indefinitely continued existence of the human race, with human beings such as we currently know them. A self-transformation of these human beings, on the other hand, would shatter the temporal symmetry, open up a new field of possibilities, and multiply the potential combinations correspondingly. This is precisely what happens with the inventions of life, the bifurcations of evolution, or historical events.

Even in the case of an infinite system of finite and identical elements, Leibniz does not exclude innovation. Always supposing that 'the human race survives long enough', it suffices for innovation that certain messages be frequently repeated, while others remain in a state of potentiality. A large number of repetitions preserves the inexhausted potentiality of 'things that can be said but never have been'. Leibniz pushes his model of logical repetition to an extreme, in order to contrast with it the behaviour of reality where, as in the planetary year, there are never 'perfect recurrences'. Like language, history is 'one enormous open utterance'.[28] Hypothetical necessity is the result of its incompletion.

In the infinitely long book of which it is the narrative, previous histories would return only when all possible public histories had been exhausted. The same applies to private histories, except that, the greater the detail, the longer the book becomes. The transition to the limit of *La Restitution universelle* changes the register. In the order of logic and reason, repetition is inevitable. In that of empirical truths and existential experience, this is no longer the case: 'Empirical truths, which pertain not to reason but to experience, can be infinitely differentiated.'[29] Existential and singular, historical truths are concerned not with possibilities outside time, but with earthly events that are all too temporal.

In so far as Leibniz ignores 'real time', and hesitates before the transition from the combinatory to history, *De l'horizon de la doctrine humaine* offers no escape from repetition. *La Restitution universelle* abolishes this perfect circularity. Every singular assertion is historical. Its truth is to have existed, or to have to exist, 'in a determinate time and place'. Like the Last Judgement in Walter Benjamin's *Theses on the Philosophy of History*, the *Apokatastasis* becomes the inaccessible vanishing point of a final great encirclement, in which the retrospective secret of universal History is disclosed.

The experience of real history remains open to the minute variations that break the circle of the eternal return, and permit a glimpse of something 'better', heralding the themes of progress:

Even if a previous century recurs as regards the perceptible facts, it will not recur in all respects. For there will always be some differences, albeit imperceptible, which could never be satisfactorily described by any book. This is so because the continuum is divided into an actual infinity of parts, such that in each part of matter there exists a world of an infinity of creatures which cannot be described by any book, however long. . . . And for this reason it could turn out that things improve gradually, though imperceptibly, following revolutions. . . . Moreover, it may also be concluded from this that the human race will not always remain in its present state, because it does not conform to the divine harmony always to sound the same chord. Instead, we must believe that, for natural reasons of congruence, things are due to improve, either gradually or, sometimes, by leaps. For although they often appear to get worse, this should be regarded as occurring in the same way as we sometimes take a step back before advancing more securely.[30]

Trapped in the iron circle of repeated defeats, following in the tracks of Leibniz, and rediscovering his words, Blanqui clung on to the fragile wick of the passing moment to declare that, in spite of everything, the 'chapter of bifurcations' remained open to hope.

'What is actual is possible': in Hegelian logic, the being-in-itself of the actual possesses the character of possibility to perfection. Possibility contains two moments, one positive – 'a reflectedness into itself' – the other negative, which determines possibility as an imperfection: 'that possibility lacks something, that it points to an other, to actuality in which it completes itself'. In its positive mode, possibility is simply logical or formal: '*everything is possible that is not self-contradictory*'. As 'actuality reflected in itself', it remains meagre and merely tautologically registers the being of being, its self-identity. Positive possibility thus constitutes something that is 'as superficial and empty as the law of contradiction itself'.[31]

Over and above this empty assertion of identity, possibility is at the same time a contradiction or impossibility. Once formal, it now becomes actual. The Hegelian distinction between formal and actual possibility (or formal/actual necessity) echoes the Leibnizian opposition between absolute necessity and hypothetical necessity. The potential power of the actual always exceeds its immediate determinateness. Any effective reality is in fact possibility on two counts. On the one hand, factual determinateness is contingent with respect to other possible determinacies: 'the actual is itself only one possibility'.[32] On the other hand, possibility is the essential actuality.

The necessity delineated is thus no longer the exclusive opposite of contingency, but precisely its other, its shadow, *its* necessity: 'Real possibility and necessity are therefore only *seemingly* different; this is an identity which does not have to *become* but is already *presupposed* and lies at their base.' Consequently, actual necessity is 'at at the same time *relative*'. It begins with a presupposition, and it is the contingent or accidental that constitutes its starting point:

For the real actual as such is the *determinable* actual, and has first of all its *determinateness* as *immediate* being in the fact that it is a multiplicity of existing circumstances; but this immediate being as determinateness is also the *negative* of itself, is an in-itself or possibility, and thus it is real possibility.

Real possibility thus becomes necessity, but the latter begins 'that unity of the possible and the actual which is not yet reflected into itself'. The really necessary thus remains a limited reality which, 'on account of this limitation', also constitutes, in some respect, a 'contingent reality'.[33] When all is said and done, what is designated as 'absolute necessity' is nothing other than 'the unity of necessity and contingency'.

Contingency, or the existence of something that might not exist. But understanding why the contingent exists is immediately to make it disappear as contingent, with the result that the contingent is doomed to vanish. For Hegel, there is a necessity of contingency, the two mutually determining each other while constantly vanishing into one another. The contingency of a thing consists in its isolation, hence its submission to an external constraint (like Spinoza's stone, plaything of a heteronomous will); whereas free necessity is the perfect connection of autonomous determination. Necessity is no longer the relational concept of an external, strict determinism, but the index of the sufficiency of a *causa sui*. The task of science (and philosophy specifically) then consists in attaining knowledge of the reality concealed beneath the appearance of contingency.

This dialectic of the necessary and the possible remains incomprehensible to those who castigate a dull, determinist Marx, bent as they are on imputing to him a mechanical concept of necessity. His position emerges as early as his doctoral thesis on the *Difference between the Democritean and Epicurean Philosophy of Nature*:

> this much is historically certain: *Democritus* makes use of *necessity*, *Epicurus* of *chance*. And each of them rejects the opposite view with polemical irritation . . . Necessity appears in finite nature as *relative necessity*, as *determinism*. Relative necessity can only be deduced from *real possibility*, i.e., it is a network of conditions, reasons, causes, etc., by means of which this necessity reveals itself. Real possibility is the explication of relative necessity . . . Chance, for [Epicurus], is a reality which has only the value of possibility. *Abstract possibility*, however, is the direct *antipode of real possibility*.[34]

Full of whirlwinds and turbulence, the atomistic thought of Democritus, Epicurus and Lucretius favours discontinuities, ruptures, the *clinamen* by which novelty creeps into the sequence of cause and effect: 'If atoms never swerve and make beginning / Of motions that can break the bonds of fate, / And foil the infinite chain of cause and effect, / What is the origin of this free will / Possessed by living creatures throughout the earth?'.[35]

No watertight barrier separates necessity from contingency determined by the relation to the law of which it is contingency. Thus:

> With the transformation of the magnitude of value into the price this *necessary relation* appears as the exchange-ratio between a single commodity and the money commodity which exists outside it. This relation, however, may express both the magnitude of value of the commodity and the greater or lesser quantity of money for which it can be sold *under the given circumstances.*[36]

Numerous circumstances act likewise on the course of historical development. Thus, the balance of class forces depends upon the previous history, social gains, organizational capacities, and the memory and culture of the social movement. It is therefore not arbitrary. But it is none the less contingent with respect to the laws of capitalist production. This contingency relative to a given mode of production is not an absence of causes. The paradoxical notion of 'objective chance' is apposite here.[37] Eugène Fleischmann stresses that contingency, error, chance are 'necessary from the standpoint of the rational order of society': 'Without contingency, there would be no such thing as either reason or necessity.' He notes ironically that, 'despite this categorical position on the necessity of contingency, Hegel is still treated as a pan-logicist and a purely deductive philosopher'.[38]

The same applies to Marx's 'determinism', and for the same reasons. The relation of contingency and necessity is perfectly illustrated by the problematic of economic crises. In *Capital*, Marx introduces their logical possibility at several points. In Volume One, with the division between sale and purchase, whose 'internal unity' is affirmed by crisis: 'These forms ... imply the possibility of crises, though no more than the possibility. For the development of this possibility into a reality a whole series of conditions is required, which do not yet even exist from the standpoint of the simple circulation of commodities.'[39] Their possibility – but possibility only – reappears in Volume Two, with the gap between the cycle of production and the cycle of circulation (new commodities can flood on to the market before those of the previous cycle have been sold), or with the asynchrony between the cycle of circulating capital and that of fixed capital (whose fits and starts punctuate the industrial cycle). Hence the potential crisis, *in potentia*, which is not yet an actual crisis.

It then remains to explain the transition from the possible to the real, the potential to the actual. For this purpose, traditional economists sometimes make do with sheer chance, elevated to a *deus ex machina*, and sometimes deduce the crisis from the disjunction between sale and purchase, which boils down (Marx ironizes) to explaining, in its most abstract form, 'the crisis by the crisis'. The separation of the acts of purchase and sale only determines the possibility of crisis. What determines the transition from possibility to actuality is found in neither Volume One nor Volume Two of *Capital*, but at the level of reproduction.

Michel Vadée justly concludes that 'the Marxian conception of historical necessity was at the same time a conception of historical possibility'.[40] At the same time, and in one and the same movement. What is stated as 'historically necessary' [*historisch notwendig*] – the reversal of capitalism, the abolition of exploitation, the establishment of a classless society – is first of all necessary because it is possible. In contrast to natural necessity, this necessity is historical. To understand it as a blind, external necessity – a sort of legal or divine prescription applied with the force of destiny – involves misinterpretation pure and simple.

For Jindrich Zeleny, *Capital* involves neither a purely logical process nor a purely historical process, but a relation between the two governed by an internal lawfulness that is distinct from external causality. Galilean causality, which is mechanical and quantitative, has not disappeared, but Marx conceives different forms of action that are 'alien' to it. In order to capture the most varied forms of 'inner connection', Marx experiments with several forms of causal thought. He searches for a law that is no longer a mechanical 'link', but an 'inner', immanent law ('general law of exchange', 'coercive law of competition', 'immanent law of capitalist production'), or the inner and necessary connection between two things that seemingly contradict one another. Mechanical causes thus lose their privileged position in scientific explanation, making way for mediation.[41]

Gérard Duménil has inventoried the occurrences of 'law' in *Capital* in minute detail. He has particularly brought out the ambiguities of the notion of natural law. In 'accidental' exchange relations, socially necessary labour-time 'prevails after a hard-fought battle as a *regulative natural law*'.[42] On several occasions, Marx designates the law of value as 'blind natural law'. The internal bonds of social production are imposed in the form of an 'all-powerful natural law'. In these formulations, the law is dubbed 'natural', in contrast to 'free will'. The stated naturalness of the law translates its perception by the producers who endure it. But the naturalizing perception is an effect of commodity fetishism and the process of reification: 'the interconnection of production as a whole here forces itself on the agents of production as a *blind law*, and not as a law which, being grasped and therefore mastered by their combined reason, brings the productive forces under their common control'.[43] The natural law is blind in so far as it remains invisible and incomprehensible to each individual agent of protection. It is contrasted with a law (historical, not natural, and conscious, not blind) which, dominated and controlled by the reason of the associated producers, cancels itself as a law. The notion of law, then, clearly designates not some bond of mechanical causality between two phenomena, but the logic of an essence over and above the 'fortuitous accidents' perceptible on the surface of circulation and exchange.

When Marx refers to 'fixed social laws', when he evokes the 'iron necessity' of physical laws in connection with them, fixity and necessity must be construed in a wholly relative manner. Between their seeming naturalness and the social and historical reality that determines them, contradiction is at work. We are dealing with historical laws that present themselves as natural. The difficulty springs back to life. If laws pertain to the order of generality and regularity, what is a 'historical law'?

History is woven out of factual particularities. History exists only in so far as what happens need not have happened. Radically immanent, as social relations historical laws assert their necessity in the face of extreme contingencies. In this sense, they are opposed to the formalism of external causality. Thus:

> the class struggle counteracts the untrammelled exploitation of the workers by capital, but, however beneficial its effects, the value of labour-power remains determined by the labour-time required for the production of the subsistence goods that accrue to the working class. In each case, these extreme determinations operate contingently, without the content of the law being upset one iota. Quite the reverse, the law is asserted in all its rigour through such disruptions attributable to external causes, by the preservation of the necessary relation between abstract labour and value.

Duménil pertinently underlines the close kinship between the law and the concept.[44] The action of a conceptual law expresses the immanent (internal) necessity of a process, as opposed to a multiplicity of contingent external causes that are independent of one another. Thus: '[t]he exchange or sale of commodities at their value is the rational, natural law of the equilibrium between them; this is the basis on which divergences have to be explained, and not the converse, i.e. the law of equilibrium should not be derived from contemplating the divergences.'[45]

A number of critics stumble over the disorientating logic of *Capital*, in which laws are not statistical generalizations of visible phenomena, but the invisible constraints that govern their fluctuations. In a more contemporary terminology, this internal or immanent law might also be regarded as a structural or 'bathygenic' law. Commodity fetishism transforms its immanence into alien powers and compulsions that the literally subjugated producer must confront. Similarly, '[u]nder free competition, the immanent laws of capitalist production confront the individual capitalist as a coercive force external to him'. If commodities can be sold at prices that diverge from their value, 'this divergence appears as an infringement of the laws governing the exchange of commodities'.[46]

The statement of a law cannot be definitive, any more than the determination of a concept can. It pertains to the process of determination leading from the simple relation of production, and its abstractions, to the concrete complexity of reproduction as a whole. The quasi-mechanical law expressed at the level of the production process becomes a variety of organic law, enriched, rectified and complex, at the level of the whole process. What we are then dealing with is not strictly economic laws, but unusual historical laws, which constantly contradict themselves.[47]

Predisposing Necessities and Laws of Tendency

This metamorphosis of economic laws into historical laws is foreshadowed by the strange concept of 'law of tendency', introduced as early as the preface to the first edition of *Capital* to correct the 'iron necessity' of the natural laws of production. In Volume One, the law that the price of labour-power always reduces to its value meets with obstacles that allow it to be realized only within certain limits. The law is counteracted by simple mechanical factors, a kind of friction that checks it.

In Volume Three, the notion of tendency is no longer presented as accidental. It encapsulates what is distinctive about economic laws compared with physical or natural laws: 'With the whole of capitalist production, it is always only in a very intricate and approximate way . . . that the *general law prevails as the dominant tendency*.' The existence of a general rate of surplus-value is 'a *tendency*, like *all economic laws*'.[48]

This concept of 'law of tendency' now assumes its full significance. In Part three, in connection with 'the law of tendential fall in the rate of profit' [*Gesetz des tendenziellen Falls der Profirate*], the 'counteracting factors' are no longer external obstacles or mechanical friction, but the very consequence of 'the law's internal contradictions' [*Entfaltung der innern Widersprüche des Gesetzes*]. The tendential character of the law henceforth expresses the internal contradictions by which the economic law cancels itself as a law: 'Counteracting influences must be at work, checking and cancelling the effect of the general law and giving it simply the character of a tendency.' According to Marx, the 'same laws . . . produce both a growing absolute mass of profit for the social capital, and a falling rate of profit'; they are 'evident in the relative fall of variable capital as a proportion of the total capital, and the accelerated accumulation that follows from this'; and they 'make the profit rate fall [and] also promote accumulation, i.e. the formation of additional capital'. What we have here is a 'double-edged law of a decline in the profit *rate* coupled with a simultaneous increase in the absolute *mass* of profit, arising for the same reasons'.[49] Tendential, the law nevertheless remains coercive. It is not annulled by the factors that counteract it. It is expressed and imposed in and through them. The increase in the rate of surplus-value does not cancel the general law. It simply has 'the effect that this law operates more as a tendency, i.e. as a law whose absolute realization is held up, delayed and weakened by counteracting factors'. An 'inner and necessary connection between two apparently contradictory phenomena', the 'law operates . . . simply as a tendency, whose effect is decisive only under certain particular circumstances and over long periods'.[50] Its innermost contradiction expresses the fact that capital itself is the real barrier to capitalist production. The third part of Volume Three logically concludes with the inevitability of crises ('Hence crises', Marx tersely concludes), which constitute the limit and horizon where the 'double-edged' character of the law is resolved.

'Laws of tendency' are laws, 'not . . . in the naturalistic sense or that of speculative determinism, but in a "historicist" sense, valid, that is, to the extent that there exists the "determined market" or in other words an environment which is organically alive and interconnected in its movements of development'. Gramsci clearly understood the significance of this category. Does not the

> discovery of the formal logical principle of the 'law of tendency' . . . imply a new 'immanence', a new conception of 'necessity' and of freedom, etc.? Translation into these terms seems to me precisely the achievement of the philosophy of praxis, which has universalised Ricardo's discoveries, extending them in an adequate fashion to the whole conception of history and thus drawing from them, in an original form, a new conception of the world.[51]

Whereas Marx explores a different form of causality and a different mode of predictability, a novel articulation of the real and the possible, Althusser, blind to the role of critique, unimaginatively summons him back to the order of normal science. It is Althusser, not Marx, who reduces the law of tendency to a mechanical law counteracted by complexity, checked by a kind of external friction. Marx's terms indicate that he is torn between Galilean rationality and a different rationality, dictated by his object (political economy). Although he still speaks of the checking and weakening of the law by circumstances, he tackles the 'law's internal contradictions' in accordance with his logic of immanence. This tentative approach illustrates the unresolved tension between positive science and German science mediated by critique. It clarifies the contradictions between the determinist temptation (of the preface to *Capital*) and open-ended historical development (the polemics against the 'supra-historical'). It underscores the fundamental logical difference between a mechanical causality, formal and external, and a law of tendency, immanent and internal, in the tradition of Hegelian 'antithetical tendencies'. In an open system that is not fully determined, like political economy, the empirical regularities and constant conjunctions of events are in fact manifested as tendencies. Unlike causal judgement, 'legal' judgement expresses historically delimited tendencies that can never arrive at their term, but are essential to a dynamic understanding of social relations.[52]

Conscious of the ambiguities of 'law of tendency', and its possible mechanistic interpretations, Ernst Bloch endeavoured to separate the terms, going so far as to counterpose law and tendency. A tendency is not a frustrated law. A law closes with its repetition. A tendency is open to innovation: 'A tendency is the structure in which the strange pre-existence of its orientation and anticipation is expressed. In other words, a tendency is the way in which the content of a goal that does not yet exist pushed itself forward.'[53] Gramsci maintains that 'the tendential nature cannot refer just to the counteracting forces in the real situation . . . It seems that the meaning of "tendential" must . . . be of a real "historical", and not a methodological nature.' Alert to any vulgar mechanistic interpretation of *Capital*, he notes that the tendency for the rate of profit to fall represents 'the contradictory aspect of another law, that of the production of relative surplus value'.[54] The technological progress that makes it possible to increase this relative surplus-value has the conjoint effect of increasing the organic composition of capital and lowering the rate of profit – except that, in Volume Three, this contradictory law no longer operates on the abstract relation of exploitation strictly in the sphere of production, but through competition between many capitals.

What a number of interpreters take for a formal evasion (a law that is not a law), or a scientific abdication, in reality conveys a necessity that is peculiar to the 'critique of political economy', to the laws immanent in its object, to its very limits. Once again, it is Gramsci who has the best grasp of the import of these new causalities:

The counteracting forces of the tendential law, which are summed up in the production of ever greater relative surplus value, have limits that are given, for example, technically by the extension of the elastic resistance of matter and socially by the level of unemployment that a society can stand. That is to say, *the economic contradiction becomes a political contradiction and is resolved politically by overthrowing praxis.*[55]

Those who claim to deduce a theory of the automatic and imminent collapse of capitalism from the tendency of the rate of profit to fall are mistaken about what the tendential involves according to Marx, and the transition from economic law to political strategy. Construed in a historical perspective, the tendency for the rate of profit to fall underlies the phenomena of Americanization and Fordism as attempts to surmount or avoid it.

Reviewing the polemical biases of a critical, engaged *œuvre*, Engels wrote to Franz Mehring two years before his death:

in the first instance we all laid, and *were bound to lay*, the main emphasis on the *derivation* of political, juridical and other ideological notions, and of actions arising through the medium of these notions, from basic economic facts. But at the same time we have on account of the content neglected the formal side – the manner in which these notions, etc., come about.[56]

Yet this 'formal side' affects the necessity involved in the 'derivation', corrects it as an iron necessity, and problematizes it into a 'contingent necessity'. The result – notes Lenin, reading Hegel – is that the accidental becomes necessary, and necessity itself is determined as chance.

What is a singular, factual historical necessity? Responding to one aporia with another, it might be ventured that the same applies to historical necessity as to laws of tendency: in addition to injunctive laws, history knows permissive laws.[57]

A 'free necessity', said Spinoza; an 'inclining necessity', said Leibniz: a contingent necessity. Historical necessity has contingency pegged on to it. It is what comes to pass while remaining hidden, only to reveal itself at the end. Like progress, it becomes itself only a posteriori. Progress affirms itself as such, as a general process, through its innermost regressions. Necessity is fully determined only from the retrospective standpoint of an impossible last judgement.

And if history never ends ending? And if its closure is only a borderline surmise? Necessity then remains indefinitely suspended, subject to contingency, just as progress remains permanently conditional. This is what is indicated by the third of Walter Benjamin's *Theses on the Philosophy of History*: 'To be sure, only a redeemed mankind receives the fullness of its past – which is to say, only for a redeemed mankind has its past become citable in all its moments. Each moment it has lived becomes a *citation à l'ordre du jour* – and that day is Judgment Day.'[58] This improbable day concludes the journey of negative theology. Then, and then only, necessity, a category of the past, reveals itself as the possibility that has come to pass, and cannot now be cancelled. A category of the future, possibility is a necessity still in a state of potentiality. As for reality, a category of the present, it indissolubly combines necessity and possibility.

This present is the time of politics: the time of Marx's 'second voice', 'brief and direct', impatient and excessive, because 'excess is its only measure' – the time when, as Benjamin says, politics assumes primacy over history.

Notes

1. For the first position, see Karl Lamprecht, *Moderne Geschischtwissenschaft* (1905) and his disciple, K. Breysig, *Der Stufenbau und die Gesetze der Weltgeschichte* (1904). For Eduard Meyer, see his *Zur Theorie und Methodik der Geschichte* (1902).
2. Max Weber, *The Methodology of the Social Sciences*, trans. and ed. Edward A. Shils and Henry A. Finch, Free Press, New York, 1949, p. 184.
3. Ibid., pp. 74, 80.
4. Georg Simmel, *The Problems of the Philosophy of History*, trans. Guy Oakes, Free Press, New York 1977, pp. 106–9.
5. Ibid.
6. Ibid., p. 182. As early as his *Critique of Hegel's Doctrine of the State*, Marx pierced 'the lie of [Hegel's] concept of progress', and perceived its political consequence: conservatism. The cult of historical progress is in fact fundamentally conservative.
7. Karl Marx, Preface to the First Edition, in *Capital*, vol. 1, trans. Ben Fowkes, Penguin/NLR, Harmondsworth 1976, pp. 91–2.
8. Karl Marx and Frederick Engels, letters of 7 August, 2 October, 3 October and 5 October 1866, in Marx and Engels, *Collected Works*, vol. 42, Lawrence & Wishart, London 1987, pp. 304, 320–3.
9. See Elhanan Yakira, *La Causalité de Galilée à Kant*, Presses Universitaires de France, Paris 1994.
10. Henri Denis, *Logique hégélienne et systèmes économiques*, Presses Universitaires de France, Paris 1984, p. 148.
11. G.W.F. Hegel, *Science of Logic*, trans. A.V. Miller, Allen & Unwin, London 1969, p. 734.
12. Ibid., pp. 558–9, 561, 562.
13. Ibid., pp. 562, 566.
14. Ibid., pp. 569–70.
15. Ibid., pp. 503–5, 511, 725.
16. Ibid., p. 734.
17. G.W.F. Hegel, *Phenomenology of Spirit*, trans. A.V. Miller, Oxford University Press, Oxford and New York 1977, p. 46.
18. Marx, *Capital*, vol. 1, p. 317.
19. In Gramsci, '[o]bjective always means "humanly objective"', by contrast with 'historically subjective'. Humanity 'knows objectively in so far as knowledge is real for the whole human race *historically* unified in a single unitary cultural system' (Antonio Gramsci,

Selections from the Prison Notebooks, ed. and trans. Quintin Hoare and Geoffrey Nowell Smith, Lawrence & Wishart, London 1971, p. 445).

20. Jean-Paul Sartre, *Notebooks for an Ethics*, trans. David Pellauer, University of Chicago Press, Chicago and London 1992, p. 40.

21. Roy Bhaskar, *Dialectic: The Pulse of Freedom*, Verso, London and New York 1993, pp. 53, 90.

22. Ilya Prigogine, *Les Lois du chaos*, Flammarion, Paris 1994, p. 11.

23. Ibid., p. 35. As early as the 1930s, Whitehead stressed the difference between scientific induction and historical prediction. Classical science deals with generalities. Our knowledge of scientific laws is sadly deficient and our knowledge of the significant facts of the present and past is extremely sparse. The 'purely descriptive' character of natural laws in their positive conception had the advantage of a seductive simplicity compared with the difficulties of immanent laws or injunctive laws (whose ambiguities lead back to the abandoned paths of metaphysics in the Aristotelian sense of the term). Law becomes synonymous with the statement of observed facts, but statistics have nothing to say about the future, without the introduction of postulates of stability and a calculated risk of error.

24. Georges Friedmann, *Leibniz et Spinoza*, Gallimard, Paris 1975, pp. 314–22.

25. G.W. Leibniz, *Theodicy*, trans. E.M. Huggard, Open Court, La Salle, IL 1985, p. 152.

26. Ibid., p. 71.

27. See Yvon Belaval, *Leibniz*, Vrin, Paris 1969, p. 162.

28. G.W. Leibniz, *De l'horizon de la doctrine humaine/La Restitution universelle*, J. Vrin, Paris 1991, p. 57.

29. Ibid., p. 65.

30. Ibid., pp. 74–5. In *L'éternité par les astres*, Blanqui pursued (inadvertently?) a line of reasoning analogous to that of Leibniz. In Blanqui, the iron circle of the eternal return of defeats is broken by the chapter of 'bifurcations', the only one 'open to hope'. Similarly, in the final version of *Apokatastasis*, Leibniz did not preserve this passage from the first draft: 'A day will come when the very life of individuals will repeat the same circumstances almost in detail. Myself, for example, living in a town called Hanover, situated on the bank of the River Heine, writing letters with the same meaning to the same friends.' In Blanqui, we find practically word for word this idea of the eternal revival of defeats and confinement to the fort of Taureau, where he wrote *L'éternité par les astres*. The Blanquist theme of bifurcations is virtually contemporaneous with the consequences of thermodynamics for temporal reversibility: the shattered symmetry of time is illustrated by points of bifurcation where possibilities branch out. Thus is sketched a non-linear, ramified and bush-like history, which Henri Lefebvre, long before rhizomes became fashionable, illustrated by 'trellis-like' development (see his *Logique formelle, logique dialectique*, Éditions Sociales, Paris 1947).

31. Hegel, *Science of Logic*, pp. 542–9.

32. Herbert Marcuse, *Hegel's Ontology and the Theory of Historicity*, trans. Seyla Benhabib, MIT Press, Cambridge, MA and London 1987, p. 95. Taking this two-dimensionality of the real and the possible seriously, Musil observed that if a sense of reality exists, a sense of potentiality is equally justified and necessary. Similarly, comments Marcuse, '[t]hrough this motility of the actual, an "identity of the same" throughout all contingencies is established: this identity is actuality's necessity. In its very transition from possibility to possibility, actuality constitutes itself as *necessity*' (ibid.).

33. Hegel, *Science of Logic*, pp. 549–50.

34. Karl Marx, 'Difference between the Democritean and Epicurean Philosophy of Nature', in Marx and Frederick Engels, *Collected Works*, vol. 1, Lawrence & Wishart, London 1975, pp. 43–4.

35. Lucretius, *On the Nature of the Universe*, Bk Two, ll. 235–7, trans. Sir Ronald Melville, Clarendon Press, Oxford 1997, p. 43.

36. Marx, *Capital*, vol. 1, p. 196; emphasis added. In the words of Eugène Fleischmann:

We must be very careful with the dialectical notion of contingency. A thing is regarded as contingent because it might have been different. But things actually exist and, despite the fact that they could have been different, they are not. On the contrary, they are necessarily as they are because they are possibilities realized by a cause that has conjured up their reality and explains it. These three notions – possibility (contingency), necessity and reality – are only separable with the aid of an abstraction. The standpoint of possibility envisages the future while ignoring the present and the past; reality is the present; and necessity is characteristic of the past (which can never be other than what it is). (*La Philosophie politique de Hegel*, p. 35)

37. This is the opinion of Michel Vadée: 'The determinist interpretation of Marxism, which seeks to explain everything dogmatically by economic necessity and the laws of production, suppresses the role of objective chance into which the individual human will is inserted' (*Marx penseur du possible*, Klincksieck, Paris 1992, p. 149). Much less happy is the idea that Marx's contingency is virtually equivalent to Cournot's: an encounter between independent causal series. For Marx, unlike Cournot, all causal series issue from a world of which they are only aspects. People sometimes have the impression that the link between the apparent chance of isolated cases and the internal law that inscribes them in the totality is revealed by statistical results. Thus:

the sphere of competition . . . is subject to accident in each individual case; i.e. where the inner law that prevails through the accidents and governs them is visible only when these accidents are combined in large numbers, so that it remains invisible and incomprehensible to the individual agents of production themselves. Further, however, the actual production process, as the unity of the immediate production process and the process of circulation, produces new configurations in which the threads of the inner connection get more and more lost, the relations of production becoming independent of one another and the components of value ossifying into independent forms. (Karl Marx, *Capital*, vol. 3, trans. David Fernbach, Penguin/NLR, Harmondsworth 1981, p. 967)

Possibly we should detect in this assertion the influence of Adolphe Quételet (*On Man and the Development of his Faculties*), of whom one finds traces in Marx's notebooks in 1851 and whose rule of 'governing averages' is evoked by Marx in *Capital*, vol. 3, p. 1000.

38. Fleischmann, *La Philosophie politique de Hegel*, p. 233.
39. Marx, *Capital*, vol. 1, p. 209.
40. Vadée, *Marx penseur du possible*, p. 19.
41. Jindrich Zeleny, *The Logic of Marx*, trans. Terrell Carver, Blackwell, Oxford 1980. This is also Lenin's reading of Hegel's *Logic*: 'When one reads Hegel on causality, it appears strange at first glance that he dwells so relatively lightly on this theme, beloved of the Kantians. Why? Because, indeed, for him causality is only *one* of the determinations of the universal connection' (V.I. Lenin, 'Conspectus of Hegel's Book *The Science of Logic*', in Lenin, *Collected Works*, vol. 38, trans. Clemens Dutt, Progress Publishers, Moscow 1961, p. 162).
42. Gérard Duménil, *Le Concept de loi économique dans le Capital*, Maspero, Paris 1978.
43. Marx, *Capital*, vol. 3, p. 365; emphasis added.
44. Duménil, *Le Concept de loi économique dans le Capital*, p. 49.

What distinction should we keep in mind between the concept of value and the law of value? At first sight, the difference seems very slight. The paradox that initially held our attention – the absence of the term 'law of value' in Part I of *Capital* – thus finds the beginning of an explanation. To expound the concept of value is to formulate its laws (or law). This is trivially conveyed by the fact that the formulas 'value is such and such a thing', or 'the law of value implies such and such a thing', may, in an initial approximation, be regarded as equivalent . . . The interiority of the law is thus defined in relation to the concept. (p. 40)

45. Marx, *Capital*, vol. 3, p. 289.
46. Marx, *Capital*, vol. 1, pp. 381, 261.
47. 'It is thus that economic laws assume the guise of historical laws. In economic laws, historical mutation represents that beyond which they continue to obtain. The law expresses what is intangible within the mutation itself and conveys the permanent explanatory value of a conceptual system': Duménil, *Le Concept de loi économique dans le Capital*, p. 150.
48. Marx, *Capital*, vol. 3, pp. 261, 275; emphasis added.
49. Ibid., p. 339, 325–6, 331.
50. Ibid., pp. 341–2, 331, 346.
51. Gramsci, *Selections from the Prison Notebooks*, p. 401.
52. Bhaskar, *Dialectic*, pp. 226, 404.
53. Ernst Bloch, *Experimentum mundi*, Payot, Paris 1981, pp. 138, 142.
54. Antonio Gramsci, *Further Selections from the Prison Notebooks*, ed. and trans. Derek Boothman, Lawrence & Wishart, London 1995, pp. 432, 429.
55. Ibid., p. 430.
56. Frederick Engels, letter of 14 July 1893 to Franz Mehring, in Marx and Engels, *Selected Correspondence*, Progress Publishers, Moscow 1975, pp. 433–4.
57. Françoise Proust, who proposes this distinction in the light of Kant, adds that permissive laws (*Erlaubnisgesetz*) do not authorize not beginning, but state that a beginning has always begun excessively and yet insufficiently, has always begun too soon and yet too late: see *Kant, le ton de l'histoire*, Plon, Paris 1991.
58. Walter Benjamin, 'Theses on the Philosophy of History', III, in Benjamin, *Illuminations*, trans. Harry Zohn, Fontana, London 1982, p. 256.

10

Choreographies of Chaos

The critique of political economy leads Marx into unknown territory, where logical behaviour deviates from the classical model. Without as yet superseding the ideal of causality bound up with it, his understanding of capital breaks with representations of a homogeneous space and linear time.

Subsequent scientific developments clarify his experimentation. In the mid-nineteenth century, three simultaneous but logically heterogeneous innovations helped to undermine the Newtonian paradigm: the Darwinian theory of evolution, the principles of energy conservation and loss, and the Marxian critique of political economy. These 'sciences' of transformation no longer refer to factual certainties, but to probabilities, choices and bifurcations. They tackle instability and disequilibrium, aperiodic motion and time's arrow.

Classical laws no longer operate in certain domains, where a novel rationality takes shape; where events and inventiveness return in force; where probability is no longer a token of ignorance tied to the position of the observer, as in Laplacean mechanics, but an intrinsic property of a random system. The very meaning of ignorance is transformed: it ceases to be residual, and determines a new representation of science.

Mediated by rhythms, mechanical causality is not cancelled. It is inscribed in the lawfulness of complex structures and the reciprocal determination of the whole and its parts. Their systemic causality eludes any decisive experiments that would definitively close history and abolish contradiction. These systems, which presuppose themselves, possess reasons that are unknown to classical reason. Mechanical causes and probabilistic contingencies now combine; they are no longer mutually exclusive.[1]

In classical theories of equilibrium, systems tend to rediscover their dynamic stability by resolving disruptions. In the logic of disequilibrium, dynamic stability and structural instability are compatible. Without possessing the requisite mathematical instruments – something he explicitly bemoaned – Marx precisely sought to combine the dynamic stability of cyclical reproduction schemas with the structural instability of the system (technological, social and political mutations). Hence crises are apprehended as so many forks, junctions and critical points. Temporal symmetry is shattered, without it being possible to foresee which of the determinate possibilities will prevail.

The Footprints of Chaos

The intelligibility of the Galilean universe presupposes a strict causal structure. Banking on a world governed by laws and regularities, one causalist metaphysics expelled another. But the triumph of this classical ideal was (relatively) short-lived. Shaken in the second half of the nineteenth century, it tottered in the interwar period under the combined effect of a major cultural shock (war and the 'decline of the West'), and a scientific controversy (over quantum mechanics in physics and psychoanalysis in the social sciences). In part, the moral crisis preceded the scientific upheaval. As early as 1918, in *The Decline of the West*, Spengler contrasted destiny, requiring creation, with causality, demanding dissection, the former bound up with life and the latter with death.

All scientific thought includes causality in its explanatory modes. Classical physics, however, gives it a restrictive meaning: scientific thought and determinist causality become synonymous. Natural events are rigorously and completely determined. Any phenomenon is the necessary result of a cause preserved in the effect. In theory at least, everything is predictable. In the absence of friction, the past wholly determines the present (and vice versa). The metaphor of Laplace's demon exemplifies this determinism, which is based on the logical equivalence of two propositions of Newtonian dynamics at two distinct moments:

> We must regard the present state of the universe as the effect of its prior state, and as the cause of what will ensue. An intellect which at any given moment knew all the forces that animate Nature and the mutual positions of the beings that comprise it, if this intellect were vast enough to submit its data to analysis, could condense into a single formula the movement of the greatest bodies of the universe and that of the lightest atom: for such an intellect nothing could be uncertain; and the future just like the past would be present before its eyes.[2]

The formula expresses with admirable concision the ideal of a physics unified, from the largest bodies to the smallest atoms, in the eyes of a panoptic, omniscient ('vast enough') intellect.

Differential equations determine the predictable evolution of a system when the initial positions and velocities of all of its elements are known. Laplace was conscious of the borderline character of this hypothetical ideal. In practice, the behaviour of physical systems diverges from the mathematical model, and requires a 'science of chance and probabilities'. The causal structure subsists, but it is only approximated to, and is divided between 'regular causes' and 'accidental causes'.

If the classical determinist picture is conventionally associated with Laplace's demonic intellect, the term 'determinism' itself was diffused later, starting with the works of Claude Bernard. In his *Introduction à la médecine expérimentale*, the principle of determinism dominated study of the phenomena of life, as it did all natural phenomena. At stake was establishing the legitimacy of the experimental approach against the metaphysical consequences of vitalism. Like every physical phenomenon, each vital phenomenon resulted from a set of 'determining conditions' that should be substituted for the 'old and obscure spiritualist notion of cause'. Intent upon founding the laws of living beings against the obscure survivals of magical causes, this plea remained subject to the constraints of its particular object. At a moment when Marx was searching for a specific concept of economic law, Bernard described a causal relation, which was biological and not mechanical, in the categories of 'determining conditions' or 'directing forces': 'In living bodies, the *directing or evolutionary forces* are morphologically vital, whereas their *executive forces* are the same as in crude bodies.' The 'morphological law' generating 'organized matter' thus subjugated general physico-chemical forces.[3]

Impotent when confronted with the logic of organic or economic systems, the dream of classical predictability next came under attack on the very terrain of physics and mathematics. At the end of the century, Hadamard's geometry and Poincaré's topology shook the epistemological base. Geodetics pertain to a model in which the system's sensitivity to initial conditions becomes essential. Freeing the visual imagination from its analytical vice, isoclinal folds form a sort of extraordinarily densely woven trellis, tissue or lattice. Determinist prediction then becomes impossible:

> A very small cause which escapes our notice determines a considerable effect that we cannot fail to see, and then we say that the effect is due to chance. If we knew exactly the laws of nature and the situation of the universe at the initial moment, we could predict exactly the situation of that same universe at a succeeding moment ... But it is not always so; it may happen that small differences in the initial conditions produce very great ones in the final

phenomena. Prediction becomes impossible, and we have the fortuitous phenomenon.[4]

Describing the behaviour of a system sensitive to initial conditions, Poincaré's topology discovers the 'footprints of chaos'.

In the same period, Volterra's works on population statistics challenged the 'restrictive hypothesis' that a system's future depends exclusively on its current state, not on its previous states. His idea of a 'hereditary mechanics' introduced a random historical dimension into determinist logic.

The Crisis of the European Sciences

In the Galilean world, continuous and homogeneous time underpins the order of causal relations, whose formal expression is supplied by mathematical functions. Quantum discontinuity shakes the reference points of this linear temporality, and disrupts the causal picture of the universe. Quantum probabilism discloses 'tunnel effects' whereby an object can suddenly pass in stages from one state to another. In the case of the smallest objects, the possibility of such effects increases. Henceforth it becomes practically impossible to organize phenomena in a univocal linear succession. This break in the temporal sequence of cause and effect persuaded Niels Bohr definitively to abandon the classical ideal of causality and the simultaneously causal and spatio–temporal description peculiar to ordinary causality. Heisenberg, more radical, offered scientific support to Spengler's theses by insisting that quantum mechanics had conclusively invalidated the principle of causality [*Kausalgesetz*].

The upheaval was considerable. Grounded in the continuity of an abstract homogeneous time, the duo of cause and effect seemed tried and tested. The lacunae of scientific prediction appeared to be attributable simply to incomplete initial information. An inventory of hidden variables and greater calculating capacity would end up conquering this invisible frontier. But quantum mechanics inscribes chance at a deeper level, from which it cannot be dislodged solely by a cumulative progress in knowledge. It then has to be conceded that classical causality describes only a part of physical reality. The introduction of the notion of probability wave seems to legitimate a certain indeterminism. At least it makes it necessary to clarify the relation between determinism and uncertainty, since an event can be both non-arbitrary and unpredictable.[5]

If the uncontrollable action between objects and measuring instruments no longer allows causal description in every reference system, modern science risks collapse. Einstein's rationalist vertigo when he was confronted with such a perspective is understandable. The challenge prompted a critical exploration of random phenomena (historical, biological, economic, ecological), which seemed to be excluded from the field of classical rationality. A world sealed up by pre-programmed progress excluded in principle the untimely irruption of some Messiah impotent before the iron wall of the facts. Yet atoms suddenly revealed a world of potentialities and possibilities, rather than a world of facts.[6]

However, the path spanning the indeterminist abyss in which reason might come to grief is a narrow one. Confronted with quantum discontinuity, the standpoint of complementarity, according to Bohr, aims at 'a logical generalization of the notion of causality', rather than abandoning it for a drift into mysticism. Similarly, according to Kojève, challenging classical causality does not lead to an arbitrary universe. Each possible result remains subject to a determinate probability, since modern physics, while rejecting the 'idea of precise causal determinism', ultimately accepts 'statistical determinism and approximate causal determinism'. No satisfactory explanation of the indivisibility of transition processes can in fact be given in the framework of classical determinist descriptions. Accordingly, drawing the consequences of temporal discontinuity for causal relations, the thing to do is to reform the threatened rationality the better to salvage it.[7]

The controversy extended well beyond physics. Indeterminacy can justify a strange complicity between science and myths. Hence Einstein's stubborn determination to defend a 'modern causality': renovated, local, differential and instantaneous. Helping to challenge the classical paradigm, this open causality is closely akin to a non-linear historical causality, in which the event constantly modifies the rules of the game.[8]

At a time when the Stalinist terror was carrying the pretension to make history scientifically to a frenzy, and its tribunals were taking the notion of 'objective guilt' to absurd lengths, quantum mechanics blurred the boundary between subject and object. Physicists preceded politicians in observing that the motives for a decision cannot be known in full. Upon examination, the facts altered.

In its turn, physical knowledge took on a strategic cast.

In the 1920s, the crisis of physics thus combined with moral and political crisis, and then economic crisis, to challenge the dominant causal paradigm. It is significant that the works of Freud (*Civilization and its Discontents*, 1930), Kojève (*L'idée de déterminisme*, 1932), Whitehead (*Adventures of Ideas*, 1933), Popper (*The Logic of Scientific Discovery*, 1934), Carnap (*The Unity of Science*, 1934), and Husserl (*The Crisis of the European Sciences*, 1935) appeared well-nigh simultaneously, seeking to redefine scientific rationality or to salvage its unity.

Of these endeavours, Husserl's is the most moving. Without abandoning the 'absolute foundation' of the sciences, he registered a historical displacement in the general idea of science deriving from the existing sciences, which had become hypothetical sciences.[9] The aporias of the Cartesian revolution – or, more precisely, the failed attempt at a total reform of philosophy to make it a science with absolute foundations – were at the root of this 'crisis of the European sciences', in so far as the ideal of geometry and mathematical physics had exercised a baneful influence for centuries.

As catastrophe approached, the world of the 1930s was torn between the unleashing of calculative reason and the dark revenge of daytime magicians. The impasse of positive science as a science of being that had lost itself in the world foreshadowed the end of an epoch. In this *Krise*, where everything threatened to 'succumb to skepticism, irrationalism and mysticism',[10] Husserl could see no other exit than a radical return upon ourselves. It was first of all necessary to bracket the world so as subsequently to rediscover it, and salvage what could still make sense.

If necessary, this must be at the cost of an agonizing revision of the way in which science was practised. For '[m]erely fact-minded sciences make merely fact-minded people'. The positivist paradigm was indeed at the heart of the torment. The anguished question uttered by Husserl on the threshold of disaster still echoes in our ears, more piercing and more desperate perhaps: 'Can we console ourselves with that? Can we live in this world, where historical occurrence is nothing but an unending concatenation of illusory progress and bitter disappointment?' Against the fossilization of humanity in facticity, reason's critical labour begins by contesting the positivist model:

> It was not always the case that science understood its demand for rigorously grounded truth in the sense of that *sort* of objectivity which dominates our positive sciences in respect to method ... The specifically human questions were not always banned from the realm of science ... Thus the positivistic concept of science in our time is, historically speaking, a *residual concept*. It has dropped all the questions which had been considered under the now narrower, now broader concepts of metaphysics ...

In disqualifying these unanswered questions, in fashioning the idea of a 'rational infinite totality of being with a rational science systematically mastering it', in imposing this 'unprecedented idea', modern science, 'in a manner of speaking, decapitates philosophy'.[11]

The result was that humanity risked losing its head and seeing instrumental rationalism turn into a vindictive irrationalism. In fact, one-sided rationality opened the way to 'the greatest danger of drowning in the skeptical deluge'.[12]

Despite some misleading sunny spells, the deluge had not ceased. The perverse alliance between immoral technology and moralizing opinion attested to its ravages.

'Knowing the world in a seriously scientific way' demanded a systematic construction of the world and its causalities, 'starting from the meagre supply of what can be established only relatively in direct experience'. Made conceivable by the mathematical idealization of the world of bodies (construed for the first time as an *objective* world), and the unprecedented development of the art of measurement, the 'universal causal style' of the Galilean revolution founded the possibility of hypotheses, inductions and predictions. Like any conquest, this new age of knowledge entailed its share of sacrifices. Its forced march required numerous concessions on the way. With Galileo, 'the greatest discoverer of modern times', the disquieting idea of a separate world of self-enclosed bodies 'appears for the first time, so to speak, full-blown'. The world of mathematical idealities becomes the only world of real or possible experience, 'our daily life-world'.[13]

Originally split, this rational world spelt the end of 'philosophy as a rigorous science', in favour of the disciplinary sciences. '[I]n the area in which it began', in mathematics and physics, the new ideal of rationality and universality represented significant progress. But:

> It is something else to ask *how far* the exemplary character of these sciences should be stretched ... in his haste to ground objectivism and the exact sciences as affording metaphysical, absolute knowledge, [Descartes] does not set himself the task of systematically investigating the pure ego ... with regard to what acts, what capacities, belong to it and what it brings about, as intentional accomplishment.[14]

His radical objectivism thus had as its flipside a scarcely contained subjectivism.

The explosion of knowledge into disciplinary sciences ('bourgeois professions', in Husserl's words) meant that they 'completely lost the important sense which was alive in them ... of being branches of philosophy': 'What had been sciences in that other sense, the only genuine one, had turned unnoticed into remarkable new arts', disciplines that 'could be taught and learnt'. Poles apart from the proclaimed end of philosophy, this Husserlian critique seems to revive nostalgia for philos-

ophy as the 'ultimately grounding and universal science', the 'strict
science' [*strenge Wissenschaft*] of Nietzsche, whose advent, at a dangerous
moment, is urgent in the face of Enlightenment rationalism, 'laden with
hidden absurdity'.[15]

In the name of the vanquished and victims of positive knowledge,
'German science' thus tirelessly laments the poverty of a 'geometry of
forms', bereft of a non-mathematizable 'second geometry' of 'plena'.
Lucidly, Husserl was convinced that there would be no restoration of the
old 'rationalism'. Instead, its impasses risked licensing the rejection of all
rationality in favour of mythical discourses on 'the community spirit, the
will of the people, the ideal and political goals of nations' which, 'arising
out of a transposition by analogy of concepts that have a genuine
meaning, only in the sphere of individual persons' amounted to so much
'romanticism and mythology'. But 'Reason is a broad title'. It is not
exhausted by its mutilated fragments.[16]

In 1935, this moving defence of a menaced rationality was literally a
life-and-death question, and was all the more poignant in that the argument was not always equal to the task. Despite the demand for a reflection
that would rise above the ground, this flirted perilously with the jargon of
authenticity. The great danger of weariness announced by Husserl veered
towards exhaustion.

Spiritual hatred and barbarism are always just around the corner. On
the other hand, even if the narrow exit necessarily passes through a
philosophical (or theoretical) renaissance, there is no strictly philosophical solution to the *Krise*.

Swirling Logics

Four centuries after Galileo, a science of disorder has asserted itself
alongside a science of order. It is no longer always possible to predict the
behaviour of systems governed by precise, immutable laws. The order that
can 'generate its own chaos' is no longer synonymous with law, or disorder
with its absence. Nor is it any longer the case that each system obeys
specific rules, in accordance with some sensible coexistence between
determinist laws for simple systems and statistical laws for complex systems. Postulated by classical determinism, the unity of the universe and
the homogeneity of its organization are no longer self-evident in overlapping systems and subsystems where local and regional sets of laws inter-
penetrate. Governing heterogeneous levels, a 'transversal principle'
becomes necessary to maintain the universe in its entirety as a unified

scientific object. The Baconian age of knowledge fades; the modern idea of science falters.

In so far as the future's relative independence from the past no longer ensures the reproducibility of experience, the experimental method is undermined in its inductive principle and in the postulated symmetry of explanation and prediction.[17] On the bare ground of classical science, systems theory and determinist chaos trace the unfinished contours of a new paradigm, and passageways to an expanded rationality.

Hadamard's geodetics, Poincaré's isoclinal folds, and Picard's 'hereditary mechanics' explored access to systems that are sensitive to initial conditions. Nevertheless, unpredictability generally continued to be attributed to defective measurement, rather than to the irreducibly random character of turbulence and vortices. It was a long time before the unpredictability of turbulent flows was attributed to the mixture of dynamically stable and dynamically unstable regimes – and exclusively to it. In dramatic evolutionary developments from one state of equilibrium to another, non-linearity obtains. In a system sensitive to initial conditions, slight variations in the initial data induce a difference that increases exponentially over time. To predict what the weather will be like in a few weeks, it would, for example, be necessary to be able to account for the effect of an electron 10^{10} light years away. Although it is determined, the behaviour of the system is no longer predictable.

In 1986, a Royal Society conference in London settled on the notion of 'stochastic behaviour occurring in a determinist system' to define chaos. Stochastics evokes random behaviour in scholarly mode. Among the Greeks, *stochastikos* referred to a master in the art of applying or using the laws of chance to attain his objective. In effect, chaos describes 'lawless behaviour wholly governed by a law'. Chaotic dynamics carve out a series of forks and junctions in irreversible time, where possibilities can bud, open out and wither. Under the impact of the Versaillais reaction, Blanqui had already employed the notion to ward off the spectre of the eternal return of defeat: only 'the chapter of bifurcations' seemed open to historical hope. Introduced into the study of instability by Poincaré, the notion of bifurcation has since become established among physicists and mathematicians.

The atomists of Antiquity had had a poetic intuition of these chaotic tempests. Democritus superbly evokes the vortex as 'the substance of necessity'. Lucretius recommends careful observation of the 'particles of matter' dancing in disorderly fashion in a ray of sun, for 'their dancing shows that within matter/Secret and hidden motions also lie': 'For many you will see are struck by blows/Unseen, and changing course are driven back/Reversed on all sides, here, there, everywhere'. Thus, the wind gusting in the sea provokes a 'wondrous boiling'. And thus,

> Clouds form when in the expanse of sky above
> Many flying atoms come together
> All at once, and these are rougher, and so although
> They tangle together lightly, that is enough
> To hold them firmly fixed and joined together.

At first, 'small clouds' are formed. But they then condense, 'and the winds drive them on/Until in time a furious storm builds up'.[18] With the vortices of gas and liquids, with the infinite mutability of meteorological patterns, came a renewed interest in loops and vibrations, plaits and coils.

In the 1860s, thermodynamics and the theory of evolution opened up contradictory perspectives. Clausius reconciled the seemingly incompatible principles of the conservation and dissipation of energy with the 'incredibly abstract' notion of entropy (measure of the dispersal of thermic energy in a system). He demonstrated that the universal tendency in the material world is the dissipation of energy, increasing disorder, a levelling of differences up until the point of final extinction, when all energy will be transformed into evenly distributed, low-temperature heat.

On the one hand, the physical world is relentlessly running down. On the other, the living world is improving. It thus seems to contradict the sombre verdict of entropy, by developing a counter-tendency to a higher order, more heterogeneity, greater organization, making evolutionary biology 'the primary science of history'.[19]

In a closed physical system, the end-state is determined univocally by the initial conditions; entropy is always positive; order is continually destroyed. Time's arrow seals the irreversibility of phenomena. Open (living) systems are fundamentally characterized by a permanent exchange of matter and energy with their environment. In them, thermodynamic tendencies are constantly contradicted by the introduction of negative entropy. Organisms thus maintain themselves in a fantastically improbable condition. Traditional physics and chemistry, static structures, and the motions of horology represent closed systems; living organisms, the dance of flames, and ecological wholes are open systems.

The contradiction between evolutionary theory and thermodynamics disappears if the second principle applies exclusively to closed systems. In an open system, where self-organization, increased order, and reduced entropy are compatible, the maintenance of a high degree of organization (through the supply of energy-rich matter) is thermodynamically possible.

In contrast to the reductionist procedures of classical science, the contemporary sciences have reinstated holism. They have rediscovered the importance of transactions, interactions, organization, and teleology. Long regarded as a typically metaphysical notion, foreign to properly scientific work, the totality is back. The isolable causal series of classical physics have proved inadequate for understanding the organism as a whole and organized, complex systems. While the system remains a unified whole, any disturbance in fact leads to a new stationary state, owing to internal interactions. If it is divided into independent causal chains, the specialized parts become independent, and regulation disappears. New problems arise, requiring new modes of mathematical thought.

Bertalanffy's theoretical biology explicitly refers to Claude Bernard and to Whitehead's 'organic mechanism'. Whereas mechanistic physics is associated with partial processes, components, linear causal sequences, the dynamics of the living being are concerned with growth and self-regulation, features of open systems. Irreducible to static models and mechanical structures, the cell and organism participate in a continuous process of destruction and regeneration, regulated to establish a steady state. Such is indeed the 'fundamental mystery of living systems'. '[A] pale, abstract and empty concept' at first sight, the colourless notion of system is in fact the core, 'full of hidden . . . potentialities', of an '*Organic Revolution*' offering for our inspection '*the world as organization*'.[20]

Systems theory brings into play the specific categories of metabolism, equifinality, homeostasis, and teleology. Metabolism refers to the operations of assimilation and rejection of organic exchange [*Stoffwechsel*]. In a closed system, the end-state is determined univocally by the initial state; in an open system, starting from different initial conditions, it can be arrived at by different routes. Accordingly, against essentialist determinism, equifinality appears to be constitutive of any strategic thinking. Finally, oscillating between trial and error, homeostatic behaviour translates the adaptation of the system according to circular chains of information. In retroaction, unidirectional causal series are closed in a loop of regulation.[21]

Bertalanffy defines a system by a certain number of elements that interact with one another and their environment according to a set of equations. His formal definition casts a new light on concepts that previously had a whiff of vitalism or metaphysics about them: 'In modern science, dynamic interaction appears to be the central problem in all fields of reality.'[22] As the scientific study of systemic totalities, his 'general systems theory' expresses a fundamental tendency in modern thought, at work in cybernetics (with the phenomena of retroaction and circular causality), information theory and game theory (antagonistic dynamics and rational competition), and strategic theories of decision-making, as well as the mathematical topology of relations or the factor analysis of phenomena possessing numerous variables. Traditional physics and chemistry treat closed systems tending to a state of dynamic equilibrium. The theory of open systems applies to a large set of biological and social phenomena. Living systems are in fact governed by ongoing relations of entry and exit, construction and destruction, with their environment.

A general change in attitudes and scientific conceptions is taking shape under the influence of the biological and social sciences. The scientific picture of a mechanical world governed by isolated causal chains is disintegrating. Against the unhealthy glorification of sovereign technology, the vision of a 'vast organization' is taking shape, one whose complexity demands new categories and concepts. Devalued by the explanatory principles of the nomothetic sciences, overshadowed by the preference for cliometric research, the comprehensive narrative of the narrative sciences is once again claiming a legitimate place in the activity of knowledge.

In the aftermath of the war, J.D. Bernal gave a clear description of the symptoms of this mutation in the dominant scientific paradigm:

> No one who knows what the difficulties are now believes that the crisis of physics is likely to be resolved by any simple trick or modification of existing theories. Something radical is needed, and it will have to go far wider than physics. A new world outlook is being forged, but much experiment and argument will be needed before it can take a definitive form . . . It must have a different dimension from all previous world views, and include in itself an explanation of development and the origin of new things. In this it will naturally fall in line with the converging tendencies of the biological and social sciences in which a regular pattern blends with their evolutionary history.[23]

The unity of scientific knowledge is now no longer guaranteed, as in Carnap, by the hegemony of the language of physics. It results more modestly from the isomorphism of domains and discourses. Under the influence of the social practice of science and technology, the divide between sciences of nature and sciences of the spirit is reduced with the humanization of nature and the acknowledged naturalization of the human. The three pillars of Laplacean determinism – belief in a natural causal structure bound up with an ideal of intelligibility; faith in the predictive capacity of mathematical laws; and confidence in the fertility of mechanical reductionism – are tottering. Alongside a science of order, a science of disorder emerges. The behaviour of systems governed by immutable laws is not always predictable. Order, 'which can breed its own kind of chaos', is no longer synonymous with law. Disorder is no longer 'lawless'.[24]

For a long time, people were satisfied with the compromise whereby mechanical determinism was applicable to simple systems and statistical determinism to complex systems. It was supposedly enough to respect their territory and arrange their peaceful coexistence. But systems overlap and blend. The historical singularities of evolution cut across the regular models of physics. Instead of the unified universe posited by classical determinism, there emerges a perspectivist *feuilleté* of different levels of organization, overlapping systems and subsystems, possessing local and regional sets of laws. Thus, the second principle of thermodynamics does not apply identically in isolated systems prone to the dissipation of energy and in living systems, where organic exchange occurs. The very concept of science is at stake. In so far as the scientific ideal banks on a determinist principle of universal intelligibility as a condition of its own adventure, abandonment of predictive capacity hits it head-on. Yet: 'chaos tells us that even when our theory is deterministic, not all of its predictions lead to repeatable experiments'.[25]

The Fancy Dress Ball of Commodities

The middle of the nineteenth century witnessed a veritable irruption of narrative sciences. Around 1850, the so-called Devonian controversy was greeted by palaeontologists as the authentic '"establishment of history"'. The 'primary science of history', evolutionary biology was taking its first steps.[26] The works of Christian Jorgensen Thomsen, whose *Guide to Antiquities* appeared in 1856, opened up the field of prehistory. In 1867, the Universal Exhibition in Paris for the first time contained a pavilion dedicated to the history of work, with a collection of instruments. The same year, the first international conference on prehistory was held. In *Pre-Historic Times* (1865), Darwin's disciple John Lubbock introduced the neologisms 'Paleolithic' and 'Neolithic'. In 1870, Morgan published his *Systems of Consanguinity and Affinity of the Human Family*. The first congress of international statistics was held in Brussels in 1854. When Adolphe Quételet, pioneer of 'moral statistics', died in 1864, research on the 'average man' was still in its infancy. The 1840s and 1850s were equally marked by intense research into the conservation of energy and electromagnetism, although mathematical topology, theories of relativity, and *a fortiori* the quantum revolution were still to come. Marx's theory took its place amid this excitement, at the junction of rapidly developing historical research and a physics on the verge of major changes. Volume One of *Capital* appeared in 1867, eight years after *The Origin of Species* and two years after the formulation of Clausius's laws. The ordered disorder of capital likewise required the invention of a different rationality.

Classical economics is in fact directly inspired by Newtonian physics. Locke's founding letter to a Member of Parliament, *Some Considerations of the Consequences of the Lowering of Interest and Raising the Value of Money* (1691), is contemporaneous with Newton's *Principia* (1687).[27] To the physical abstraction of space corresponds the economic abstraction of the market, which renders different types of labour and wealth commensurable through the monetary relation. To homogeneous, empty physical time corresponds the linear time of circulation and accumulation, whose harmony is interrupted only by fortuitous disruptions and natural calamities. The utopia of equilibrium is common to both classical mechanics and economics. Engendered by the multiplication of exchange, the uniform economic and monetary space-time of the market grounds the possibility of measurement and law reduced to a rule of sequence. It presents an economic causality based on the physically measurable character of labour and capital, which is modelled on physical causality. Constitutive of classical thought, the concept of 'institutionalized market' makes it possible to consider theoretically the unity of a space of exchange and a juridico-monetary institution of regulation, and to register its theoretical difference *vis-à-vis* the simple empirical development of commercial relations. It is part and parcel of the very emergence of economic laws.

Walras's neoclassical economics forms part of the tradition of determinist equilibrium, endeavouring to integrate the contribution of energetics into it. His attempt to preserve the classical model of the market as the object of economic science persists even in chaos economics, which seems to offer a possible salvation for the neoclassical research programme.[28] Chaos derives (to some extent) from the economy, and returns to it. Market inconsistency and stock exchange turbulence have always inspired its theoreticians in return. Under the influence of quantum mechanics, stochastic processes got a hold over economics with the econometric revolution of the 1930s. In 1963, Benoît Mandelbrot published an article on price variations that has since come to be regarded as one of the 'sources of fractal geometry'. Conscious of non-mechanical price fluctuations, and especially their discontinuous variations, he abandoned linearity. The random was no longer conceived as a fortuitous disruption, but as structurally constitutive of economic experience. A year later, the 'fractal manifesto' developed this position. Contrary to common sense, it stressed the fundamental difference between economic time and Newtonian time. Aperiodic fluctuations in climatic conditions and prices prompted investigation of the shifting terrain of a 'second stage of indeterminism': 'The new models will nessarily differ in kind from the old ones. In other words, they will usher a new stage of indeterminism into science. The change will not only affect the details of the answers but the very characterization of what makes a question well-posed, or capable of being answered, and henceforth asking.'[29]

Conversely, it was inevitable that chaos or systems theories would shake up a discipline strongly marked by the paradigm of classical physics and reared on its metaphors. According to neoclassical economics, in a system of pure, perfect competition a price system guaranteeing a balance of supply and demand on all markets, and thus maintaining general equilibrium, would exist. This state of equilibrium is as ideal and hypothetical as the sequences of mathematical determinism. Its static approach does not permit integration of either the analysis of growth, or the dynamic behaviour of fluctuations. Spontaneous equilibrium, to which perfect competition is supposed to tend, leads to attributing responsibility for the onset of crises resulting from distorted competition to factors exogenous to the system, not immanent laws of its development.

Crises have no place in the laws of neoclassical equilibrium; yet they break out as surely as the Earth revolves!

Instead of an abstract space, the critique of political economy discovers a turbulent topology, divided up into basins, springs, wells, flows; an articulated space, imbricated and interlocking, whose fault-lines and fractures organize the metabolism of unequal exchange. Rosa Luxemburg underscored the dynamic function of the spatial heterogeneity of the world market. But the heterogeneity of the national market itself (access to raw materials and transport, availability and skill of manpower) is constantly used by the mobility of capital, whose investment and location shift in search of greater profitability. Hence the phenomena of ecological spoliation and uneven regional development which constitute one of the springs of accumulation. Similarly, the critique of political economy explores not a homogeneous but a rhythmical time, interspersed with intervals, hiccoughs and crises, a time of increases and decreases. Faced with the stochastic behaviour of capital, classical reason loses its grammar.

Mechanical equations and economic equations do not pertain to the same logic. For Ludwig von Mises, we know of no constant relation between magnitudes in the domain of social exchange; and the only magnitudes we can determine possess a historical significance that cannot be generalized. The result is that even if we could determine the present conditions, it would remain impossible to formulate predictions of a quantitative sort. According to von Mises, the quantitative treatment of economic problems was the preserve of economic history, not economic theory; and today's preferences could only be assessed in so far as they were expressed in today's prices.[30] Yet today's prices retroactively determine yesterday's value. The labour-time socially necessary for the production of commodities emerges a posteriori in the formation of market prices. The circular relation of value and prices, which misleads so many economists intent on conceiving it in terms of transformation, operates in the manner of information theory in Marx. Information on prices retro-determines value:

> Price therefore is distinguished from *value* not only as the nominal from the real; not only by way of the denomination in gold and silver, but because the latter appears as the law of the motions which the former runs through. But the two are constantly different and never balance out, or balance only coincidentally and exceptionally.[31]

Just as Spinozist substance is prior 'in nature' (and not chronologically) to the affections that determine it, value is logically prior to the prices that determine it.

In fact, the economy resembles an open, non-linear system. Econometric models have enormous difficulty integrating the irreducible uncertainty of investments, technological changes, monetary crises, and stock exchange crashes. In strategic reasoning, the hypothesis of a single, stable equilibrium price no longer holds. As an open system, the economy is permanently confronted with the question of the 'externalities' where its own borders become blurred. Thus, for a neoclassical economist like Arthur Pigou, the weakness of desire for distant satisfaction justifies the corrective intervention of the state. Private agents, behaving exclusively in accordance with private utility and disutility, are incapable of determining an optimal allocation of resources that takes account of the social marginal product and external effects such as pollution, health and unemployment.[32] The distinction between private product and social product is crucial and revealing. Market failures disclose an intrinsic contradiction irreducible to the faulty information so dear to Hayek.

Under the constraint of their specific object – political economy – the aporias of *Capital* foreground one way of doing science and its limits. They raise problems that could not be answered in the nineteenth century's epistemological terms of reference, and whose fecundity is obvious today. Nevertheless, the unsustainable legend of Marx as a Newtonian economist dies hard:

> [The] 'inexorable laws of physics' on which . . . Marx tried to model his laws of history, were never really there. If Newton could not predict the behaviour of three balls, could Marx predict that of three people? Any regularity in the behaviour of large assemblies of particles or people must be *statistical*, and that has quite a different philosophical taste. In retrospect we can see that the determinism of pre-quantum physics kept itself from ideological bankruptcy only by keeping the three balls of the pawnbroker apart.[33]

Contrary to these incautious assertions, Marx knew full well that social relations comprise more than three billiard balls and three bodies. For him, the economy was not a closed system, with autonomy from the political, but a sort of 'hereditary mechanics' that recounted a history inscribed in the still unsettled determinants of class struggle. That is why, in the calvary of the commodity, today's value is measured by the retroactive effect of tomorrow's prices, which are themselves conditioned, not by a purely linear economic causality, but by political and social relations. Hence the logical circularity of determination and the permanent anticipation of a future (prices) which, as in homeostatic systems, continues to act on the present (value).

Obviously, it would be ridiculous as well as anachronistic to metamorphose Marx into a pioneer of determinist chaos. On the other hand, it is legitimate to clarify his problems, declared impasses, and acknowledged experimentation by means of the subsequent development of scientific culture and the vision of the world that it helps to sketch. His interest in the atomism of Democritus and Epicurus prepares him for the questions of modern atomism. If he seems to adhere to the determinist picture, he in fact remains attached to the interplay of the future that cracks and opens out under the 'flying lance': 'The upshot is/That nowhere in the universe can be/A final edge, and no escape be found/From the endless possibility of flight.'[34]

In what respect is this Marx, so sensitive to the unruliness of the struggle, still a determinist? Contrary to what Jean-Paul Sartre, Karl Popper and

Jean-Yves Calvez claim in unison, Marx is not a representative of philosophical determinism.[35] The economic laws of *Capital*, internal and immanent, are also historical, changing and modifiable. Nature, which cannot be determined by anything other than itself, determines itself through the conflictual development of dormant powers and forces, potential capacities, and potentialities – through an interplay of interdependency and interaction from which any sovereign will or understanding is absent.

In this perspective, the social sciences fall within the sciences of evolution, where the future, subject to variable parameters, is unpredictable without being indeterminate; where historical singularities divide the future and ramify it into numerous channels. Hence a historical knowledge, more interpretative than predictive, of the glimmerings of reality. It takes little for forks and bifurcations to open up, affording a multiplicity of possible outcomes to each situation.

Introducing history into economics in the way in which Hegel temporalized logic, Marx conceptualizes a swirling economy, whose circles of circles and dizzy shapes fascinate chaos physicists today:

> In fact, economic cycles that are approximately periodic have been observed. At still higher levels of technological development, one might have a superimposition of two or three sufficiently elevated levels of development that there is a *turbulent economy with irregular variations and acutely dependent on initial conditions*. It is not unreasonable to maintain that we live in such an economy at present . . . [so that] if a more quantitative analysis is attempted, it immediately stumbles over the fact that economic cycles and other fluctuations occur against a general background of growth.[36]

In *Capital*, the conceptual organization of time precisely foregrounds this superimposition of different periodicities (labour-time distinct from production time, asynchronic cycles of production, circulation and reproduction, articulated turnovers of fixed and circulating capital). It renders intelligible the irregular variations of a turbulent, disequilibrium economy, under the retroactive effect of the temporal determination of value by prices.

Marx's dynamic economy already presents itself as an unstable system sensitive to initial conditions. It foreshadows, within its own limits, general systems theory, eco-dynamics and ecological thought. Capital revolves around itself, breaks into torsions and flexions. In these fractured forms, social relations exhibit their astonishing choreography.[37] These chaotic motifs are those of the dialectical logic of *Capital*. Like Claude Bernard's 'directing forces', its laws of tendency reinstate multiple causalities (functional, structural, reciprocal, morphological, cyclical, accidental, metonymic, symbolic), long disregarded in favour of an exclusively mechanical causality. Price curves are wrapped up in a virtual value. The equalization of market value to arrive at actual value occurs through 'constant oscillations' in the former. Unlike the abstract laws of classical physics, the law of value imposes itself as an 'inner connection' and a 'secret inner structure'. 'Order of disorder', the law of value thus governs the play of appearances from within, like a sort of strange attractor controlling market deviancy. At the singular points of bifurcations that are open to hope, strategic choices, the aim of the archer skilled at attaining possibilities in full flight, are applied.

The often obscure controversy over teleology then appears in a different light. Marx warmly greeted the fatal blow dealt to teleology in the natural sciences by Darwin. This enthusiasm is consistent with his admiration for Spinoza, whose philosophy of substance excludes any recourse to final causes, which emerge as mere human fictions once it is granted that nature has no prescribed end.

What Marx defends in Darwin is his struggle against the old religious teleology, assigning a providential destiny and end to the history of the world. But a systemic behaviour that is self-regulated, conditioned and orientated by the stability of an end-state can be described as teleological in a quite different sense. Systems theory sheds new light on an old problem. 'German science' never abandoned teleology for an exclusively mechanical causality. Kant reclaimed this teleology as a strict 'internal finality'. Schelling evoked nature as a whole organized on its own basis, and self-organizing. The Hegelian doctrine of the concept develops the *teleology of the living being*:

> Teleology is especially contrasted with *mechanism*, in which the determinateness posited in the object, being external, is essentially one in which no *self-determination* is manifested . . . It can therefore be said of the teleological activity that in it the end is the beginning, the consequent the ground, the effect the cause, that it is a becoming of what has become . . .[38]

Conceived as goal-directed, action inscribed in the immanence of real processes, what we now have is a secularized teleology, whose content is renewed by the contributions of contemporary science on self-organization, looped regulation, and homeostatic controls.

For Marx, the relation between prices and value, the role of money as a presupposition of circulation, and the role of the market as a presupposition of abstract labour are so many signs of the transition from the mechanical viewpoint to a teleological viewpoint thus construed. Capital as a subject, organic exchange, and the self-determination of value appear as moments of a totality whose strictly immanent dynamic does not allow for the survival of any exteriority.[39] Similarly, the average profit of individual capitals is not immediately determined by the surplus labour directly extracted from production, but a posteriori, by the sum of total surplus labour extorted by capital as a whole. Individual capitals thus receive a share proportional to their share in the total capital. From this standpoint, the order of capital is teleological.

In eliminating final causes (as well as the concepts of organization, totality and directionality), the classical determinist paradigm was remarkably fertile for the physical sciences. Vitalism, on the other hand, continued to be suspected of teleological nostalgia, and had a hint of mysticism about it. This temptation, inherent in the life sciences, nevertheless accounted in its fashion for the retroactive functioning and reciprocity effects of systems. Unidirectional mechanical causality does not capture adaptive behaviour that is regulated by the search for an end-state. Teleology thus re-emerges not as the accomplishment of a destiny, or as the pursuit of some externally fixed goal, but as the self-regulation immanent in the search for a stationary state. Although interpreting events in the light of this end-state is conducive to the religious phantasmagorias of the best of all possible worlds, such finality can possess a non-anthropomorphic sense. As the index of a 'dependency on the future', it betokens an effect of 'inverted causality', whose future conditions determine the orientation of the process.

Regarding capital as a dynamic social relation in chronic disequilibrium, Marx glimpsed 'the footprints of chaos on the sands of time',[40] but was not yet able to decipher them. On the track of plena and historical singularities that are inaccessible to improved calculation on its own, his science is, in the first instance, a critique of commodity forms.

If it is no longer a question of merely interpreting the world, what is at stake? Changing it, of course. Marx sometimes seems to anticipate philosophy becoming a science, as if the positive certainty of the Enlightenment was due to prevail conclusively over the obscure uncertainties of hermeneutics. His preface to *Capital* thus begins by paying homage to the natural laws of physics, but concludes by emphasizing the polemical character of knowledge as a social product: 'In the domain of political economy, free scientific inquiry does not merely meet the same enemies as in all other domains.' A prisoner of earthly constraints, this free inquiry remains, in accordance with heroic images of science and scientists, squarely on the battlefield, where it encounters 'the most violent, sordid and malignant passions of the human breast, the Furies of private interest'.[41] Scientific in a certain sense and to a certain extent, the critique of political economy is thus condemned to confronting the ideological illusions of opinion, without itself being able to escape the snares of fetishism completely. It evokes and calls for the subtleties of a future 'organic mechanism', the undulating knowledge of an ordered disorder – in short, a different way of doing science.

Notes

1. At points of bifurcation, prediction assumes a probabilistic character, whereas between points of bifurcation, we can speak of deterministic laws (see Ilya Prigogine, *Les Lois du chaos*, Flammarion, Paris 1994).
2. Pierre Simon de Laplace, *Philosophical Essay on Probabilities*, quoted in Ian Stewart, *Does God Play Dice?*, Penguin, London 1990, pp. 10–12.
3. See Claude Bernard, *Rapport sur la marche et les progrès de la physiologie générale en France* (1867); and also his *Leçons sur les phénomènes de la vie communs aux animaux et aux végétaux* (1878). The controversies over physical and physiological determinism obviously did not evade the philosophical issues. In distinguishing 'directing forces' from 'executive forces', Bernard intended to arrange a modest niche for freedom. Determinism was supposedly absolute 'in the executive phase', while free agency obtained 'in the directive phase of the phenomenon'. At the same time, Boussinesq formulated an analogous compromise by combining an intermittent freedom, exercised at the bifurcation points of unique solutions, with the strict determinism of differential equations when the system was stable (*Conciliation du véritable déterminisme mécanique avec l'existence de la vie et de la liberté morale*, 1878). In *Les Lois du chaos*, Prigogine makes some comparable suggestions.
4. Henri Poincaré, *Science and Method*, trans. Francis Maitland, Thomas Nelson & Sons, London 1914, pp. 67–8. The phrase 'small error' could give the impression that what was at stake was mere imprecision, whereas it involved configurations in which any causal variation, any development, in essence produces an effect distinct in kind from the preceding one. Pierre Duhem immediately glimpsed the significance of the problem by writing in 1906 on this precise point some magnificent pages that anticipate current theories of chaos: see *The Aim and Structure of Physical Theory*, trans. Philip P. Wiener, Princeton University Press, Princeton, NJ 1954.
5. According to wave mechanics, the spatial determination of a configuration point remains bound up with uncertainty: see Max Planck, *The Universe in the Light of Modern Physics*, trans. W.H. Johnston, Allen & Unwin, London 1937. Niels Bohr stressed that 'in quantum mechanics, we are not dealing with an arbitrary renunciation of a more detailed analysis of atomic phenomena, but with a recognition that such an analysis is *in principle* excluded': *Atomic Physics and Human Knowledge*, Wiley and Sons, New York 1958, p. 62. Planck and Bohr might seem thus to retreat to an 'essentially statistical' (or weakened probabilistic) causality. In reality, they demanded a general re-examination of the very notion of *Kausalgesetz*, believing that the principle of causation had proved much too narrow a framework to encompass the very specific laws governing individual atomic processes. The individuation of atomic processes does not subtract them from any form of law, but the law governing them can no longer be superimposed on that of classical causality. See Bohr, *Atomic Physics and Human Knowledge*, and Erwin Schrödinger, *Science and Humanism: Physics in Our Time*, Cambridge University Press, Cambridge 1951.
6. See Werner Heisenberg, *Physics and Philosophy*, Allen & Unwin, London 1959.
7. See Bohr, *Atomic Physics and Human Knowledge*; and Alexandre Kojève, *L'idée du déterminisme dans la physique classique et dans la physique moderne*, LEG, Paris 1932. Conscious of the

possible effects of discontinuity on any scientific representation, René Thom adheres to a 'metaphysics of continuity': 'My basic belief is in the continuous character of the universe and phenomena, and of the substratum of phenomena. And the essence of catastrophe theory is precisely to reduce apparent discontinuities to the manifestation of an underlying, slow evolution': *Prédire n'est pas expliquer*, Flammarion, Paris 1993.

8. In *Les Théories de la causalité* (Presses Universitaires de France, Paris 1971), Françis Halbwachs distinguishes a 'simple causality' that links a cause to an effect by a 'why' in linear fashion; a reciprocal causality and circular causality; 'a homogeneous or formal causality' that describes the 'how' internal to a class of phenomena, without it being possible to dissociate cause from effect; a 'bathygenic causality' that involves a change of level, with an underlying mechanism, invisible most of the time, accounting for the phenomenon under consideration (the microscopic level for the macroscopic level in physics; the genetic level for the cellular level in biology).

9. Edmund Husserl, *Cartesian Meditations* (1936), trans. Dorian Cairns, Nijhoff, The Hague 1960. From the beginning of the 1930s, Whitehead likewise emphasized the limits of the scientific model, and reinstated the function of philosophy. Science was at a turning point: 'The stable foundations of physics have broken up: also for the first time physiology is asserting itself as an effective body of knowledge . . . The old foundations of scientific thought are becoming unintelligible'. The scientific explosion of the seventeenth century, and the emergence of mathematics as a sovereign power, assumed an instinctive faith in a rational order of nature and access to truth via analysis of the nature of things. The principal contribution of the nineteenth century to the heritage of the modern sciences consisted in 'the invention of the method of invention' bound up with the 'new scientific information' and 'the change [in status of scientists] from amateurs to professionals'. The result was an upheaval in the field of knowledge and an orgy of scientific triumph. The crises of physics and the quantum revolution dictated a new sobriety. Novel truth-relations dictated moves towards a new representation of science:

> I would term the doctrine of these lectures, the theory of *organic mechanism*. In this theory, the molecules may blindly run in accordance with the general laws, but the molecules differ in their intrinsic characters according to the general organic plans of the situation in which they find themselves . . . an individual entity, whose own life-history is a part within the life-history of some larger, deeper, more complete pattern, is liable to have aspects of that larger pattern dominating its own being, and to experience modifications of that larger pattern reflected in itself as modifications of its own being. This is the theory of organic mechanism. (A.N. Whitehead, *Science and the Modern World*, Cambridge University Press, Cambridge1926, pp. 23, 136–7, 112, 151).

See also Whitehead, *Adventures of Ideas*, Cambridge University Press, Cambridge 1933, chapter 12.

10. Edmund Husserl, *The Crisis of European Sciences and Transcendental Phenomenology*, trans. D. Carr, Northwestern University Press, Evanston IL 1970, p. 3.

11. Ibid., pp. 6, 7, 7–9, 22, 9.

12. Ibid., p. 14.

13. Ibid., pp. 32, 31, 53, 57.

14. Ibid., pp. 66, 82.

15. Ibid., pp. 194, 197.

16. Ibid., pp. 294, 290.

17. '[C]haos tells us that even when our theory is deterministic, not all of its predictions lead to repeatable experiments': Stewart, *Does God Play Dice?*, p. 289.

18. Lucretius, *On The Nature of the Universe*, Bk Two, ll. 125–31 and Bk Six, ll. 451–6, trans. Sir Ronald Melville, Clarendon Press, Oxford 1997, pp. 39–40, 192.

19. Stephen Jay Gould, *An Urchin in the Storm*, Penguin, London 1990, p. 24. At the beginning

of the century, Bernard Brunhes identified the contradiction between evolution and the dissipation of energy as a beneficial slowing down of the latter by living organisms (a sort of reverse effect), which was nevertheless insufficient to cancel it (see his *La Dégradation de l'énergie*, Flammarion, Paris 1909).

20. Ludwig von Bertalanffy, *General Systems Theory*, Penguin, Harmondsworth 1973, pp. 165, 198–9.

21. Homeostasis and allometry are principles of retroaction and regulation: the allometric equation expresses the simplest relation between the size of a body and its metabolic processes.

22. Von Bertalanffy, *General Systems Theory*, p. 89.

23. J.D. Bernal, *Science in History*, quoted in ibid., p. 4.

24. Stewart, *Does God Play Dice?*, pp. 5, 17. If it seems reasonable to pass from the idea of a single science unified by a dominant paradigm to that of distinct systems of scientific knowledge whose isomorphism permits the circulation and exchange of concepts only with due precaution, these different ways of doing science nonetheless remain under the exacting constraint of their specific objects.

25. Ibid., p. 289.

26. Gould, *An Urchin in the Storm*, pp. 77, 25.

27. 'The classical political economy that was to be born in the eighteenth century is one of the fruits of the upheaval in conceptions of scientific knowledge that occurred in the seventeenth century': Henri Denis, *Histoire de la pensée économique*, Presses Universitaires de France, Paris 1977.

28. Philip Mirowski, 'From Mandelbrot to Chaos in Economic Theory', *Southern Economic Journal*, July 1980.

29. Benoît Mandelbrot, 'Towards a Second Stage of Indeterminism in Science', *Interdisciplinary Science Review*, vol. 12, no. 2, 1987.

30. See Ludwig von Mises, 'Economic Calculation in the Socialist Commonwealth', in F.A. von Hayek, ed., *Collectivist Economic Planning*, George Routledge and Sons, London 1935.

31. Karl Marx, *Grundrisse*, trans. Martin Nicolaus, Penguin/NLR, Harmondsworth 1973, p. 137.

32. Arthur Cecil Pigou, *Economics of Welfare*, Macmillan, London 1919–20. Conceiving the economy as an open system modifies the terms of certain debates, like the discussion of endogenous and exogenous factors in the onset and resolution of crises. In an open system, effects continually become causes, so that it no longer makes much sense to classify technological innovation or wars as endogenous or exogenous.

33. Stewart, *Does God Play Dice?*, p. 40.

34. Lucretius, *On the Nature of the Universe*, Bk One, ll. 982–5, p. 31.

35. 'As to the question of whether Marx was a determinist, for me the answer is not problematic, but categorical: it is "no", in so far as he knew determinism and rejected it' (Michel Vadée, 'Marx était-il déterministe?', *M*, no. 73, October 1994, replying to an article by Yvon Quiniou, 'Marx penseur déterministe', *M*, no. 71, June 1994).

36. David Ruelle, *Hasard et chaos*, Odile Jacob, Paris 1991, p. 110.

37. 'Turbulences, overlapping cyclones and anti-cyclones, like on the weather map. Wisps of hay tied in knots. An assembly of relations. Clouds of angles passing. Once again, the flames' dance': Michel Serres with Bruno Latour, *Conversations on Science, Culture, and Society*, trans. Roxanne Lapidus, University of Michigan Press, Ann Arbor 1995, p. 122.

38. G.W.F. Hegel, *Science of Logic*, trans. A.V. Miller, Allen & Unwin, London 1969, pp. 734, 748.

39. Gramsci acutely perceived this ambivalence of teleology: 'Might one not trace to a teleological root the expression "historic mission"? In many cases indeed this expression has acquired an equivocal and mystical meaning. But in other cases it does have a meaning, which, in the light of the Kantian conception of teleology, could be maintained and justified by the philosophy of praxis' (Antonio Gramsci, *Selections from the Prison*

Notebooks, ed. and trans. Quintin Hoare and Geoffrey Nowell Smith, Lawrence & Wishart, London 1971, p. 471).
40. Stewart, *Does God Play Dice?*, p. 113.
41. Karl Marx, *Capital*, vol. 1, trans. Ben Fowkes, Penguin/NLR, Harmondsworth 1976, p. 92.

The Torment of Matter
(Contribution to the Critique
of Political Ecology)

Productivist evil genius or ecological guardian angel? Whether we blame him for bureaucratic productivism and its catastrophes, or conveniently claim him as a Green, dicta to support the verdict can easily be found in Marx. From the early works to the 'Marginal Notes on Wagner', his *œuvre* is certainly not homogeneous. But faced with the test of the present, some trails long obstructed by the dead weight of didactic vulgarizations are once again open.

Obviously, it would be anachronistic to exonerate Marx of the Promethean illusions of his age. But it would be just as inaccurate to make him a heedless eulogist of extreme industrialization and unidirectional progress. We must not confuse the questions he posed with the answers subsequently given by social-democratic or Stalinist epigones. On this point as on others, the bureaucratic counter-revolution in the USSR marked a rupture.

The research of Vernadsky, Gause, Kasharov and Stanchisky paved the way for a pioneering ecology, which could have been integrated into the promise of a 'transformation in the way of life' in the 1920s. The dates speak for themselves. As early as 1933, Stanchisky was in prison, his venture wrecked and his ideas banished from Soviet universities. The productivist delirium of forced collectivization, the craze for accelerated industrialization, and the Stakhanovite frenzy became incompatible with any innovative ecological critique. At a time when the regime's ideologues were inventing 'the construction of socialism in one country', this would have entailed conceiving the development of the Soviet economy within the constraints of its global environment. It would have required democratic choices over priorities and the mode of growth, which were utterly incompatible with the confiscation of power and crystallization of privileges. Finally, a certain idea of the interdependence of humanity and nature, a consciousness of its dual – social and natural – determination, would have clashed head-on with the bureaucratic voluntarism that made 'man the most precious capital'.

Since the Second World War, the renaissance of critical ecology has helped to wreck belief in a redemptive end of history, when a humanity reconciled with itself will savour the plenitude of the times. If we drill through the ideological deposits to rediscover abandoned theoretical seams, contemporary lines of inquiry will make it possible to understand those of yesteryear differently.

A Human Natural Being

Marx conceived the production relation as a conjoint relation of human beings with nature and with one another, mediated by labour. The irreducibility of the living individual does not end with the socialization of nature. Thus: '[t]he first premise of all human history is, of course, the existence of living human individuals.'[1] As early as the 1844 *Manuscripts*, nature constitutes 'man's *inorganic body*'.[2] As a human natural being, '[m]an is directly a *natural being*':

> *Man* is directly a *natural being*. As a natural being and as a living natural being he is on the one hand equipped with *natural powers*, with *vital powers* . . . On the other hand, as a natural, corporeal, sensuous, objective being he is a *suffering*, conditioned and limited being, like animals and plants.[3]

The formula from *Capital* according to which labour is the father of material wealth, and nature its mother, is therefore not a chance utterance: it is in a line of strict continuity.

The young Marx's approach in fact inaugurates a long critical journey through political economy. Humanity's membership of nature – or, more precisely, its 'natural being' – means that the labour-power used up in the production process is, originally, a vital power. The natural being is a 'human natural being'. In humanity, natural determination is denied without being cancelled. Commodity fetishism does not merely transform human relations into things: it also degrades the natural into the 'animal'. The inversion of roles and values is general:

> The result is that man (the worker) feels that he is acting freely only in his animal functions – eating, drinking and procreating, or at most in his dwelling and adornment – while in his human functions he is nothing more than an animal. It is true that eating, drinking and procreating, etc., are also genuine

human functions. However, when abstracted from other aspects of human activity and turned into final and exclusive ends, they are animal.[4]

Rather than enriching humanity, the needs determined by capital are one-sided and compulsive. It is they that possess human beings, not vice versa. This negation of freedom consigns humanity not to some original or natural bestiality, but to a social brutishness that can easily prove to be a good deal more savage.

The negation of the humanity in human beings posits the restoration of their naturalness as a condition of emancipation. That is why, after having affirmed the identity of humanism and a consistent naturalism, the young Marx simply designates communism a 'fully developed naturalism'.[5]

This problematic leads on to the critique of economics as a field of fragmented rationality, of illusory autonomy. The capacity of living human beings to produce surplus labour refers, in the final analysis, to an 'extra-economic' fact: that human beings do not need to spend all their time producing the goods required for their subsistence, and that the free time at their disposal can be employed for surplus labour. Marx insists with remarkable consistency on the exuberance of living labour, whose impetuousness overflows economic calculation, and bursts the confines of its measurement.

At work as early as 1844, this logic is not suppressed with the liquidation of the 'erstwhile philosophical consciousness'. Quite the reverse.

1. Positing the principle of a radical monism, Marx affirms the primacy of the living being and cuts mind down to size, reminding it of its wretched dependency on matter. First of all eat and clothe ourselves, said Hegel. In the first instance, a human being is a walking, breathing body, adds Marx. 'In the beginning is nature', an 'objective natural being'. Everything starts from that.

2. The classical philosophical antinomies (between materialism and idealism, nature and history) are resolved in this radical monism. Marx breaks the vicious circle of fallacious oppositions. Whereas a certain contemporary ecology resurrects the quarrel between naturalism and humanism, he postulates that a consistent naturalism and humanism are one and the same thing. The formal contradiction between materialism and idealism is resolved in their unity. From the standpoint of this close unity, 'only naturalism is capable of comprehending the process of world history'. The result is an upheaval in the relation between subject and object, a transformation in the notions of subject and subjectivity, object

and objectivity: 'A being which has no object outside itself is not an objective being.'[6] Objectivity assumes the incompleteness and alterity of the . . . subject.

3. Humanity's original membership of nature – or more precisely, its 'natural being' – also implies that it is first of all 'equipped with natural powers, with vital powers'. What appears as labour-power in the production process is originally a 'vital power'. This natural determination persists in the social determination of labour-power. Whatever its pride, *Homo sapiens sapiens* remains an animal and a plant. While profit seems to arise *ex nihilo*, the theory of exploitation and surplus-value illuminates the mystery of this nothingness. But the capacity of labour-power to furnish more than is necessary for its own reproduction reveals, by the same token, an enigmatic property of that 'vital power'.

4. Humanity's irreducible 'dependence' on its initial determination is revealed in natural need, which is the starting point for the whole system of needs. It expresses the relation of incompleteness between humanity and nature, as a relation of part to whole. Human beings are incessantly reminded of their finitude by lack – and first of all by hunger, an unquenchable corporeal demand that continues to bring the mind back down to earth, forcing it to 'confess' its wretched material condition.[7]

5. What has been abased must be raised up again. Marx finds the angel ever ready to play the beast. The human being is a natural being, but a 'human natural being'. In this humanity, nature is denied without being effaced. It is cracked and differentiated without being broken. Just as being and nothingness are united in evolution, the natural and the human are united in the history that is their specific evolution. For '[n]either objective nor subjective nature is immediately present in a form adequate to the *human* being'. In its particularity, distinct from its natural universality, humanity is thus specifically determined by its historicity: history is its birth certificate. That is why, far from being opposed to nature in some insurmountable antinomy, '[h]istory is the true natural history of man'.[8]

Notwithstanding subsequent theoretical revisions, the young Marx's approach persisted. Under all forms of production, human labour-power is always conceived as the 'expression of a natural power'. In labour, man 'confronts the materials of nature as a force of nature . . . he acts upon external nature and changes it, and in this way he simultaneously changes his own nature. He develops the potentialities slumbering within nature'.[9]

The critique of a natural in-itself, unmediated by humanity, and of the alleged autonomy of consciousness *vis-à-vis* nature, is to the fore here. History is neither a chaotic set of facts (as in Schopenhauer) nor a unified meaningful structure (as in Hegel). As an articulated totality, the world is not subject to any unitary idea which confers sense on it. Anti-utopian facticity *par excellence*, ultimate reminder of natural finitude, death illustrates the impotence of any metaphysics and any theodicy. At its bourne, the particular determination of human freedom comes to an end. This is also why death remains outside the philosophical field. Much might be said of it, but little can be thought.

The path opened up by the 1844 *Manuscripts* and the *Theses on Feuerbach* led, ten years later, to the magisterial elaborations contained in the *Grundrisse*. The creation of absolute surplus-value by capital pushes the sphere of circulation to expand constantly. Production dominated by capital involves '*a constantly widening sphere of circulation*, whether the sphere itself is directly expanded or whether *more points within it are created as points of production*'. Accordingly, the 'tendency to create the *world market* is directly given in the concept of capital itself'.[10]

The production of surplus-value based on growth of the productive forces, on the other hand, requires 'the production of new consumption' – first by a 'quantitative expansion of existing consumption'; secondly by the extension of existing needs to a larger circle; thirdly by the 'production of *new* needs and [the] discovery and creation of new use values'. Hence 'exploration of all of nature in order to discover new, useful qualities in things; universal exchange of the products of all alien climates and lands; new (artificial) preparation of natural objects, by which they are given new use values'. Hence, finally:

> The exploration of the earth in all directions, to discover new things of use as well as new useful qualities of the old; such new qualities of them as raw materials etc.; the development, hence, of the natural sciences to their highest point; likewise the discovery, creation and satisfaction of new needs arising from society itself . . .[11]

Production based on capital simultaneously creates universal industry and a universal system of exploitation of natural and human properties. Nothing seems any longer to possess a higher value in itself, to be justified for its own sake outside this circuit of production and social exchange. It is thus capital alone that 'creates the bourgeois society, and the universal appropriation of nature as well as of the social bond itself by the members of society'. Hence its 'great civilizing influence'. It generates a level of social development in comparison with which all previous development looks like local and limited nature-idolatry. With capitalist production proper, 'nature becomes purely an object for humankind, purely a matter of utility; ceases to be recognized as a power for itself; and the theoretical discovery of its autonomous laws appears merely as a ruse so as to subjugate it under human needs, whether as an object of consumption or as a means of production'. The dynamic of capital 'drives beyond national barriers and prejudices'. It tears down 'all the barriers which hem in the development of the forces of production, the expansion of needs, the all-sided development of production, and the exploitation and exchange of natural and mental forces'.[12]

If capital surmounts each such obstacle '*ideally*', 'it does not follow . . . that it has *really* overcome it'. Its production 'moves in contradictions which are constantly overcome but just as constantly posited'. The universality to which it aspires comes up against the limits inherent in its own nature, rendering it, at a certain stage of its development, 'the greatest barrier to this tendency [to universality]'.[13]

This decisive text goes to the heart of the contradiction that haunts the capitalist mode of production:

1. The creation of absolute surplus-value is the key to the historical acceleration inherent in expanded reproduction and globalization of general commodity production. They are 'directly given in the concept of capital'. In 1858, such an understanding displayed an astonishing capacity for theoretical anticipation.

2. The primacy of exchange-value, in its contradictory unity with use-value, allows a distantiation (an 'uprooting') *vis-à-vis* nature and its constraints. The 'moment' of production is subordinate to that of trade, which has become the necessary mediation between forms of production that are immediately heteronomous and indirectly interdependent. The result is a metamorphosis of agriculture, which is emancipated from its natural conditions and regulation to fall under the implacable law of commodity production. It is a matter for regret that Marx did not extend this understanding to raw materials, energy and the environment. In his defence, however, let us recall the still determinant place of agriculture in the most developed countries of his time, and the limits of industrialization. *Capital* predates the appearance of modern finance imperialism.[14]

3. The production of relative surplus-value and the hunt for productivity gains not only demand a constant expansion of the sphere of production, and a headlong productivist flight, but also a correlative expansion

in the sphere of circulation and a constant metamorphosis of needs. The unlimited growth of production cannot, in fact, be absorbed solely by the quantitative expansion of consumption. It prompts the 'production of new needs and discovery and creation of new use values'. The peculiar logic of capital thus heralds the development of the so-called consumer society.

4. This vortex, in which production and circulation are mutually swept up, has as an unprecedented consequence the 'exploitation of all of nature'. The term does not have a necessarily pejorative sense here by analogy with the exploitation of human labour. It points up a fertile dynamism, pressing towards the discovery of 'new things of use', and the universalization of needs (and hence of humanity itself) beyond natural barriers and climatic particularities. The result is an insatiable curiosity, a feverish search for 'new qualities' in matter, an unprecedented development of science and social needs themselves. Even so, applying the notion of exploitation to nature is scarcely fortuitous. It marks a contradiction, and suggests paths – rapidly renounced by orthodoxy – which Walter Benjamin rediscovered at the moment when the most acute danger heightened the sense of peril: 'The new conception of labor amounts to the exploitation of nature, which with naive complacency is contrasted with the exploitation of the proletariat . . . Nature, . . . as Dietzgen puts it, "exists gratis," is a complement to the corrupted conception of labor.' These complementary conceptions of labour and nature are pitted against the 'products [of labour] benefit[ing] the workers' and the idea of a labour which, 'far from exploiting nature, is capable of delivering her of the creations which lie dormant in her womb as potentials'.[15] This is a labour that is no longer compulsory, no longer really labour, but a creative, free activity.

5. Under the lash of capital, the formation of 'a system of general exploitation of the natural and human qualities' sets in motion a process of desacralization of nature. If this desacralization inevitably takes the alienated form of disenchantment, the observation contains no trace of backward-looking nostalgia for an enchanted world. In the still religious forms of fetishism, capital merely creates the preconditions for a secularization of human existence freed of its mystical nightmares.

6. Swept along by its momentum, this Promethean enthusiasm passes directly from the demythification of nature to its 'universal appropriation', and salutes, in the integral socialization of human relations, capital's unilaterally 'civilizing influence'. Long endured as a mysterious and

tyrannical power, nature at last 'becomes purely an object for humankind, purely a matter of utility'. Even science goes through the motions of submitting to its laws the better to steal its secrets, and place them at the service of production and consumption.

7. One of the essential indices of civilization is its degree of universalization. The tendency to 'create a world market' ineluctably tears down the cramped barriers of tradition, and rends existing horizons. It seems to shake up 'national prejudices' irremediably, and to put an end to the magical deification of nature. Here once again we encounter the admiring tones of the *Communist Manifesto* confronted with capital's energy for destroying and constant revolutionizing, for liberating the expansion and diversification of needs. For human beings are not some intemporal essence, but the unity of their own needs, which determine them in a relation of exchange and mutual enrichment, with both their natural milieu and their social milieu. The quantitative and qualitative development of needs is thus an enrichment of their generic and individual personality. No trace of a Robinsonnade is to be found here; nor the least regret for an original humanity living in basic harmony with nature.

8. For all that, Marx does not lapse into a blind apologia for 'progress'. The development of needs is certainly a potential enrichment of the personality. But their determination by the constraints of capital, the alienation of labour, and commodity reification make them mutilated needs. The desacralization of labour thus foreshadows an act of emancipation, only to succumb at once to the tyranny of new fetishes and the naked disenchantment of market relations. The universalization in question is a truncated one, which constantly negates itself as it encounters the barriers of capital, now become its own limit.

These elaborations illustrate Marx's variations on the concept of nature. His early distaste for Romantic naturalism and its dubious mythologies was sufficient for numerous hasty interpreters to impute to him an unbridled will to the possession and domination of nature. Unlike vulgar and productivist socialists, however, he never believed that nature is offered 'gratis'. Thus:

> The first premise of all human history is, of course, the existence of living human individuals. Thus the first fact to be established is the organisation of these individuals and their consequent relation to the rest of nature. Of course, we cannot here go either into the actual physical nature of man, or into the natural conditions in which man finds himself – geological, orohydrographical,

climatic and so on. All historical writing must set out from these natural bases and their modification in the course of history through the action of men.[16]

Contrary to Lukács's claim, natural determination is not extinguished in historical socialization. 'Man's inorganic body', nature in the young Marx, has similarities with Spinozist substance. Moreover, Marx does not reduce the source of material wealth to labour alone. The formula according to which labour is its father, and the earth its mother, is literally adopted by Engels: 'Labour is the source of all wealth, the political economists assert. And it really is the source – next to nature, which supplies it with the material that it converts into wealth.'[17] The *Critique of the Gotha Programme* hammers the point home: 'Labour is *not the source* of all wealth. Nature is just as much the source of use-values . . . as labour. Labour is itself only the manifestation of a force of nature, human labour power.'[18]

Alfred Schmidt argues convincingly that for Marx, nature is irreducible to a social category. In *The Holy Family*, Marx and Engels wrote:

> Among the qualities inherent in *matter, motion* is the first and foremost, not only in the form of *mechanical* and *mathematical* motion, but chiefly in the form of an *impulse*, a *vital spirit, a tension* – or a '*Qual*' [torture of matter], to use a term of Jakob Böhme's. . . . In its further evolution, materialism becomes *one-sided* . . . Knowledge based upon the senses loses its poetic blossom, it passes into the abstract experience of the *geometrician. Physical* motion is sacrificed to *mechanical* or *mathematical* motion . . . Materialism takes to *misanthropy*. If it is to overcome its opponent, *misanthropic, fleshless* spiritualism, and that on the latter's own ground, materialism has to chastise its own flesh and turn *ascetic*. Thus it passes into an *intellectual entity*; but thus, too, it evolves all the consistency, regardless of consequences, characteristic of the intellect.[19]

In effect, the early works develop a non-mechanical conception of nature. Mechanics and mathematics are moments of motion, whose concrete totality involves a logic of the living being, evoked by the notions of 'impulse', 'vital spirit' and 'tension'.

Nature could not be external and subordinate to the human, any more than humanity could set itself up as a domineering subject. The opposition between subjects of right and objects of knowledge is utterly alien to the dialectical unity of subject and object. That is why it is theoretically scarcely conceivable to 'internalize' within economic calculation a nature that has first of all been abstractly and arbitrarily excluded from it. Historical development is a general process of hybridization (naturalization/humanization). 'Hybrid objects' (simultaneously natural and social), and an understanding of 'science as a social relation', thus converge with the inaugural rejection – as early as the *Theses on Feuerbach* – of passive materialism and mystical activism alike. Marx's practical categories are 'hybrids' of matter and knowledge. He, too, was never modern.[20]

The popular discourse on the crisis of Marxism confines Marx to the limited horizons of his century, affixes him to an outmoded 'epistemological base'. He is supposedly the late representative of a narrowly determinist and mechanistic philosophy. This expeditious characterization clashes foursquare with the intrinsic logic and architecture of *Capital*.

As early as *The Holy Family*, a non-mechanical conception of matter inspired by the Hegelian critique of the understanding is pitted against abstract geometrization and distanced from the 'French science of nature'. The reference to Jakob Böhme and the mystical sources of the German dialectic is by no means fortuitous. The mysteries of the capitalist economy cannot be solved exclusively on the terrain of economics.

Labour attests to the 'torment of matter', the painful irruption of life in non-life. As the creator of use-values, as useful labour, labour is one of the conditions of existence of humanity regardless of social forms: it constitutes a natural, necessary and external mediation between humankind and nature. In labour, human beings are not only objectified, but also alienated. Their bodies are literally stolen from them, and their existence is reduced to its economic function. The separation of labour from its natural conditions results in the destruction of the natural condition of humankind, living off the earth and its own labour. However, '[l]abour time itself exists as such only subjectively, only in the form of activity': 'this statement means, subjectively expressed, nothing more than that the worker's particular labour time cannot be directly exchanged for every other particular labour time'. For this general exchange to become possible, it must assume 'a form different from itself'. In a word, it must become abstract, objectified, alienated, become abstract general labour that makes individuals mere 'instruments of labour'. And then, 'time is everything, man is nothing; he is, at most, time's carcass'.[21]

Through the mediation of abstract labour, the living, individual element, which possesses a uniqueness irreducible to economic abstraction, becomes a *common measure*. It will end up rebelling for, as the necessary relation of humankind to nature, 'labour-power exists only as a capacity of the living individual'.[22] In insisting on the individuality of the living being, Marx lays the foundation for any resistance to abstract, formal universalization. The 'vital power' breaks through in labour-power reduced to the lot of a commodity, and subject to factory despotism. Economic categories are thus never self-sufficient. Use-value is denied in exchange-value. The reversal of a vital teleology into an economic teleology is reversed in its turn. The inability of circulation to produce a valorization of value sends us back to the hidden abode of production – in other words, to the secret laboratory of the body that produces surplus-value.

Michel Henry sees in this the index of a separation between 'a sphere of appearance and a secret sphere of subjectivity', in which capital itself is produced.[23] The capacity of the living human being to produce surplus-labour is, in the final analysis, an 'extra-economic' fact – 'the sole extra-economic fact', as Marx claims. This capacity to dispose of time beyond the strict constraints of reproduction thus refers to a decisive property of the living being (of nature). The exuberance of 'living labour' recalls the enigma of the natural determination: labour is the living, form-giving fire; it is the transitoriness of things, their temporality, as their formation by living time:

> Living labour must seize on these things, awaken them from the dead, change them from merely possible into real and effective use-values. Bathed in the fire of labour, appropriated as part of its organism, and infused with vital energy for the performance of the functions appropriate to their concept and to their vocation in the process, they are indeed consumed . . .[24]

In capital, *le mort saisit le vif.* In labour, life obstinately rebels against the death that awaits it.

The details in *Capital* about the death of the young milliner Mary-Ann Walkley, at first sight anecdotal, are in fact wholly appropriate. This phenomenology of life and death on the field of toil is part of the requisite demystification: 'for a full elucidation of the law of accumulation, [the worker's] condition outside the workshop must also be looked at, his condition as to food and accommodation'. For the basis of the capitalist world is the existence of the worker, and capital has a 'vampire thirst for the living blood of labour'.[25] Exploitation is, in the first instance, the subjugation and maiming of living bodies. Hence certain passages in *Capital* in the style of a martyrology of physically tortured proletarians.

The notion of 'organic exchange' or metabolism [*Stoffwechsel*] appears as early as the *Economic and Philosophical Manuscripts.* It refers to a logic of the living being that counters mechanical causality and heralds the nascent ecology. Marx arrived at it via the legacy of the German philosophy of nature conceived as a totality in motion and a unity of subject and object. Contemporaneous with the composition of *Capital,* Jacob

THE TORMENT OF MATTER

Moleschott's books (*Physiologie des Stoffwechsel in Planzen und Tieren*, 1851; *Der Kreislauf des Lebens*, 1857; *Die Einheit des Lebens*, 1864) defend a naturalistic-scientific materialism inspired by Schelling's philosophy of nature. They analyse nature as a vast process of transformation and exchange. Influenced by this tradition, Marx considered the organic exchange between humankind and nature, mediated by labour, as 'the strategic crux of social being'.[26]

In Hegel, Nature is not a determinate being in itself, but the moment of the idea alienated as universal abstraction before returning to itself in Absolute Spirit. Mediation between Logic and Spirit, it is divided into three moments, which tend to be singular: mechanics, to which the categories of space and time, matter and motion pertain; physics, with which the categories of the universal, the particular and the singular are articulated; and finally, organic physics (or the living being), which is subdivided, in increasing order of concreteness, into geological, vegetable and animal nature. According to this philosophy of Nature, mechanics and physics are moments of the concrete organicism of the living being, not the consummate model of scientific rationality. Similarly, Life pertains to the logic of the concept and, in the logic of the concept, to the moment of completion of the totality: that of the Idea.

The logic of *Capital* likewise covers the moments of production (characterized by a linear, mechanical organization of time); circulation (characterized by a circular, physical organization of time); and reproduction as a whole (characterized by an organic temporality of the living being). In the course of these determinate abstractions, capital is gradually revealed to be like a living being and, what is more, a 'vampire'. The competition between many capitals evokes the metabolism of 'organic exchange'. Thus, it is not by chance that in Volume Three we find the metaphors of the body and the circulation of blood proliferating.

This logic of the living being does not sit well with the mechanical image of the cog-wheel of progress. Breaking with the technological optimism of his time, Marx rejects the idea of a homogeneous progress advancing at an even pace in some course of history. Instead, he insists upon the 'uneven development of material production relative to e.g. artistic development'; or again, on the fact that 'relations of production develop unevenly as legal relations'. More fundamentally, he recommends that 'the concept of progress [is] not to be conceived in the usual abstractness'.[27]

Progress is not condemned as such, but for its abstractness and formalism:

all the progress of civilization, or in other words every increase in the *powers of social production . . .*, if you like, in the *productive powers of labour itself* – such as results from science, inventions, division and combination of labour, improved means of communication, creation of the world market, machinery etc. – enriches not the worker but rather *capital.* Since capital is the antithesis of the worker, this merely increases the *objective power* standing over labour.[28]

This critique of the image of progress glorified by the dominant ideology has nothing accidental about it. It contradicts the cliché of a scientistic and productivist Marx, complacently confident about the future guaranteed by the course of history: 'The starting-point of the development that gave rise both to the wage-labourer and to the capitalist was the enslavement of the worker. *The advance made consisted in a change in the form of this servitude, in the transformation of feudal exploitation into capitalist exploitation.*'[29] Subject to determination by capital, progress remains potential – conditional – progress, which continually negates itself. Thus: 'all progress in capitalist agriculture is a progress in the art, not only of robbing the worker, but of robbing the soil; all progress in increasing the fertility of the soil for a given time is a progress towards ruining the more long-lasting sources of that fertility'. More generally: '[t]he productivity of labour is also tied up with natural conditions, which are often less favourable as productivity rises . . . We thus have a contrary movement in these different spheres: progress here, regression there.'[30] This decisive passage not only asserts the ambivalence of capitalist 'progress'. It articulates it with the contradictory relation between unlimited exploitation and natural constraints. In so far as the labourer remains a natural being, and raw materials, instruments and environment remain, in the final analysis, component parts of 'organic exchange', natural determination continues to exercise constraints upon social determination. That is why Marx envisages the cancellation of the 'progress' in social productivity through the *exhaustion* of 'natural conditions' and their decreasing yield. Human beings are thus given a harsh reminder of their finitude and 'dependence' as human natural beings:

> On the one hand, there have started into life industrial and scientific forces which no epoch of former human history had ever suspected. On the other hand, there exist symptoms of *decay*, far surpassing the horrors recorded of the latter times of the Roman empire. In our day everything seems pregnant with its contrary. Machinery, gifted with the wonderful power of shortening and fructifying human labour, we behold starving and overworking it. The new-fangled sources of wealth, by some strange weird spell, are turned into sources of want. The victories of art seem bought by the loss of character. At the same pace that mankind masters nature, man seems to become enslaved to other

men or to his own infamy. Even the pure light of science seems unable to shine but on the dark background of ignorance. *All our invention and progress seem to result in endowing material forces with intellectual life, and in stultifying human life into a material force.*[31]

In his trial for productivism, Marx does not cut a docile figure in the dock. He is criticized for the ambiguity of the notion of 'productive forces'.[32] But in his work, they do not represent a unilateral factor of progress regardless of their concrete imbrication with the given mode of production. They can as easily be enriched by new knowledge and new forms of social co-operation as negated by being transformed into their opposite: destructive forces.

Exposing the progressivist ideology that undermined the nascent working-class movement, the fetishism of labour pertains to 'bourgeois formulations':

> Man's labour only becomes a source of use-values, and hence also of wealth, if his relation to nature, the primary source of all instruments and objects of labour, is one of ownership from the start, and if he treats it as belonging to him. There is every good reason for the bourgeoisie to ascribe *supernatural creative power* to labour, for when a man has no property other than his labour power it is precisely labour's dependence on nature that forces him, in all social and cultural conditions, to be the slave of other men who have taken the objective conditions of labour into their own possession.[33]

According to Ted Benton, however, 'there is a crucial hiatus between Marx's and Engels's materialist premisses in philosophy and the theory of history, on the one hand, and some of the basic concepts of their economic theory, on the other'.[34] These concepts supposedly mark a regression compared with the critical intuitions about the abstractions of progress. Natural determination tends to be absorbed into the strict social determination of economic categories. This confusion diverted Marx from an understanding of ecological crises, which was present in some of his texts.

Marx and Engels, thinkers of their time, were, in short, supposedly loath to acknowledge natural limits. In their polemic against Malthus, they maintained that, even if he were correct, a social transformation would be all the more urgent to create the social conditions for the mastery of instincts. They thus avoided pronouncing on the fundamentals of the demographic question. Engels was content strongly to recommend its reduction to a question of economics: 'Thanks to this theory, as to economics as a whole, our attention has been drawn to the productive power of the earth and of mankind; and after overcoming this economic

despair we have been made for ever secure against the fear of overpopu-
lation.' He recognized transient social limits, inherent in the 'barriers' to
itself erected by capital, but rejected 'natural limits', which were regarded
as the apologetic alibi of political economy.[35]

The reduction of the natural qualities of land to the function of 'raw
materials' likewise precluded a critical deepening of this category. They
are thus assimilated into the instrumental evolution of an agriculture
henceforth subject to the industrial production process:

> In agricultural labour-processes, by contrast with productive, transformative
> ones, human labour is not deployed to bring about an intended transformation
> in a raw material. It is, rather, primarily deployed to sustain or regulate the
> environmental conditions under which seed or stock animals grow and develop.
> There *is* a transformative moment in these labour processes, but the transfor-
> mations are brought about by naturally given organic mechanisms, not by the
> application of human labour. Agriculture and other 'eco-regulatory' labour-
> processes thus share an intentional structure which is quite different from that
> of productive, transformative labour-processes.[36]

Marx, in contrast, is said to have assimilated every labour process to the
productive-transformative model. Yet if hunting, gathering and mining
appear, at first sight, to pertain to production rather than eco-regulation,
'[i]n these practices, the place of principal and accessory raw materials is
taken by "naturally given" materials or beings, whose location and availability are relatively or absolutely impervious to intentional manipulation'.[37]
Thus, simple appropriation does not transform the natural conditions on
which it remains strongly dependent.

Finally, the Marxian conceptualization of the productive/transforma-
tive labour process remained defective – for several reasons, according to
Benton:

(a) the material nature of instruments of labour and raw materials will
    sooner or later limit their utilization-transformation according to
    human intentions;
(b) even if these instruments are the product of a previous labour-process,
    they nevertheless continue to depend – albeit indirectly – on the
    appropriation of nature;
(c) labour itself, as consumption of labour-power, remains constrained
    by natural determination.

Thus Marx underestimated the relative autonomy of naturally given, non-
manipulable conditions.[38] This criticism can doubtless draw on the productivist credo expressed in certain of Engels's texts:

The whole sphere of the conditions of life which environ man, and which have hitherto ruled man, now comes under the dominion and control of man, who for the first time becomes the real, conscious lord of Nature, because he has now become master of his own social organisation. The laws of his own social action, hitherto standing face to face with man as laws of Nature foreign to, and dominating him, will then be used with full understanding, and so mastered by him.[39]

The instrumental logic of Cartesian reason takes lyrical flight here; and Mr Hyde breaks through in Dr Jekyll.

In Search of Dissipated Energy

It would be ridiculous, relying on quotations, to pit a productivist Marx against a precociously ecological Marx. It is better to take up a position in his contradictions, and take them seriously. From this problematic location, various reading strategies clash. If he shared the prevalent scientific and technological optimism, Marx was neither a pure visionary nor a mere child of his century. The year he put the finishing touches to Volume One of *Capital*, the notion of 'ecology' appeared in Ernst Haeckel's work.

Ecology is defined today as the science of ecosystems, that is to say, of subsets, whatever their size (pool, lake, forest), exhibiting a certain functional unity between organism and biosphere. Its object emerged slowly with the development of modern science: from the 'economy of nature' proposed by Linnacus, via Fraas's studies of flora and climate, Liebig's critique of modern agriculture, and Wallace's understanding of the living organism in terms of dynamic interaction, to Haeckel's *General Morphology of Organisms*:

> In societies swept up in the conquering, predatory dynamic of capitalism, the need was expressed for a more profound understanding of the workings of nature, with the avowed aim of expanding and increasing the efficiency of its exploitation. Ecology was to be engendered by this imperative and this need. The idea that the same natural equilibrium governs the workings of society and those of nature would ground ecology, just as it had grounded economics.[40]

By ecology, Ernst Haeckel understood the science of the relations between organisms and the outside world, where the factors of the 'struggle for existence' were discernible. Born in an age which displayed confidence in science and progress, ecology would nevertheless become established, branching into plant and animal ecology, oceanography and limnology. From the 1850s and 1860s onwards, the development of theories of energy led to the quantification of its flows. It made it conceivable to determine the portion of solar energy intercepted by Earth, dissipated again in space, and the portion that plants can transform into carbons.

For Marx, expanded social reproduction (which, in the capitalist mode of production, takes the form of capital accumulation) relied on the extraordinary capacity of labour-power to furnish more energy than it consumed for its own reproduction. He did not, however, seek to elucidate this mystery.

In 1880 a Ukrainian socialist, Serge Podolinsky, published a short article in *La Revue socialiste* entitled 'Le socialisme et l'unité des forces physiques'. He posed the question directly:

> According to the theory of production formulated by Marx, and accepted by socialists, human labour, *expressed in the language of physics*, accumulates a greater quantity of energy in its products than has had to be expended for the production of the labour force. Why and how is this accumulation performed?

And by what miracle was human labour able to function for longer than the time required for its own reproduction? Podolinsky recalled the laws of the distribution of energy and the constancy of the solar flux. It was in humanity's power to 'produce certain modifications in this distribution of solar energy', for it could increase the quantity of solar energy accumulated on Earth and reduce the quantity that is dispersed, particularly by improving agriculture and the biological productivity of nature. On the basis of an energy audit of French agriculture, he demonstrated that each calorie of labour expended to cultivate an acre of artificial meadow restored, in the conditions of productivity of the period, about forty.[41]

What, then, is the reduction factor? According to the laws of thermodynamics, although the energy in the universe is constant, it tends to be dissipated. Entropy refers to the growing quantity of energy that cannot be converted into other forms of energy. The first principle of the conservation of energy, formulated virtually simultaneously by Joule, Mayer and Helmholtz in the 1840s, asserts that the quantity of energy in a closed system is constant. The second principle, anticipated by Carnot as early as 1824 (*La Puissance motrice du feu*), and formulated in 1865 by Clausius, asserts that every transformation of energy is accompanied by dissipation. Without ever being destroyed (quantitative conservation), energy thus changes form (qualitative dissipation) up to the point where it is transformed into heat, without it – conversely – being possible to transform this heat wholly into labour.[42] Podolinsky makes no distinction between open and closed systems. Nor does he broach the relation between thermodynamics and natural selection (although he polemicized against Social Darwinism). In his view, poverty was not the result of a lack of energy, but in the first instance a social phenomenon bound up with inequality and waste. However, he ventured the hypothesis of two concurrent processes: plants accumulating energy through photosynthesis, and animals dissipating it. When the former prevailed, storage occurred; when the latter prevailed, destocking. Participating in the animal process of destocking, humankind altered the balance between the production and accumulation of energy through its useful labour. Human labour-power and its exploitation were indeed the origin of surplus-value in social relations, but did not constitute its ultimate source. Human labour acted in the last instance as a simple converter of energy. The social surplus product thus originated in the destocking of plant and fossil energy.

In a letter to Marx of 8 April 1882, Podolinsky presented his initiative as 'an attempt to harmonize surplus-labour with current theories in physics'. He ventured the hypothesis of a reciprocal relation between energy and 'forms of society'. Like the neoclassical economists, he examined economic processes from a thermodynamic viewpoint. The theory of the conservation of energy indicated that human labour cannot derive something from nothing, but can only alter existing energy flows in order to adapt them to the satisfaction of needs. Living beings were thus the agents of a precarious balance between accumulation (plant) and dissipation of solar energy absorbed by the system of life:

> Here we find ourselves facing two parallel processes that together constitute what is called the *life cycle* [*Kreislauf des Lebens*]. Plants have the faculty of accumulating solar energy, whereas animals, feeding off plant substances, transform part of this accumulated energy into mechanical labour, and thus dissipate it in space. If the quantity of energy accumulated by plants were greater than that dissipated by animals, one would have a sort of energy storage, for example in the period of formation of coal, when plant life was obviously preponderant over animal life. If, on the other hand, animal life got the upper hand, energy stocks would be rapidly dissipated and plant life itself would regress to the limits fixed by the plant kingdom. There would thus be a certain equilibrium between accumulation and dissipation of energy: the energy balance-sheet on the earth's surface would correspond to a more or less stable magnitude, but the net accumulation of energy would drop to zero, or, in any case, to a much lower level than during the epoch of plant preponderance.[43]

Podolinsky thus moved towards an interpretation of labour productivity in terms of energy. Convinced that human beings had the capacity to transform one-fifth of the energy accumulated into muscular energy through the absorption of foodstuffs, he dubbed this relation the 'economic coefficient', and concluded that the human body acts as a more efficient converter of energy than the steam engine:

> Humanity is a machine that not only transforms heat and other physical forces into labour, but in addition it succeeds in realizing the reverse cycle – that is to say, transforming labour into heat and other physical forces necessary for the satisfaction of our needs – so that it is, as it were, capable of heating its own boiler through its own labour converted into heat.

As long as the energy productivity of labour was at least equal to the economic coefficient, it could accumulate a greater quantity of energy than was expended for survival. Such was the primary material basis of any society.[44]

Engels, often blamed for the missed rendezvous between the critique of political economy and ecology, enjoys a solid reputation as a hard-bitten scientist.[45] Between 1875 and 1886, *Anti-Dühring, Ludwig Feuerbach*, and the *Dialectics of Nature* sought to formalize a unity of method and content, at the price of unquestionable slides into positivism: 'If we deduce world schematism not from our minds, but only *through* our minds from the real world, if we deduce principles of being from what is, we need no philosophy for this purpose, but positive knowledge of the world and of what happens in it; what this yields is also not philosophy, but *positive science*.'[46] The *Dialectics of Nature* justly owes its notoriety to the famous formalization of the 'laws of the dialectic', deduced from nature, and from the scientific credo that all of nature now lay before humanity as a system of series and processes that had been explained and understood in broad outline. Consulted by Marx on the theses of his Ukrainian correspondent, Engels gave a categorical reply. Himself convinced that the principle of the conservation of energy dictated a revision of traditional conceptions, he nevertheless rejected energeticist proposals:

> This is how I see the Podolinsky business. His real discovery is that human labour is capable of retaining solar energy on the earth's surface and harnessing it for a longer period than would otherwise have been the case. All the economic conclusions he draws from this are wrong. . . . Podolinsky went astray *after his valuable discovery*, because he sought to find in the field of natural science fresh evidence of the rightness of socialism and *hence has confused the physical with the economic.*[47]

While he salutes the importance of the discovery, Engels thus rejected the conclusions drawn from it. The best and the worst of reasons were mingled in this verdict.

Engels's reasons were essentially of two sorts. The first reason for his distrust was directly ideological. It was aimed at religious extrapolations from the theory of entropy as to a 'thermic death sentence on the universe'. Like the updating of Malthusian discourse on natural limits and Haeckel's racial theses heralding the problematic of living space, the success of thermodynamics was in fact feeding mystical speculation. The second law in particular was exploited by a pessimistic theology. Against these visions of apocalypse, Engels devoted himself to defending the permanence of material substance. He adhered to the first principle (conservation of energy), while rejecting the second (its progressive dissipation). He regarded entropic dissipation as an appearance bound up with the provisional limits of our knowledge:

> Hence we arrive at the conclusion that in some way, which it will later be the task of scientific research to demonstrate, it must be possible for the heat radiated into space to be transformed into another form of motion, in which it can once more be stored up and become active. Thereby the chief difficulty in the way of the reconversion of extinct suns into incandescent vapour disappears.[48]

In its own time, this hypothesis of energy lost and found again was not a mere whim. It responded to the difficulty of reconciling quantitative conservation and qualitative degradation, as well as that of combining the entropic perspective of thermodynamics with the creative perspective of evolution. For a long time to come, physicists would question whether reconcentration of the enormous quantity of energy radiated in all directions was possible. Some readily conceded dissipation in a closed system, but pondered whether the material universe is in fact a closed system. William Thompson thus envisaged processes that were impossible under the dominion of the laws governing the known processes currently occurring in the material world. More generally, an intellectual elite convinced of conservation, and sceptical about dissipation, persisted in the late nineteenth century in thinking that if something was lost every day, it would return later, and that dissipated energy would be reconcentrated.[49]

Endeavouring to assimilate Joule's discoveries on the conversion of heat and Lyell's development of geology, Engels, for his part, stuck to 'Descartes' principle', according to which 'the universe always contains the same quantity of motion'. Although he preferred it to that of 'force', he greeted the notion of energy itself with reservations. On the one hand, it grasped only one aspect of the whole relation of motion: action, but not reaction. On the other, it dubiously evoked 'something external to matter'. Engels understood the transformations of energy as conversions between various forms of motion, insisting on the law of the 'quantitative equivalence of motion in all its transformations'. He perceived in it the promotion to the status of 'scientific fact' of what had hitherto been merely a philosophical hypothesis: the unity of all motion in nature. But he obstinately declined to accept Clausius's principles: 'Newtonian attraction and centrifugal force – an example of metaphysical thinking: the problem not solved but only *posed*, and this preached as the solution. – Ditto Clausius' dissipation of heat.' The law of entropy seemed to him manifestly to be a breach through which religion could make a return. This is a leitmotiv of the notes on physics in the *Dialectics of Nature*: 'The question as to what becomes of the apparently lost heat has, as it were, only been *nettement posée* since 1867 (Clausius).' Engels envisaged that much time might pass before it was solved, but 'it will be solved, just as surely as it is certain that there are no miracles in nature and that the original heat of the nebular ball is not communicated to it miraculously from outside the universe'. The cycle would not be traced before 'the possibility of the re-utilisation of the radiated heat is discovered'. Clausius proved that the universe has been created, and that the matter created can also be destroyed. However his second principle was formulated, it 'shows energy as lost, qualitatively if not quantitatively': 'The world clock has to be wound up, then it goes on running until it arrives at a state of equilibrium from which only a miracle can set it going again.'[50]

The stakes are clear. Engels rejected the second principle of thermodynamics on account of its possible theological consequences. In condemning a scientific discovery on account of the putative ideology of the scientist, he thus situated himself on the terrain of ideology. The tone becomes that of a profession of faith:

> It is an eternal cycle in which matter moves . . . a cycle in which every finite mode of existence of matter . . . is equally transient, and wherein nothing is eternal but eternally changing, eternally moving matter and the laws according to which it moves and changes. But . . . however long it may last before, in one solar system and only on *one* planet, the conditions for organic life develop; however innumerable the organic beings, too, that have to arise and pass away before animals with a brain capable of thought are developed in their midst, and for a short span of time find conditions suitable for life, only to be exterminated later without mercy – we have the certainty that matter remains

eternally the same in all its transformations, that none of its attributes can ever be lost, and therefore, also, that with the same iron necessity that it will exterminate on the earth its highest creation, the thinking mind, it must somewhere else and at another time again produce it.[51]

To the creationist temptations of thermodynamics, Engels responds with a cosmological credo on the eternity of matter. He thus doubly violates his own recommendation to accept the validity of systems of scientific knowledge only with regard to their field of application: 'Our whole official physics, chemistry, and biology are exclusively *geocentric, calculated for the earth.*'[52] This healthy principle should have allowed him to accept Clausius's laws at the level of this (closed) system, without speculating about some possible recuperation of dissipated energy at the level of a vaster (open) system whose specific laws were (as yet) unknown. The theory of evolution could have provided him with some useful arguments against the vision of a universe reduced to ashes. While William Thompson had published his sensational article on the 'universal tendency to the dissipation of mechanical energy in nature' in 1852, according to Darwin the law of evolution implied a better adaptation to surrounding conditions in the race for life. In their turn, physicists proved reluctant about this increase in vital forces contrary to the laws of thermodynamics. Some sought to salvage the compatibility of the two approaches by explaining the dynamic of life through the conversion of dissipated energy into mental energy.

In part, the contradiction attaches to a reduction of the social to the physical – a danger to which Engels was alert. Theories of open systems, information and organization have subsequently provided some elements of an answer to what was, at the time, a disconcerting contradiction between thermodynamic entropy and the creativity of evolution. Natural selection selects social instincts on the same basis as other instincts, favouring an increase in rationality and privileging behaviour that involves solidarity and assistance:

A further effect of natural selection supervenes to thwart another, primitive effect that is more widely recognized since it merges with natural selection itself, which had previously presided through the elimination of those less fit for the improvement of the species. One thus passes from elimination to protection, from extermination to assistance. In its own historical evolution, natural selection thus ends up cancelling itself.

This is what Patrick Tort calls the 'reversive effect', or 'reversal without rupture' in the logic of selection as extended to humankind.[53]

More generally, evolution neutralizes, or partially corrects, thermodynamic tendencies. The 'reversive effect' thus makes it possible to face up to the ecological consequences of the accelerated consumption of non-renewable forms of energy, without being resigned to the inevitability, at our level of space and time, of thermic death. Plant photosynthesis supposedly uses only about one per cent of solar energy; the industrial system wastes more than 50 per cent of the energy consumed; and only between 10 and 20 per cent of energy expenditure is justified in relation to the goals being pursued. One can therefore imagine that a 'reversive effect' bound up with the development of information (knowledge and social co-operation) might make it possible to counteract entropic tendencies through greater efficiency in energy consumption, the use of renewable energy, and energy expenditure that proceeds more slowly than the reconstitution of supplies.

Physical Labour, Social Labour

Engels's second critique is of an epistemological nature. In direct line with his polemic against the vulgar materialism of Büchner or Moleschott, he criticizes Podolinsky for having wanted to 'find . . . fresh evidence of the rightness of socialism'. What is at stake, and what is decided, in the class struggle is never reducible to a quarrel between experts, whether they intervene to plead the innocence of technology or to ground an ecological politics scientifically. If, on several occasions, Marx proclaimed that it was the vocation of the social and natural sciences to merge into a single historical science, this tendency was a protracted process. For now, Engels refused to 'confuse the physical with the economic', to confuse the notions of 'forces' specific to each of them, to 'apply the theory of natural science to society'. Excluding the possibility of measuring manual labour and capital in 'joules', he combated the then fashionable energeticist dogmatism (which inspired Walras and the neoclassical economists), and the reduction of individuals to mere converters of energy.

Podolinsky's error thus consisted in an illegitimate translation of economics into the language of physics. His ingenious hypothesis bore the brunt of the refutation of vulgar materialism and its 'pretension to apply the theory of natural science to society'. In *Anti-Dühring* and his notes for an 'Anti-Büchner' (*Dialectics of Nature*), Engels in fact constantly came up against the confusion of physics and economics. Opening up the path to the concept of energy and thermodynamics, the notion of work made its appearance in physics in the 1820s to conceptualize the economy of machines.[54] It articulated physics and economics theoretically, seeking to measure the production and consumption of men and machines in order to optimize their use. It thus revived the problematic of a vast universal mechanics present in the Leibnizian argument on live forces.

In 1778, Coulomb's dissertation on *La Force des hommes* sought to 'determine the amount of activity that men can furnish through their daily work, depending on the different ways in which they use their strength'.[55] In a process of labour rationalization, what was involved was measuring the ordinary capacities of the average man doing an 'honest day's work', rather than exceptional performances. The social measurement of value progressively imposing its law by the abstraction of work (Coulomb's average) was thus reduced to its physical quantification, the professed concern being to maximize the result/fatigue relation that expresses the economic efficiency of labour. Indeed, *physical* fatigue – not the social power of labour – was what was supposedly being remunerated. Unless human beings were conceived as machines for converting energy, however, only the market metabolism determining the 'normal' working day made it possible to evaluate it.

The early nineteenth century's infatuation with physics came to the aid of classical economics. Searching for a common measure for different types of labour, Navier referred to it as a mechanical currency allowing measurement of a machine's capacity regardless of the content of the work it performed. Coriolis, on the other hand, began by distinguishing between physical formalism and economic significance. In the first place, labour was the 'correct measure of the action of machines and the output in useful labour that of their efficiency'. Used to refer to both effort and the result of effort, the term 'labour' remained ambiguous. If labour was preserved physically, part of it was lost economically inasmuch as it deteriorated in the course of realizing its productive effect.[56] Here we approach the limits of the physico-economic project of engineers based on the Enlightenment's mechanical knowledge. Confronted with capitalist development, their concepts are stretched to their maximum potential, calling for the advent of the new thermodynamics:

> The treatment of the question of time is at the heart of this transition from the old to the new physics via economics ... To conceptualize the transformation of live force into labour is, in fact, to conceive an irreversible process, an energy transformation that cannot, even theoretically, occur without loss. A category of physico-economic, and not specifically physical, thought, the concept of labour presupposes the arrow of time that was soon conceptualized by thermodynamics.[57]

In proposing to determine the 'quantity of action' as a physiologico-economic magnitude by labour-effort, Coulomb mixed mechanistic materialism with biblical symbolism. Marx, by contrast, planted himself in the social contradiction of the quantification of labour-power, which is both necessary from the standpoint of abstract labour and impossible from that of concrete labour. Despite formal similarities with Navier's mechanical currency as 'expenditure of human power', his labour theory of value shifted ground and ruptured the equivalence between physics and economics, by integrating the energy dimension into the social dimension. If the goal – discovering a common measure between heterogeneous commodities and the commodity of labour-power – remained the same, the critique of political economy was constructed against the conflation of physics and economics. Engels's vigilance when he was confronted with what seemed to him to be a theoretical relapse and regression is then easier to understand.

That is also why, unlike Marx, he insisted on the distance between natural science and human 'science', social determination and natural determination. For him, the critique of political economy fixes its orientation towards history and culture. In so far as the sciences of complexity (systems theory and chaos theory) introduce a new holistic paradigm of scientific knowledge, the controversy might seem outdated. But in the nineteenth century, intransigent defence of the specific relationship of a science to its object was part of a necessary struggle to free scientific procedures from their ideological envelope. Contrary to received ideas, then, we must do justice to Engels when he rejects the fusion of economics and physics in the name of an energeticist fad, or when he inveighs against the Spencerian extension of the 'struggle for existence' to the human sciences. His discourse is still inscribed in the great divide between the natural sciences and the human or social sciences (he speaks of political economy as a 'historical science'), which dominated classification of the sciences at the time. The 'sciences of nature' (mechanics, physics, chemistry) had as their object 'investigation of [the] different forms of motion'. Mechanics deals exclusively with quantities, while physics and chemistry tackle the conversion of quantity into quality. The organism is 'certainly the *higher unity which within itself unites mechanics, physics, and chemistry into a whole*, where the trinity can no longer be separated'.[58] The problem is precisely to understand how complex systems of knowledge, such as the critique of political economy, ecology and history, articulate the knowledge that classificatory reason separates. Judging from his works, Engels seems more inclined than Marx to respect the autonomy of the hard, positive sciences. After his retirement from business and installation in London, he declared that he 'went through as complete as possible a "moulting" . . . in mathematics and the

natural sciences'.[59] Against all idealist temptations, he nevertheless maintained that scientific knowledge, including mathematics, is rooted in
history through the mediation of human needs.

In sum, Engels criticized Podolinsky for wanting to translate economics
into the language of physics, and for once again confusing the physical
notion of labour (as 'measure of motion') with its social concept. This
critique echoed Marx's polemics (particularly in the *Critique of the Gotha
Programme*) against the simplistic idealization of the manual labourer, on
the pretext that his labour possessed the miraculous faculty of producing
wealth as a quasi-natural, rather than as a social, product. The link
between the labour performed and a just social distribution of goods
could lead to an illusory socialism of distribution, as opposed to tackling
the roots of exploitation.

Engels reacted all the more sharply in that thermodynamics, transposed without precaution on to the economic field, can threaten the
labour theory of value. He looked to maintain the distinction between
economic labour and mechanical labour. Having registered the formal
affinities between theories of energy and value theory, he clearly understood that any confusion of the two could lead, by extension of the law
of entropy, to the idea of a negative surplus-value, of a net loss threaten-
ing the very coherence of the relation of exploitation as an answer to
the mystery of profit and accumulation. Quantifying social exchange in
terms of energy can lead to the conclusion that the labourer consumes
more energy than he is capable of restoring through productive labour.
Were that to be the case, the mystery of accumulation would remain
intact, unless it is conceived as sheer physical deduction and destocking
of natural reserves. Refuting Podolinsky's hypotheses by a *reductio ad
absurdum*, Engels emphasized that human beings cannot produce more
energy through their labour than is contained in its consumption, their
energy output being necessarily inferior to 1. Economic activity can result
in production that is superior in energy terms to the human labour
expended – not by virtue of any particular human energy productivity,
but through the *social* exploitation of labour-power, the deduction and
conversion of other energy resources, whose appropriation and allocation are socially mediated through the organization of labour.

In the specific context of a historically determinate mode of production, Podolinksy's hypothesis thus does not threaten the labour theory of
value. Accumulated capital is indeed the crystallization of unpaid labour.
This approach makes it possible to illuminate the springs and dynamics
of social conflict, to distinguish antagonistic interests, and to take sides.

In the light of the principles of thermodynamics, Engels categorically refuses any energy theory of value whereby calculation in energy terms provides a scientific basis for the labour theory of value. But one determination does not cancel the other. They operate at different levels. The validity of the theory of value in the context of specific relations of production does not negate the interest of energy audits on a different time-scale.

Conflictual class relations shape the underlying contradiction between storing and destocking of energy, with human labour playing the role of converter. Just as the abolition of class exploitation does not mechanically betoken the end of sexual oppression, so the end of class conflict is insufficient to resolve that contradiction. In other words, ecological devastation does not derive exclusively from the chaos of capitalist competition. Bureaucratic ecocide is capable of disasters that are at least equivalent. If radical ecology is necessarily anti-capitalist, what is necessary is not necessarily sufficient.

These criticisms diverted Engels from fruitful hypotheses. And this is all the more regrettable in that he himself succeeded in extracting an ecological problematic. In a passage from his famous text on 'The Part Played by Labour in the Transition from Ape to Man', he wrote these significant words:

> Let us not . . . flatter ourselves overmuch on account of our human victories over nature. For each such victory nature takes its revenge on us . . . Thus at every step we are reminded that we by no means rule over nature like a conqueror over a foreign people, like someone standing outside nature – but that we, with flesh, blood and brain, belong to nature, and exist in its midst, and that all our mastery of it consists in the fact that we have the advantage over all other creatures of being able to learn its laws and apply them correctly . . . But the more this progresses the more will men not only feel but also know their oneness with nature, and the more impossible will become the senseless and unnatural idea of a contrast between mind and matter, man and nature, soul and body . . .[60]

Engels expressed an acute sense of the ambiguities of progress: 'each advance in organic evolution is at the same time a regression, fixing *one-sided* evolution and excluding the possibility of evolution in many other directions'.[61] Progress is thus not measurable in terms of advances and regressions, on the uniform axis of the passage of time, but rather in comparative terms, of possibilities temporarily abandoned and potentialities forever lost. Development is never mere quantitative increase. It is also always a choice.

Consequently, progress cannot be reduced to a weighing up of immediate gains, discounting medium- and long-term losses. Yet capital con-
summates the one-sided rationality of previous modes of production,
which 'aimed merely at achieving the most immediately and directly
useful effect of labour. The further consequences, which appear only
later and become effective through gradual repetition and accumulation,
were totally neglected.' Indeed: '[i]n relation to nature, as to society, the
present mode of production is predominantly concerned *only about the
immediate, the most tangible result*'.[62] Posing the question of a 'common
measure' between 'immediate results' and 'further consequences', Engels
raised the thorny problem of the commensurability of needs and wealth
between generations. Energy calculation on its own cannot provide a
response. On the other hand, it can furnish some valuable indications.[63]

In the 1920s, the idea of a dual thermodynamic process (accumulation
and dissipation of solar energy), structurally characterizing an ecological
community, became established. At the time, Soviet researchers were in
the forefront of the emergent thinking. In 1926, Vladimir Vernadsky
studied life on earth as a totality in *The Biosphere*. As a result of this book,
he is considered the father of global ecology. As early as 1930, it was
reviewed by Raymond Queneau in *La Critique sociale*. Queneau stressed
'the importance of the quantitative study of life in its indissoluble relations with the planet's chemical phenomena'.[64] Vernadsky stressed a disturbing degradation, to which the only solution was a change in food
models and energy sources. Numerous research and teaching institutions
devoted to ecology opened in the young Soviet republic.

In 1930, the fourth Pan-Russian congress of zoologists registered 'the
extraordinary importance of ecology, not only for its applications, but
also from a theoretical viewpoint'. It demanded that ecology be granted
a place in the colleges of agronomy and pedagogy. In 1931, D.N.
Kasharov published a manual on the ecology of communities, *Environment and Communities*, and provided the impetus behind the appearance
of the *Journal of Ecology and Biocoenology*. Gause's works on populations
and ecological niches studied 'the dynamic and evolutionary structure of
living communities, in the myriad strategies of their various populations:
attack, defence, evasion, flight, co-operation, symbiosis, parasitism, etc.'.[65]
If the works of Vernadsky and Gause were known and won recognition
almost immediately outside the Soviet Union, the same was not true of
those of the Ukrainian Vladimir Stanchisky. He started from the fact that
the quantity of living matter in the biosphere is directly dependent on
the quantity of solar energy transformed by autotrophic plants, which
constituted the economic base of the living world. The biosphere was

itself composed of subsystems (biocoenoses). The dynamic equilibrium of each biocoenosis was explicable by the existence of definite, proportionate relations between autotrophic and heterotrophic components, herbivores and carnivores, hosts and parasites, which had practically been ignored up until then. In an article written in 1931, Stanchisky presented a mathematical model describing the annual energy balance-sheet of a theoretical biocoenosis.[66] His intellectual venture was over by 1933. A victim of bureaucratic persecution, he was sacked and then imprisoned, and his ideas were kept under wraps for the duration.

This pioneering ecology in the country of the soviets, whose richness was revealed by the 1931 International Congress of the History of Science and Technology, could have played its part in the 'transformation of the way of life' promised in the 1920s. But it did not escape the bureaucratic reaction – for understandable reasons.

- A consistent ecology would not have been compatible with the productivist delirium of forced collectivization and accelerated industrialization, or with the Stakhanovite frenzy of the 1930s.
- It would have made it necessary to conceive the development of the Soviet economy within the constraints of its global environment, at the very moment when the regime's ideologues were inventing 'the construction of socialism in one country'.
- It would have necessitated a genuine democratic choice about priorities and modes of development, in outright contradiction with the crystallization of bureaucratic privileges and confiscation of power.
- Finally, a certain idea of the interdependence between humankind and nature, and a consciousness of its dual determination, social and natural, would have clashed head-on with the bureaucratic voluntarism that had just decreed 'man' to be 'the most precious capital'.

The nascent Soviet ecology thus experienced the fate of the new art, attempts to surmount the divide between country and city, and avant-garde pedagogy. After the bureaucratic Thermidor, there was no longer any question of changing life, only of 'catching up with and overtaking' the achievements of capitalism itself, according to the competitive maxim of industrial and sporting productivism.

Some perceptive readers had, however, glimpsed the perspectives opened up. In his presentation of Vernadsky, Queneau insists on the differences between biological time and astronomical time. In another issue of *La Critique sociale*, the Austrian economist Julius Dickmann sought to identify a relation between 'the exhaustion of natural resources' and the brutality of the social upheavals that were shaking the planet at the time. He went so far as to suggest that socialism would be not the result of an impetuous development of the productive forces but, rather, a necessity dictated by the 'contraction of the pool of natural resources' squandered by capital. He highlighted the relations of reproduction as a whole: 'It is precisely because the viewpoint of reproduction is neglected that people are completely mistaken about the capacity for growth of the productive forces.'[67] According to Dickmann, what characterized the current phase of capitalism was less its obstacles to the growth of the productive forces than to their 'reckless' expansion, to the detriment of their 'permanent conditions of reproduction', which undermined the very conditions of existence of the human race. That was why it would be appropriate to treat the possibility of a continuous increase in the productivity of labour with a good deal of scepticism.

The Ecological Irrationalities of Economic Reason

Proposed by Raymond Lindemann in the middle of the Second World War, the notion of ecosystem (as a unit of energy exchanges in nature) inaugurates the age of modern ecology. The link between the globalization of the economy and the emergence of a 'world ecology' is obvious. The constitution of a global space of production is in fact the vehicle of the ecological unification of the world. This tendency aided a growing awareness of the risks of rupture in biochemical processes, climate change and demographic developments:

> Human civilization involves a series of cyclically interdependent processes, most of which have a built-in tendency to grow, except one – the natural, irreplaceable, absolutely essential resources represented by the earth's minerals and the ecosphere. A clash between the propensity of man-dependent sectors of the cycle to grow and the intractable limits of the natural sector of the cycle is inevitable.[68]

In a context marked by recession, the Six Day War, and soaring petrol prices, the 1970s were characterized by growing ecological consciousness and appeals from such rebel outsiders as René Dumont, as well as the official alert from the Club of Rome. Our civilizations remembered that they were mortal.

Today, it is clear that the model of growth and consumption of the richest countries is not generalizable to the whole planet. The production of a food calorie consumes eight to ten fossil calories in these countries. At this rhythm, the risk of 'ecological crisis' becomes practically unavoidable: 'When the temporalities of human history take precedence over the temporalities of ecological history, thresholds are definitively crossed in the non-reproduction of eco-systems or towards their increasing entropy.'[69]

Even so, the debate is not over. Studies of the biosphere tend to demonstrate the vulnerability of its balances and its fine-tuning. Thus, liberation from natural constraints (which we proudly claim as our freedom) risks being paid for with an irremediable disturbance. But even so, must we take the idea of a limited flow of material and available energy as established?

According to the hypothesis that the expenditure of animal and human energy destocks solar energy accumulated in the form of plant or fossil energy, industrial options, demographic evolution, and the damage that has already been done are accelerating this depletion at a breathtaking rate. Nevertheless, it does not follow from this that we are threatened with an absolute energy shortage. On the scale of the human species, the energy flow received is enough to respond to expanding consumption until the extinction of the solar fires or the Big Crunch. The forecast shortage is thus relative. Provided that energy is also 'stored time', what is at issue is indeed a problem of temporalities. The danger consists not in a sharp breakdown, but in the exhaustion of certain forms of energy, which are depleted much more quickly than they are renewed. This is certainly sufficiently serious for us to consider energy policies, and the priority given to renewable forms of energy, as so many issues of the greatest importance. But it is not a sufficient reason for succumbing to crepuscular ideologies and Robinsonnades. It is always possible that humanity will discover other energy sources, and identify different modes of consumption.

Meanwhile, a conscious and agreed self-limitation of consumption is perfectly conceivable (and indispensable). The problem lies, obviously, in the consciousness and consent. No consistent ecological option could accept the perpetuation of inequalities, where the sacrifice demanded of some would offset and exonerate the licence granted to others.

Going beyond electoral episodes, the ecological debate has the merit of brutally posing some basic societal questions. Some of the replies are not only critical of capitalist or bureaucratic productivism, but bluntly anti-productivist and naturalistic. Their logic could result in lamenting that the progress of medicine, by eradicating such and such an illness, distorts natural demographic regulation. For, after all, it is nowhere decreed that humanity has an interest or a wish to live ever longer in ever greater numbers. In such penitent returns to a nurturant nature, religiosity is sometimes close at hand.

This is not a new pitfall. In 1850, in the *Neue Rheinische Zeitung*, Marx reviewed Daumer's book *Die Religion des neuen Weltalters*, which typified a nostalgic medievalism. Nature and woman, wrote Daumer, 'are the really divine, as distinct from the *human* and *man*'. The submission of the human to the natural, of the masculine to the feminine, was 'the genuine, the only true meekness and self-externalisation, the highest, nay, the only virtue and piety'. This inversion of perspective had some legitimacy. Modern science and technology had imposed themselves in tandem with the exclusion of women from the public sphere and knowledge. Their procedures and categories were impregnated with a masculine monopoly. Marx nevertheless detected in Daumer accents of a reactionary naturalism. His reply was stinging:

> Herr Daumer flees before the historical tragedy that is threatening him too closely to alleged nature, i.e. to a stupid rustic idyll. . . . He tries to restore the old pre-Christian natural religion in a modernised form. . . . He tries to console women for their civil destitution by making them the object of a rhetorical cult which is as empty as it would fain be mysterious. Thus he seeks to comfort them by telling them that marriage puts an end to their talents through their having to take care of the children . . ., that they retain the ability to suckle babes even until the age of sixty . . ., and so on. Herr Daumer calls this 'the devotion of the male to the female'.

Thus emerged the hidden face of a naturalist ecology ready to resurrect the pagan cults of nature, and to contest the emancipation of women in the name of the natural functions of maternity.[70]

Ecological events pertain to the *longue durée*, even the very long *durée*. There is no obvious common measure between their temporal register and that of social exchange in a determinate mode of production. Discouraged by this incommensurability, Jean-Baptiste Say consigned natural resources to a beyond that remained inaccessible to economic rationality. For him, natural resources were inexhaustible, and that was why they could be freely drawn upon. Incapable of being multiplied or exhausted, they thereby lay outside the field of economic science. This reasoning is manifestly circular. If natural resources are gratis, it is because they are not scarce. If they are not scarce, they are inexhaustible. *Ergo*: so-called natural resources are not economic wealth.

Say presupposes an 'economy' defined as the management of scarce resources. Yet his notion of what is gratis is an economic category (bound up with the exchange of limited goods), exported without due care to the 'extra-economic' sphere (according to his own conception) of natural wealth. Can what is deemed economically free, within the limits of a determinate mode of production, remain free on another spatio-temporal scale?

The quarrel between ecology and economics (as understood by classical and neoclassical economics at least) refers to the divorce between two heterogeneous temporalities: an economic temporality punctuated by the reproduction of capital and labour-power; and an ecological temporality governed by the storing and consumption of energy, which is also stored time. Recommending to Engels that he read a book by Nikolaus Fraas, a 'Darwinian before Darwin', Marx stressed the long-term ravages of certain forms of agriculture (desertification). He returned to the subject in Volume Two of *Capital*, insisting on the disarticulation between the *longue durée* of forestry and that of the market economy: 'The long production time (which includes a relatively slight amount of working time), and the consequent length of the turnover period, makes forest culture a line of business unsuited to private and hence to capitalist production, the latter being fundamentally a private operation'.[71]

Without arriving at a calculation in terms of energy flows, and without taking into account the energy cost of fertilizers, Liebig sought a promising transition from an exploitative agriculture to a restorative agriculture as early as 1840. It was becoming possible to determine the portion of solar energy transformed into carbon by plants. At the beginning of the 1880s, Podolinsky endeavoured to introduce the problem of energy into the critique of political economy. In his 1885 brochure *On Energy Stocks and their Use in the Service of Humanity*, Clausius raised alarm over the 'coal question', emphasizing that human beings were behaving like extravagant heirs when they consumed stocks immediately, without a thought for tomorrow.

However, the discoveries concerning the transformation and dissipation of energy had scarcely any immediate repercussions on economic theory. The obstacles to the 'critique of political ecology' were considerable, the expansion of capitalism favouring the division of labour and the ascendancy of instrumental reason. Unfortunately, the diffusion of Marxism conduced to the same result. The majority of orthodox theoreticians in the Second International did indeed conceive nature as a windfall offered gratis to a sovereign humanity. Positivism and scientism required it.

Capital lives from day to day, on instant gratification, and is reckless of tomorrow. Only the bureaucracy can compete with its short-sighted egotism. Against its pretension to immortality, political ecology returns a pitiless verdict. Faced with the received ideas of commodity fetishism, it represents a formidably effective anti-myth. Thus, the market does not satisfy needs, but demand. Money is not reality, but its fantastic represen-tation. Collective utility is not reducible to a sum of individual utilities. The economic does not necessarily involve the social, and today's profits are not necessarily tomorrow's jobs. Finally, the sphere of the market economy is not equivalent to the biosphere: it is only ever a small bubble whose partial rationality operates to the detriment of the whole.[72]

Market reductionism operates as if real and monetary flows, being exchanged against one another, obeyed the same logic. It would then suffice to internalize the social cost of ecological expenditure to restore the harmony of market regulation. This sort of solution assumes the compatibility of market optimization and reproduction of the natural environment on the basis of a common measure – energy as the common denominator of all goods, regardless of whether they belong to the market sphere. Any material good could then be expressed by the quan-tity of energy it contains.[73]

The problem, objects René Passet, is that:

the economic sphere and the biosphere have never operated according to the same logic and, while this fact could be ignored as long as the first did not threaten the existence of the second, this is no longer the case today. Into natural rhythms occurring and harmonizing over millennia (and sometimes millions of years), economic management introduces the rupture of brief maximizations, a rupture whose effects will only be felt in generations to come.[74]

This critique invokes a non-market measurement, foreign to an auto-matic economy bereft of political conscience and social scruple. It would involve reintegrating the economy into a totality of ecological and social determinants. Without completely replacing monetary information, cri-teria such as material and energy audits would furnish information ignored by market rationality. The insertion of the economic into an eco-social whole would thus require 'a normative management under duress': in other words, a civic choice determined by needs and inscribed in a long time-frame should prevail over market automatism.

For some, the notion of 'normative management', like the temporal dimension involved in the confused notions of durable or sustainable development, resurrects the spectre of bureaucratic planning. This is one of the main liberal complaints against radical ecology. Opposing the effects of blind competition, it supposedly reawakens the old fantasies of totalitarian planning. Normative ecological management does indeed runs the same risks as socialist planning. It can assume the form of a new technocratic authoritarianism, or of a self-managing, democratic planning that remains to be invented.

René Passet's logic is impeccable. Long-range forecasting, an economy of non-renewable resources, the definition of a new mode of consumption – these involve an upheaval in the mode of production itself, and are incompatible with the dictatorship of short-term market criteria. Only a radical political democracy could introduce a medium term between spheres that lack any direct common measure. Such is indeed the nub of the question: 'The fundamental fact emphasized by ecological economics against orthodox economics is nothing other than *incommensurability*. We are incapable of assigning to the goods we consume monetary values that take account of forecast ecological costs.'[75] Often only visible in the long – or even very long – term, these costs would have to be assessed by generations to which we cannot attribute our priorities or assessment criteria.

How are they to be reckoned today, with the aid of measuring instruments that themselves vary with time? Some bluntly conclude that 'commensurability does not exist'.[76] Indeed, it cannot exist on the cramped terrain of 'political economy'. Exposing the historical relativity of its rationality, the ecological critique of political economy reinforces its social critique. Thus, Georgescu-Roegen does not merely highlight the partiality of the classical economic viewpoint: he reveals its incapacity (already exposed by Henryk Grossmann) to think in terms other than equilibrium. This impotence bears the stamp of a dated mechanistic epistemology to which analytical economics, conceiving the economic process as a closed system, remains wedded.[77]

The construction of the market economy as a closed system in fact involves a separation between factors internal and 'external' to the object thus defined. 'Externalities' are then treated as shortcomings in comparison with the ideal of perfect competition and the environment as a particular instance of them. The monetary evaluation of environmental goods and services expresses their 'true value' only inadequately. It is in fact impossible to establish such an evaluation 'correctly' without passing via production and exchange, via abstract labour, which grounds the social commensurability of commodities. 'Welfare economics' for Pigou already proposed taxes that no longer represented a market measure, but an estimate of social costs by the state, and hence a directly political judgement. For him, tax is equivalent to a price-signal which, when taken into account, is thought to restore perfect competition. These attempts at internalization take account of forms of pollution approximately converted into market criteria, rather than of the lasting damage inflicted on the biosphere on another time-scale. As against the outlines of a social economics, competitive rationality and the search for maximum profit constantly push firms to externalize costs and internalize benefits. The extra-economic establishment of an 'environmental norm' thus remains an uncertain operation – a matter, in the last instance, of democratic arbitration.[78]

The Miserable Measure of All Wealth

One can combine distinct rationalities without confusing them, as does André Gorz when he provides an environmental foundation for the tendency for the rate of profit to fall. The decreasing yield or relative exhaustion of natural resources can indirectly bring about a rise in the organic composition of capital. But the environmental effect does not supervene without mediations in the specific tendencies of capitalist accumulation. It is expressed through the intermediary of its specific conceptual categories (organic composition, surplus-value, average profit rate), in whose formation energy audits cannot intervene directly. The incommensurability between economic and ecological levels is not absolute. It is nevertheless real enough in the framework of the capitalist mode of production, and therewith attests to its historical limits.

The passage from the *Grundrisse* that we have already quoted at length illustrates Marx's farsightedness on this point. As capitalist production develops, as the organization of labour becomes complex, as labour itself incorporates more accumulated social knowledge, 'the creation of real wealth comes to depend less on ... the direct labour time spent on ... production, but depends rather on the general state of science and on the progress of technology': 'Real wealth manifests itself, rather ... in the monstrous disproportion between the labour time applied, and its product, as well as in the qualitative imbalance between labour, reduced to a pure abstraction, and the power of the production process it superintends.' The living worker becomes more and more alien to work itself. He is expelled 'to the side of the production process instead of being its chief actor'.[79]

The explosive consequence of this transformation is that the measure of all wealth (and consequently the common measure of the whole social relation connecting isolated and fragmented labours) becomes derisory and 'miserable':

The theft of alien labour time, on which the present wealth is based, appears a miserable foundation in face of this new one, created by large-scale industry itself. As soon as labour has ceased to be the great well-spring of wealth, labour time ceases to be its measure, and hence exchange value [must cease to be the measure] of use value. . . . On the one side, then, [capital] calls to life all the powers of science and of nature, as of social combination and social intercourse, in order to make the creation of wealth independent (relatively) of the labour time employed on it. On the other side, it wants to use labour time as the measuring rod for the giant social forces thereby created, and to confine them within the limits required to maintain the already created value as value.[80]

This 'miserable foundation' carries within it a general dissolution of human beings' relations with one another, as well as their relation with nature.

That is where we are! Massive structural unemployment, general under-employment and marginality, and social exclusion on a planetary scale are devastating testimony to the inadequacy of labour-time as a measure of 'giant social forces'. The ecological critique adds to this diagnosis that labour-time appears *a fortiori* too 'miserable' a unit of measurement to govern exchanges between humankind and nature, or to establish a bond of solidarity between generations. In other words, if it is dangerous purely and simply to conflate the particular temporalities and criteria of economics and ecology, to amalgamate their interdependent but specific fields of knowledge, they are closely akin in their common critique of incommensurability, in their understanding of the general crisis of measurement by labour-time, and in their demand for a different regulation of social relations. If a non-formalistic, organic, logical link can be established between the metamorphoses of work, the accelerated squandering of labour-power, and the parameters of the planetary ecological crisis, this encounter can become the starting point for a new theoretical alliance.

According to Joan Martinez-Allier, in highlighting the limits of political economy, the ecological critique reveals two flaws in Marxian theory.

1. The ecological viewpoint challenges the notion of productive forces, but proposes no new theories of economic value.[81] It provides a more adequate definition of the concept of productive forces, by supplying it with a clear empirical reference. An uncritical acceptance of the notion of productive forces supposedly fed the chimera of a communism in which the trump card of abundance abolished the contradictions of distribution and the problem of non-monetary information. In fact, Marx

scarcely defined these productive forces. Proceeding by determinants, most of the time he made do with a descriptive inventory, comprising raw materials, technical equipment and the organization of labour, as well as the development of scientific knowledge and the institutional conditions of its production. Like social classes or productive labour, the productive forces thus possess neither the same content, nor the same significance, when they are considered in the *broad sense*, common to different modes of production, and in the sense *specific to the capitalist mode of production*. Productive from the standpoint of capital, they can prove destructive for the future of humanity.

As one passes from the most abstract determinants (natural and technical) to the most concrete (including the social relations of labour, the production and application of scientific knowledge, etc.), the contradiction no longer concerns only the productive forces and relations of production. It is inscribed at the very heart of the productive forces, and brings into play notions such as growth and development. There is in fact such a thing as 'growth without development', when the quantitative craze of instrumental reason negates its social ends.

The idea of a transformation of forces that are potentially productive into forces that are actually destructive, in another temporal register, is unquestionably more fertile than the mechanistic schema of the opposition between the development of the productive forces and the relations of production fettering them. It opens the way to a critical elaboration of the very concept of progress, as 'differentiated progress' (according to a formula of Ernst Bloch's), as opposed to the one-sided abstractness of the illusions of progress.

2. In looking to calculation in energy terms for a 'contribution to critiques of theories of value', Martinez-Allier partially contradicts his own profession of faith: 'Those of us who are ecological economists are not proposing a new theory of value: we are challenging commensurability, whether in terms of price, calories, or production time.'[82] While he affirms the incommensurability of temporalities that are heterogeneous with respect to one another, he does not draw the logical consequences. The labour theory of value does not claim to found a new economic science. It remains a negative knowledge, a critique of political economy immanent to its specific object (the economy as a separate sphere), destined to disappear with its supersession. By contrast, the ecological critique, in terms of material or energy audits, requires a change of terrain, a supersession of political economy from the standpoint of the

biosphere. It is situated on a different logical plane, and pertains to a different rationality from value theory, which it cannot invalidate at its own level of determination.

Gaia emerges from the recovery of the living being in its organic unity as a seductive, poetic hypothesis. Humankind is no longer detached from its environment, but integrated into it as part of the whole. Hence the enveloping and tender Gaia. But a goddess remains a goddess. The professed refusal of anthropocentrism inadvertently sustains an anthropomorphic re-enchantment of nature, which has once again become a woman, mysterious and maternal as befits it. An underhand religiosity worms its way into the diction, troubling the father of Gaia himself – James Lovelock – who maintains that he 'in no way see[s] Gaia as a sentient being, a surrogate God':

> When I wrote the first book on Gaia I had no inkling that it would be taken as a religious book. Although I thought the subject was mainly science, there was no doubt that many of its readers found otherwise. Two-thirds of the letters received, and still coming in, are about the meaning of Gaia in the context of religious faith.[83]

His disquiet seems all the more justified in that denunciation of human freedom as a disruptive element in the ecosystem can lead to unexpected 'new alliances', the premisses of which include authoritarian birth control, forced sterilization, the rejection of procreative technologies (not on account of their market logic, but in the name of nature as opposed to artifice), campaigns against contraception and the right to abortion in the name of the naturalness of maternal functions. More generally, it is no accident that a radical naturalism can lead on to an anti-humanist 'realism': 'Our humanist concerns about the poor of the inner cities or the Third World, and our near-obscene obsession with death, suffering, and pain as if these were evil in themselves – these thoughts divert the mind from our gross and excessive domination of the natural world.'[84]

A change of direction and priorities. The last act of the Copernican and Darwinian revolution. The end of the great Promethean dream. Expelled from the centre of the universe towards its infinite frontiers, humanity is no longer the secret of man, or its password. Its poverty, epidemics, sufferings and death are merely the incidents and misadventures of a vast equilibrium, without understanding or volition, which had already caused Leibniz to take fright. It took the deranged egotism, pretensions and hubris of the human animal for it to grant itself such precedence at the heart of Gaia, which is equally receptive to all her creatures. According to this logic, nature ends up taking everything that is thrown at it. If its relation to human beings always passes through the mediation of their relations with one another, the declared primacy of nature over humankind remains the alibi of very precise social interests. In its fashion, the Rio Earth Summit illustrated the implication of ecology in the social relations of exploitation, dependency and domination.

Pregnant with various possible lines of development, it is not some new open sesame. 'Eco-development' calls for a conscious, collective mastery of science, technology, and decisions about production and consumption; and hence opting for radical democracy and a global approach that does not reduce ecology to the role of simple crutch for a deformed progress. 'Ecocracy', by contrast, could take the shape of a reformist, technocratic environmentalism that perpetuates the demobilization of citizens stripped of their responsibility, on the pretext of expertise. Ecology does not vouchsafe a response to the question: who decides and by what criteria? When the scientific community is divided, competence cannot stake an exclusive claim to settle controversies.

Ecology does not escape politics. The alternative between naturalistic ecology and political ecology involves basic questions, where falsely obvious answers risk getting in the way. The very term ecology tends to substantiate the idea of a well-defined, established scientific discipline. Yet Popper would have ranged it, by the same token as Marxism or psychoanalysis, among the irrefutable sciences, and hence among the non-sciences. The specific object of what declares itself to be ecology is certainly difficult to identify. Either it tends to define it; and then it flirts with various partial disciplines that are already established. Or it takes on the role of knowledge of an organic totality, and tends to be erected into meta-history, meta-science and metaphysics simultaneously.

Between the two, ecology should define its relations with economics and existing theories more modestly. From the standpoint of long time, Jean-Paul Deléage regards energy systems as weighty determinants, common to different productive systems. An energy system can subordinate various modes of production to itself. Thus, nuclear energy supposedly determines the dynamic of capitalist market economies, just as it did the bureaucratic command economies.[85] Fostered by historical works on long time, this hypothesis shares the same paradoxical consequences. Authors like Pierre Chaunu or Emmanuel Le Roy Ladurie, who criticize Marx for his economic determinism, lapse into a climatological, geological, demographic ultra-determinism, to the point of reducing events to accidental incidents, about which there is nothing more to be said in historical terms. Proposing long-range periodizations, in which the differences between modes of production are erased and the social choices that are *essential on a human scale* are blurred, an ultra-determinism of ecology and energy would have similar consequences. The critique of political economy would then be engulfed in the bottomless and shoreless ocean of general ecology. If the energy choice of the windmill or the nuclear power station has irreversibly set humanity off for several centuries on an adventure it no longer controls, specifically political responsibilities, which are strongly conditioned and dreadfully limited, are henceforth exercised only at the margin. What we are left with is moderating the immediate effects of a predatory growth and praying to avert ultimate catastrophe.

Alternatively, we can turn the suggestion round and demand, in the name of a critique of political ecology, more free responsibility and responsible freedom for humankind as 'human natural beings'.

Affirming the identity of humanism and consistent naturalism, the young Marx conceived communism as 'fully developed naturalism':

> *Communism* is the *positive* supersession of *private property* as *human self-estrangement,* and hence the true *appropriation* of the *human* essence through and for man; it is the complete restoration of man to himself as a *social,* i.e. human, being, a restoration which has become conscious and which takes place within the entire wealth of previous periods of development. This communism, as fully developed naturalism, equals humanism, and as fully developed humanism equals naturalism; it is the *genuine* resolution of the conflict between man and nature, and between man and man, the true resolution of the conflict between existence and being, between objectification and self-affirmation, between freedom and necessity, between individual and species. It is the solution of the riddle of history and knows itself to be the solution.[86]

This historical supersession of philosophical antinomies involves an audacious conclusion about scientific knowledge:

> *Society* is therefore the perfected unity in essence of man with nature, the true resurrection of nature, the realized naturalism of man and the realized humanism of nature ... History itself is a *real* part of *natural history* and of nature's becoming man. Natural science will in time subsume the science of man just as the science of man will subsume natural science: there will be *one* science.[87]

Anyone who is attached to the idea of a scientistic Marx, promoting the positive sciences of nature into an absolute model of scientificity, cannot but be confounded by this perspective. It upsets the great classificatory frontier separating experimental sciences and human sciences, natural and social sciences, nomographic and idiographic sciences. The idea of an integral socialization of nature, of 'nature's becoming man', suggests that natural science is set to merge into human science. Yet this is not what Marx says. Instead, he indicates a third way, involving a mutual envelopment in which natural science 'subsumes' the human science that 'subsumes' it. This epistemological credo expresses a cognitive strategy. Whereas an inconsistent naturalism subordinates the human sciences to a natural meta-science, 'consistent naturalism' makes socialized nature the genuine object of knowledge.

Marx returned to the subject a few months later in *The German Ideology*:

> We know only a *single science*, the *science of history*. One can look at history from two sides and divide it into the history of nature and the history of men. The two sides are, however, inseparable; the history of nature and the history of men are dependent on each other so long as men exist.

This idea forms part of the break with Feuerbach: 'the nature that preceded human history . . . no longer exists anywhere (except perhaps on a few Australian coral islands of recent origin)'.[88] It is now humanized and historicized by human labour. If, by nature, is understood not only the Earth and its immediate environment, but the universe, the hypothesis is factually false. But it remains pertinent in a perspective inspired by Vico and his 'new science', where the part of nature that can be known is precisely the nature that has been humanized by labour, the nature where praxis has stamped its recognizable mark.

From this point of view, there could be no definitive separation between nature and society. Against his own reiterated assertion that social determination does not cancel natural determination, Marx thus seems to consider that no natural limit exists outside of social limits. That, at least, is the interpretation of Lukács who, at a determinate stage of historical development, reduced nature to a social category in *History and Class Consciousness*. Assuming the active share of idealism, such an interpretation subjectivizes nature by reducing it to its self-organization under the impact of historical praxis. Conversely, the positivist orthodoxy of Stalinized Marxism reduced historical praxis to a mere aspect of objective natural relations.

This dual temptation reflects an unsurmounted problem in which the uncertain relation between nature and history masks the equally problematic relation between what is dead and what is alive, between nature as a universal form of 'non-living matter in motion' (Engels) and history as the dynamic self-organization of living matter. In the epistemological context of his epoch, Marx did not ground the unity of science, as

Carnap would later do, on the reducibility of all scientific reasoning to its physical model. Nor was he resigned to the great divide between physical and historical sciences. He located himself in a real contradiction. The unity of science could not be proclaimed arbitrarily. It was itself a historical process of mediated unification of subject and object.

Thus construed, the prospect of 'one science' is rather confirmed by the deep epistemological tendencies of our times: a convergence of the life sciences and social sciences thanks to information and systems theory; exchanges and confrontations between economic subsystems open to ecological systems (ecosystems and the biosphere); structural and hermeneutic dialectics; the development of the sciences of form.[89]

The critique of political economy does not profess to found a general science of the economy. It does claim to be a critique of capital. By this token, it could not exhaust the constraints of natural determinations and have done with the torment of matter.

For its part, the critique of political ecology cannot in all rigour absorb the critique of political economy. On the other hand, the two of them can form a productive relationship starting from different temporalities. Their dialogue is then strictly incompatible with the canons of 'methodological individualism', since the private calculation of interest in principle ignores universalist, altruistic relations between generations: 'Based exclusively on exchanges between agents whose conduct reposes on a postulated rationality and utilitarian calculation, economic theory cannot deal with the inter-generational allocation of finite resources.'[90]

In the absence of monetary commensurability, this relation must be conceptualized in ethical, aesthetic, or quite simply political terms. When it comes to the use and distribution of finite resources, it is in fact impossible to separate economic efficiency from social criteria. Thus we rediscover ways of thinking that do not recognize the idea of the economy *tout court*, a naked economy, or raw market logic. We once again receive the message of Coupé de l'Oise, member of the 1793 Convention, speaking of a 'social economy', or the historian E.P. Thompson referring to a 'moral economy'.[91] Social or moral, this economy cannot be measured in exclusively monetary or energy terms. It endeavours to hold the two ends of the chain through democratic choice. If illusions about an integral socialization of nature, as of an integral naturalization of humankind, are renounced, the contradiction emerges in its stubborn reality.

It is impossible to elude the torment of matter. Knowledge introduces a principle of evolution (information, self-organization, negative entropy) that is in conflict with sombre thermodynamic forecasts. The question is whether, in the evolution of species, the 'reversive effect' of collective consciousness is capable of resolving the antinomy between economics and ecology. In other words, whether a *moral and ultimately political econ-omy* can harmonize the rhythms of renewal of natural resources, official levies, and environmental self-purification, while awaiting the discovery of novel renewable forms of energy, or the means of recycling the great mass of energy that is dissipated unproductively.

In Volume Three of *Capital*, Marx wrote:

> The real wealth of society and the possibility of a constant expansion of its reproduction process does not depend on the length of surplus labour but rather on its productivity and on the more or less plentiful conditions of production in which it is performed. The realm of freedom really begins only where labour determined by necessity and external expediency ends; it lies by its very nature beyond the sphere of material production proper. Just as the savage must wrestle with nature to satisfy his needs, to maintain and reproduce his life, so must civilized man, and he must do so in all forms of society and under all possible modes of production. This realm of natural necessity expands with his development, because his needs do too; but the productive forces to satisfy these expand at the same time. Freedom, in this sphere, can consist only in this, that socialized man, the associated producers, govern the human metabolism with nature in a rational way, bringing it under their collective control instead of being dominated by it as a blind power; accomplishing it with the least expenditure of energy and in conditions most worthy and appropriate for their human nature. But this always remains a realm of necessity. The true realm of freedom, the development of human powers as an end in itself, begins beyond it, though it can only flourish with this realm of necessity as its basis. The reduction of the working day is the basic prerequisite.[92]

Attributing to Marx a prophetic conception of the end of history in the realm of freedom is a commonplace. This banality rests on a trivial interpretation of 'necessity' confused with fatality. We have seen that for Marx, necessity is not the positive certainty of the future, but a negative perception of the innermost limits of capital. The critique of political ecology can reinforce that of political economy. Capital can survive and decay in the iron circle of these limits, without succeeding in transgressing them. It cannot change scale and dimension without convulsions, because it is incapable of yielding the new social measures that make it possible to harmonize human beings' relations with one another and with nature.

The market exploitation of labour-power, and the reduction of social relations to the common measure of social labour-time, reveals the loss of functionality prophesied in the *Grundrisse* in endemic mass unemployment, new insecurities and marginality, and crises of overproduction, but also in the growing incommensurability of social activities that are irreducible to abstract labour. This was already true of works of art, whose market value is determined speculatively, outside any conceivable relation with the labour-time socially necessary for their production. It is more and more the case with intellectual and scientific works. 'To the degree that science is directly applied to production, '[l]abour no longer appears so much to be included within the production process; rather, the human being comes to relate more as watchman and regulator to the production process itself.' The 'product of mental labour – science – always stands far below its value, because the labour-time needed to reproduce it has no relation at all to the labour-time required for its original production'.[93] Political economy is indeed stymied by the incommensurability of heterogeneous temporalities (the cycle of capital and natural cycles, temporal relations between generations), and by the 'miserable' character of its own forms of measurement – something that is confirmed by its ecological critique.

Notes

1. Karl Marx and Frederick Engels, 'The German Ideology', in Marx and Engels, *Collected Works*, vol. 5, Lawrence & Wishart, London 1976, p. 31.
2. Karl Marx, 'Economic and Philosophical Manuscripts', in Marx, *Early Writings*, trans. Rodney Livingstone and Gregor Benton, Penguin/NLR, Harmondsworth 1975, p. 328.
3. Ibid., p. 389.
4. Ibid., p. 327.
5. Ibid., p. 348.
6. Ibid., pp. 389–90.
7. See Dionys Mascolo, *Le Communisme: révolution et communication ou la dialectique des valeurs et des besoins*, Gallimard, Paris 1953; Agnes Heller, *The Theory of Need in Marx*, Allison & Busby, London 1976; and Philippe Bayer, 'Besoin radical et contradiction radicale chez Marx', photocopied text, Poitiers 1992.
8. Marx, 'Economic and Philosophical Manuscripts', p. 391.
9. Karl Marx, *Capital*, vol. 1, trans. Ben Fowkes, Penguin/NLR, Harmondsworth 1976, p. 283.
10. Karl Marx, *Grundrisse*, trans. Martin Nicolaus, Penguin/NLR, Harmondsworth 1973, pp. 407–8.
11. Ibid., pp. 408–9.
12. Ibid., pp. 409–10.
13. Ibid., p. 410.
14. See Ted Benton, 'Marxism and Natural Limits', *New Left Review*, no. 178, November/ December 1989.

15. Walter Benjamin, 'Theses on the Philosophy of History', XI, in Benjamin, *Illuminations*, trans. Harry Zohn, Fontana, London 1973, p. 261.
16. Marx and Engels, 'The German Ideology', p. 31.
17. Frederick Engels, *Dialectics of Nature*, trans. Clemens Dutt, Progress Publishers, Moscow 1954, p. 170. This attitude disposed Marx to receive Liebig's ecological intuitions favourably. While rejecting the notion of decreasing yields, he was sensitive to the distinction between a despoiling agriculture and a restorative agriculture, as well as to the opposition between large-scale rural exploitation and small-scale agriculture, large urban areas and dispersed urbanization.
18. Karl Marx, 'Critique of the Gotha Programme', in Marx, *The First International and After*, Penguin/NLR, Harmondsworth 1974, p. 341.
19. Karl Marx and Frederick Engels, 'The Holy Family', in Marx and Engels, *Collected Works*, vol. 4, Lawrence & Wishart, London 1975, p. 128. See Alfred Schmidt, *The Concept of Nature in Marx*, trans. Ben Fowkes, New Left Books, London 1971.
20. See on this subject, Bruno Latour, *We Have Never Been Modern*, trans. Catherine Porter, Harvester Wheatsheaf, London 1993. See also the articles of Bruno Latour and Catherine Larrère in *Écologie et politique*, no. 5, 1991.
21. Marx, *Grundrisse*, p. 171; Karl Marx, 'The Poverty of Philosophy', in Marx and Engels, *Collected Works*, vol. 6, Lawrence & Wishart, London 1976, p. 127.
22. Marx, *Capital*, vol. 1, p. 274.
23. Michel Henry, *Marx, une philosophie de la réalité*, vol. 1, Gallimard, Paris 1991, p. 241.
24. Marx, *Grundrisse*, p. 361; *Capital*, vol. 1, p. 289.
25. Ibid., pp. 367, 807.
26. André Tosel, 'Philosophie de la praxis et ontologie de l'être social', in *Idéologie, symbolique, ontologie*, Éditions du CNRS, Paris 1987, p. 96. Alfred Schmidt stresses that this concept of organic exchange in Marx introduces a new understanding of the relations between humanity and nature, alien to the cultural horizons of the Enlightenment (*The Concept of Nature in Marx*).
27. Marx, *Grundrisse*, p. 109.
28. Ibid., p. 308.
29. Marx, *Capital*, vol. 1, p. 875.
30. Ibid., Karl Marx, *Capital*, vol. 3, trans. David Fernbach, Penguin/NLR, Harmondsworth 1981, pp. 369, 638.
31. Karl Marx, 'Speech at the Anniversary of the *People's Paper*', in Marx, *Surveys from Exile*, Penguin/NLR, Harmondsworth 1973, pp. 298–9; emphasis added.
32. 'The ecological vision of the conditions of human existence', writes Martinez-Allier, 'could easily have been connected with Marxism through an adequate definition of the productive forces. But this is what Marx did not do': Joan Martinez-Allier, *La Ecologia y la economia*, Editions Efe, Mexico 1991.
33. Marx, 'Critique of the Gotha Programme', p. 341.
34. Benton, 'Marxism and Natural Limits', p. 55.
35. Frederick Engels, 'Outlines of a Critique of Political Economy', in Marx & Engels, *Collected Works*, vol. 3, Lawrence and Wishart, London 1975, p. 339. In the debate on demography, mediatized by world population conferences, the discussion of Malthus retains an undeniable relevance. See on this subject the collective volume *Les Spectres de Malthus*, ORSTOM-EDI-CEPED, Paris 1991; C. Reboul, *Monsieur le Capital and Madame La Terre*, EDI–INRA, Paris 1989; Hervé Le Bras, *Les Limites de la planète*, Flammarion, Paris 1991; and Michel Husson, *Sommes-nous trop?*, Textuel, Paris 2000.
36. Benton, 'Marxism and Natural Limits', p. 67.
37. Ibid., p. 69.
38. See ibid., pp. 71–2.
39. Frederick Engels, 'Socialism: Utopian and Scientific', in Karl Marx and Engels, *Selected Works*, vol. 3, Progress Publishers, Moscow 1970, p. 149.
40. Jean-Paul Deléage, *Histoire de l'écologie*, La Découverte, Paris 1991, p. 58.

41. See Serge Podolinsky, 'Le socialisme et l'unité des forces physiques', *La Revue socialiste*, 1880.
42. See Bernard Brunhes, *La Dégradation de l'énergie*, Flammarion, Paris 1909.
43. Serge Podolinsky, 'Menschliche Arbeit und Einheit der Kraft', *Die Neue Zeit*, 1883. On Podolinsky, in addition to Jean-Paul Deléage, see Joan Martinez-Allier and Klaus Schlupman, *La ecologia y la economia*; Martinez-Allier, 'La confluence dans l'éco-socialisme', in 'L'idée du socialisme a-t-elle un avenir?', *Actuel Marx*, Presses Universitaires de France, Paris 1991; and Tiziano Bagarolo, 'Encore sur marxisme et écologie', *Quatrième Internationale*, May 1992.
44. See Martinez-Allier and Schlupman, *La ecologia y la economia*, pp. 66–72.
45. In *Marxism and the Status of Philosophy* (trans. Kate Soper and Martin Ryle, Harvester, Brighton 1980), Georges Labica has judiciously drawn attention to the received ideas and clichés that make it difficult to get at the human and theoretical personality of Engels, which was nevertheless decisive and endearing. He insists on the risks inherent in any 'Marxist' research that downgrades Engels's contribution.
46. Frederick Engels, *Anti-Dühring*, trans. Emile Burns, Progress Publishers, Moscow 1947, p. 51.
47. Frederick Engels, letter to Marx of 19 December 1882, Marx and Engels, *Collected Works*, vol. 46, Lawrence & Wishart, London 1992, pp. 410–12. On Engels and the conservation of energy, see Éric Alliez and Isabelle Stengers's fascinating article, 'Énergie et valeur: le problème de la conservation de l'énergie chez Engels et Marx', seminar at the Collège international de philosophie, 1984.
48. Engels, *Dialectics of Nature*, pp. 38–9. The conservation of energy posed as many problems as it resolved:

> For some (this was true of Poincaré and Duhem), the conservation of energy (there is something that remains constant) was a principle of investigation whose truth had no other measure than fertility. For others (like Ostwald), the qualitative difference between the various forms of energy was irreducible and mechanics was thus simply one science among others. For yet others, the conservation of energy implied the possibility of reducing all forms of energy to a single form: mechanical energy. Located in its historical context, the discovery of the conservation of energy thus did not seem conducive to a model that other sciences must emulate. Rather, it constituted a problem that each of the protagonists latched onto and used as a basis for their own conception of science. Engels was one of these protagonists. (Alliez and Stengers, 'Énergie et valeur')

49. Bruhnes, *La Dégradation de l'énergie*, pp. 370–4.
50. Engels, *Dialectics of Nature*, pp. 245, 273, 284–5.
51. Ibid., p. 39.
52. Ibid., p. 238.
53. Patrick Tort, *La Raison classificatoire*, Aubier, Paris 1991, pp. 406–8.
54. The notion of labour was officially introduced into physics by Coriolis in 1829. On this point, see François Vatin's valuable study *Le Travail: économie et physique*, Presses Universitaires de France, Paris 1993.
55. Coulomb, quoted in ibid., p. 41.
56. Ibid., p. 78. Coriolis perceived the economic degradation of labour at a time when physics was still ignorant of the law of entropy. He was thus prompted to establish a valuable distinction between labour itself and the 'labour's capacity for producing', which heralds the decisive distinction between labour and labour-power.
57. Ibid., p. 91.
58. Frederick Engels, letter of 30 May 1873 to Marx, in Marx and Engels, *Selected Correspondence*, Progress Publishers, Moscow 1975, p. 264; *Dialectics of Nature*, p. 250.
59. Engels, *Anti-Dühring*, p. 16.
60. Engels, *Dialectics of Nature*, pp. 180–1.

61. Ibid., p. 307.
62. Ibid., pp. 182–3.
63. In the name of the energy imperative, Wilhelm Ostwald attempted to redefine progress as an increase in the availability of energy, the replacement of human energy by other, alternative energies, and augmentation of thermodynamic yield in the use of energy.
64. Raymond Queneau, *La Critique sociale*, reprinted Éditions de la Différence, Paris 1983.
65. Deléage, *Histoire de l'écologie*, pp. 166–72.
66. See Jean Batou, 'Révolution russe et écologie (1917–1934)', *XXᵉ Siècle*, no. 35, 1992.
67. Julius Dickmann, 'La véritable limite de la production capitaliste', *La Critique sociale*, no. 9, September 1933. Queneau's review of Vernadsky appeared in the third issue of the same journal in October 1931.
68. Barry Commoner, *The Closing Circle*, Jonathan Cape, London 1972, p. 122.
69. Deléage, *Histoire de l'écologie*, p. 250.
70. Karl Marx, review of Daumer's *Die Religion des neuen Weltalters*, in Marx and Engels, *Collected Works*, vol. 10, Lawrence & Wishart, London 1978, pp. 244–5. The affinities between green fundamentalism and religion are not circumstantial. André Gorz cites a symptomatic text by Jürgen Dahl, 'The Last Illusion', from *Die Zeit*, 23 November 1990:

> It would be presumptuous to dare to predict where the weak point might lie from which the . . . collapse will develop. The world . . . is the victim of the opulence which has been enjoyed at its expense but, in falling victim to that opulence, . . . it also renews itself and will regain a balance, though with fewer inhabitants, less beauty and less wealth. As a necessary consequence of the opulence, there will be great poverty. . . . Only poverty can save us . . . enforced renunciation. And since no one will choose the state of poverty of his own free will while such wealth is easily to hand . . . that poverty will have to come about as ineluctable fate' (quoted in Gorz, *Capitalism, Socialism, Ecology*, trans. Chris Turner, Verso, London and New York 1994, p. 14 n. 3)

To the ambiguities of a romantic ecology, Gorz counterposes an ecological rationality consisting in the maximum satisfaction of material needs with as low a quantity of goods as possible, of high use-value and durability, and thus in mobilizing a minimum of labour, capital and natural resources.
71. Karl Marx, *Capital*, vol. 2, trans. David Fernbach, Penguin/NLR, Harmondsworth 1978, pp. 321–2.
72.
> Whereas nature maximizes stocks (biomass) starting from a given flow (solar radiation), the economy maximizes commodity flows while exhausting non-commodity natural stocks, whose diminution does not appear in any economic balance-sheet and thus exercises no corrective action over these flows. Whereas nature obeys a logic of interdependence and circularity, economic decision-making is based on a simple linear causal relation, comparing the variation of an expenditure and a result. Now, according to this logic, every element introduced into the economic sphere spreads into the various compartments of the biosphere, and continues to perform its work there'. René Passet, 'Limites de la régulation marchande', *Le Monde diplomatique*, June 1992.

73. René Passet, *L'économique et le vivant*, Payot, Paris 1979.
74. René Passet, 'Régulation marchande au temps des pollutions globales', in 'Le Monde est-il un marché?', *Actuel Marx*, Presses Universitaires de France, Paris 1991.
75. Martinez-Allier and Schlupman, *La ecologia y la economia*, p. 222.
76. See William Kapp, *Les Coûts sociaux dans l'économie de marché*, Flammarion, Paris 1976.
77. '[N]o other conception could be further from a correct interpretation of facts. Even if only the physical facet of the economic process is taken into consideration, this process is not circular, but *unidirectional*. As far as this facet alone is concerned, the economic process consists of a continuous transformation of low entropy into high entropy, that is, into *irrevocable waste*': Nicholas Georgescu-Roegen, *The Entropy Law and the Economic Process*, Harvard University Press, Cambridge, MA 1971, p. 281.

360   THE ORDER OF DISORDER

78. See Kapp, *Les Coûts sociaux dans l'économie de marché*.
79. Marx, *Grundrisse*, pp. 704–5.
80. Ibid., pp. 705–6.
81. Martinez-Allier, 'La confluence dans l'éco-socialisme'.
82. Martinez-Allier and Schlupman, *La ecologia y la economia*, p. 180.
83. James Lovelock, *The Ages of Gaia*, Oxford University Press, Oxford 1988, pp. 204, 191.
84. Ibid., p. 198.
85. See Jean-Paul Deléage, in collaboration with Jean-Claude Debeir and Daniel Hémery, *Les Servitudes de la puissance: une histoire de l'énergie*, Flammarion, Paris 1987.
86. Marx, 'Economic and Philosophical Manuscripts', p. 348.
87. Ibid., pp. 349–50, 355.
88. Marx and Engels, 'The German Ideology', pp. 28–9, 40; emphasis added.
89. This analogy between economics and the 'life sciences' (rather than the mechanical sciences) has been highlighted since the beginning of the last century by researchers as varied as Boulding, Daly, Passet, Lovelock and Mandelbrot.
90. Martinez-Allier and Schlupman, *La ecologia y la economia*, p. 209.
91. In *The Theory of Need in Marx* (Allison & Busby, London 1978), Agnes Heller likewise stresses that the category of needs transgresses the limits of political economy, precisely in that, through the historicity of needs, it sutures the natural and the social. Consequently, it functions as a kind of category critical of the horizons of political economy and transitional towards the horizon of communism.
92. Marx, *Capital*, vol. 3, pp. 958–9.
93. Marx, *Grundrisse*, p. 705; *Theories of Surplus-Value*, vol. 1, trans. Emile Burns, Lawrence & Wishart, London n.d., p. 343.

Bibliography

General

Althusser, Louis, *Essays in Self-Criticism*, trans. Grahame Lock, New Left Books, London 1976.

—— *Essays on Ideology*, trans. Ben Brewster and Grahame Lock, Verso, London 1984.

—— *For Marx*, trans. Ben Brewster, Verso, London and New York 1990.

—— *The Future Lasts a Long Time and The Facts*, trans. Richard Veasey, Chatto & Windus, London 1993.

—— and Balibar, Étienne, *Reading Capital*, trans. Ben Brewster, New Left Books, London 1970.

—— and Balibar, Étienne, Establet, Roger, Macherey, Pierre and Rancière, Jacques, *Lire le Capital*, Presses Universitaires de France, Paris 1996.

Anderson, Perry, *Considerations on Western Marxism*, New Left Books, London 1976.

—— 'The Antinomies of Antonio Gramsci', *New Left Review*, no. 100, November 1976/January 1977.

—— *In the Tracks of Historical Materialism*, Verso, London 1983.

Andréani, Tony, *De la société à l'histoire*, 2 vols, Klincksieck, Paris 1989.

Arendt, Hannah, *The Origins of Totalitarianism*, Harcourt, Brace, New York 1951.

Aron, Raymond, *Marxismes imaginaires*, Gallimard, Paris 1970.

Assoun, Paul-Laurent and Raulet, Gérard, *Marxisme et théorie critique*, Payot, Paris 1978.

Bailly, Jean-Christophe, *Adieu*, Éditions de l'Aube, Paris 1993.

—— and Nancy, Jean-Luc, *La Comparution*, Christian Bourgois, Paris 1992.

Balibar, Étienne, *Écrits pour Althusser*, La Découverte, Paris 1991.

—— *The Philosophy of Marx*, trans. Chris Turner, Verso, London and New York 1995.

Bataille, Georges, *The Accursed Share*, 2 vols, trans. Robert Hurley, Zone Books, New York 1991–93.

Bhaskar, Roy, *Dialectic*, Verso, London and New York 1993.

Bidet, Jacques, *Que faire du 'Capital'?*, Klincksieck, Paris 1984.

—— *Théorie de la modernité, suivi de Marx et le marché*, Presses Universitaires de France, Paris 1992.

Blanchot, Maurice, *Friendship*, trans. Elizabeth Rottenberg, Stanford University Press, Stanford, CA 1997.

Bloch, Ernst, *The Principle of Hope*, 3 vols, trans. Neville Plaice, Stephen Plaice and Paul Knight, Blackwell, Oxford 1986.

Brohm, Jean-Marie *et al.*, *Marx ou pas?*, EDI, Paris 1986.

Bukharin, Nicolai, *Historical Materialism*, International Publishers, New York 1925.

Chavance, Bernard *et al.*, *Marx en perspective*, EHESS, Paris 1985.

Colletti, Lucio, *From Rousseau to Lenin*, trans. John Merrington and Judith White, New Left Books, London 1972.

—— *Marxism and Hegel*, trans. Lawrence Garner, New Left Books, London 1973.

—— 'Marxism and the Dialectic', trans. John Mathews, *New Left Review*, no. 93, September/October 1975.

—— 'A Political and Philosophical Interview', in *New Left Review*, ed., *Western Marxism: A Critical Reader*, New Left Books, London 1977.

—— *Le Déclin du marxisme*, Presses Universitaires de France, Paris 1984.

Cornu, Auguste, *Karl Marx et Friedrich Engels*, 4 vols, Presses Universitaires de France, Paris 1955–70.

De Giovanni, Biagio, *La Teoria politica delle classi nel Capitale*, De Donato, Bari 1976.

Della Volpe, Galvano, *Rousseau and Marx and Other Writings*, trans. John Fraser, Lawrence & Wishart, London 1978.

—— *Logic as a Positive Science*, trans. Jon Rothschild, New Left Books, London 1980.

Denis, Henri, *Logique hégélienne et système économique*, Presses Universitaires de France, Paris 1984.

Derrida, Jacques, *Specters of Marx*, trans. Peggy Kamuf, Routledge, New York and London 1994.

D'Hont, Jacques, *De Hegel à Marx*, Presses Universitaires de France, Paris 1972.

—— ed., *La Logique de Marx*, Presses Universitaires de France, Paris 1974.

Dognin, Paul-Dominique, *Les Sentiers escapés du Capital*, 2 vols, Cerf, Paris 1977.

Dosse, François, *History of Structuralism*, 2 vols, trans. Deborah Glassman, University of Minnesota Press, Minneapolis and London 1997.

Duménil, Gérard, *Le Concept de loi économique dans 'Le Capital'*, Maspero, Paris 1978.

Dussel, Enrique, *La Produccion teorica de Marx*, Siglo XXI, Mexico 1985.

—— *Hacia un Marx desconocido*, Siglo XXI, Mexico 1988.

Économie et Société, nos 6–7, 'Marx et la fin de la préhistoire', Presses Universitaires de Grenoble, Grenoble 1994.

Elster, Jon, *Making Sense of Marx*, Cambridge University Press/Éditions de la Maison des Sciences de l'Homme, Cambridge and Paris 1985.

Farjoun, Emmanuel and Machover, Moshe, *Laws of Chaos*, New Left Books, London 1981.

Fausto, Ruy, *Marx, logique et politique*, Publisud, Paris 1986.

Furet, François, *Marx et la Révolution française*, Flammarion, Paris 1986.

Godelier, Maurice, *Rationality and Irrationality in Economics*, trans. Brian Pearce, New Left Books, London 1972.

—— *The Mental and the Material*, trans. Martin Thom, Verso, London 1986.

Goldmann, Lucien, *Recherches dialectiques*, Gallimard, Paris 1967.

—— *Marxisme et sciences humaines*, Gallimard, Paris 1970.

Gramsci, Antonio, *Selections from the Prison Notebooks*, ed. and trans. Quintin Hoare and Geoffrey Nowell Smith, Lawrence & Wishart, London 1971.

——*Further Selections from the Prison Notebooks*, ed. and trans. Derek Boothman, Lawrence & Wishart, London 1995.

Grossmann, Henryk, *Marx, l'économie politique classique et le problème de la dynamique*, Champ Libre, Paris 1975.

——*The Law of Accumulation and Breakdown of the Capitalist System*, trans. Jairus Banaji, Pluto Press, London 1982.

Guibert, Bernard, *La Violence capitalisée*, Cerf, Paris 1986.

Habermas, Jürgen, *Communication and the Evolution of Society*, trans. Thomas McCarthy, Heinemann, London 1979.

——*The Philosophical Discourse of Modernity*, trans. Frederick G. Lawrence, Polity, Cambridge 1987.

Hegel, G.W.F. *The Science of Logic*, trans. A.V. Miller, Allen & Unwin, London 1969.

——*The Encylopaediu Logic*, trans. T.F. Geraets, W.A. Suchting and H.S. Harris, Hackett Publishing Company, Indianopolis and Cambridge 1991.

Heller, Agnes, *The Theory of Need in Marx*, Allison & Busby, London 1976.

Henry, Michel, *Marx, une philosophie de la réalité*, 2 vols, Gallimard, Paris 1976.

Hobsbawm, E.J. *et al.*, *Storia del marxismo*, 5 vols, Einaudi, Turin 1978.

Hyppolite, Jean, *Studies on Hegel and Marx*, trans. John O'Neill, Heinemann, London 1969.

Jakubowski, Frantz, *Ideology and Superstructure in Historical Materialism*, trans. Anne Booth, Pluto Press, London 1990.

Joshua, Isaac, *La Face cachée du Moyen Age*, La Brèche, Paris 1988.

Kautsky, Karl, *Karl Marx Oekonomische Lehren*, Stuttgart 1894.

Kolakowski, Leszek, *Main Currents of Marxism I: The Founders*, trans. P.S. Falla, Oxford University Press, Oxford 1978.

Korsch, Karl, *Karl Marx*, Russell & Russell, New York 1963.

——*Marxism and Philosophy*, trans. Fred Halliday, New Left Books, London 1970.

——*L'Anti-Kautsky*, Champ Libre, Paris 1973.

——*Escritos politicos*, 2 vols, Folios Ediciones, Mexico 1982.

Kosik, Karel, *Dialectics of the Concrete*, trans. Karel Kovanda with James Schmidt, D. Reidel, Dordrecht 1976.

Labica, Georges, *Marxism and the Status of Philosophy*, trans. Kate Soper and Martin Ryle, Harvester, Brighton 1980.

——*Le Marxisme–Léninisme*, Bruno Huisman, Paris 1984.

——*Karl Marx: Les thèses sur Feuerbach*, Presses Universitaires de France, Paris 1987.

——*Le Paradigme du Grand-Hornu*, La Brèche, Paris 1987.

——and Bensoussan, eds, *Dictionnaire critique du marxisme*, second edition, Presses Universitaires de France, Paris 1985.

——*et al.*, *L'oeuvre de Marx un siècle après*, Presses Universitaires de France, Paris 1985.

——and Texier, Jacques, eds, *Labriola d'un siècle à l'autre*, Klincksieck, Paris 1988.

Labriola, Antonio, *Essays on the Materialist Conception of History*, trans. Charles H. Kerr, Monthly Review Press, New York and London 1966.

Lazarus, Sylvain, *Politique et philosophie dans l'oeuvre de Louis Althusser*, Presses Universitaires de France, Paris 1993.

Lefebvre, Henri, *Logique formelle et logique dialectique*, Éditions Sociales, Paris 1947.

——*Au-delà du structuralisme*, Anthropos, Paris 1971.

Lenin, V.I., *Philosophical Notebooks, Collected Works*, vol. 38, Lawrence & Wishart, London 1961.

Löwy, Michaël, *La Théorie de la révolution chez le jeune Marx*, Maspero, Paris 1970.

——*Dialectique et révolution*, Anthropos, Paris 1973.

——*Paysages de la vérité*, Anthropos, Paris 1985.

Lukács, Georg, *History and Class Consciousness*, trans. Rodney Livingstone, Merlin, London 1971.

Luxemburg, Rosa, *The Accumulation of Capital*, trans. Agnes Schwarzschild *et al.*, Routledge & Kegan Paul, London 1951.

——*What is Economics?*, trans. T. Edwards, Merlin Press, London 1973.

Maler, Henri, *L'utopie selon Karl Marx*, L'Harmattan, Paris 1994.

——*Convoiter l'impossible*, Albin Michel, Paris 1995.

Mandel, Ernest, *Marxist Economic Theory*, trans. Brian Pearce, Merlin Press, London 1968.

——*Late Capitalism*, trans. Joris de Bres, New Left Books, London 1975.

——*The Formation of the Economic Thought of Karl Marx*, trans. Brian Pearce, New Left Books, London 1977.

——*Long Waves of Capitalist Development*, Cambridge University Press, Cambridge 1980.

——*Marxismo abierto*, Grijalbo, Barcelona 1982.

——ed., *Ricardo, Marx, Sraffa*, Verso, London 1984.

——Introduction to Karl Marx, *Capital*, vol. 3, trans. David Fernbach, Penguin/NLR, Harmondsworth 1981.

Markus, Gyorgy, *Language and Production*, D. Reidel, Dordrecht 1986.

Mascolo, Dionys, *Le Communisme*, Gallimard, Paris 1953.

——*À la recherche d'un communisme de pensée*, Fourbis, Paris 1993.

Mehring, Karl, *Karl Marx*, trans. Edward Fitzgerald, Harvester, Brighton 1981.

Merleau-Ponty, Maurice, *Humanism and Terror*, trans. John O'Neil, Beacon Press, Boston, MA 1969.

——*Adventures of the Dialectic*, trans. Joseph Bien, Northwestern University Press, Evanston, IL 1973.

Naïr, Sami, *Machiavel et Marx*, Presses Universitaires de France, Paris 1984.

Negri, Antonio, *Marx beyond Marx: Lessons on the Grundrisse*, trans. Harry Cleaver *et al.*, Pluto Press, London 1991.

Papaioannou, Kostas, *De Marx et du marxisme*, Gallimard, Paris 1984.

Potier, Jean-Pierre, *Lectures italiennes de Marx*, Presses Universitaires de Lyon, Lyon 1986.

Proust, Marcel, *Remembrance of Things Past*, 3 vols, trans. C.K. Scott Moncrieff and Terence Kilmartin, Penguin, Harmondsworth 1983.

Riazanov, David, *Karl Marx and Friedrich Engels*, trans. Joshua Kunitz, Monthly Review Press, New York and London 1973.

Robelin, Jean, *Marxisme et socialisation*, Klincksieck, Paris 1989.

Rosdolsky, Roman, *The Making of Marx's 'Capital'*, trans. Pete Burgess, Pluto Press, London 1977.

Rubel, Maximilien, *Marx critique du marxisme*, Payot, Paris 1974.

Rubin, Isaac, *Essays on Marx's Theory of Value*, trans. Milos Samardzija and Fredy Perlman, Black and Red, Detroit 1972.

Sacristan Manuel, *Sobre Marx y marxismo*, Icaria, Barcelona 1983.

—— *Papeles de filosofia*, Icaria, Barcelona 1984.

Salama, Pierre, *Sur la valeur*, Maspero, Paris 1975.

—— and Valier, Jacques, *Une introduction à l'économie politique*, Maspero, Paris 1973.

—— and Hac, Tan Haic, *Introduction à l'économie de Marx*, La Découverte, Paris 1992.

Sartre, Jean-Paul, *Critique of Dialectical Reason I: Theory of Practical Ensembles*, trans. Alan Sheridan-Smith, New Left Books, London 1976.

—— *Situations philosophiques*, Gallimard, Paris 1990.

Schmidt, Alfred, *The Concept of Nature in Marx*, trans. Ben Fowkes, New Left Books, London 1971.

Sebag, Lucien, *Marxisme et structuralisme*, Payot, Paris 1964.

Sève, Lucien, *Une introduction à la philosophie marxiste*, Éditions Sociales, Paris 1980.

Smith, Tony, *The Logics of Marx's Capital*, State University of New York Press, New York 1990.

—— *Dialectical Social Theory and its Critics*, State University of New York Press, New York 1993.

Sorel, Georges, *Les Illusions du progrès*, Slatkine, Paris–Geneva 1981.

—— *Matériaux d'une théorie du prolétariat*, Slatkine, Paris–Geneva 1981.

—— *Décomposition du marxisme*, Presses Universitaires de France, Paris 1982.

Tombazos, Stavros, *Les Catégories du temps dans l'analyse économique*, Cahiers des saisons, Paris 1994.

Tort, Patrick, *Marx et le problème de l'idéologie*, Presses Universitaires de France, Paris 1988.

Tosel, André, *Praxis: Vers une refondation en philosophie marxiste*, Éditions Sociales, Paris 1984.

Tran Duc Thao, *Phénoménologie et matérialisme dialectique*, Gordon & Breach, Paris 1971.

Vadée, Michel, *Marx penseur du possible*, Klincksieck, Paris 1992.

Valier, Jacques, *Une critique de l'économie politique*, Maspero, Paris 1982.

Vincent, Jean-Marie, *Fétichisme et société*, Anthropos, Paris 1973.

—— *Critique du travail*, Presses Universitaires de France, Paris 1987.

Yovel Yirmiyahu, *Spinoza and Other Heretics*, 2 vols, Princeton University Press, Princeton, NJ 1989.

Zeleny, Jindrich, *The Logic of Marx*, trans. Terrell Carver, Basil Blackwell, Oxford 1980.

Part I

Actuel Marx, 'Fin du communisme, actualité du marxisme', Presses Universitaires de France, Paris 1991.

Alliez, Éric, *Capital Times*, trans. Georges Van Den Abbeele, University of Minnesota Press, Minneapolis and London 1996.

Aristotle, *Physics*, trans. Robin Waterfield, Oxford University Press, Oxford 1996.

Aron, Raymond, *La Philosophie critique de l'histoire*, Vrin, Paris 1969.

Bachelard, Gaston, *La Dialectique de la durée*, Bibliothèque de Philosophie contemporaine, Paris 1950.

Barsoc, Christian, *Les Lendemains de la crise*, La Brèche, Paris 1986.

——*Les Rouages du capitalisme*, La Brèche, Paris 1994.

Benjamin, Walter, *Illuminations*, trans. Harry Zohn, Fontana, London 1973.

——*The Arcades Project*, trans. Howard Eiland and Kevin McLaughlin, Harvard University Press, Cambridge, MA 1999.

Bensaïd, Daniel, *Walter Benjamin: sentinelle messianique*, Plon, Paris 1991.

Bergson, Henri, *Durée et simultaneité*, Presses Universitaires de France, Paris 1992.

Blanqui, Auguste, *L'éternité par les astres*, La tête de feuille, Paris 1972.

Bonnaud, Robert, *Les Alternances du progrès*, Kimé, Paris 1992.

Bourdieu, Pierre, *The Political Ontology of Martin Heidegger*, trans. Peter Collier, Polity, Cambridge 1991.

Boyer, Robert, *La Théorie de la régulation*, La Découverte, Paris 1986.

——and Durand, Jean-Pierre, *L'après-fordisme*, Syros, Paris 1993.

Brossat, Alain, *La Théorie de la révolution permanente chez le jeune Trotsky*, Maspero, Paris 1972.

Canguilhem, Georges, *The Normal and the Pathological*, trans. Carolyn R. Fawcett, Zone Books, New York 1991.

Centre d'études et de recherches marxistes, *Le Mode de production asiatique*, Éditions Sociales, Paris 1967.

——*Les Sociétés précapitalistes*, Éditions Sociales, Paris 1967.

Cohen, G.A., *Karl Marx's Theory of History: A Defence*, Clarendon Press, Oxford 1978.

Colliot-Thélène, Catherine, *Max Weber et l'histoire*, Presses Universitaires de France, Paris 1990.

Cournot, Antoine-Augustin, *Considérations sur la marche des idées et des événements dans les temps modernes*, Vrin, Paris 1973.

——*Matérialisme, vitalisme, rationalisme*, Vrin, Paris 1987.

Darwin, Charles, *The Origin of Species By Means of Natural Selection*, Penguin, London 1985.

Dastur, Françoise, *Heidegger et la question du temps*, Presses Universitaires de France, Paris 1990.

Derrida, Jacques, *Glas*, Denoël, Paris 1981.

Desanti, Jean-Toussaint, *Réflexions sur le temps*, Grasset, Paris 1993.

Dockès, Pierre and Rosier, Bernard, *Rythmes économiques*, La Découverte, Paris 1983.

Dumont, Louis, *Homo aequalis*, Gallimard, Paris 1977.

Économies et sociétés, nos 7/8, 'Les mouvements de longue durée dans la pensée économique', Presses Universitaires de Grenoble, Grenoble 1993.

Englander, Jean-Loup, *Pour l'incertain*, Syllepse, Paris 1990.

Feuerbach, Ludwig, 'Principles of the Philosophy of the Future, in Feuerbach, Karl Marx and Friedrich Engels, *German Socialist Philosophy*, Continuum, New York 1997.

Fitousssi, Jean-Paul and Sigogne, Philippe, *Les Cycles économiques*, Presses de la Fondation Nationale des Sciences Politiques, Paris 1993.

Fleischmann, Eugène, *Hegel et la politique*, Gallimard, Paris 1993.

Fukuyama, Francis, *The End of History and the Last Man*, Hamish Hamilton, London 1992.

Futur Antérieur, 'École de la régulation et critique de la raison économique', L'Harmattan, Paris 1994.

Gardiès, Jean-Louis, *La Logique du temps*, Presses Universitaires de France, Paris 1975.

Goldmann, Lucien, *Lukács and Heidegger*, trans. W.Q. Boelhower, Routledge & Kegan Paul, London 1977.

Gould, Stephen J., *Time's Arrow, Time's Cycle*, Penguin, London 1990.

—— *Wonderful Life*, Hutchinson Radius, London 1990.

——*An Urchin in the Storm*, Penguin, London 1990.

——*Dinosaur in a Haystack*, Jonathan Cape, London 1996.

Habermas, Jürgen, *Knowledge and Human Interests*, trans. Jeremy J. Shapiro, Heinemann, London 1972.

Hawking, Stephen, *A Brief History of Time*, Bantam Books, London 1988.

——*Black Holes and Baby Universes and Other Essays*, Bantam Press, London 1993.

Hegel, G.W.F., *Reason in History: A General Introduction to the Philosophy of History*, trans. Robert S. Hartman, Bobbs-Merrill, New York 1953.

——*Introduction to the Lectures on the History of Philosophy*, trans. T.M. Knox and A.V. Miller, Clarendon Press, Oxford 1985.

Heidegger, Martin, *Being and Time*, trans. John MacQuarrie and Edward Robinson, Basil Blackwell, Oxford 1962.

Horkheimer, Max, *Les Débuts de la philosophie bourgeoise de l'histoire*, Payot, Paris 1980.

Husserl, Edmund, *The Phenomenology of Internal Time-Consciousness*, trans. James S. Churchill *et al.*, Martinus Nijhoff, The Hague 1964.

——*The Crisis of European Sciences and Transcendental Phenomenology*, trans. D. Carr, Northwestern University Press, Evanston, IL 1970.

Itoh, Makotoh, *The World Economic Crisis and Japanese Capitalism*, Macmillan, Basingstoke 1990.

Kondratieff, Nicolai D., 'The Long Waves in Economic Life', *Review of Economic Statistics*, no. 17, 1935.

Koyré, Alexandre, *Études d'histoire de la pensée philosophique*, Gallimard, Paris 1981.

Kracauer, Siegfried, *History: The Last Things before the Last*, Oxford University Press, New York 1969.

Lefebvre, Henri, *La Fin de l'histoire*, Minuit, Paris 1970.

Lewin, Moshe, *The Making of the Soviet System*, Methuen, London 1985.

Louça, Francisco, *Cycles and Growth*, doctoral thesis, Lisbon 1994.

Maimonides, Moses, *Epistles of Maimonides*, trans. Abraham Halkin, Jewish Publication Society, Philadelphia 1993.

Mariategui, Jose Carlos, *Invitacion a la vida heroica*, Lima 1989.

Marramo, Giacomo, *Il Politico e le transformationi*, De Donata, Bari 1979.

Meillassoux, Claude, *Maidens, Meals and Money*, Cambridge University Press, Cambridge 1981.

Missac, Pierre, *Passage de Walter Benjamin*, Seuil, Paris 1987.

Moses, Stéphane, *L'Ange de l'Histoire*, Seuil, Paris 1991.

Nietzsche, Friedrich, *Untimely Meditations*, trans. R.J. Hollingdale, Cambridge University Press, Cambridge 1983.

Popper, Karl, *The Open Society and its Enemies*, 2 vols, Routledge & Kegan Paul, London 1945.

—— *The Poverty of Historicism*, Routledge & Kegan Paul, London 1957.

—— *Conjectures and Refutations*, Routledge & Kegan Paul, London 1963.

—— *Objective Knowledge*, Clarendon Press, Oxford 1972.

—— *Unended Quest*, Fontana, London 1976.

—— *The Open Universe*, Hutchinson, London 1982.

—— *The Lesson of this Century*, trans. Patrick Camiller, Routledge, London 1997.

Proust, Françoise, *Kant, le ton de l'histoire*, Payot, Paris 1991.

—— *L'histoire à contretemps*, Cerf, Paris 1994.

Renan, Ernest, *L'avenir de la science*, Calmann-Lévy, Paris 1949.

Ricoeur, Paul, *Time and Narrative*, 3 vols, trans. Kathleen McLaughlin and David Pellauer, University of Chicago Press, Chicago 1984–86.

Rosier, Bernard, *La Théorie des crises*, La Découverte, Paris 1987.

Ruelle, David, *Hasard et chaos*, Odile Jacob, Paris 1991.

Samary, Catherine, *La Crise, les crises, l'enjeu*, La Brèche, Paris 1987.

Serres, Michel, *Le Passage du Nord-Ouest*, Minuit, Paris 1986.

Simmel, Georg, *The Problems of the Philosophy of History*, trans. Guy Oakes, Free Press, New York 1977.

Stirner, Max, *The Ego and its Own*, ed. David Leopold, trans. Steven Tracy Byington, Cambridge University Press, New York 1995.

Thom, René, *Paraboles et catastrophes*, Flammarion, Paris 1989.

Traverso, Enzo, *Siegfried Kracauer*, La Découverte, Paris 1994.

Trotsky, Leon, *The First Five Years of the Communist International,* Monad Press, New York 1972.

—— *The Permanent Revolution & Results and Prospects,* Pathfinder Press, New York 1978.

Weber, Max, *General Economic History,* ed. I.J. Cohen, Transaction, New Brunswick, NJ 1981.

Wright, Erik Olin, *Interrogating Inequality,* Verso, London and New York 1994.

Yerushalmi, Yosef Hayim, *Zakhor,* La Découverte, Paris 1984.

Zea, Léopoldo, *El Positivismo en Mexico,* Fondo de Cultura Economica, Mexico 1984.

Part II

Actuel Marx, 'Le marxisme analytique anglo-saxon', Presses Universitaires de France, Paris 1990.

—— 'L'idée du socialisme a-t-elle encore un avenir?', Presses Universitaires de France, Paris 1992.

—— 'Le nouveau système du monde', Presses Universitaires de France, Paris 1993.

—— 'Paradigmes de la démocratie', Presses Universitaires de France, Paris 1994.

Anderson, Perry, *Passages from Antiquity to Feudalism,* New Left Books, London 1974.

—— *Lineages of the Absolutist State,* New Left Books, London 1974.

Andréani, Tony and Feray, Marc, *Discours sur l'inégalité parmi les hommes,* L'Harmattan, Paris 1993.

Arrighi, Giovanni, Amin, Samir, and Gunder Frank, André, *Le grand tumulte,* La Découverte, Paris 1990.

Bahro, Rudolf, *The Alternative in Eastern Europe,* trans. David Fernbach, New Left Books, London 1978.

Barcellona, Pietro, *Le Retour du lien social,* Climats, Montpellier 1992.

Baudelot, Christian, Establet, Roger, and Malemort, Jacques, *La Petite Bourgeoisie en France,* Maspero, Paris 1974.

Baudelot, Christian, Establet, Roger, Toisier, Jacques, and Flavigny, P.-O., *Qui travaille pour qui?,* Maspero, Paris 1979.

Berman, Marshall, *All That is Solid Melts into Air: The Experience of Modernity,* Verso, London 1983.

Berthoud, Arnaud, *La Théorie du travail productif et improductif chez Marx,* Maspero, Paris 1974.

Bihr, Alain, *Du grand soir à l'alternative,* L'Harmattan, Paris 1990.

Bloch, Marc, *Feudal Society,* Routledge & Kegan Paul, London 1961.

Bourdieu, Pierre, *Distinction,* trans. Richard Nice, Routledge & Kegan Paul, London 1984.

—— *Sociology in Question,* trans. Richard Nice, Sage, London 1993.

—— *The Weight of the World,* trans. P.P. Ferguson, Polity, Cambridge 2000.

Bourdieu, Pierre and Passeron, Jean-Claude, *Reproduction in Education, Culture and Society*, trans. Richard Nice, Sage, London and Beverly Hills, CA 1977.

Carse, James P., *Finite Games and Infinite Games*, Penguin, Harmondsworth 1987.

Collective, *Individu et justice sociale*, Éditions du Seuil, Paris 1988.

Coutrot, Thomas, and Husson, Michel, *Les Destins du tiers monde*, Nathan, Paris 1993.

Dahrendorf, Ralf, *Class and Class Conflict in Industrial Society*, Stanford University Press, Stanford, CA 1957.

Duménil, Gérard, *La Position de classe des cadres et employés*, Presses Universitaires de Grenoble, Grenoble 1975.

Dumont, Louis, *Homo Hierarchicus*, trans. Mark Sainsbury, Weidenfeld & Nicolson, London 1970.

El marxismo y los estudios clasicos, Akal, Madrid 1981.

Giddens, Anthony, *The Class Structure of Advanced Societies*, Hutchinson, London 1973.

——*A Contemporary Critique of Historical Materialism*, Macmillan, London and Basingstoke 1981.

Gilly, Adolfo, *Sacerdotes y burocratas*, Siglo XXI, Mexico 1981.

Gorz, André, *Strategy for Labour*, trans. Martin A. Nicolaus and Victoria Ortiz, Beacon Press, Boston, MA 1967.

——*Farewell to the Working Class*, trans. Michael Sonenscher, Pluto Press, London 1982.

——*Critique of Economic Reason*, trans. Gillian Handyside and Chris Turner, Verso, London and New York 1990.

——*Capitalism, Socialism, Ecology*, trans. Chris Turner, Verso, London and New York 1994.

Habermas, Jürgen, *The Theory of Communicative Action* I: *Reason and the Rationalization of Society*, trans. Thomas McCarthy, Heinemann, London 1984.

——*The Theory of Communicative Action* II: *Lifeworld and Style*, trans. Thomas McCarthy, Polity, Cambridge 1989.

——*Moral Consciousness and Communicative Action*, trans. Christian Lenhardt and Shierry Weber Nicholsen, Polity, Cambridge 1990.

Hegedus, Andreas, *Socialism and Bureaucracy*, Allison & Busby, London 1976.

Kotarbinski, Jozef, *Leçons sur l'histoire de la logique*, Presses Universitaires de France, Paris 1964.

MacNally, David, *Against the Market*, Verso, London and New York 1993.

Morin, Edgar, *De la nature de l'URSS*, Fayard, Paris 1983.

Muguerza, Javier, *Desde la perplexidad*, FCE, Madrid 1990.

Nove, Alec, *The Economics of Feasible Socialism*, Allen & Unwin, London 1983.

Parkin, Frank, *Marxism and Class Theory*, Tavistock, London 1979.

Pla, Alberto, *Mode de produccion asiatico y formaciones économico-sociales Inca y Azteca*, El Cabilito, Mexico 1982.

Polanyi, Karl, *The Great Transformation*, Beacon Press, Boston, MA 1944.

Portis, Larry, *Les Classes sociales en France*, Éditions ouvrières, Paris 1988.

Poulantzas, Nicos, *Political Power and Social Classes*, trans. Timothy O'Hagan, New Left Books, London 1973.
—— *Classes in Contemporary Capitalism*, trans. David Fernbach, Verso, London 1975.
Rakovsky, Christian, 'The "Professional Dangers" of Power', in Rakovsky, *Selected Writings on Opposition in the USSR, 1923–30*, Allison & Busby, London 1980.
Rawls, John, *A Theory of Justice*, Oxford University Press, Oxford 1971.
—— *Political Liberalism*, Columbia University Press, New York 1993.
Roemer, John, *A General Theory of Exploitation and Class*, Harvard University Press, Cambridge, MA 1982.
—— ed., *Analytical Marxism*, Cambridge University Press/Éditions de la Maison des Sciences de l'Homme, Cambridge and Paris 1986.
Saint-Croix, Geoffrey de, *The Class Struggle in the Ancient Greek World*, Duckworth, London 1981.
Schumpeter, Joseph, *Capitalism, Socialism and Democracy*, Routledge, London 1994.
—— *Imperialism and Social Classes*, Basil Blackwell, Oxford 1951.
Simmel, Georg, *Le Conflit*, Circé, Strasbourg 1992.
Staniszkis, Janis, *La Révolution autolimitée*, Presses Universitaires de France, Paris 1982.
Therborn, Göran, *Science, Class and Society*, New Left Books, London 1976.
—— *What Does the Ruling Class Do When it Rules?*, New Left Books, London 1978.
Tort, Patrick, *La Raison classificatoire*, Aubier, Paris 1989.
Trotsky, Leon, *In Defense of Marxism*, Pathfinder Press, New York 1973.
van Parijs, Philippe, *Qu'est-ce qu'une société juste?*, Seuil, Paris 1991.
Veblen, Thorstein, *The Engineers and the Price System*, Huebsch, Boston, MA 1919.
Vozlensky, Mikhail, *Nomenklatura*, Overseas Publishing House, London 1985.
Weber, Max, *The Protestant Ethic and the Spirit of Capitalism*, trans. Talcott Parsons, Routledge, London 1992.
Wittfogel, Karl August, *Oriental Despotism*, Yale University Press, New Haven, CT 1955.
Wright, Erik Olin, *Class, Crisis and the State*, New Left Books, London 1978.
—— *Classes*, Verso, London 1985.
—— *Interrogating Inequality*, Verso, London and New York 1994.
—— et al., *The Debate on Classes*, Verso, London and New York 1989.

Part III

Aboulafia, Abraham, *Épître des sept voies*, Éditions de l'Éclat, Paris 1985.
Bachelard, Gaston, *The New Scientific Spirit*, trans. Arthur Goldhammer, Beacon Press, Boston, MA 1985.
Bacon, Francis, *The Advancement of Learning*, ed. G.W. Kitchin, Dent, London 1973.
Badiou, Alain, *L'être et l'événement*, Seuil, Paris 1988.
—— *Conditions*, Seuil, Paris 1992.

Badiou, Alain, *Manifesto for Philosophy*, trans. Norman Madarasz, State University of New York Press, Albany, NY 1999.

Bagarolo, Tiziano, *Marxisme ed ecologia*, Neve Edizioni Internazionale, Milan 1989.

Bernal, J.D., *Science in History*, Watts, London 1957.

Bertalanffy, Ludwig von, *General System Theory*, Penguin, Harmondsworth 1973.

Biard, J. *et al.*, *Introduction à la lecture de la Science de la logique de Hegel*, 3 vols, Aubier, Paris 1983–91.

Bohr, Niels, *Atomic Physics and Human Knowledge*, Wiley and Sons, New York 1958.

Brunhes, Bernard, *Le Dégradation de l'énergie*, Flammarion, Paris 1909.

Buey, Francisco Fernandez, *La Illusion del método*, Editorial Critica, Barcelona 1991.

Collective, *Chaos et déterminisme*, Seuil, Paris 1992.

Colliot-Thélène, Catherine, *Le Désenchantement de l'État*, Minuit, Paris 1993.

Deléage, Jean-Paul, *Histoire de l'écologie*, La Découverte, Paris 1991.

——Debeir, Jean-Claude, and Hémery, Daniel, *Les Servitudes de la puissance*, Flammarion, Paris 1986.

Deleuze, Gilles, *Spinoza*, trans. Robert Hurley, City Lights Books, San Francisco 1988.

Denis, Henri, *Logique hégélienne et systèmes économiques*, Presses Universitaires de France, Paris 1984.

Fleischmann, Eugène, *La Science universelle ou la logique de Hegel*, Plon, Paris 1968.

Foucault, Michel, *The Order of Things*, Tavistock, London 1970.

—— *The Archaeology of Knowledge*, trans. A.M. Sheridan Smith, Tavistock, London 1972.

Freud, Sigmund, 'The Future of an Illusion', in Pelican Freud Library, vol. 12, *Civilization, Society and Religion*, Penguin, Harmondsworth 1985.

—— 'Civilization and its Discontents', in *Civilization, Society and Religion*.

Friedmann, Georges, *Leibniz et Spinoza*, Gallimard, Paris 1975.

Geymonat, Ludovico, *Filosofia e filosofia della scienza*, Feltrinelli, Milan 1966.

—— *Storia del pensiero filosofico e scientifico*, Aldo Garzanti, Milan 1972–76.

—— *Scienza e realismo*, Feltrinelli, Milan 1977.

—— *Galilée*, Seuil, Paris 1992.

Gleick, James, *Chaos*, Heinemann, London 1988.

Halbwachs, Francis, *Les Théories de la causalité*, Presses Universitaires de France, Paris 1971.

Hegel, G.W.F., *Phenomenology of Mind*, trans. A.V. Miller, Oxford University Press, Oxford and New York 1977.

Heisenberg, Werner, *Physics and Philosophy*, Allen & Unwin, London 1959.

Husserl, Edmund, *Cartesian Meditations*, trans. Dorian Cairns, Martinus Nijhoff, The Hague 1966.

Iacono, Alfonso, *Le Fétichisme*, Presses Universitaires de France, Paris 1992.

Jonas, Hans, *The Imperative of Responsibility*, trans. Hans Jonas with David Herr, University of Chicago Press, Chicago and London 1984.

Joshua, Samuel and Dupin, Jean-Jacques, *Introduction à la didactique des sciences et des mathématiques*, Presses Universitaires de France, Paris 1993.

Kapp, K.W., *Les Coûts sociaux dans l'économie de marché*, Flammarion, Paris 1976.

Kojève, Alexandre, *L'idée de déterminisme dans la physique classique et dans la physique moderne*, LGF, Paris 1990.

Latour, Bruno, *We Have Never Been Modern*, trans. Catherine Porter, Harvester Wheatsheaf, London 1993.

Leibniz, G.W., *Theodicy*, trans. E.M. Huggard, Open Court, New York 1985.

—— *Monadology*, ed. Nicholas Rescher, Routledge, London 1991.

—— *De l'horizon de la doctrine humaine/La Restitution universelle*, ed. Michel Fichant, J. Vrin, Paris 1991.

Lindenberg, Daniel, *Le Marxisme introuvable*, Calmann-Lévy, Paris 1975.

Lovelock, James, *The Ages of Gaia*, Oxford University Press, Oxford 1979.

Lucretius, *On the Nature of the Universe*, trans. Sir Ronald Melville, Clarendon Press, Oxford 1997.

Mandelbrot, Benoît, *Les Objets fractals*, Flammarion, Paris 1990.

Marcuse, Herbert, *Hegel's Ontology and the Theory of Historicity*, trans. Seyla Benhabib, MIT Press, Cambridge, MA and London 1987.

Martinez-Allier, Joan and Schlupman, Klaus, *La Ecologia y la economia*, Efe, Mexico 1991.

Passet, René, *L'économique et la vivant*, Payot, Paris 1979.

Planck, Max, *The Universe in the Light of Modern Physics*, trans. W.H. Johnston, Allen & Unwin, London 1937.

Poincaré, Henri, *Science and Hypothesis*, Walter Scott Publishing Co., Newcastle-on-Tyne and London 1905.

—— *Science and Method*, trans. Francis Maitland, Thomas Nelson & Sons, London 1914.

—— *La Valeur de la science*, Flammarion, Paris 1970.

Prigogine, Ilya, *Les Lois du chaos*, Flammarion, Paris 1994.

—— and Stengers, Isabelle, *La nouvelle alliance*, Gallimard, Paris 1983.

—— and Stengers, Isabelle, *Entre le temps et l'éternité*, Fayard, Paris 1988.

Roche, Claude, *La Connaissance et la loi dans la pensée économique libérale*, L'Harmattan, Paris 1993.

Roegen, Nicholas Georgescu, *The Entropy Law and the Economic Process*, London 1971.

Sartre, Jean-Paul, *Notebooks for an Ethics*, trans. David Pellauer, University of Chicago Press, Chicago and London 1992.

Schrodinger, Erwin, *Science and Humanism: Physics in Our Time*, Cambridge University Press, Cambridge 1951.

Selleri, Franco, *Le grand débat de la théorie quantique*, Flammarion, Paris 1994.

Serres, Michel (with Bruno Latour), *Conversations on Science, Culture, and Time*, trans. Roxanne Lapidus, University of Michigan Press, Ann Arbor 1995.

Spinoza, Benedict de, *The Ethics*, trans. Edwin M. Curley, Penguin, London 1999.

Stengers, Isabelle, *La volonté de faire science*, Les empêcheurs de penser en rond, Paris 1992.

—— *L'invention des sciences modernes*, La Découverte, Paris 1993.

Stewart, Ian, *Does God Play Dice?*, Penguin, London 1990.

Thom, René, *Prédire n'est pas expliquer*, Flammarion, Paris 1993.

Tosel, André, *Du matérialisme, de Spinoza*, Kimé, Paris 1994.

Vatin, François, *Le Travail: économie et physique, 1780–1830*, Presses Universitaires de France, Paris 1993.

Vernadsky, V.I., *La Biosphère*, Félix Alcan, Paris 1926.

Vivien, Franck-Dominique, *Économie et écologie*, La Découverte, Paris 1995.

Weber, Max, *The Methodology of the Social Sciences*, trans. Edward A. Shils and Henry A. Finch, Free Press of Glencoe, New York 1964.

Whitehead, A.N., *Science and the Modern World*, Cambridge University Press, Cambridge 1925.

——*Adventures of Ideas*, Cambridge University Press, Cambridge 1933.

Yakira, Elhanan, *La Causalité de Galilée à Kant*, Presses Universitaires de France, Paris 1994.

Index